CW00541891

The Clyde

MAPPING THE RIVER

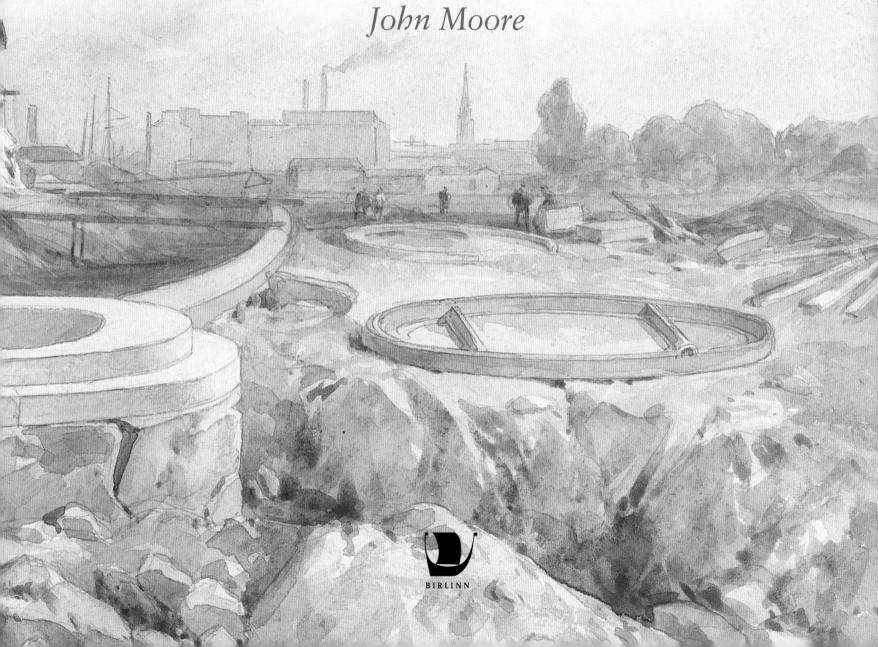

The Clyde

MAPPING THE RIVER

John Moore

BIRLINN

First published in 2017 by
Birlinn Limited
West Newington House
10 Newington Road
Edinburgh
EH9 1QS

www.birlinn.co.uk

ISBN 978 178027 482 9

British Library Cataloguing
in Publication Data
A catalogue record for this book is
available from the British Library.

Designed and typeset by Mark Blackadder

Printed and bound by PNB Print Ltd, Latvia

Contents

Defence, security and conflict: maps of strategy and war

Using the river: industry, agriculture and commerce

Crossing the river: fords, ferries, bridges and roads

Tourism, leisure and recreation

Life by the river: towns and settlements

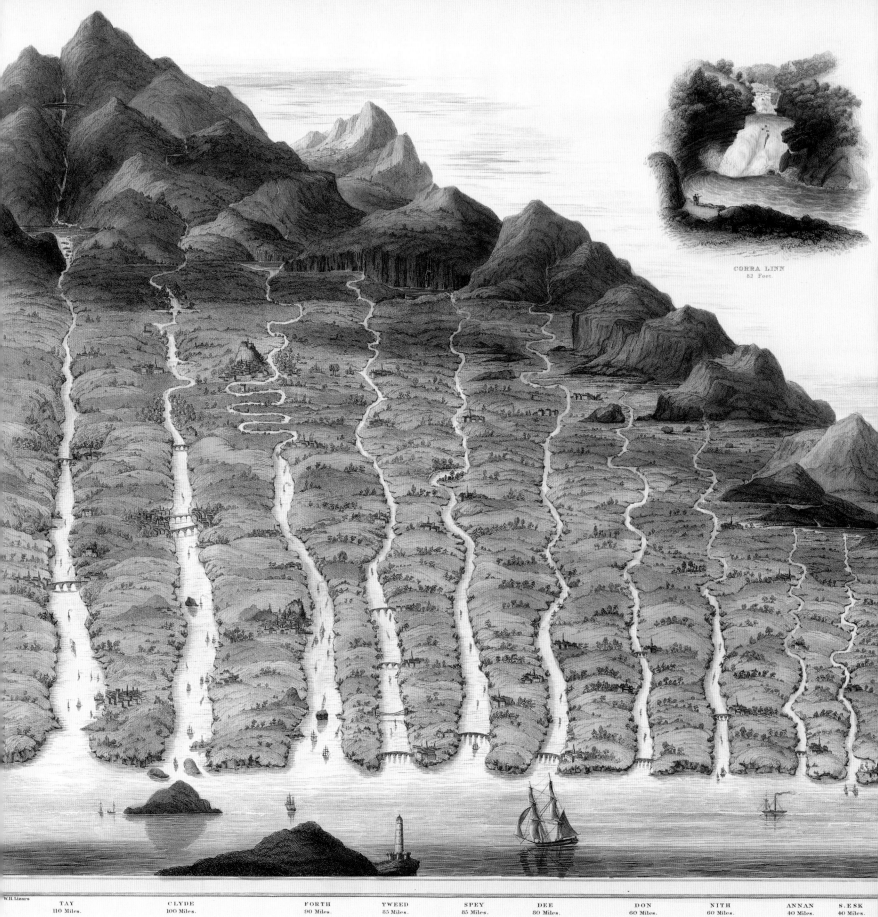

CORRA LINN
82 Feet.

W.H. Lizars

TAY	CLYDE	FORTH	TWEED	SPEY	DEE	DON	NITH	ANNAN	S.ESK
110 Miles.	100 Miles.	90 Miles.	85 Miles.	85 Miles.	80 Miles.	60 Miles.	60 Miles.	40 Miles.	40 Miles.

Introduction

Any place is affected by its immediate geography through the influence of such physical features as structural geology, topography and climate, as well as the long-term impact of those who live and work there. A river is no different but, by its very nature, it is possibly characterised by a greater number of different elements. Scotland has many rivers and there is a serious challenge to any estimation of either their number or length. While the Clyde is recorded as the second longest after the Tay, it is frequently considered to have had a greater impact on the lives of more people than any other water body in the country. This is hardly surprising given the population densities of the authority areas through which it runs in its lower reaches. There is, however, more to its influence than the merely geographical. The Clyde has had a profound effect on the national psyche and its mention still conjures up those images of strength, reliability, ingenuity, enterprise and a determination to succeed against the odds which strike a chord in the minds of many Scots.

Over the centuries, it has played a variety of roles in the history of west central Scotland from recreational playground for those who holidayed 'doon the watter' or sailed the estuary to a source of power to drive various industrial mills. The challenges it has posed to those living along its banks have, at times,

disguised the fact that it has never been a particularly useful river for navigation or as a routeway. For much of its early length, it travels through mostly agricultural land and while its flood plain facilitated road links both locally and as the major western route south to the English border, the river itself proved more of a handicap than an asset. The considerable number of fords and ferries which developed along its course is testament to the need to cross rather than travel along the Clyde.

Part of the configuration of the Clyde is the tortuous journey it takes on its way to the sea. After passing Roberton the river swings in a north-easterly direction, running to the east of Symington before commencing a curve westwards at Wolfclyde Bridge. This major loop is caused by the prominent feature of Tinto, a large domed hill of felsite rock lying directly in the river's path. At Thankerton, local geography in the shape of the Carmichael and Chester Hills influences its course as it turns north to the west of Quothquan Law. On the relatively flat lands surrounding the small village of Pettinain, the Clyde meanders considerably as it swings below Carstairs before heading south towards Crookboat, where the confluence with the Douglas Water results in a hairpin bend north. While the Clyde by this stage is of considerable size, it is more broad than deep and changes in its configuration over time were not only

Opposite. A comparative view of the lengths of the principal rivers of Scotland (1820) *from John Thomson's* Atlas of Scotland (1832)

mentioned in the *Statistical Account* of Pettinain parish by the Revd James Ferguson but can also be deduced from the number of oxbow lakes in this extended loop.

As it reaches Bonnington Linn, the combination of a quite sudden change as the river enters a gorge and the first in a series of waterfalls adds to the problems in negotiating it. Beyond Stonebyres, it continues to twist and turn, most notably between Bothwell and Rutherglen. The valley is restricted once again near Bowling where lava intrusions reduce its width to little more than a couple of miles. The Renfrewshire Heights which hindered the growth of those settlements facing the Tail of the Bank have also had an impact on how the river developed. Downriver from Dalmarnock, the changes made to the Clyde's bed and banks have been the focal points of many discussions of the river. The triumph of engineering over the immediate geography of the area resulted in the growth of Glasgow and the development of an industrial ascendancy based largely on shipbuilding and engineering which led to the conurbation's position as the Second City of the Empire.

Times change but geography continues to influence the area's situation in what is a markedly different world where commerce is less reliant on sea transport and focuses on different links. As one of the leading historians of the river has put it, 'the Clyde is in the wrong place in the days of motorways, Europe and speed'. Nonetheless, while Glasgow itself has discovered new ways in which to regenerate its economy, it has yet to find a satisfactory purpose for a river which is, possibly, a painful reminder of a past heritage. Elsewhere, the Clyde is now considered as a recreational and educational asset where the considerable numbers of local residents have opportunities for diversion, relaxation and a reconnection with the environment.

There is need, however, for a more vigorous, coherent and imaginative approach to its integration as it passes through the city with which it is so closely associated.

In other ways, there have been considerable improvements in the river. Population change and the decline in heavy industry have had an impact on pollution levels. Following European Union legislation, domestic sewage is no longer dumped in the estuary. In addition, significant investment by Scottish Water and regulation by the Scottish Environment Protection Agency have contributed to marked improvements in water quality. The return of Atlantic salmon to the river system in 1983 has been regarded as a major indication of its improving health, while the work of the Clyde River Foundation, a charity dedicated to research and education throughout the catchment area, has done much to improve fish stocks and invertebrate habitats, as well as raising public awareness in local communities.

This book considers an assortment of maps, plans and other documents which either depict the Clyde itself or indicate some particular aspect of the places, industries or other features closely associated with it. Like others in this series, the choice of what is discussed has proved challenging and is inevitably affected by availability, a need for a degree of variety but, particularly, personal preference. Many books have been written about the river, its towns and trade but little on its cartography. This work provides only a limited selection of the vast heritage of images of the river but, once again, I have drawn on an extensive range of resources to bring their availability to the attention of a wider audience. The Clyde has posed many challenges and it is left to the reader to decide how ably this text has been equal to meeting the task.

Acknowledgements

Once again, I would like to record my thanks to Hugh Andrew and his staff at Birlinn, in particular, Andrew Simmons for the commissioning of this book and for their support throughout the production process. The work has posed considerable challenges and has required my reliance on the expertise of a markedly broad range of individuals in providing either access to or information on particular depictions of the River Clyde.

There are, however, two individuals who merit especial recognition for their guidance, sage counsel and knowledge of the collections under their charge. Both Chris Fleet, Map Curator at the National Library of Scotland and Jane Brown, Head of Maps and Plans, National Records of Scotland have given freely of their time and unique understanding of my somewhat idiosyncratic requests. They should be given much credit for any value this work may have. In addition, I want to record my thanks and appreciation to Professor John Hume for his deep knowledge so freely shared, for his kind words and inspiration.

Many others have all assisted me in my wide-ranging search for relevant material and I want to record my indebtedness to the following colleagues, friends and professionals: Elaine Anderson, Sonny Maley, Niki Russell, Moira Rankin (University of Glasgow Library), Dr Irene O'Brien and the staff at Glasgow City Archives, Emily Malcolm (Glasgow Museums), Monika Woisin-Mikelsen and Antje Schröder (Bundesamt für Seeschifffahrt und Hydrographie, Rostock), Paul Archibald, Fiona Baker, Martin Davis, David Ferguson (Royal Troon Golf Club), Anne Lappin, Ian Mack, John McMillan (Turnberry), Lyndsay Mark, Lena Moser, Lisa Otty, Jon Reid (RNYC), Campbell Russell, Anne Taylor, Sue Walker and Stuart Wilson (SEPA).

I also wish to record my indebtedness to David Cranstoun of that Ilk and Corehouse and the Right Honourable The Earl of Eglinton and Winton for permission to reproduce maps from their family papers.

A considerable number of institutions have provided illustrative material to support the text. A full list of picture credits can be found on p. 273.

I would like to offer my thanks to all for their help and assistance. Their generosity has been both heartening and encouraging. It is my hope that this work is a testament to their own expertise. However, any errors in the text are of my own making for which I take full responsibility.

Kirk
Killpatrick
Pleasant
Nether closs
Draw Bridge
Fern Dike
Manse
Sandy ford
Gateside
Relief Meeting Hous
Upper Dalnotter
Red
Spouts Green
Park
Hill
Drain Bridge

opton
Gillespie Esqr
West Longhaugh
East Longhaugh
Freeland
Erskine House
Lord Blantyre
Offices
Dalnotter
Mount Blow
Donald Esqr

Cockhill
Duckmoss
Slateford
Coldside
Wraisland
Dryknow
Ritchieston
School
Kirktown of Erskine
Kirk
Manse
Mossid
Carts Moss
Back o' the Hill

Top
West Porton
Bishopton Inn
North Porton
Drumcross
Hillhead
North Barr
Buchannan Esqr
Barr Mill
Dalmuir Canal

Newton
Inglestone
Crossgate
Cartmpan
Ford
Rosland Town
Rosland Castle
West Rosland
South Porton
East Rosland
Bareloch
Dambreast
Bargarran
Kilts
Rashylee
Oldbar Castle in ruins
Soap House
Quarry

chinnoch
Ditch
Craigton
Burn
Rosland
Old Toll
Burnside
Ale House
Craigton
Little Graigton
Auchennain
Shilton
Bourtree Bush
Cold Gable
Mounthead
Umquhat
Garnyland Mill

PARH
Low
Glenshinnoch
Rashiecrook
Barangry
Craighead
Stonehouse
Greenwells
Park
Fulton Esqr

Dikenuk
Dargavell
Maxwell Esqr
Maxwellfield
South Barr
Alexander Esqr
Gateside
Turnyland
Freestone
High Park
Barsail
Craighe
Looking
Schoo
Wri

INCH
Reddan Lodge
Wardhouse
Freeland
Greenhead

MOSS
The New Road from Greenock to Gla

Mickle Commonside
Newmains
Inchinn
Allans

Haveshaw
Rannochshiel
Wheelburn
Little Commonside
Barnsford Toll

MOSS
PARISH

Stotterie
Netherfield
Fulwood Townhead
Fulwood Mill
Brownfield
Barnhill
Barnsford Bridge

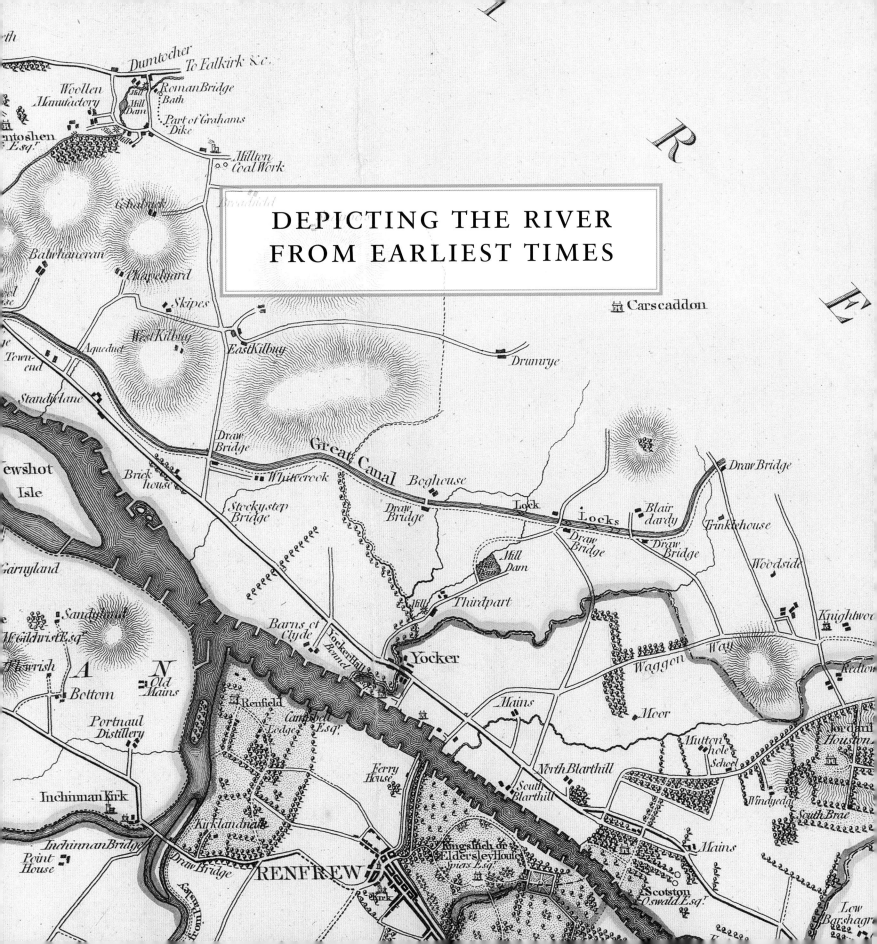

DEPICTING THE RIVER
FROM EARLIEST TIMES

INSVLÆ
ALBION
et
HIBERNIA
cum minoribus adjacentibus

CHAPTER I

In the beginning:
Scotland according to Ptolemy

Claudius Ptolemaeus, more familiarly known as Ptolemy, was a Greek mathematician, astronomer and geographer who lived in Alexandria in Egypt between about AD 90 and 168. In around AD 150, he compiled an extensive eight-volume gazetteer, atlas and treatise on cartography, frequently called *Geographia,* as a comprehensive digest of the geographical knowledge of the Roman Empire of his day. The work is now considered to be a revision, with later additions from Roman and Persian sources, of an atlas by Marinus of Tyre (*c.* AD 70–130), which is no longer extant. Marinus was one of the first to develop the concept of longitude and latitude for the location of places. It is through the translation of the *Geographia* into Arabic in the ninth century and Latin in 1406 that the work became a major influence on the concept of geography in both the Arab world and Renaissance Europe.

No Greek manuscript of the original *Geographia* survives from earlier than the thirteenth century and scholars continue to debate whether or not the textual references to maps in the work were later additions. Regardless of this, the earliest known printed depiction of Scotland appears on *Insulae Albion et Hibernia,* a map covering the whole of the British Isles which was included in the first published edition of Ptolemy's cartography, produced in Bologna in 1477. This was also the first printed book to include illustrations. The version depicted here appears as the first map in the fifth volume of Blaeu's great *Atlas Novus* from 1654 and its inclusion by the Dutch cartographers gives a sense of the high regard in which Ptolemy's work was held.

Like many other geographers of their time, both Marinus and Ptolemy relied on earlier writers, as well as the accounts of contemporary merchants and travellers, particularly for the regions well beyond the Mediterranean. The map reflects the contemporary knowledge of an area very remote from the centre of the Empire and the details are most likely based on the experience of the Roman occupation of south Scotland, being most informative about the east and Galloway coasts. This occupation had begun under Agricola in AD 79 and it is highly likely that both Marinus and Ptolemy would have been aware of the description of the area written by Agricola's son-in-law, Tacitus nearly 20 years later. Although limited in what he says about Caledonia, Tacitus is clear about the land stretching as a vast tract and tapering off in a wedge-like form. More importantly, he also mentions that the Roman fleet sailed round the coast and discovered what were then called the Orcades (or Orkneys).

What is immediately noticeable about the map is the orientation of Scotland in relation to the rest of the British Isles. Although correctly located to the north of England, it stretches eastward, with the west coast facing north. Why was this?

Opposite. Ptolemy, *Insulae Albion et Hibernia* from the Blaeu atlas *Theatrum Orbis Terrarum* (1654)

There has been much scholarly discussion on the reasons for this unusual distortion but it is very unlikely that it reflects any ignorance of the geography of the British Isles. It is now generally accepted that the right-angled orientation of Scotland is probably more due to mathematics and the need of the geographers to accommodate what they knew into their established ideas about the shape of the known world being a rectangle rather than a sphere. In consequence, the information at hand was made to fit a predetermined idea in the same way that many inexperienced hill-walkers today try and make their map fit what they think should be there. Detail was manipulated to fit a particular shape and identified places were often selected more for the overall purpose of mapping the known world rather than for any intrinsic importance.

Despite this odd interpretation of facts, which may also reflect an element of cartographic conservatism, the general outline of what was to become Scotland is clearly recognisable and the map names 57 individual locations, such as coastal features, native sites (including Vanduara and Colania, which have been suggested to be Paisley and Lanark or Carstairs) and some Roman forts (for example, Bremenium or Rochester) lying to the south. More importantly, the map carries the first printed indication of the Clyde (*Clota aestuarium*) flowing from the south and entering a wide estuary on the west coast. The river runs through an area occupied by the Damnonii, a Britonnic people for whom there is no other record than that of Ptolemy.

In many respects, this image of Scotland is more understandable than earlier manuscript maps which included Scotland, such as the diagrammatic depiction of the country on John Hardyng's *Chronicle* from the middle of the fifteenth century or the somewhat oddly-shaped medieval representations which appear on the maps prepared by Matthew Paris or the creators of the Gough map. The limited information provided on Ptolemy underlines a significant and recurring feature in the cartography of much of the west of Scotland, namely that its lack of strategic importance and distance from the centre of political power resulted in far fewer and frequently less detailed representations of the local topography.

Opposite. Detail of Clyde area

et Cherſoneſus

O

Rerigonius ſinus

Nouan te A

Epidium prom:

Rerigonium

Vidogara Sinus

Epidij

Lucopibia

Longus fl.

Cer

Lelanonius ſinus

flu.

Vanduara

Carbantorigum

Gadini

Dam-

Corda

Cale

N I

Lindum

Banatia

Fluu.

nij

Clota æſtuarium

A N N

Alauna

Tamia

ellum

goue.

Colania

Coria

Vacem

Victoria

Trimontium

T A

Orrea

Curia

Bremenium

Tina flu.

H A

Otadeni

Bod

Venni

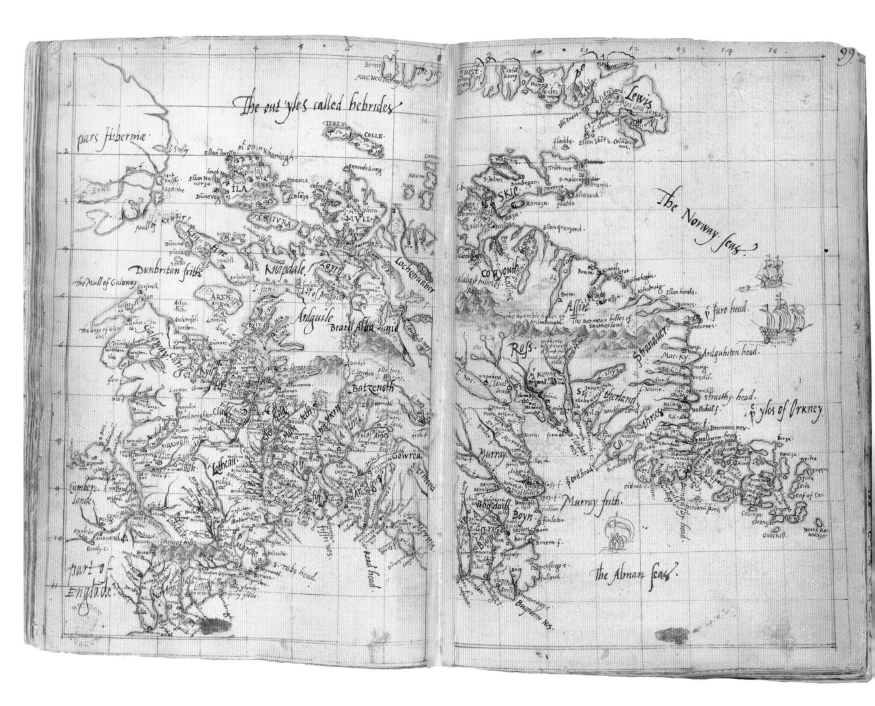

The out yles called hebrides

pars Hibernie:

The Norway seas

pars Hibernie

TIRIE COLLE

Carndeburg

Lewis
Mac Leod Lewis

ILA

IVRA

MVLL

SKIE

Dunbritan frith

Knapdale

Lochenaaber

Ardguile

Braid Alban

Assin

The Mull of Galoway

AREN

Ross

Strananyer
Mac Ky Ardquhiten head

faro head

Galoway

Batzenoth

Sutherland

strathy head

yles of Orkney

Cumber-lande

Lothean

Gowrea

Murray

Murray frith

part of Englade

Boyn

the Alman seas

CHAPTER 2

An English depiction of Clydesdale from the 1560s

This remarkably detailed image of the area of the River Clyde comes from an impressively accurate map of Scotland drawn by Laurence Nowell (*c.*1515–*c.*71), an Oxford scholar who was a friend and fellow law student of William Lambarde (1536–1601). Lambarde is celebrated as the author of the first county history of England, *A Perambulation of Kent*, published in 1576. Nowell had accompanied his friend in his travels around Britain gathering information on early manuscripts and place names in the period following the dissolution of the monasteries, when much antiquarian material was lost. It is possible that they visited Scotland during this tour in 1559. Lambarde's first book was a collection of Anglo-Saxon laws and it is now believed that Nowell was the cartographer of the map which accompanied this work, the first to be designed, printed and published in England.

More significantly, by 1563, Nowell was resident in Sir William Cecil's household as tutor to Edward de Vere, Cecil's future son-in-law. He had been recommended as a scholar and cartographer to Cecil, Queen Elizabeth I's chief advisor and Secretary of State by Thomas Randolph, an English ambassador who spent most of his professional life in Scotland at the courts of Mary, Queen of Scots and James VI. Randolph had met Nowell in Paris five years earlier and had introduced him to some Scotsmen with whom Nowell collaborated to make a map of the Scottish borders. In the same year that he entered Cecil's household, Nowell had addressed a letter to him complaining about the general inaccuracy of the maps of England and seeking support in his intention to construct improved maps of the provinces. He is also known to have prepared a small map of Britain for Cecil that the secretary was known to have carried with him everywhere.

Nowell remains a somewhat shadowy figure and is probably better known for his work on the Anglo-Saxon language, but his maps show a true artistry which provided a considerably more accurate depiction than many of his contemporaries. There is a body of evidence to support the belief that this map's greater detail is based on a large manuscript map of the British Isles which has not survived but was prepared in the mid 1550s by another and equally little-known geographer, the Scot, John Elder. Cecil knew of Elder's abilities and Nowell could have had access to a wide range of sources in the statesman's library.

The Clyde is depicted here as beginning its journey from roughly the same area as the Rivers Annan and Tweed, with some sense of its length and the widening of the channel only when it reaches Newark. Nowell has identified a considerable number of important properties along its course, including the castles of Crawford, Avondale, Bothwell, Crookston and Dumbarton, which may indicate the purpose behind the map's creation.

Opposite. Laurence Nowell, *Map of Scotland*

Overall, the information is far greater than that appearing on, for example, the map produced by the native Scot, Bishop John Leslie, which was published in 1578. Like many of the maps Cecil used during his time in power, Nowell's depiction, dated from about 1564–66, has the names of the leading landowners superscribed in red. In Clydesdale, the Earls of Arran and Lennox, as well as Lord Fleming are identified.

Interestingly, in 1563 Randolph was heavily involved in the negotiations to arrange a marriage between Mary Stuart and Lord Robert Dudley, later Earl of Leicester, which was strongly advocated by Cecil himself. This may have some relevance in the background to Nowell's map. Dudley was the son of John Dudley, Henry VIII's Lord Admiral and first Duke of Northumberland. He had negotiated a peace treaty between England and France in 1546. During his stay in Paris, Dudley met Nicolas de Nicolay, a French cosmographer, who in the dedication of his book, published in 1583, *La Navigation du Roy D'Escosse Jaques Cinquiesme du Nom* to the French admiral, the Duc de Joyeuse, describes how he was persuaded to return with Dudley to London where he was shown 'a small book written by hand in the Scottish language, containing the voyage of the King of Scotland . . . around his kingdom . . . together with the marine chart'. Robert Dudley himself took an interest in cartography and his library at Kenilworth had a range of local maps and charts.

The map which accompanied Nicolay's book was a considerable improvement on earlier depictions of Scotland, particularly in the shape of the coastline, and scholars believe it to be based on the work of James V's pilot, Alexander Lyndsay. Of far greater significance is the close similarity between Nowell's and Nicolay's outline of Scotland. Nowell's map provides further evidence of the way Tudor statesmen gathered geographical information but it is likely that it was confined to government circles and not widely shared. Whether it was Elder, Randolph or Dudley who provided him with the information, Nowell was moving in a circle of people who fully appreciated the power of cartography in the diplomacy of the period.

Opposite. Detail of Clyde estuary

SkipInce

L. fien.

L. farlan ca.

Erl of Ardguile

ailza .

AREN.

Arenca.

L. Reuenza.

L. Skriuan.

Ardguile

Ardshnsel.

Lamlas,

BVIT.

Hck.

Kilmon.

Brai

carlton.

Broa ca.

L. Goil.

Fidnus

lord Mügty

Curas

tyrue

Crosregal al. also.

dunure

S. Mary Ile

Kilwenig mo ab

Goth

L. Gare

Blackan nan.

accessls.

Egisto

Air.

Iudo

Irwin.

Clyd. f.

L. Lomonde

Roskoy

Kyir

Newark

Don

Cuprito

finlai stou

Ni

okilb

fail.

Akilmarso

Arda

Dubrito

Kilmoronak.

conwar.

Conokirk

Glascou

Buyhanan.

Newmils

Sempil

Erl of Monco

Erl of Lenox

Jenox

mok

L. Ern.

Craxstan

inceshene

intemoco

Erl of March

Baquhider

saquher

Erl of Aren

Glasco

Erl of

Erwod

perhok.

Lord knighton.

Cluds

Hamilton

Stu Mon

Publan

Ern f.

Inner meghe

Ale

Aucdale.

Bothwel.

Drime

Disdeir

Duglasdal Dramm

Hemming

faukirk

Incchefra ab.

craford fton

Cumirnal

Sterlin

clackinan

Mallar

Mocrim

craford c.

Tarwod

kinkarne

Cragy.

Clyd.

flaminto

lanrick

Mant

Garuy

Ark

Alway c.

Strathord

Beggar.

Tweda

torfecan

Blackn

kulros

Brug of Ern

S Jonlton

L. ami

nerue

Arge

DEVCALEDONIVS OCEANVS

Septentrio

ORCADES
insulæ

SCOTIA,
Regnum.

Miliaria
Scotica

Strath

Sutherlandia

Rofsia

HEBRI

DES

insulæ

Morauia

Buqu
hania

MARE

GERMANICVM

Loquha

Perth

bria

Mula

Argadia

Mentcith

Ylaa
insula

Laudonia

Cumn

Clides

ham

Mar

IRLANDIAE fiue HIBERNIAE
PARS

Meridies

Per Gerardum Mercatorem
Cum Priuilegio

Occiduus

Ortus

CHAPTER 3

'Clidesdaill' on Mercator's map of *c.* 1595

While it is recognised that the publication of the Blaeu atlas of 1654 did result in Scotland becoming one of the best mapped countries in the world, the depiction of the nation had been slowly improving since the middle of the previous century. In particular, two maps produced by Gerhard Mercator in 1564 and 1595 reflect a growing knowledge of its geography. Mercator (1512–94) is frequently referred to as the first and greatest of the Dutch cartographers who dominated the map world from the end of the sixteenth century. Most people know his name through the cylindrical map projection he first presented in his world map of 1569, but he is also recognised as the first cartographer to apply the word 'atlas' in a geographical context. Initially, this was intended to denote a description of the creation and form of the whole universe, not simply as a collection of maps. However, as Mercator died the year before his *Atlas Sive Cosmographicae Meditationes de Fabrica Mundi et Fabricati Figura* was completed, subsequent editions became bound volumes of maps alone in the form of a book and, by the middle of the following century, the word became synonymous with such publications.

Resident in Duisburg from 1552, Mercator was very much a scholar geographer, travelling very little and basing his work on his extensive library and conversations and correspondence with a wide network of contacts, which included merchants, mariners and statesmen. While his large-format world map was typical of his earlier work, his later career saw him turn to the production of more than a hundred regional maps suitable for binding into single volumes. This change may reflect a widening of the market beyond the requirements of diplomacy alone. In 1564, Mercator published a vast eight-sheet map covering the British Isles entitled *Angliae Scotiae et Hibernia nova descriptio*, which was a considerable improvement on earlier delineations and was to be copied by later cartographers, including Abraham Ortelius. The depiction of the Scottish coast was markedly better than most of its predecessors and the greater detail of place names and features of the interior suggest a local source for the topographic information.

It is increasingly considered likely that John Elder was the source of this more accurate detail. At some time before the summer of 1547, Elder had presented the English authorities with a map of Scotland which described the chief towns, castles and abbeys in each county. Mercator himself noted on his map that a friend offered him a draft with the request that it should be engraved. Certainly, the number of place names in Elder's home county of Caithness and in other areas where he is known to have been resident (e.g. Aberdeen and Glasgow) add weight to this argument. The influence of Elder on the manuscript map prepared by Nowell has been discussed already and it is possible

Opposite. Gerhard Mercator, *Scotia Regnum ...* (c.1595)

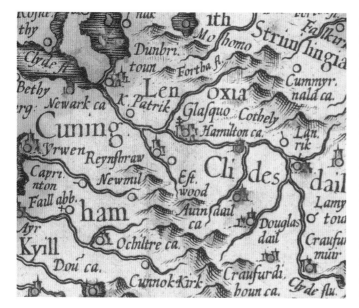

that information passed from Nowell to Mercator. Regardless of the means whereby Mercator gathered the knowledge which improved his map, its influence on subsequent depictions was relatively short-lived.

Over 30 years later, Scotland appears in the third part of Mercator's 1595 atlas in far greater detail than ever before in print. The country is covered by three maps which present a notable improvement on the 1564 depiction. The single-sheet map *Scotia Regnum*, drawn at a scale of about 25 miles to the inch, provides a more accurate coastal outline than previous depictions, particularly for the western seaboard. It is likely that this was based on the Nicolay map which had first appeared in 1583. In fact, this outline became the basis for nearly all the depictions of Scotland for the next six decades, largely through the survival of the original plates and their reuse by Jodocus Hondius and his heirs. Much of the landward detail which had been a feature of the earlier map of the British Isles was retained and enhanced by some additions and corrections.

Mercator's original three maps were to appear unaltered up to 1634 but, by 1638, the two sheets covering northern and southern Scotland separately were no longer published. Looking carefully at the depiction of the Clyde and the adjacent countryside, one of the most striking features is the width of the Firth of Clyde and the markedly narrow entrance to the upper river. On the other hand, on both the single sheet and that covering southern Scotland, there is a very clear identification of how quickly the channel is reduced upriver from Dumbarton. Unsurprisingly, neither map identifies the still minor fishing village of Greenock, but the larger-scale version includes additional place names along the banks of the river (e.g. Finlaston, Ynchman (Inchinnan), Bodwel and Draffen).

The Clyde is shown running in a generally north-westerly direction from Glasgow to the estuary but upriver from the city there are marked distortions in the alignment and positions of features. Hamilton is placed almost due east of Glasgow and Lanark is similarly placed too far north. Despite the larger scale, the map of southern Scotland only indicates one additional location (Biggar) in the Upper Ward and both versions mark the source of the Clyde as a water body lying to the west of the same group of hills which hold the sources of the Tweed and Annan.

Mercator's map had a far wider impact than merely improving the outline of the Scottish coastline. It was included as the first map of Scotland engraved in Great Britain when, in 1607, William Hole added a crudely produced copy to the first version of William Camden's *Britannia* to be illustrated with maps. Four years later, John Speed published *The Theatre of the Empire of Great Britaine*, a volume of maps based on the work of Christopher Saxton but also including a map of Scotland dated 1610. The maps were engraved in Amsterdam but the printing of the work took place in London. A close scrutiny of the Speed map and its depiction of the Clyde shows it to be a direct copy of Mercator down to the selection and orthography of the place names. Due to its popularity, there were several reprints of the *Theatre* through the seventeenth century, thereby perpetuating Mercator's influence well after his death.

Opposite and above. Detail of Clyde area

Bailmoir
Douart a.
Iula

I. strik
Dunstafage ca.
Bergomum ca.
Foir

Lo
I. Nawel
Efill
Leaue Logh
Lorne
Tar.
at
b.
Eyl
Forlan ca.
Forlan fl.
rna
Brẽ ad
Albayn
Lomond hilles
Grampius mo

Atole
Perth
ey. ca.
L. Loquhen
L. Lion
Strath
Amunde
L. Docber
L. Tay
Tay flu.
Dunkell
ia
St Johns toun
Inuer
megy ca.
Mefyn
Strath Erne
Gafk L
L. Erne
Erne fl.
Drumyn ca.
Leuy
Kinkardin

kar
uay
Lady
well
Core
breken
St Ma
chare
Swyn
ca.
Braig
Ofcir
Lofouter
les
Knapdayl
Ge
gay
Skapinche
Sandell
ca.
Karray
Can
tyr

Forlan
ca.
Kylleran
Nadayn
L. Eyn
Ymuse
Duglyn
Dunnyn ca.
Marnoch
Kil
mon
Neyum
Rofdoy
ca.
Rofne
thy
Clyde fl.
Argadia

L. Lomond
Cambel
ca.
Kerr
ca.
Kilmoro
nak
Dunbri
toun
Forthe fl.
Monoch
ca.
Dunblain
Sterling
Mente
ith
Mo
homo
Len
oxia
Cummyr
nald ca.
Lan
ruk
Stru
lingia
Fallkirk
Fortha fl.

Rofay
ca.
Bethy
K. Patrik
Glafquo
Cothely
Hamilton ca.
Cli des
daill
Lamyn
toun
Craufurd
muir

Re
uenfa.
Arren
Bute
Ardroffen ca.
Larg
as
Newark ca.
Cuning
Yrwen
Reynfbraw
Newmul
Eft.
wood
Auinsdail
ca.
Douglas
dail
Cut
ca.

Gilleia
ren
Kirk
morich
Lamalafche
tan fyrth
Dunniger
ca.
Capri
nton
Faull abb.
ham
Ochiltre ca.
Craufurdi
houn ca.
Clyde flu.

Pradda
Ar
Duna
uart ca.
Sanda
Aulea
Gudzen
ca.
Ardun
ton
Ayr
Kyill
Doú ca.
Cunnok Kirk

Cantyr mul
als Lorne
toonge
Dunbri
Caulton
Ardftin
fel
ncta
Bargany
Blaquhen
ca.
Cunnok ca.
Saucher
Dundanryk
Nythes
daill
Anan
Anan fl.
Apilga

Owyndurg
Cofwel
L. Kyan
Beloche
Ca.
Loghmuar ca.
Glanfcar
Mor
toun
Nyth flu.
Maban c.

BERNICVM
The Mul
of Gallo
way
Glenlus abb.
Gal louu:
dra
Garueis ca.
Freiff ca.
Dundra
nam abb.
Ouer flu.
Dunfr

The
Maydens
Salfid ab.
Wygton
Kirken
brik
Solway
Ana

The
Kowe
Laune
Gregu.
rgan
New ab.
bay
Carla

Copmans
ile
The Bryalle
C. Penningham
Whithorne
Meridie
Sulway

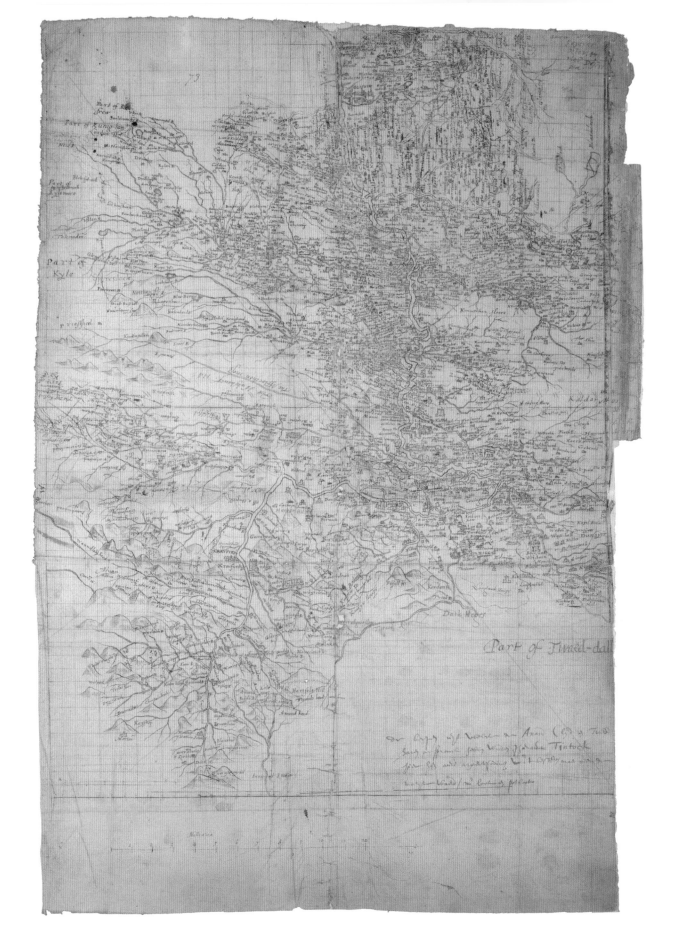

Pont's survey of Clydesdale

Like many other parts of Scotland, the earliest detailed mapping of the Clyde valley is to be found in the surviving manuscript maps drawn by Timothy Pont at the end of the sixteenth century and which are held in the National Library of Scotland in Edinburgh. Clydesdale itself is depicted on what is now described as Pont 34, perhaps the most impressive of all of his work that has come down to the present day. In addition to almost 1,400 features identified on the map, it is the only manuscript to bear a date (Sept. et Octobr. 1596 Descripta). Researchers have suggested that as this map is a later and more legible draft of original smaller pieces of fieldwork, and the autumn of 1596 may be an indicative date of the end of Pont's active surveying. Certainly, the map has variant alignments of names in different parts, probably the result of such amalgamation of earlier work while a grid of small squares over its surface hints at some form of editorial process.

Much more importantly, this map again gives some indication of how Pont went about his mapping and also of how different areas of Scotland were perceived at the time. Its coverage encompasses most of the Clyde's drainage basin and is a significant example of mapping based along a major river valley. Working largely on his own or possibly assisted by his brother Zachary, Pont's technique of valley traverses followed what was a standard practice of the day where the relationship of individual places to each other was of greater importance than precision of geodetic accuracy. This is also in accord with what is now generally accepted as the methodology behind Pont's work, namely chorography. This was the recording of not only the geographical features of an area in map form but also the written descriptions of its landed families and their genealogy, its mineral and other resources and its overall character – in other words, a form of state political survey. Pont's textual description of the district of Cunningham in Ayrshire is the only part of his writings to survive. This forms part of a collection of topographical writings gathered by Sir James Balfour of Denmilne (1600–57), Lyon King of Arms and a noted antiquary, and its existence strengthens the argument for Pont being such a chorographer. This approach may possibly have been influenced by the appearance of William Camden's *Britannia*, published in 1586, only three years after Pont had graduated from St Andrews University.

He remains one of the unsung heroes of sixteenth-century Scotland and his remarkable achievement in mapping much of the country still poses many questions. Little survives to suggest what the motivation was for such a comprehensive survey. Pont's father Robert was a well-connected and leading figure in both church and state circles, being moderator of the early Reformed church on six separate occasions between 1570 and

Opposite. Timothy Pont, [*Glasgow and the county of Lanark*] (1596)

Pont's depiction of the Clyde in its middle stretches between Lanark and Dalzell Castle indicates the level of place-name detail on this manuscript

1597. Both Timothy and Zachary were churchmen, but there is no evidence to back up any suggestion that the maps were prepared to aid better ecclesiastical government. In fact, Pont generally took far greater pains over the depiction of significant castles than church buildings, frequently providing elevations drawn from ground level with some attempt to retain a recognisable form of the building. This can be seen in the comparison of the sketch of St Mungo's Cathedral in Glasgow with that of, for example, Crawford Castle.

Significantly, the southern section of this manuscript shows both the 'Poutrail' and Daer Waters meeting just south of 'Crukenston' to form the river itself, suggesting some familiarity with the sources of the Clyde. In addition, the creation of a single map of a major river basin is important. While Scottish counties did have their origins in the medieval shires created

in the reign of Alexander I (1107–24), sheriffdoms based on distinct geographical areas (such as river valleys) were often the more recognisable units. Both Clydesdale and the neighbouring Tweeddale were names in more common usage at the time than the concept of the counties of Lanark and Peebles.

Over 1,000 of the map's place names identify human settlements, ranging from the detailed sketches of Glasgow, Hamilton, Biggar and Lanark through the careful depictions of Avondale and Craignethan Castles to more remote locations in the hills around Crawford (O. Southwood). Drawn well before the development of any road system, the map also indicates several bridges, including an ornate and buttressed bridge across the Clyde downstream from Hamilton at 'Clydesbrig'. While the manuscript maps overall show very few roads, the location of bridges is an important indicator to the routes used in Pont's

Image of St Mungo's Cathedral (left) in comparison with the detail of Crawford Castle (right)

day and of the comparatively limited movement of goods and people.

The over-riding impression of the map is that the valleys of both the Clyde and its main tributaries were densely settled by the late medieval period. Tower houses and sizeable castles emphasise that the area had a considerable representation of the aristocracy resident in the immediate area. Regardless of what we know and what we can only surmise, Pont 34 is a fascinating, challenging and rich source of information on the geography of Clydesdale more than 400 years ago.

Right. Pont's depiction of the meeting of the 'Poutrail' and Daer Waters suggests some knowledge of the immediate geography of the sources of the Clyde

GLOTTIANA
PRÆFECTVRA
SVPERIOR.
Auct. Timoth: Pont.

THE VPPER WARD of
CLYDS-DAYL.

Scala Miliaria
1 2 3 4 5

CHAPTER 4

Pont's work engraved: Joan Blaeu's atlas *Theatrum Orbis Terrarum* of 1654

Recent research suggests that Timothy Pont died sometime in the early 1610s without seeing much of his work published. Although it is possible that his map of Lothian and Linlithgow was engraved at some date around 1610–12, it would take another 40 years and the combined efforts of several key individuals before the bulk of Pont's cartographic efforts were to appear in the fifth volume of the great world atlas *Theatrum Orbis Terrarum* or *Atlas Novus*, published by the Blaeu family of Amsterdam in 1654. Through this landmark publication, Scotland was to become one of the best-mapped countries in the world, based largely on Pont's original fieldwork. Certainly, the maps which appear in the atlas and its many reproductions are better known (and more easily available) than the original manuscripts, but the time gap between Pont's death and the publication date is extremely important in understanding the story behind his work, what the atlas maps show and, more importantly, what they do not show.

Given the extensive coverage of the atlas maps, it is clear that the surviving manuscripts reflect only a fraction of what was surveyed and the story of their survival is an intriguing account of achievement and loss, dogged by neglect, disinterest, copyright restrictions, the ravages of time and civil war. When Sir James Balfour acquired Pont's maps from his heirs in or shortly before 1628, his neighbour, Sir John Scot of Scotstarvit

(1585–1670), Director of Chancery and a Privy Councillor, was already in correspondence with the Dutch publishers, Willem Jansz and Joan Blaeu regarding the publication of a volume of Latin poems by Scottish writers which was eventually published in 1637 under the title *Delitiae Poetarum Scotorum*. Surviving letters indicate that Blaeu, who had already begun work on his world atlas, sought Scot's assistance in providing him with relevant maps. It would now appear that Balfour passed some of Pont's work on to the Blaeus through Scot before the summer of 1631. At about the same time, Sir Robert Gordon of Straloch (1580–1661) became involved in editing certain maps which Blaeu had found difficult to interpret. These he had returned to Scotland and the map of Clydesdale was one such document, as confirmed by an entry in Dutch on the original manuscript. Gordon redrafted the Clydesdale map some time prior to 1642 but it is based entirely on Pont's original work. Subsequently, Blaeu was to divide the map into two; namely *Glottiana Praefectvra Inferior* and *Glottiana Praefectvra Svperior* or the Nether and Upper Wards of Clydesdale, justified in his own address to the atlas reader as separating 'into several what was one confused map'. The various wars between King and Parliament and the English and Dutch further delayed progress and it would be another 12 years before the atlas appeared eventually in print – with 49 maps and 154 pages of descriptive text.

Opposite. Joan Blaeu, *Glottiana praefectura superior* (1654)

Detail of configuration around Chappell from Joan Blaeu, *Glottiana prefectura inferior* (1654)

Looking at the two engraved maps, there is a sense that the lower Clyde basin was a noticeably densely populated area. Nearly 950 places taken from Pont's manuscript are named on the Nether Ward map – although the Dutch engravers clearly had some problems with the transliteration of the original text, as evinced by 'Broorasyd' for Broomsyd and 'Daltel Cast' for Dalzell Castle. East of Hamilton, the engravers may have omitted some places because of their density but they have also made a poor job of reproducing the policies of the substantial building to the north-east of Carfin, possibly the chapel used as a burial ground. This site is no longer extant but was located beside

what became Chapelhall Iron Works. There is a considerable area of overlap between the two maps to the extent that 150 names are common to both depictions. However, while Lanark is clearly identified and coloured on the Nether Ward version, its name is completely missing and a blank space is left above the symbols which locate the burgh on the other depiction. This Upper Ward map shows a much lighter settlement pattern across what is a more upland area, with only 695 names identified.

Of much greater importance is the omission of more than 90 names from the original Pont manuscript which have not

Joan Blaeu, *Glottiana praefectura inferior* (1654), detail of Lanark

been reproduced on either of the engraved sheets. Not only is this a loss in information transfer but it means that this area was even more densely settled than the printed maps suggest. In addition, the engravers have reduced Pont's elevations and sketches to a more standard use of symbols, thereby diminishing the amount of building detail of both country houses and small burghs. A comparison between Pont's image of the layout of Lanark and that on the atlas map emphasises that the Blaeu version is a poorer source. On both of the engraved maps, the river system is shown in considerable detail and provides a locational framework for the settlement pattern. There are cases

where the alignment of the Clyde, particularly between Lanark and Crawford, is noticeably incorrect but this again emphasises that the survey focused more on the location of places in relation to each other.

The accompanying text to these atlas maps has little on the Clyde itself but much on the history of the local landed gentry. However, the one sentence on Glasgow states 'this is the most famous market in this area, in a lovely situation, praised for its apple trees, and has a beautiful bridge' and this provides key elements in the relationship of the river to the settlements on its banks which will be discussed in later sections.

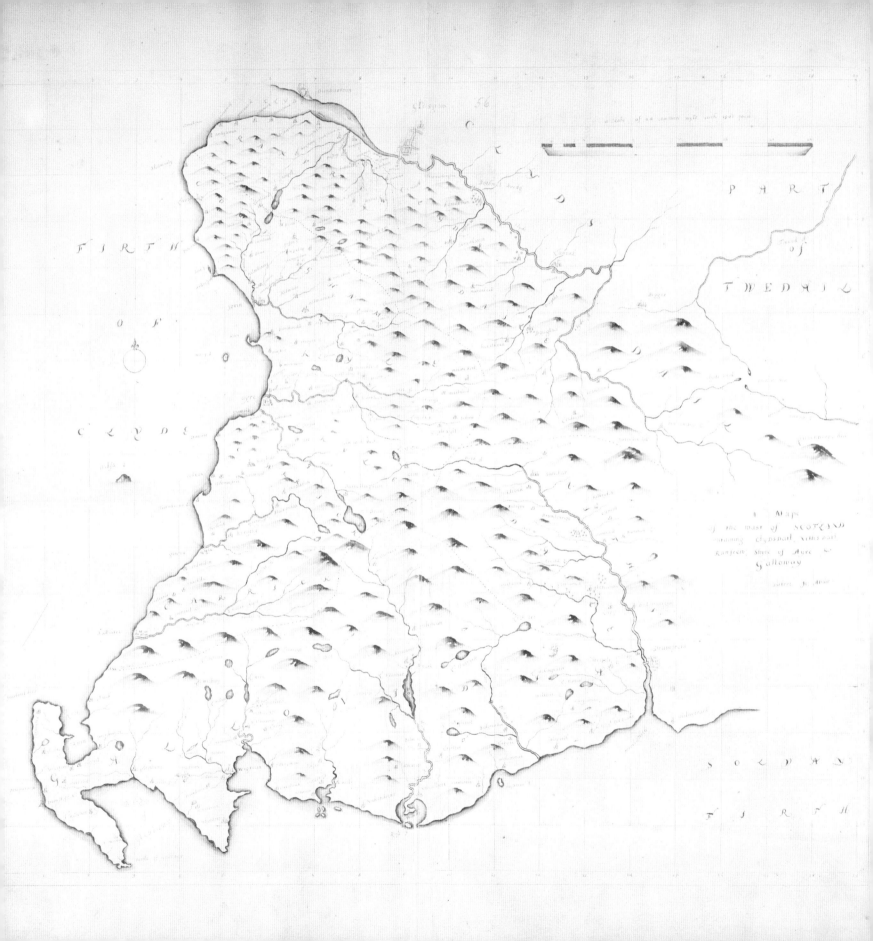

CHAPTER 6

John Adair's map of the west of Scotland

Towards the end of the seventeenth century, Scotland produced a map-maker of exceptional talent. This was John Adair (1660–1718), whose interests covered natural history and antiquarianism as well as the mapping of estates, counties and the coastal waters of the kingdom. Much has been written about Adair and the difficulties he faced in financing his surveys at a time when the political climate was affected by the turmoil of the Glorious Revolution of 1688 and its consequences. It is also clear that Scotland in the 1690s was badly affected by the economic disaster of the Darien scheme and may not have had either the finances or administrative resources to support his work over the demands of others, most notably Sir Robert Sibbald and John Slezer.

One difficulty in assessing Adair's contribution is the confused and contradictory evidence regarding the background to his activities. It is assumed that the initial motivation for his surveys was a request from Moses Pitt, a London bookseller, to prepare maps of the Scottish counties for a projected *Great Atlas*. This resulted in an application for support to the Scottish Privy Council which, in May 1681, gave Adair authority 'to take a survey of the whole shires of the Kingdom, and to make up maps thereof'. Adair had appended a new map of Clackmannanshire to his submission which clearly demonstrated a talent and quality of draftsmanship all the more impressive given his age.

With this support, Adair promptly set about surveying the Lothians, completing the three counties by 1682 but at this point the picture becomes far less clear. Pitt's atlas project was beginning to fail and Charles II's newly appointed Geographer for Scotland, Sir Robert Sibbald, was tasked with producing a geographical description of the country with accompanying maps. Sibbald's claim in his *Account of the Scottish Atlas*, dated 1683, that Adair's commission to survey was related to this project is suspect and his description of him as a 'skilful mechanic' rather smacks of condescension. Regardless of this, Adair appears to have been tied into a contractual agreement with Sibbald which prohibited anyone else from publishing maps.

By this date, Adair was having problems with the promised financial support – a difficulty which was to plague the rest of his career. Despite this, the period between 1683 and 1685 saw him produce maps of the Forth, Strathearn and the Carse of Gowrie, East Fife and the country around Stirling. Following this, he turned his attention to the west, and this map which covers Clydesdale, Nithsdale, Renfrewshire, Ayrshire and Galloway on one sheet probably dates from 1686. It is also possibly the last landward survey Adair made as part of his obligations to Sibbald for, in the May of that year, he appealed to the Privy Council to be paid the balance of the monies due

Opposite. John Adair, *A mape of the west of Scotland* (c.1685)

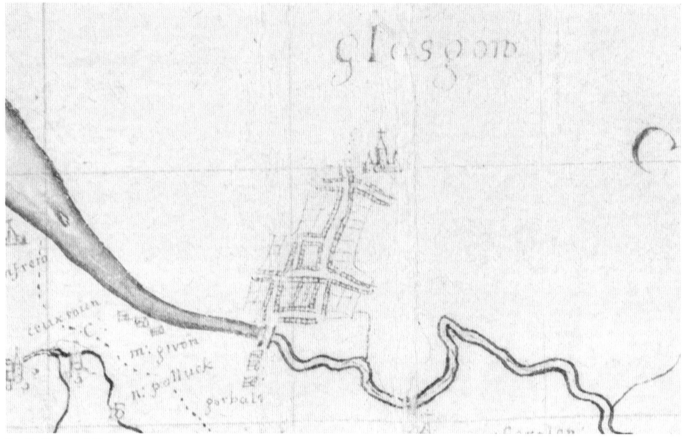

Detail of layout of Glasgow

him. The following month, the Scottish Parliament passed an Act in his favour to provide sufficient funding, through a tunnage levy on shipping, to defray any expenses incurred by a hydrographic survey of the Scottish coast.

From then on, Adair appears to have focused his efforts on maritime mapping, spending several summers charting the Solway and Clyde coasts and the Western Isles. In a submission to the Privy Council in February 1698, a list of his maps, as opposed to charts, showed that little else had been surveyed in the intervening 12 years. This lack of achievement was to be repeated in subsequent records, and it is difficult to avoid the assumption that Adair promised much but finished relatively little when compared with, for example, Timothy Pont's achieve-

ment. While some of his work appears to have been lost in the intervening years, Adair's widow compiled an inventory of his papers following his death which clearly shows that he produced hardly any other topographical maps after 1686.

In that 1723 inventory is recorded one map of the 'Inland Counties of the South and West part of Scotland, with the Coast thereof, viz. from Dumfries round the Mull of Galloway, and northward along the Coasts of Carrick, Kyle, and Cunningham, and up the River Clyde to Crawford, &c. to a Scale of 4 computed Miles in the Inch', along with a smaller map of the area around Hamilton and another covering an area from Douglas to the southern shore of the Forth. Neither of these two latter depictions appears to have survived and all that is

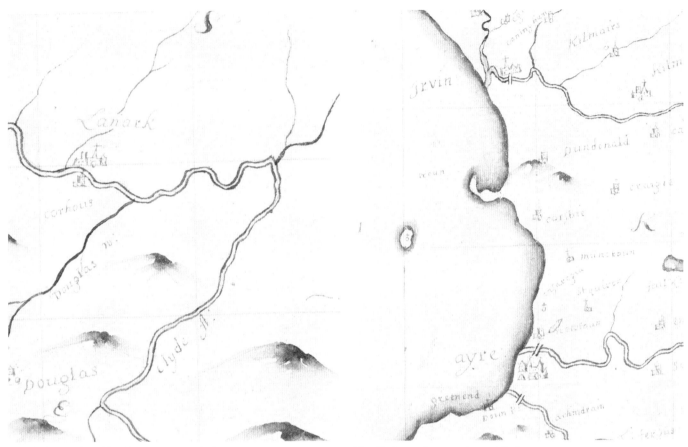

Detail of Lanark and bend in river at Pettinain

Detail of coast between Ayr and Irvine

left of Adair's work of the western counties is this very general coverage of the whole of the south-west.

General it may be, but it does provide some fascinating, if limited, details. The first thing to notice is the marked lack of features on the north bank of the Clyde, apart from the identification of Glasgow, Lanark and Biggar. Glasgow, however, is shown in a plan form, which is the only image of the city's layout that survives from the seventeenth century and it stands in contrast to much of the rest of the map. Like several other of Adair's surviving manuscript maps, the sheet is covered by a grid and has a margin, suggesting that this was a finished state of the work.

Later scholars have dismissed some of its cartography because Adair clearly copied the Solway coast outline from the Blaeu map *Gallovidia*, but this was not the case for the Ayrshire section which gives a far superior impression than even the later Clyde chart published by George Scott in 1731. Much of the sheet is covered in groups of hill images which bear little resemblance to reality but Adair has taken pains to indicate the turns of the river, particularly its great sweep around Tinto and Pettinain, possibly indicating that, like others, his surveying was based on traverses along river valleys. However, this may have been limited in the case of the Clyde for, unlike Pont, he suggests its source at 'Clyds head' near to the start of both the Annan and the Tweed.

P.Dornick
ardentenie
P.Chapell
Luss
Cameden
Gartur
Card ross
Loggs M.
alva
Delaemirbray
Cumbell

Balmaha
Buchannan
Drymen
Bucklive
Holm
Sterling
S.Ninians
Cambus
Aloa
Clackmanan
Kincardin
Blair
Cedros
Tom

CUMB
Ros lue
Row
Caple
Ross
Kilmarnok
Camrons
Gartness
Duntraith
Strathblain
Moork
Craig anet
Herbert
Towfouls
Stony house
Kinnardin
Salinhill

arden
tenie
Glen Freoe
Clochan
Bon
Hill of
Ardmore
Balloch
Lesinside
Dumbrtton
Dunglas
Kilpatrik
Woodhead
Glorat
Kilsyth
Falkirk
Beancross
Bonefs
Blackni

ruel
ercaple
Ouig
Rozneth
Gouran
Green
Crafardyk
Pt.Glass
Newrark
Bishopton
Erskine
Renfren
Scotstoun
Calder
Munklandk
Deerdyke
Jan
Stamanou
Tarfichen
Newliston
Bathgate
Queens

Duncon
Kilmand
Arden
Artine
Inverkip
Kelly
Finlaystoun
Houston
Partich
Glasgow
Roughsoles
Munkland
Kirkintillo
Cumbernauld
Calender
Glen
Westguard
Lithgon

Rothsay
M.Steuart
U.Cumbra
Skellmarly
Knok
N Paisley
Johnstone
Ellensley
Gavin
Gorbells
Cardanal
Barrenfuld
Tovcens
Boghal
Bradyskolm
Roschall
Ardree
Farskin
Moorhead
whiteburn
Crawfordloch
Calder
hall

Largo
Serapls C.
Iocwin
Beith
Hulkhead
Cathcart
Pottokhous
Ruglon
Milk Cast.
Bathwel
Orbistoun
K of Shots
Const

Kelburn
S.Annan
Nielston
Egglisham
Clandeston
Kilbride
Hamilton
Niesland
Torran
Mother well
Dalzil
Carfin
Winshan
Rashiehill
Castle greg

Huntersloun
Pencors
Scamilth
Dunlop
Blacklan
HAM
Kingnell
Raplock
Strain
Birknood
Clyster
Camneham
Carluke
Jariswood
Forth
Fala
Cobinsha
Kensnell
Newbigen

L.Cumbra
Horse Ic.
Saltcols
Ardgowan
Kilwining
Eglintoun
Irvin
Corsill
Steuertoun
Moorgett
Emnick
CLYDESDALE
Dolserf
Corstair
Lochtarthall
Kirt
Skirti

Broduk C.
Blacktellyr
Lapith
Burtnhill
Kilmars
Kilmarnok
Dean
Cranfordland
Cast.
Evermuir
Achokan
Douglass
Mead
Middintele
Boighall
Biggar
Kilbucho

Lamlash I.
L.Mary I.
C.Dundonald
Konsby
C.Craigy C.
Symington
Cairn
hill
Loudon Cast.
Newmilt
Loudon hill
Gaursbrahead
Crawford I.
Harside
Lamington
Birok
Newhall
Routhier
Glenholm

Kitskiddel
Kingscass
Prostvick
Failaby
Auchingute
Ayre
Torbolton
Yeaston
Jesnoch
Brantwood
Woodhead
Soirn C.
Holthous
Mochline
Boig house
Crawford
Newton
Lindsay
Glenbreck
PEE

Dounon
Plada I.
Grennan
Craighall
Stair
Bars
Ochiltra
Wallwood
Auchenseck
Whithaugh
Stanhill
Skeel
Crawford
oleverias

Nivark
Auchendrain
Sundrum
Glencord
Drungan
Dalrymple
Cats C.
Bonningtoun
Whiteholm
Darnill
Auchinorn
Garf
Lead Mines
Tweedsha

Demure
Hilton
Monknod
Cassils
Shankton
Barlish
Glen kynner
Laicht C.
Waterhead
Kirkonel
Spangok
Pedvin
Koom
Wobslan

K.Maybole
CowRagnet
D'asmore
Knockblaid
Posnil
Gavils
Sanghart
Tweedsha

Covas
Thomastoun
Dilduf
Glenc'urit
Kirkmichel
Glass
Streton
Dalmellin
Cumnock
Elcok C.
Achingruch
Drumlanrik
Knok
Thornnat

Turnberry
Dolgelham
Blachan
Kilkeran
Daylykirk
Kilshonar
Bargeny
Gleanle
Streton
Arron
L.Dun
Longbrae
Longfoot
Holm
Craigny
Caronhill
Choburn
Hoomwood
Dalsinth

Girvin
Ardmillan
Tormiksbell
Dalrym
Castle
Dun
Poumeldon
Streil
Bank
Dalgisham
Laun
Bardon

CARRICK
Kiracklach R.
Sinchar R.
Pinmir
Darle
Kirkbride
Blair
Palgoun
Craiginga ulin
Dunkans ton
Mikil
Trostan
Chaples
mark
Glencairn
Dalminth

Balentrae
Kilore
rena
Gartus
Garery
Skestoun
Quare
wood

CLYDE FIRTH
Clyde Firth
Cuning
ham
KYLE
CARRICK
CLYDESDALE
AIR SHIRE
NITHS
LIGHT

CHAPTER 7

John Elphinstone's map: an improved outline but weak in detail

This depiction of the Clyde comes from a map of Scotland which was published only four months before Charles Edward Stuart landed on the island of Eriskay in 1745. It was priced at 2/6d and dedicated to Prince William Augustus, Duke of Cumberland, Commander-in-Chief of the allied forces then fighting in Europe during the War of the Austrian Succession. As the title states, it was laid down from recent surveys and the 'most approved observations' by John Elphinstone, described as a practitioner engineer. Elphinstone's career as a cartographer remains an enigma to anyone studying Scotland's maps. This map, however, is a fascinating document which indicates the growing improvement in accuracy but which also poses several questions.

Relatively little is known about the cartographer, despite him being the eldest son of Charles, ninth Lord Elphinstone. It has been suggested that he may have suffered from a physical disability, which would make his achievements all the more remarkable. He was frequently mentioned by subsequent surveyors, such as John Thomson, as one of the individuals responsible for the improved mapping of the country. The earliest record of him is in a letter sent in June 1742 to the Duke of Hamilton, requesting his support for employment as an artist or architect. Two years later, however, he entered the military branch of the Board of Ordnance as a practitioner engineer and so produced

this map while serving as a soldier. Nonetheless, in 1743 a map of Great Britain and Ireland which he had drawn was engraved by Richard Cooper and published in Edinburgh. It was dedicated to John Dalrymple, Earl of Stair, another Commander of British forces and one of the Scottish aristocrats who had made the transition to serving the British state following the Union. This map shows in outline certain errors made by Moll in the depiction of the north coast but itself provides a poor impression of the west coast and Clyde estuary. Possibly as an insight to his own character, Elphinstone noted 'I don't here pretend to have been quite free from errors but they will be found small in comparison of the above ones.'

Interestingly, at about the same time, he produced *A New & Correct Map of the Lothians* which includes an advertisement claiming that the work corrected the mistakes of 'these published already in three seperate [sic] sheets', suggesting a criticism of Cooper's earlier engravings of Adair's surveys of these counties. Although this map is dated 1744, it clearly marks the site of the battle of Prestonpans, at which Elphinstone may have been present. More significantly, the map is a close copy of Cooper's work with no obvious improvement in the mapping and as many errors as the original. Given the disparity of date and detail, it is a little uncertain when his map of Scotland did first

Opposite. John Elphinstone, *A new & correct map of North Britain* (1745), extract for the River Clyde

Detail of upper river showing Koom and Spangok

appear but, while there are many elements of the topography which are markedly inaccurate, it was the most up-to-date version available to officers on both sides in the ensuing military campaign. More significantly, several copies have survived, variously annotated to indicate the location of camps and the routes of military roads.

Turning to the map's detail of the Clyde, it is clear that Elphinstone has based his depiction on earlier maps. His spelling of place names bears some similarities to those on maps by Moll (e.g. Gouran, Pedwin) but others, such as Spangok and Koom, defy interpretation. The delineation of the course of the river is much poorer than that on the Clydesdale map in Moll's 1725 atlas and shows neither Pettinain nor the curve of the

Clyde there. In fact, the river is indicated with a markedly straight north-west alignment from the area around Lanark, which is not identified. Dalserf is incorrectly located on the north bank and there is no clear indication of the river's source. The neighbouring county of Selkirkshire is misnamed Roxburghshire and, overall, the county boundaries are inexact. The map contains a list of authorities for Elphinstone's improvements which includes Adair, Alexander Bryce and Murdoch Mackenzie. While it repeats the addition of the outline of earlier errors in marking the coast, it is the mention of Mackenzie which is surprising since he is believed to have begun his survey in the Orkneys only in 1744 and opens up the possibility of Elphinstone having a wide and up-to-date network of contacts.

Detail of river where Lanark should be

In truth, the map was of limited value for the movement of troops since Elphinstone's identification of upland areas appears to be more schematic than accurate and the scale of more than 13 miles to the inch was not detailed enough for any tactical, strategic or ordnance planning. Although Elphinstone was to accompany Cumberland during his advance north and was at the battle of Culloden, he was not to be involved in the Military Survey in any way, despite being promoted to the rank of sub-engineer in 1748. This may have been because his talents were better suited to artistic depiction, as is evinced by his collection of views of various important Edinburgh buildings and Glamis Castle, but he may also have been unfit for the exertions of field survey in the remoter areas of the Highlands. His contem-porary William Edgar had died from fatigue while surveying in the north in 1746.

The map was engraved by Thomas Kitchin, one the most prolific London engravers of the period, and published there by Andrew Millar, a Scottish publisher working in the Strand. They were to produce a close copy of Elphinstone's map of the Lothians themselves in 1745, possibly capitalising on the interest engendered by the events in Scotland at the time. A second larger-scale copy of the Scottish map, with elements in the cartouche and decoration emphasising the subjugation of the rebellious Jacobites, was to appear in 1746, dedicated to Willem Anne van Keppel, second Earl of Albemarle, Cumberland's successor as the Commander-in-Chief in Scotland.

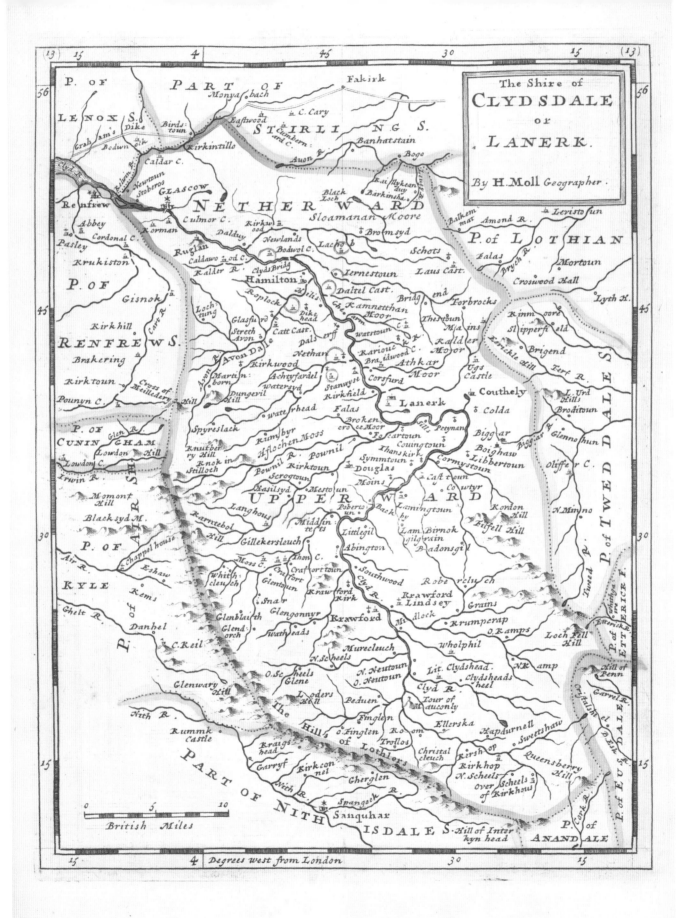

The Shire of
CLYDSDALE
or
LANERK.

By H. Moll Geographer.

CHAPTER 8

A London cartographer seizes a business opportunity: the 'Moll' atlas of 1745

In a piece of brazenly audacious self-promotion, the northern schoolteacher and land surveyor, George Mark had printed in 1728 a proposal 'For Publishing by Subscription, An Accurate Map or Geometrical Survey of the Shires of Lothian, Tweddale, and Clydesdale'. This was not a particularly unusual business approach for the period and it was a good way for a surveyor to 'test the water' to see if sufficient funds could be raised to finance any such undertaking. What is slightly more out of the ordinary is Mark's extensive comments on the contemporary cartography available to him when surveying Roman remains on either side of the border. In his own words, he found 'horrid and unaccountable Blunders and Mistakes committed in the maps . . . Rivers sometimes made to run over the Tops of the highest Mountains, and on the wrong Sides of Towns and Villages, and sometimes Rivers are represented in Places where there are none, and as often omitted where they should be represented: And in a Word, they are no more than a Parcel of crooked wavey Lines drawn at random, and not only blundered in their several Turnings and Windings, but even in their general Tendencies and Bearings.'

While Mark made an appeal to the Scottish nobility and gentry to rectify this national slight by contributing and encouraging him to 'doing their Country a Piece of common Justice',

finishing by also offering his services in surveying estates, his suggestion fell on deaf ears. There is no record of any Scottish maps or plans drawn by him, which might raise questions about his own abilities in comparison with the material he so strongly castigated. Just because one critic is scathing about the work of others does not necessarily mean that his own is any better. Nonetheless, it is worthwhile considering which Scottish maps he found so markedly incorrect.

In fact, in 1728 there were surprisingly few published maps available for the areas Mark proposed to cover by his proposal. Certainly, those maps included in the great Blaeu atlas were more than 70 years old by this date and, being in a volume for the library, they were generally not in circulation, if only through price alone. However, there was one other atlas of the period, produced three years earlier by the London cartographer, engraver and publisher, Hermann Moll (c.1654–1732). Entitled *A Set of Thirty-Six New and Correct Maps of Scotland Divided into its Shires*, it was, in effect, a companion volume to an atlas covering the counties of England and Wales produced by Moll in association with Thomas and John Bowles the previous year and reflected a growing interest in Scotland following the Union in 1707. Moll, an extremely successful businessman, was an astute judge of what might sell and he designed the work as

Opposite. Herman Moll, *The shire of Clydsdale or Lanerk* (1745)

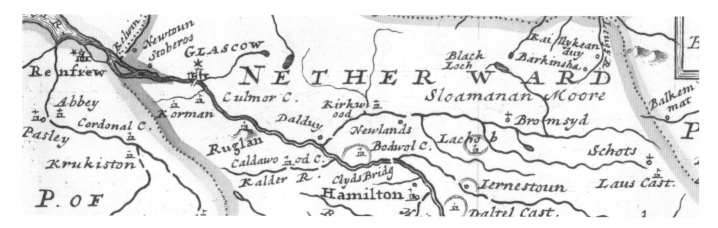

more for the pocket than the study. As the title page maintained, this was 'a Work long wanted, and very useful for all Gentlemen that Travel to any Part of that Kingdom'.

It was first advertised May 1725, generally selling for 8s, and included 34 maps of the shires and districts of Scotland. Moll informed his readers in a preliminary note that the county maps are based on those of Gordon and Pont, amended by information from the surviving manuscript work done by John Adair, although this is open to question, given how limited the topographical detail is on the Moll maps. Nonetheless, it is possible that Moll had access to Adair's work through their mutual association with Moses Pitt in his failed scheme for a new English atlas. In addition, Moll's claim that 'generous Informations' were received from 'Curious Noblemen and Gentlemen' should be viewed with considerable caution.

Moll died in 1732 but another edition of the atlas, *Scotland Delineated; Or Thirty-Six New and correct Maps of North Britain* appeared in 1745, again sold by the Bowles brothers. Despite the title change and the repeated description of the maps being 'new and correct', this is merely a reissue of the original work. However, the amended date of issue certainly suggests that the publishers calculated that its appearance would exploit a renewed public focus on Scotland following the initial success of the Jacobite Rising in 1745. It was first advertised

in September 1745, only 12 days before the battle of Preston-pans, but, by December, that early interest appears to have waned. A further version of the atlas appeared sometime after 1747 with additions showing the new military forts established in the wake of the Rising.

Given Mark's comments on the depiction of rivers, a close inspection of the relevant Moll coverage of the Clyde on *The Shire of Clydsdale or Lanerk* seems to confirm some of his criticism. In truth, the maps throughout the work are a poor shadow of the detail shown on their Blaeu sources and this underlines how limited were the resources that could have been useful to the army in Scotland. The river itself is shown initially as the coming together of three tributaries flowing west from the county boundary and lying north of Hapdurnell. Joining other streams flowing from the south, it trends north-west before turning north-east and making its wide loop around Pettinain. The size and scale of the map limits the amount of detail which it provides to the user and, as the publishers were reliant on other people's work, there are some unusual transcriptions of place names (e.g. Dalduy, Symmtoun, Bodwol C.). However, in the rush to be informed about north Britain in the troubled times of late 1745, it is doubtful if too many customers would be critical of the depiction of a country so little known.

Opposite. Detail of source of river

REWS.

Avon R. Avon Dale
Dals
Karioue C.
Kaialer
Brigend

Nethan
Braidwood C.
MOOR

Kirkwood
Athkar
Ugs Castle
Benickle Hill

Martin born
Achtyfardel
Corsfurd
Moor
Terf R.

Cross of Meilledery
watersyd
Stanwyst
Couthely
L. Urd Hills

Hill
Dungevil Hill
Kirkfield
Lanerk
Colda
Broditoun

Spyreslack
waterhead
Falas
sills
Petynan
Biggar

Kumbyr
Broken croce Moor
Foscartoun
Couingtoun
Biggar
Glenno hun

Knutberry Hill
Hflochen Moss
Thanskirk
Boighaw

Knok in Stilloth
Pownil R. Pownil
Symmtoun
Cormystoun
Libbertoun
Oliffer C.

Pownil Kirktoun
Douglas
Cast toun

Scrogtoun
Moins
Cowtyr

Hasilsyd
Mestoun
U P P E R   W A R D
Kordon Hill
N. Minno

Langhous
Pobertoun
Back
Lamingtoun
Filfell Hill

Karntebol Hill
Middin tents
Littlegil
Lam gilg by
Birnok rain

Chappel house
Gillekersleuch
Abington
Badonsgil

Eshaw
Moss C.
Thon C.
Southwood
Robe rclu ch

Kems
Whith cleuch
Crafort
Crafort toun
Clyd R.
Krawford Lindsey

Danhel
Glentoun
Krawford Kirk
Grains

Glenblaith
Snair
Glengonnyr
Krawford
Midlock
Krumperap
O. Kamps
Loch Fell Hill

C. Keil
Glendorch
Watheads
Wholphil

Glenwary Hill
O. Scheels
Glene
N. Scheels
Murecleuch
N. Neutoun
O. Neutoun
Lit. Clydshead
Clydsheads heel
NK amp

Nith R.
L oders Hill
Peduen
Clyd R.
Tour of Mauconly
Ellerska
Hapdurnell
Sweetshaw

Kummk Castle
The Hills of Lothlers
Finglen
o. Finglen
Ko om
Trollos
Christal cleuch
Kersh op
Kirkhop

Kraigs head
Garryf
Kirkcon nel
Gherglen
N. Scheels
Over Scheels of Kirkhous
Queensberry Hill

Nith R.
Spangock R.
Hill of Penn

P A R T   O F   N I T H
Sanquhar
I S D A L E S
Hill of Inter kyn head
A N A N D A L E

5   10

itish Miles

4   Degrees west from London   30   15

MAP
of the
COUNTY
of
RENFREW
Surveyed by JOHN AINSLIE in 1796

Published as the act directs June 20th 1800. and sold by Mr. Ainslie Hanover Street Edinr. Messrs Richardson & Co. Glasgow and Mr. William Faden Geographer to the King Charing Cross London

To William Macdowal Esqr OF GARTHLAND Lord Lieutenant OF THE COUNTY OF RENFREW

This Map is most humbly Inscribed by his much obliged and most obedient Servt.

John Ainslie

CHAPTER 9

The Clyde in the age of the county map

In March 1754 an influential group of noblemen, gentlemen, clergy and merchants met in a London coffee house to form the Society for the Encouragement of Arts, Manufactures and Commerce. The following September, a letter from a Cornish vicar, William Borlase, to his friend Henry Baker, one of the founder members, suggested that the society offer some reward for the best plan or survey of a city or district in an effort to improve the accuracy of the country's maps. Local historians and topographers were well aware of the deficiencies of many of the available sources, particularly those by Moll, and after some debate, a series of £100 premiums were eventually approved, with a recommendation to select a 1 inch to 1 mile scale. Although this had been a popular scale for nearly a century and had been used in several earlier surveys, it was its promotion by the society which helped establish it as a standard and, subsequently, influenced the Ordnance Survey. For almost the next 50 years, the society was to award both money and medals for a series of county surveys with an initial aspirational aim of providing a national coverage of improved mapping.

In truth, such a sum of money on offer would never provide sufficient funding for any such survey but the society did have a significant influence in establishing a better style and increasing the accuracy of county maps. More valuably, it introduced a system of appointing referees for maps and of examining field notebooks. Although no Scottish survey was supported in this way, the raising of standards had a profound influence which percolated north in the second half of the eighteenth century, partly through the work of Andrew Armstrong who had been awarded a bounty of 50 guineas for his 1769 map of Northumberland before he went on to produce maps of Berwickshire (1771), the Lothians (1773) and Ayrshire (1775).

Most county maps of the period were the result of individual ventures sponsored by subscriptions from the local gentry who would underwrite the costs of any such proposal. The history of Scottish mapping is littered with failed schemes and of surveyors being declared bankrupt through the lack of financial support. Possibly the leading example of this was the commercial failure of John Thomson's 1832 *Atlas of Scotland* which ended with the public sale of both his copper plates and the atlas volumes. Thomson may well have been influenced by the Society of Arts approach to verification, for the constituent maps of his atlas rested on the attestation by trusted authorities for their accuracy.

Thomson based several of these depictions on the best avail-

Opposite. John Ainslie, *Map of county of Renfrew* (1800)

Overleaf. William Forrest, *County of Lanark* (1818)

able county surveys and the introduction to the volume provides a valuable contemporary assessment of what those resources were. Of the counties on the banks of the Clyde, Thomson's negative comments on the Armstrongs' map of Ayrshire, which had taken four years to complete, support other criticisms of their work. Errors in their survey were deemed so great that various efforts were made to produce an improved coverage but none met with suitable encouragement. William Forrest's map of Lanarkshire, published in 1816 and based on a survey made in 1813 was, however, regarded as of the first rate. Exceptionally, Renfrewshire is the only mainland county not mentioned in Thomson's prefatory text but like Lanarkshire it had been the subject of an exceptionally fine survey by the leading Scots cartographer of his day, John Ainslie.

Both Forrest and Ainslie were experienced and talented map-makers with several other county surveys to their name. Forrest's East Lothian map was published in 1802 and he was to produce similar coverage for West Lothian in 1818. Ainslie had published 1-inch maps of Selkirkshire (1773), Fife and Kinross (1775), Wigtownshire (1782), Angus (1794) and Kirkcudbrightshire (1797) before turning to his survey of Renfrewshire in 1796. Although it took another four years before the map was published, it is a superbly detailed and comprehensive picture of the county, its human and physical features and, of course, the Clyde. In particular, the map marks the groynes built out into the river to increase its flow, but the over-regularity of their identification suggests that Ainslie's is, perhaps, not a true record of the number and size of these jetties. He also marks the ferries at Erskine and Renfrew, as well as detailing the many burns feeding into the river which have subsequently disappeared with the spread of industrial and urban development. Unsurprisingly, there is no indication of the shoals or sandbanks in the river and, while the various harbour quays are marked, there are no soundings given. What may be slightly more odd is the lack of regularity in the depiction of Helensburgh and the identification of Hilly (instead of Holy) Loch. Ainslie included a table of the 116 local subscribers who had guaranteed a prepublication sum amounting to 270 guineas. This list includes many of the local aristocracy and gentry, as well as merchants in both Paisley and Glasgow, the customs comptroller at Port Glasgow, Captain Campbell of the *Culter* and George Langlands, a fellow land surveyor.

Ainslie's map appeared on four sheets, but Forrest took twice as many for his coverage of Lanarkshire published 16 years later. In many ways, his depiction of the Clyde is a valuable corrective to the markedly notched image of the earlier work. Ferries are identified at Braehead, Govan and Blantyre, as well as fords at Dalmarnock, Bogleshole, Carmyle, Garrion and several other locations. Heights of the waterfalls at Bonnington, Corra and Stonebyres Linns are recorded. The map was produced at a time when the work of the various turnpike trusts was beginning to have a marked influence on road communications and several more bridges (for example, Hyndford) are now indicated crossing the river. Of equal value is the record of the various industries growing up along the banks of the Clyde, in particular the cotton mills located at New Lanark and Blantyre. Upstream, it can be more difficult to discern the course of the river and while Forrest does clearly show the meeting of the Powtrail and Daer Waters, he identifies the source of the Clyde to the north of Tippet Hill where the Clyde's Burn rises prior to flowing west.

Opposite. Forrest's depiction of the river at Hyndford Bridge is one of the earliest cartographic records of this important crossing.

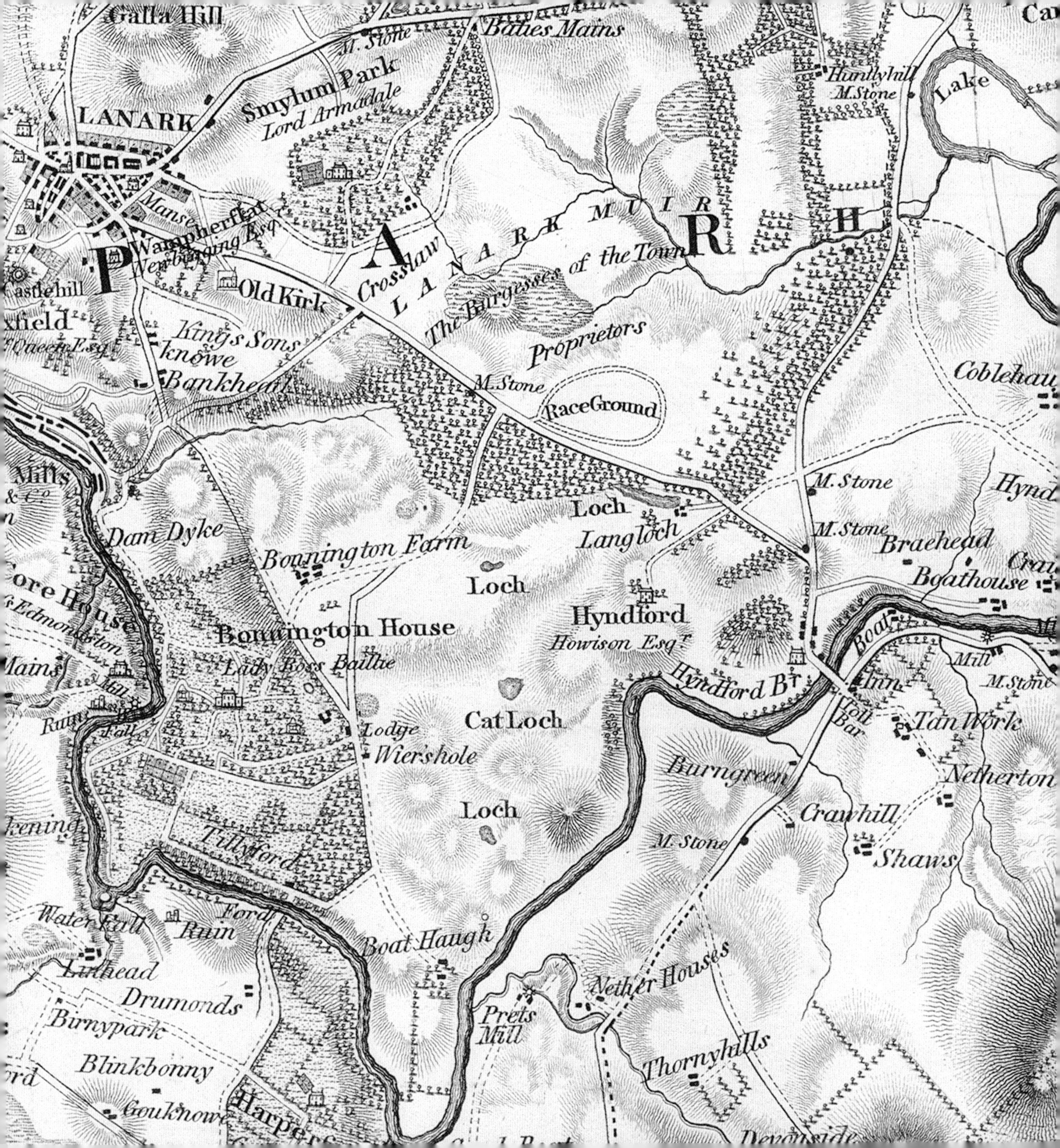

Galla Hill

Bates Mains

M. Stone

LANARK

Smylum Park
Lord Armadale

Huntlyhill
M. Stone

Lake

LANARKMUIR PARISH

Wamphersflat
Newbigging Esq.

Mans

Crosslaw

The Burgesses of the Town

Castlehill

Old Kirk

King's Sons

Proprietors

Coblehau

xfield

Queen Esq.

Knowe

Bankhead

M. Stone

RaceGround

M. Stone

Mills
& Co

M. Stone

Hynd

Dam Dyke

Bonnington Farm

Loch
Langloch

Braehead

ore House

Loch

Boathouse

Edmonton

Bonnington House

Hyndford
Howison Esqr.

Cra

Mains

Lady Ross Baillie

Boat

Ruin

Lodge

Fall

Wiershole

Cat Loch

Hyndford Br

Inn

Mill
M. Stone

Toll
Bar

Tan Work

kening

Loch

Burngreen

Netherton

Tillyford

M. Stone

Crawhill

Shaws

Water Fall

Ford

Ruin

Boat Haugh

Nether Houses

Lithead

Drumonds

Birnypark

Prets
Mill

Blinkbonny

Thornyhills

ord

Gouknowe

Harper

Devonside

CHAPTER 10

A question of balance:
James Knox's map of the Clyde

Although several thousand maps and plans exist of the River and Firth of Clyde, there are surprisingly few that stand alone in seeking to depict the whole basin. Many illustrate a particular aspect of the waterway or a significant stretch along its banks, while others form part of a more general series covering a more extensive area. This plan by the Edinburgh cartographer James Knox was published in 1836 and in it he sought to illustrate the whole of the Clyde downriver from Carstairs. It appeared as the last in a short series of maps of the three major Scottish river basins (the Forth, Tay and Clyde) drawn by him from 1828 onwards. Each map was produced at the scale of 1 inch to 2 miles but in the case of the Clyde basin it is possible that such a strict adherence to the same equivalent works against the overall legibility of the map.

Undoubtedly, there is an impressive level of information shown on it and Knox has taken pains to indicate a wide range of topographical elements, from the policies of country houses, with the owners' names included, to the identification of Roman remains and other features of historical interest. He clearly had an interest in archaeology for several of his other maps also indicate similar features. In this instance, the Roman camp at Cleghorn is clearly shown, as is the redoubt at Castle Dykes – although a very unusual oxbow lake is suggested lying to the south-west. Soundings, rocks, shoals and lighthouses are depicted in the firth, while the navigable channel is indicated by the line of ferry routes. The drainage network is shown in some detail, and Knox has carefully indicated a considerable number of tributaries. Garrion Bridge, completed in 1817, is marked but not the crossing at Crossford. It is the density of names which seems to work against the sheet's clarity. Additionally, where the map has been coloured to indicate separate parishes, it can be quite difficult to follow the line of the Clyde itself while the copious information on features, such as those around Hamilton, can make the map appear cluttered.

Other studies have commented on the number of individuals who participated in its creation, but this Clyde map is unique in having two engravers responsible for the end product. William Home Lizars (1788–1859), one of the leading Edinburgh engravers of the early nineteenth century, prepared the delineation of the parklands and the hachuring which defined the hills, whereas the slightly less challenging outline and lettering of the map was the work of John Muir. Lizars had engraved a map of the Clyde and west coast for James Lumsden's *Steam-Boat Companion* in 1820, but this is a markedly different depiction. However, little is known of Muir and his name appears in the Edinburgh directories as an engraver only from 1841 onwards, possibly indicating that he may have been learning his trade under Lizars at the time of the map's production.

Opposite. James Knox, *Map of the basin of the Clyde* (1836)

Although the maps of the Forth and Tay were separately the work of two other Edinburgh engravers (Thomson and Gellatly), there is a similarity of style within the group.

Knox had excellent credentials as a surveyor for he had trained under John Ainslie and may have worked with James Anderson, another Edinburgh figure who was to develop a later career as a civil engineer. By the time that this map appeared, Knox had been working professionally for more than 30 years, producing a range of county, estate, farm and urban plans covering lands mostly in the Lothians and southern Scotland. Nonetheless, his set of estuary maps marks a significant change in output away from more localised commissions to smaller-scale works covering more extended areas. This was to lead to him following Anderson's example into civil engineering in later years.

In many respects, his story is a mirror of the age and reflects the experience of many surveyors working in the second quarter of the nineteenth century. Although he had an obvious talent, he faced problems in raising sufficient money for some of his projects, as was the case with his county map of Midlothian. This was surveyed in 1812 and it is possible that he tried to raise funds by selling his house and its grounds in June 1813. However, it took four years before the map appeared in print, with Knox going to the expense of having it engraved by Samuel Neele, a successful figure in the London printing world. Despite the quality of the cartography, only 180 copies were sent to the subscribers and Knox was forced to sell the remaining impressions, as well as the plates and copyright, by public auction in August 1820 to meet his creditors' demands.

The map was subsequently redrawn in 1821 and later incorporated into John Thomson's *Atlas of Scotland*. As recorded above, Thomson was similarly to face bankruptcy as a result of over-stretching his finances in producing this publication and his plates, along with others by Knox, were eventually purchased and reissued by W. & A.K. Johnston. It is a significant fact that both men were based in Edinburgh and had the support of a considerable number of subscribers for their work yet failed to profit from their maps. Another side to Knox is revealed in a short additional note to the fifth volume of Francis James Child's *The English and Scottish Popular Ballads* published in 1892, where he records taking down a version of 'Johnie of Braidisbank' 'from the recitation of Mr James Knox, land-surveyor at Tipperlinne, near Edinburgh, in the month of May, 1824, when we met him in the good town of Paisley'.

Individual map users will decide whether or not Knox's map suffers from information overkill or provides a detailed picture of Clydesdale and the Clyde coast at a time when it was developing into an industrial and commercial powerhouse. What cannot be overlooked is that the map was reissued in 1837 and 1838, clearly suggesting that there was a buoyant market for good representations of the area.

Opposite. Detail of river around Crossford, showing how
the detail and colouring hinders the legibility

CHAPTER 11

Where does the Clyde begin?

As has been discussed previously, various maps through the ages have offered different interpretations for the preferred source of the Clyde. Although many people still adhere to the idea of its origin in the Lowther Hills, this is largely through the influence of Kenneth McKellar's rendition of 'The Song of the Clyde' written by R.Y. Bell and Ian Gourley. In fact, it does rise in these hills but, unfortunately, although it sounds well in the song, the river does not flow 'from Leadhills all the way to the sea'. It is now generally accepted as coming into being at the more prosaic meeting of the Potrail and the Daer Waters to the east of Glenochar at Ordnance Survey grid reference NS954136. Having said that, the Ordnance Survey itself is somewhat coy about where it starts to identify the body of water as the Clyde. On the most recent 1:500 and 1:2500 scale maps, the name first appears on a marked loop well to the north of the point where the Crookedstane Burn joins the river. As the scale of the maps reduces, the location of the first naming becomes more inconsistent and cannot be justified solely by lack of space on the map. At 1:5000, it is placed immediately to the east of Elvanfoot, whereas the 1:10,000 map only begins to identify the river on the curve lying north-west of Lady Cairn, while on the 1:20,000 scale the name covers an area on the west bank from opposite the mouth of the Bakehouse Burn to

that of the Clyde's Burn. The unsurprisingly more consistent (but less informative) OpenStreetMap marks the name just to the north of a point where the Glenlochar Burn joins the river from the west, confirming what is now generally agreed upon.

For a considerable part of its early course, the Clyde wends its way north and provides a direct route from England and eastern Galloway into central Scotland. In fact, the Caledonian Railway line between Glasgow and Carlisle, originally opened in 1848, follows the river's course very closely and, even today on leaving Glasgow Central Station, the line crosses the river half a dozen times on its journey towards Annandale. However, it is the valley of the Clyde which is the aid to road and rail transport and, given that most of the major routes in the Central Belt run east to west, the river itself has long presented a barrier to cross-country travel. This will be discussed later in a consideration of the fords, ferries and bridges that were put in place to meet the challenge.

This plan is an excellent example of how estate surveyors were turning to the Ordnance Survey as a base for their own work. It also provides a detailed illustration of the various tributaries which come together to form the Clyde. While it shows the sweep of the Caledonian Railway track crossing the Clyde just before Elvanfoot station, what is notable is the location of

Opposite and overleaf. Plan of River Clyde and Daer Water (1866)

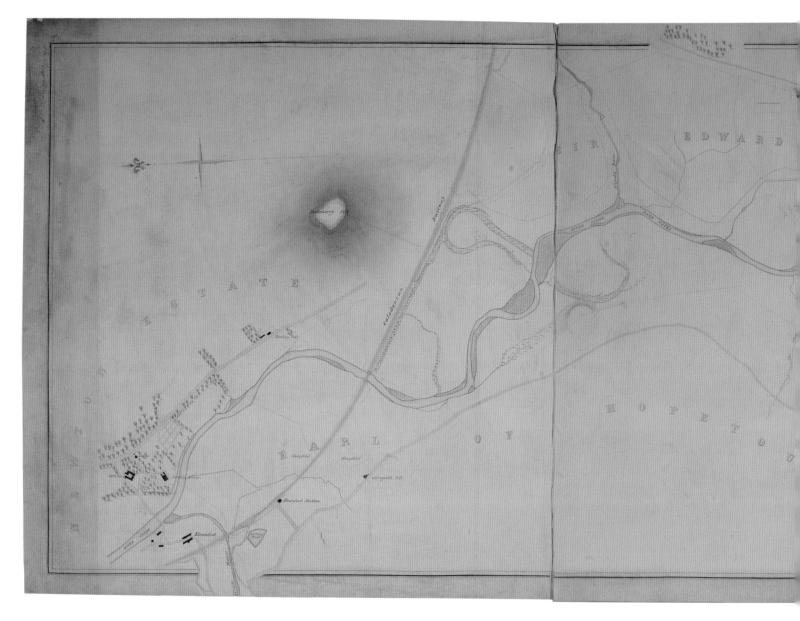

the village to the east of the line rather than today's settlement location on the slightly higher ground beside the A702. Twenty-first century Elvanfoot is something of a backwater facing across the river to the bustle of the A74. Its church has been placed on the Buildings at Risk Register and the pedestrian suspension bridge over the Clyde, the highest crossing point on the river, has been closed for the last decade. Newton House which appears on this plan is now demolished. The current Ordnance Survey maps no longer indicate the curling pond or the station but they do delineate the course of a Roman road which forded

the Elvan Water immediately east of the railway viaduct. This was the direct route from Durisdeer which was to follow the river to the fort and camp at Clyde's Bridge and thence to Lamington, Coulter and Biggar. Like several other depictions of the early course of the river, this version chooses to name it as the Clyde only after the Clyde Burn joins it from the east. Immediately before this confluence, it is still identified as the Daer.

Both Glenlochar and Watermeetings are identified on the plan, which was prepared in 1866, only two years after the

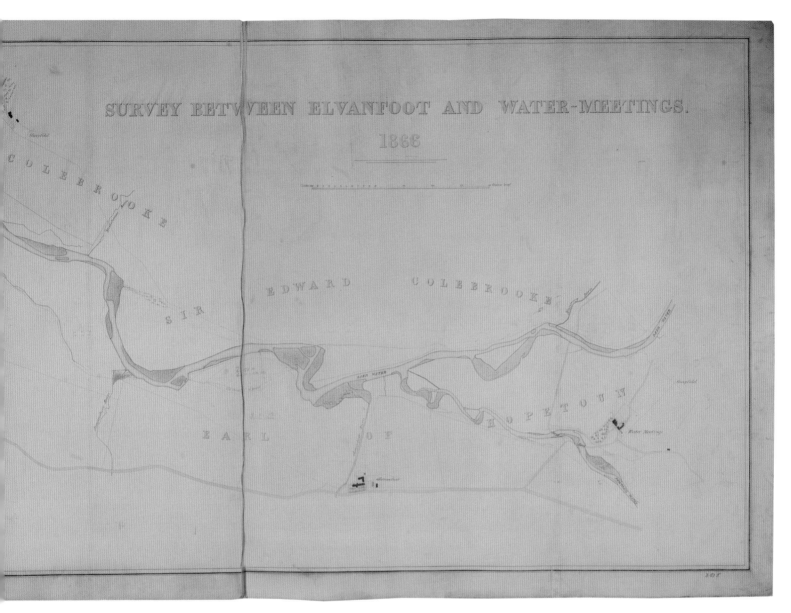

SURVEY BETWEEN ELVANFOOT AND WATER-MEETINGS.

1866

Ordnance Survey had published the relevant 25-inch map of the locality. This clearly influenced its design for the selection of colours to depict features is strongly similar to the official map. Of greater interest may be the detail of the river itself and the careful marking of the shingle and sand banks along its early course. What may be a former oxbow lake and the pencil markings showing an earlier centre of the river to the northeast of Glenlochar may be suggestive of the purpose behind the plan's production. Certainly, there are no obvious clues other than the names of the adjacent lands which belonged to Sir

Edward Colebrooke (1813–90), MP for Lanarkshire at this date, George Vere Irving, Lord Newton (1815–69), a Scottish judge and antiquary and John Hope, sixth Earl of Hopetoun (1831–73). Two years earlier, Irving had contributed the archaeological and historical section to Alexander Murray's *The Upper Ward of Lanarkshire Described and Delineated* and had an interest in ancient camps. In a fashion similar to an example discussed later, it is possible that the making of this plan had something to do with estate boundaries and the gaining or losing of land as the bed of the Clyde shifted over time.

CHAPTER 12

The Ordnance Survey map goes coloured

Although many people are familiar with Ordnance Survey maps, the complex history of the various scales and editions of the several series it has produced can be quite intimidating to anyone wanting to know what our national survey authority has produced. The early days of the Survey north of the border were characterised by a very erratic approach, particularly in the original triangulation which created the framework for the topographic detail. While parties had commenced surveying on a scale of 2 inches to the mile in the south-west of Scotland in 1819, this was discontinued nine years later and, for the next decade and a half, no topographic work was carried out here, largely as a result of Survey staff being moved to Ireland to meet the requirements for a proper map on which to base land valuations.

After much lobbying of the government by MPs, leading scientific societies and other bodies, surveying in Scotland recommenced in 1843, based on a preferred scale of 6 inches to a mile. However, further delays were caused by what is often described as the 'Battle of the Scales', an extensive but informed debate on the selection of the most appropriate degrees of representation for large-scale mapping. The earliest Scottish 1-inch map was not published until 1856 as part of what was a first edition of the series. It was based on those larger-scale surveys but, as an edition of the map, it was not completed until 1887. A second edition followed, published between 1898 and 1903. Although selected sheets covering the Highlands and Islands were subsequently colour lithographed to illustrate the Crofters' Commission report of 1892, the introduction of colour as a standard and consistent feature on all sheets only began with the production of the third edition in 1905.

Based on a national field revision carried out between 1901 and 1912, it is the first to be specifically designated as an edition on the individual sheets. The teams involved worked west and north from an area along the border around the River Tweed and, thereby, the most populated areas were covered in the earlier stages. Unfortunately, this version was discontinued before completion, with the imminent outbreak of the Great War, and the sheets which would have covered Colonsay and the Western Isles were never published. Experiments in colour printing of English sheets on behalf of the Ordnance Survey had been conducted by the Edinburgh map publishers Bartholomew and Son in the later 1890s and these were produced either from lithographic stones or zinc plates rather than the more traditional engraved plate. Bartholomew had developed an effective method of layer colouring to represent landscape relief and their 'Reduced Ordnance Maps' based on the more detailed

Opposite. Ordnance Survey, *1-inch 3rd edition, sheet 30 Glasgow and Greenock* (1906)

Ordnance mapping at 1 inch to the mile sold well, largely because they were revised every couple of years and were more up to date than their original source.

It is clear that the introduction of colour to OS mapping was one part of the effort to meet the stiff competition from such commercial map publishers. Described as 'the most significant event in the development of the Ordnance Survey one-inch . . . map', it took quite a time before the Survey mastered the technique of balancing the colours but, with the introduction of a choice of green for woodland, red contour lines, brown hachuring, blue for water and burnt sienna for roads, the resultant maps were much more attractive than previous editions and unquestionably very popular with the map-using public. The sheets of the engraved and hachured version of this edition are, unquestionably, some of the most beautiful 1-inch maps produced by the Survey.

Sheet 30 which includes Glasgow and the lower reaches of the Clyde was issued in 1905, three years after revision. In the same year, the Automobile Association was founded to serve the needs of the steadily growing number of car owners and only two years earlier, the Motor Car Act introduced the registration of cars, as well as driver licensing. It is estimated that in that same year there were 32,000 cars in the UK. By the end of the decade the figure had more than tripled to 100,000. These figures are more important than a mere reflection of the increase in road traffic for they put into perspective the reality that this edition shows a road system which had changed relatively little since the mid nineteenth century and before the radical impact which easier motor transport had on both the town and countryside.

Looking at the maps in more detail, one of the most striking features is, unsurprisingly, the noticeably fewer roads identified than the maps of today but this brings out the way in which the topography influenced the pattern of this earlier network.

The courses of rivers seem much clearer and, again, their impact on road communications can be seen in the fewer bridges shown. Railway branch lines which once served more remote settlements, such as Blackwood and Strathaven, reflect the change in transport patterns during the twentieth century. This is even more strongly seen in the depiction of the Clyde through Glasgow where the numerous docks, industries and ferries downstream from Jamaica Street Bridge give a clear impression of the bustle and busy-ness of a river at the height of its prosperity. In addition, the map clearly marks the navigable channel, as well as the various beacons, lights and shoals between Bowling and Port Glasgow.

The Ordnance Survey itself regarded the 1-inch map as essentially a touring and cycling map which had a primary objective of providing sufficient information for the average person to be able find their way about unfamiliar country without any difficulty. In effect, the third edition marks the period when the bicycle gave way to the motor car as the popular means to discover what was 'just round the next corner'. It was from this series that the earliest sequence of Ordnance Survey tourist maps was produced in the 1920s, including *Burns' Country* and *Rothesay & Firth of Clyde*, the two publications specifically covering stretches of the Clyde and which are discussed later. However, with the subsequent growth in the number of vehicles on the road, it was realised that the lack of a road classification scheme, combined with both a weakness in the depiction of hill features and a confused variety of map forms, were marked flaws in this version of the map, leading to it being replaced eventually by the Popular Edition in the 1920s. Nonetheless, the maps of the third edition reflect a move away from the merely functional to a more commercially viable product and remain an attractive record of a radically different past landscape.

Opposite. Details of Glasgow area showing the stretch
of the river downstream from Jamaica Street Bridge

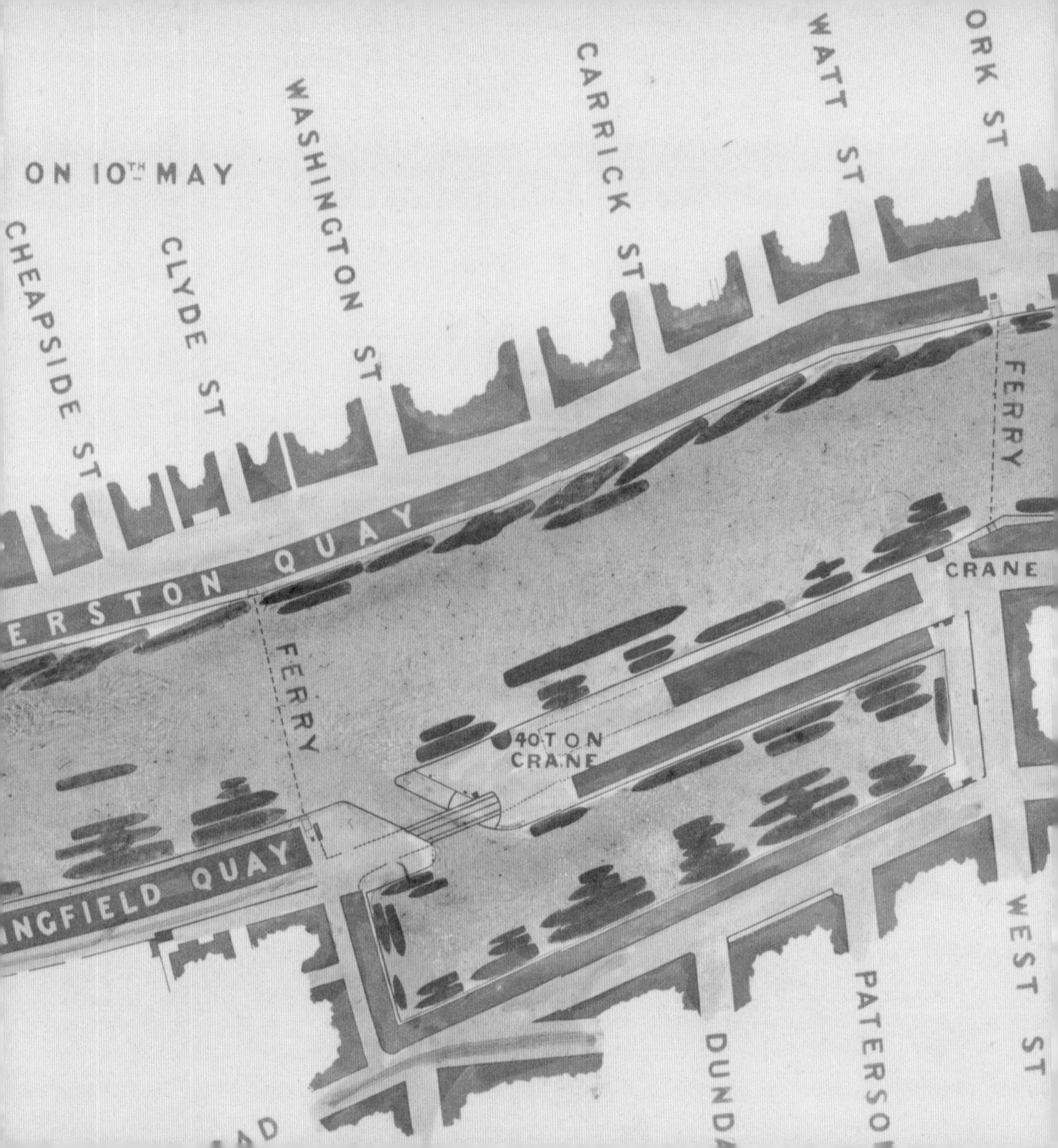

ON 10ᵀᴴ MAY

CHEAPSIDE ST

CLYDE ST

WASHINGTON ST

CARRICK ST

WATT ST

ORK ST

...ERSTON QUAY

...NGFIELD QUAY

FERRY

FERRY

CRANE

40 TON
CRANE

WEST ST

PATERSO...

DUNDA...

...AD

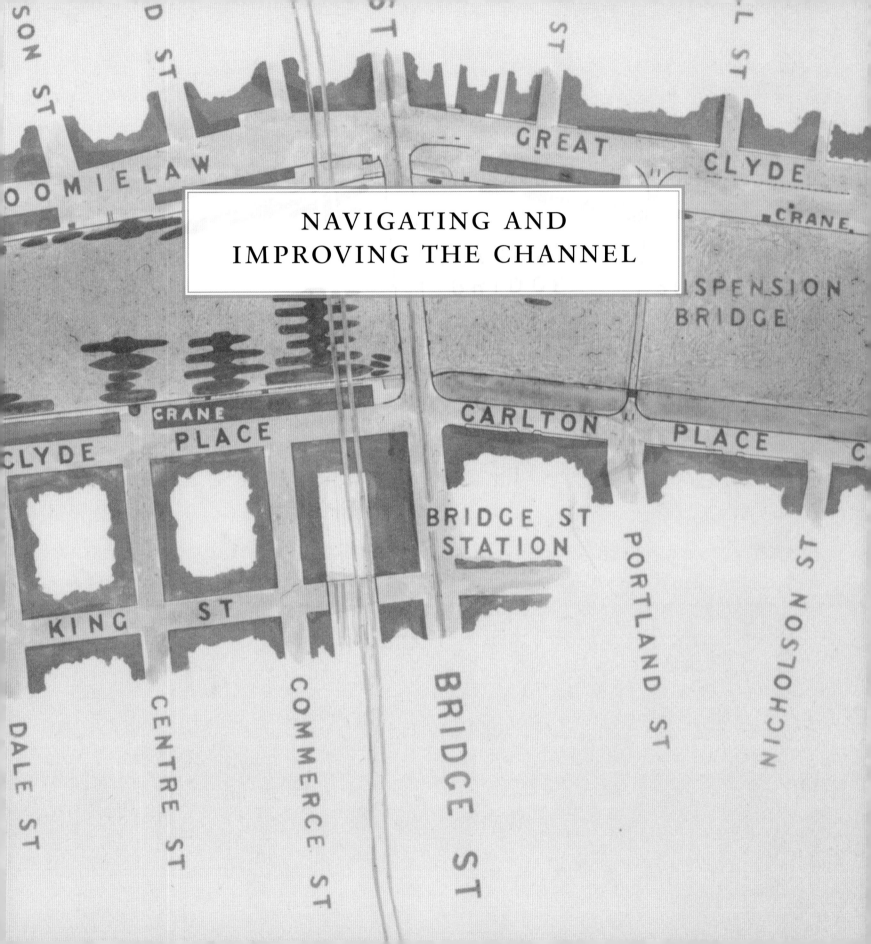

NAVIGATING AND
IMPROVING THE CHANNEL

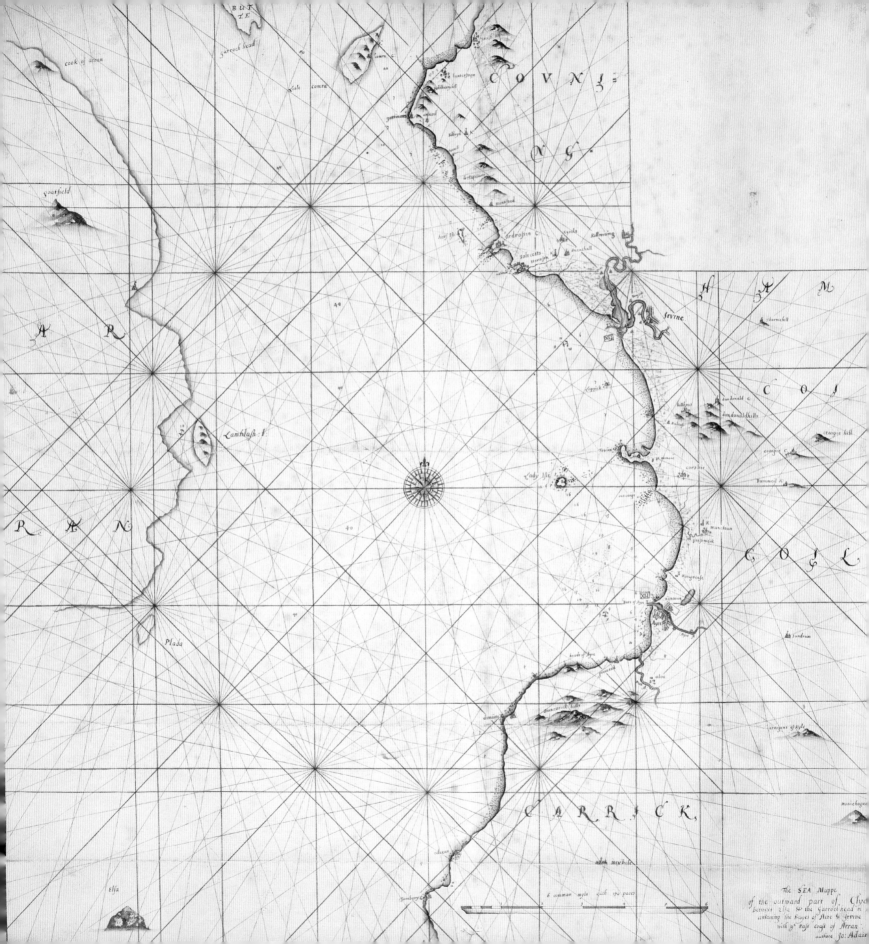

BUTE

cook of arran

Garroch head

Ile comra

comra c.

COVN =

hunterstoun

coldberryhill

N G=

goatfield

horf the

ardrossen C.

Nordo

Kilmaurng

monsfood

Salt cotts
stevenston

muirhall

H   A   M

A   R

fevine

Thornehill

COI

XII

Lamblash : I.

Coppick

hillhead

R. Ballo

dundonald C.
dundonald hills

craigie hill

craigie C.

Tenine

R.monine

corsbie

Barnweel R.

R

lady Ifle

rock cosge

Lady Isle

R.R. munckton
preffemyck

Kingcense

XII
Bars of Ayr

R. & Ms Kun

Plada

Ayr

Ayr

Sundrum

P   R   A   N

breads of Ayr

greenend

alou

Duncarrick fells

dinmure

craigins of Kyle

CARRICK,

muirhoge

Elfa

Turnberry C.

moirhole

6 common myle quch the pace

The SEA Mappe
of the outward part of Clyd
betwixt ylla & the Garroch need m
conteaning the bayes of Aire & fevine
with y' wose coast of Arran
authore Jo: Adair

CHAPTER 13

John Adair and the
charting of the Clyde

The surviving documentary evidence highlights John Adair's undeniable capabilities as both a land surveyor and hydrographer. Much has been written on his difficulties in finding sufficient financial support for his cartography but, whether through personal temperament or the circumstances of the time, the failure to have the greater part of his work published denied Scotland the opportunity to benefit from the improved accuracy of much of his mapping. This is particularly the case for the west coast of Scotland.

In 1703, Adair published *The Description of the Sea-Coast and Islands of Scotland* as the first in a projected series of volumes designed to cover the whole of the Scottish seaboard. Its contents reflect the continued focus on the east coast which had been evident in Greenville Collins's *Great Britain's Coasting Pilot*, initially published ten years earlier. This, the first home survey of Britain's coasts, had been supported by both Trinity House and the Admiralty in recognition of the paucity of coverage of the northern coasts. The Scottish Parliament's backing of Adair underlines the perceived need for good charts of home waters. However, with only five new charts included in Adair's atlas, the end result may have appeared somewhat disappointing to many mariners, particularly as his work was deemed 'most necessary for navigation'.

In truth, much of Scotland's maritime trade remained coastal or focused on the North Sea and the lack of published charts of the west coast may also have as much to do with a lack of demand than anything else. Although the 1703 volume was the only one to be published, Adair had spent several summers on various expeditions to survey the north and west coasts. In 1686, the Scottish Parliament had passed a tunnage levy on ships to provide him with financial support specifically to conduct such hydrographic work. Certainly, from this time onwards Adair appears to have turned his attention more towards maritime survey but it took another five years before he was free of a contract with the Geographer Royal, Sir Robert Sibbald, to provide him with maps for his proposed atlas of Scotland. Once free of this tie, Adair organised major trips to chart the Solway (1695), the Clyde (1696–97) and the Western Isles (1698).

In August 1696, he hired a small vessel with the intention of travelling to the small islands, presumably in the Clyde estuary, and along the south coast. The fact that the firth was charted over two summers suggests the special attention he deemed necessary for a proper survey. The following year, he aimed to map the inner parts of the estuary and requested the assistance of the local customs collectors in providing 'boatts,

Opposite. John Adair, *Sea Mappe of the outward part of the Clyde betwixt Elsa and the Garroch Head in Bute* (1696)

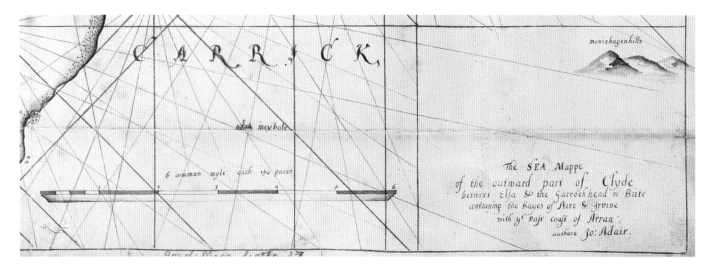

seamen and other necessares'. That summer, he spent ten weeks charting both the firth and river at the considerable cost of £200 sterling.

This depiction of the Firth of Clyde covers the Ayrshire coast and the estuary between Garroch Head on Bute and Ailsa Craig. Now held in the University of Oxford's Bodleian Library as part of the collection gathered together in the eighteenth century by the eminent topographer Richard Gough, it is one of two surviving Clyde charts by Adair. Although tentatively dated 1686, it is much more likely to be the result of Adair's survey expeditions in the mid 1690s. In comparison with a second copy held in the Admiralty Library, this version gives a better sense of the delineation of the south Ayrshire coast and, while less ornate, provides many more bearing lines and several more locations. Whereas most of his earlier work involved land surveys, Adair here focuses very much on coastal features alone, particularly those in Ayrshire.

Both the bays at Ayr and Irvine are depicted in some detail, with rocks, shoals and a considerable number of soundings given. A close inspection shows that he paid particular attention to indicating the entrances to both Ayr and Irvine harbours, as well as the plans of the two burghs. In Ayr, the layout of the citadel erected by Cromwell's troops in 1652–54, the Auld Brig and the Auld Kirk are clearly identified, as are the sizeable property and grounds which was formerly Newton Castle, situated north of the river, and two mills lying to the east. Further up the coast, the narrow entrance and the channel of the River Irvine are defined, while Saltcoats is also marked as an anchorage. Interestingly, the north-east segment of the manuscript has been almost completely blocked off as if to provide space for a map title or dedication. The lettering for Cunningham is also placed irregularly to strengthen this possibility. These features would suggest that when Adair prepared this draft, he was still working towards the publication of another volume of the atlas to cover the rest of the Scottish inshore waters.

In an account of the progress of his charting the coast prepared for a parliamentary commission in 1704, Adair recorded an additional chart of the Clyde estuary up to Dumbarton as 'done but not fully finished' and, in 1713, a further list sent to the Earl of Mar, then Secretary of State, records a chart of 'the inner part of Clyde, from Gourock to Finlastoun, surveyed and drawn out'. Neither of these seems to have survived and the only Adair work covering the Clyde to be published was to appear in Edinburgh 13 years after his death.

Opposite. Details of Ayr and Irvine

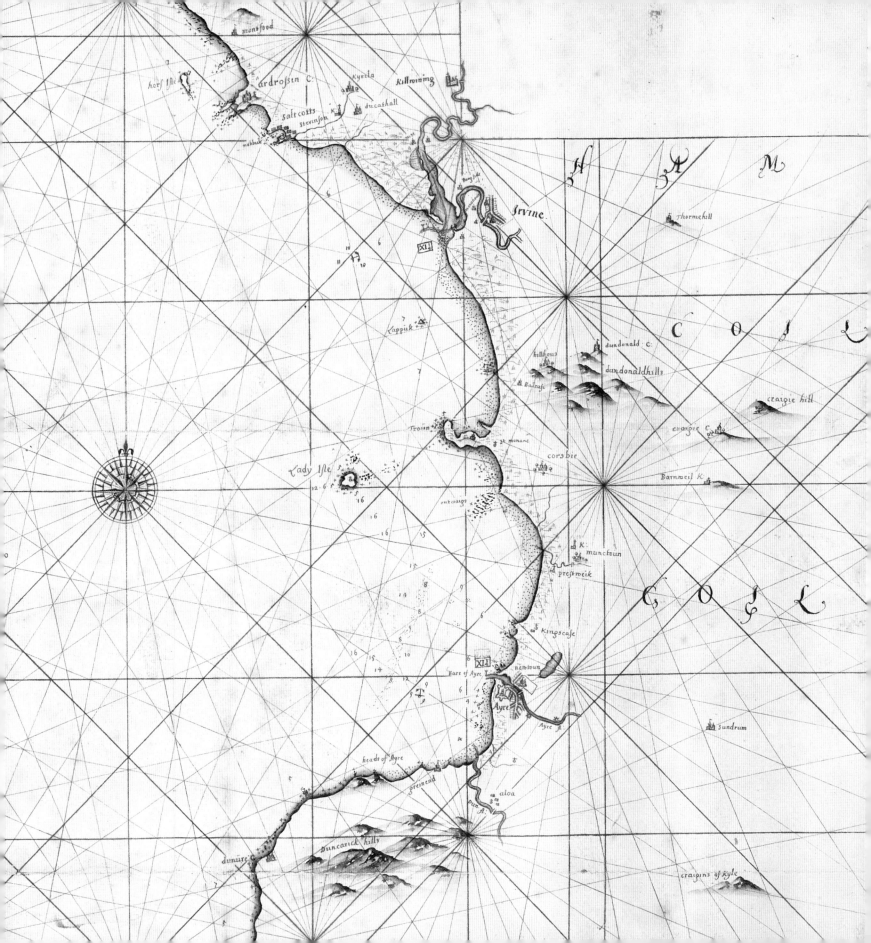

horf Ifle
mont food
ardrofsin C:
Kyrtla
Killwining
Saltcotts
K:
Stevinfon
ducathall
nebbuk

H A M

Irvine

Thornhill

XII

A

COL

rappuk

hillhous
dundonald C:
dundonaldhills

St Baltafi

craigie hill

Troin
St monanc

craigix C:

corsbie

Lady Ifle

Barnweil K:

out craigs

K:
munctoun

preftweik

COL

kingscafe

XII
Barr of Ayre
newtoun

Ayre

Sundrum

Ayre

heads of Ayre

greinend

aloa

pure A:

duncarick hills

dunure

craigins of Kyle

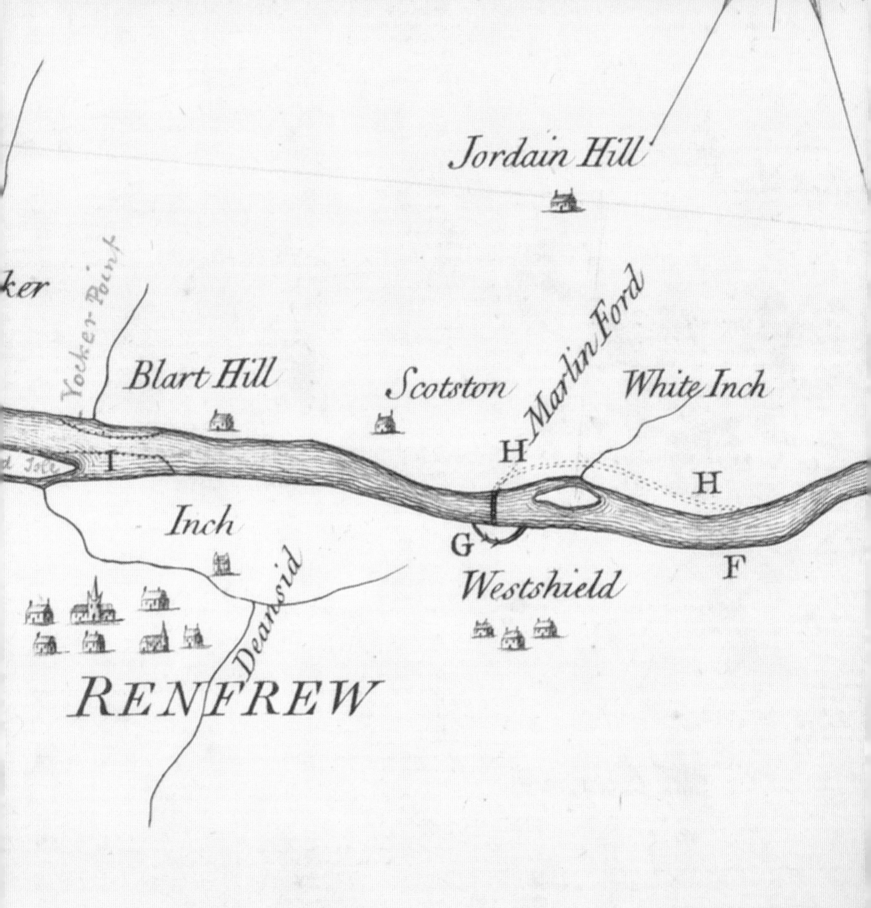

CHAPTER 14

The work of John Smeaton,
John Golborne and James Barry

Following the success of his book *A Tour in Scotland in 1769*, Thomas Pennant, the Welsh naturalist and traveller, made a second visit here in 1772 and his subsequent description of the Clyde at Glasgow is a concise contemporary record of the problems faced in improving the river's navigability. He recorded that 'the city of Glasgow, till very lately, was perfectly tantalized with its river: the water was shallow, the channel much too wide for the usual quantity of water that flowed down, and the navigation interrupted by twelve remarkable shoals.' Glasgow was a burgh with a trade which was growing beyond that of a local market but it could only develop successfully if it could ensure a safe channel upriver for vessels of even a moderate draught. During the middle decades of the eighteenth century the magistrates commissioned a series of surveys and plans from the most eminent engineers of the day to investigate an effective way to deepen the channel, thereby allowing coasting vessels and colliers to reach the city's quay at the Broomielaw. This emphasis on coasting craft is important as it reflects one of the other challenges posed to shipping, namely the vagaries of the wind and tide.

The establishment of the harbour at Port Glasgow was a significant step for the city in developing a transatlantic trade with the West Indian and American colonies. This proved a safe haven for the growing merchant fleet, but the narrowness of the upper channel, combined with those many submerged shoals and sandbanks, made for a difficult passage for all but the smallest of boats. Creating a deeper channel for ocean-going vessels would have been regarded as an unnecessary project as long as the south-westerly winds and the adverse tidal conditions hindered the working of any ship under sail. It was seen as more important for the river to be deepened to improve access for the barges and smaller gabbarts which were used for the trans-shipment of tobacco, sugar and manufactured goods between Glasgow and its port, particularly at a time when the harbour facilities in the city itself were limited. Any image of the Clyde between the two burghs shows 'the canal-like nature of Glasgow's link to the sea' and it is not surprising that the men employed in the improvement work came from the ranks of the canal engineers of the period.

Efforts to remove some of the obstructions can be traced back to the mid sixteenth century but these met with little success, largely as they were localised and had only limited financial support. Nonetheless, increasing trade, the lack of warehouse space at the deep-water port and the poor condition

Opposite. Detail of dam and lock at Scotstoun from Barry's *Plan of the River Clyde*

Overleaf. James Barry, *A Plan of the River Clyde* (1758)

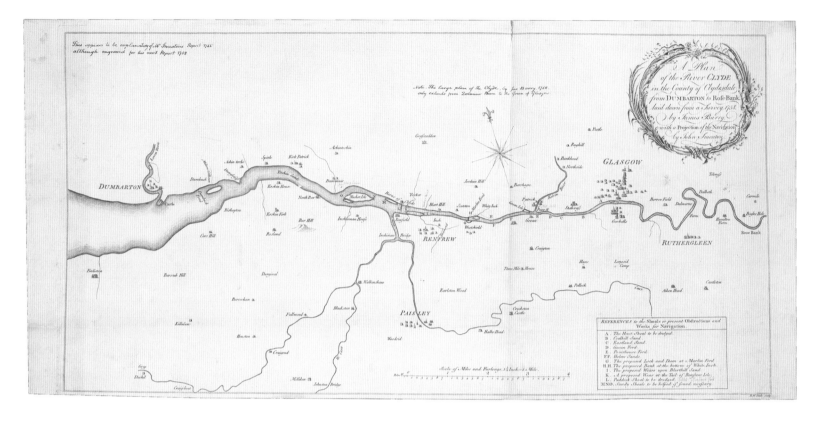

of the connecting roads convinced the major merchants and, through their powerful influence, the Glasgow Council of the need for a long-term solution. At the same time, there was an equal awareness of other hazards to shipping bound for the upper Clyde which was to lead to the establishment of a lighthouse on the Little Cumbrae, as will be discussed subsequently.

Burgh records for the period indicate an ongoing determination by the Glasgow magistrates to resolve the issue. In late 1748, Provost Andrew Cochrane travelled to London with a commission to petition parliament for financial relief for the city. The wording of his appeal specifically mentioned the need to deepen the river for the convenience of trade and navigation. It is from this point onward that an increased determination can be discerned in the action of the council, perhaps spurred by more effective competition from Greenock and the possibility of increased siltation of the Port Glasgow harbour. The chief agent for the Scotch Mines Company at Leadhills, James Stirling,

was asked to investigate the river and he proposed a system of locks and dams. Payment for his expenses was recorded in January 1752 but it is more likely that the surveying was carried out in the previous summer. A separate survey of the Clyde coast had been conducted in June 1750, overseen by the Dean of Guild. It is now thought that this was carried out by a local expert, James Barry, and as Stirling would have been well aware of his abilities he may also have been employed on this original proposal.

The details of Barry's early career are rather sketchy. In the 1760s, he gave evidence in a court case, stating that he had over 30 years of experience in surveying. Subsequently, as the city began to expand, he was to become the man that the magistrates turned to for a wide range of commissions and was to be appointed as 'surveyor and measurer for the city' in March 1773. While much has been written about the gradual improvement of the Clyde navigation, relatively little has been written

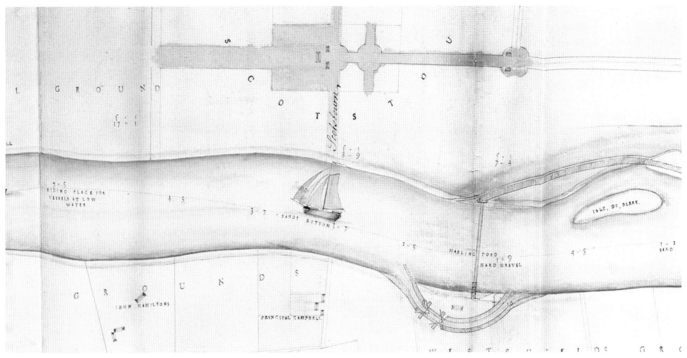

James Barry, *A Plan of the River Clyde in the county of Clydesdale from Dalmuir Burn to the Green of Glasgow* (1758), extract of manuscript plan showing the river at Scotstoun and Barry's characteristic use of letter stamps for places

on the plans and maps prepared by the engineers. It is Barry's name which makes a regular appearance throughout the surviving records and surveys, yet he is probably the least well-known figure in the story.

It took a further three years from Stirling's suggestions before John Smeaton (1724–92) was invited to investigate the feasibility of such a scheme. Smeaton was one of the leading engineers of his day and is frequently referred to as the father of civil engineering. This engraved plan of the Clyde between Dumbarton and Rose Bank was based on earlier detailed work carried out by Barry that was to be approved by the Glasgow Turnpike Road Trustees in June 1756. Forming part of the archive of Smeaton's output held at the Royal Society, it indicates the engineer's reliance on the expertise of the local man on the ground at a time when he was being consulted on a wide range of other commissions, including the rebuilding of the Eddystone lighthouse. A manuscript addition to this map written by John Farey,

junior, himself a mechanical engineer, records that it 'appears to be explanatory of Mr Smeaton's Report 1755' making it highly probable that Barry had worked with him then.

The plan is a fascinating record of the Clyde and its shoals, islands and fords prior to the many projected changes. The river itself is the main focus, with relatively little detail marked elsewhere. The only bridge is at Glasgow, but fords are marked at Pointhouse and Govan. More significantly, it marks the location of Smeaton's proposed lock and dam at Marlin Ford to the west of Whiteinch, where a bank was to be constructed. In addition, weirs were to be created on Blawarthill Sands and at the western end of Renfrew Isle. When he reported his findings to the magistrates in the autumn of 1755, the minimum depth of water from Renfrew up to the Broomielaw was found to be less than 18 inches. His report also included a suggestion of additional work to reduce shoaling by the introduction of 'a wear brought from each side of the River, so as to make a

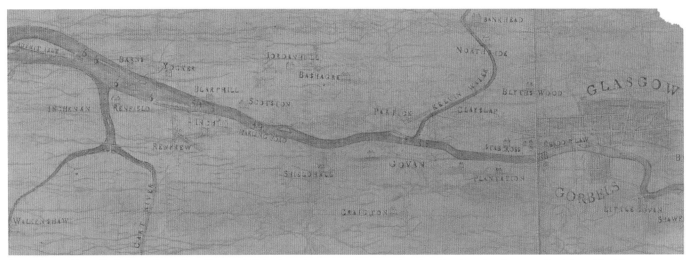

James Barry, *River Clyde from Carmyle to Rosneath Point* (1769), extract of manuscript plan showing river between Partick and Inchinnan showing depths recorded

contraction upon the shoal, which, by confining the current at low water, will be sure to carry away the sand to any depth required'.

While there was subsequent criticism of the concept of turning the river virtually into a small canal, Smeaton was merely identifying the most suitable place to site Stirling's proposal – a scheme later described as 'more than adequate for the usual vessels sailing on the Firth of Clyde and to the Western Isles'. Such major work required considerable financing and, following a petition to parliament, the final draft of the bill had a successful passage ensuring that *An Act for improving the Navigation of the River Clyde to the City of Glasgow* received royal assent in June 1759. This was the first in a sequence of local parliamentary acts designed to support Glasgow's plans to ensure easier access to the sea.

During this process, the council was also taking action on a more practical level. Smeaton was invited to return in 1758 to provide expert advice at the same time that Alexander Wilson, subsequently professor of practical astronomy at Glasgow University, was requested to survey the river, take levels and identify the best location for the lock. Wilson worked alongside Barry and their survey resulted in this detailed manuscript depiction (p. 61) of the Clyde from Dalmuir to Glasgow Green

prepared that summer. Smeaton's supplementary report of December 1758 credited Wilson with the levelling and Barry with measurements of the river's breadth on which his original choice of Marlin Ford was confirmed. Interestingly, James Watt also assisted Wilson in taking levels of the river, but of equal importance is the record of payments to the figures involved, which reflects a more generous approach than afforded to earlier improvement attempts. Smeaton himself was paid more than £200 for his reports.

Although he was contracted as chief engineer and building work commenced on the dam in 1760, the underlying soil could not support its construction. The collapse of walls, in combination with scouring and silting from spring floods, delayed any progress. Eventually, with money running out, the scheme was abandoned at the end of 1762, leaving the way open for John Golborne's more effective proposals six years later. Golborne investigated the river down to Port Glasgow and suggested a range of works to combat the problems of a river which had 'gained in breadth what is wanting in depth'. His two-pronged approach of dredging and assisting nature by contracting the channel is often repeated in the various histories of the river but, in reality, it was only a development of earlier suggestions.

Once again, Barry appears as the key figure in further surveys of the Clyde, on this occasion resuming his collaboration with James Watt. In fact, the latter records his indebtedness to Barry not only for his knowledge of the Clyde and its fords but also for his assistance in his observations. More significantly, the council minutes specifically state that before Golborne could make his calculations, he required an exact plan of the river, detailing the depths of the fords and their soil conditions. This plan (p. 62) was duly prepared by Barry and transmitted to the engineer. It is likely that this third Barry depiction of the Clyde, which is taken from a more extensive plan covering the river between Carmyle and Rosneath Point, relates to this survey, particularly as it includes the lower reaches of the channel. In his second submission to the magistrates, Golborne confirmed that his annexed plan was based on such a larger work by this local expert.

Returning to Pennant's account, it was subsequently noted that 'at length the plan proposed by my old friend, Mr John Golburne, of Chester, that honest and able engineer, was accepted, and he entered into contract with the magistrates of Glasgow to deepen the channel to seven feet at the quay, even at neap tides. He has made considerable progress in the work, and had given the stipulated depth to within four miles of the place.' In due course, craft of up to 70 tons were able to reach Glasgow and, by 1773, coasting vessels were arriving direct from Ireland. Subsequent work to tackle the problem of the Dumbuck Shoal resulted in the construction of the Lang Dyke, a constraining barrier between the two channels which is depicted in this final plan prepared by Golborne himself. The number of soundings taken on such a short stretch of the river emphasises the care and detail which went into the surveying. In addition to the delineation of the dyke, the plan also identifies the beacons built to mark its location. It is testament to the wall's effectiveness that, despite further work to deepen the Clyde, it remains a noticeable feature of the river to this day.

John Golborne, *Plan of the River Clyde to accompany report for deepening the Clyde between Longoch Point and Dumbuck Ford* (1772)

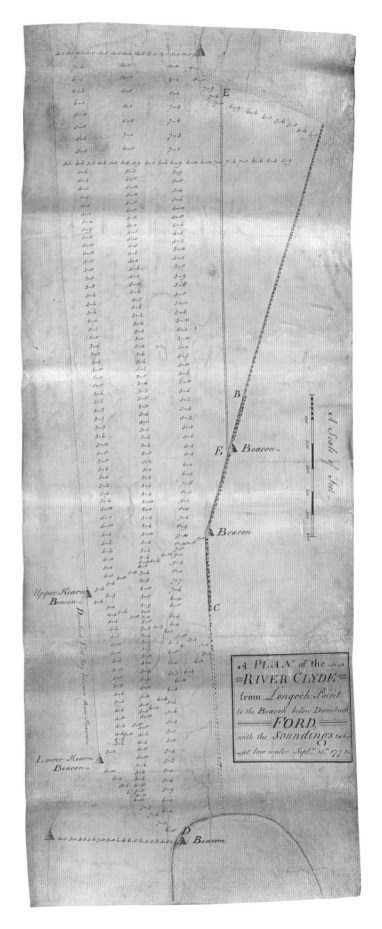

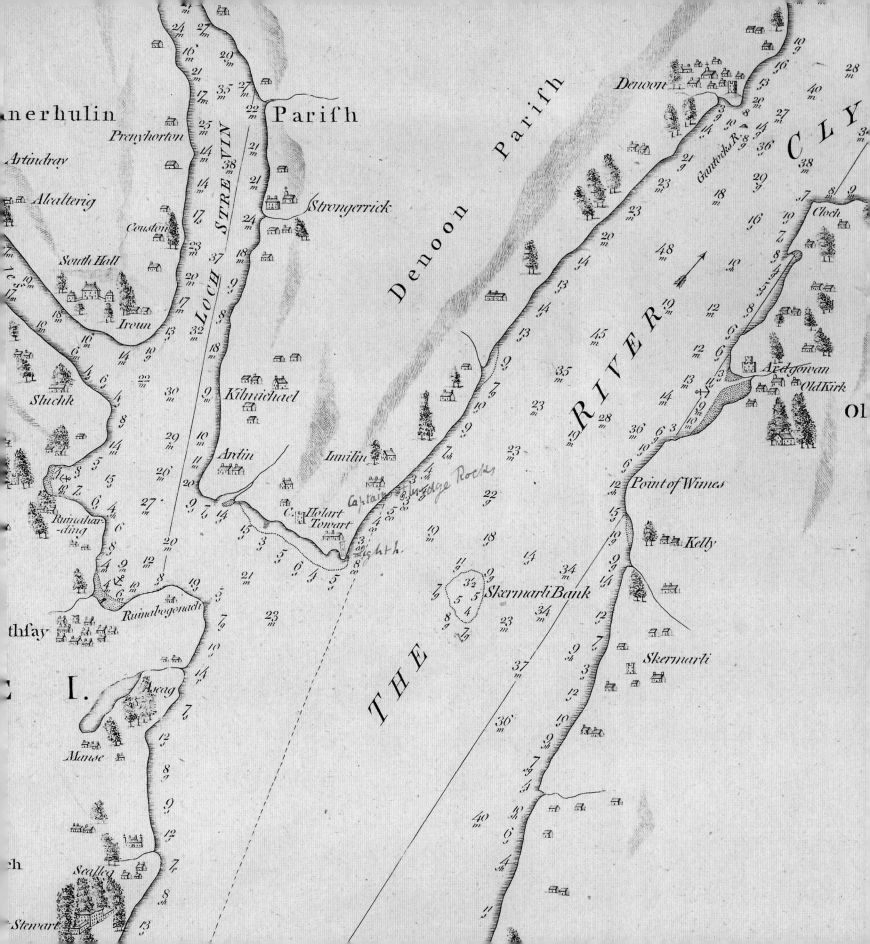

CHAPTER 15

Murdoch Mackenzie
surveys the Clyde

While a considerable amount of research has been carried out on the impact of the 1745–46 Jacobite Rising on the mapping of the Scottish mainland, comparatively little work has been done on the charting of the nation's coastal waters both prior to and following the battle of Culloden. As mentioned earlier, there were surprisingly few charts of the western seaboard of Scotland available at the time. Much of the lack of coverage was due to a dearth of sizeable, safe anchorages on the west coast and to its lesser significance in Scots maritime trade in comparison with that from Aberdeen, Dundee, the Fife ports and Leith.

Like the military establishment, the Royal Navy had been equally wrong-footed during the Jacobite campaigns, as evinced by the unchallenged landing of Spanish troops on Scottish soil in 1719 and of the Young Pretender in 1745. However, in the years after the Rising, the efforts of one surveyor in particular appear to have rectified this serious lack of coverage. This man was Murdoch Mackenzie (1712–97), of whom it is considered that 'no single person in this country made a more lasting contribution to the science of hydrography in both the theoretical and practical fields'. He seems to have had excellent credentials for the career he followed, having attended mathematics classes at Edinburgh University, and good family connections. Certainly, in November 1742 Professor Colin Maclaurin provided a testimonial on his behalf highly commending his qualifications 'to take a geometrical survey' when Mackenzie issued a proposal to begin his hydrographic work by covering the Orkney Islands, his home territory.

With financial support from the East India Company and the use of instruments on loan from the Admiralty, Mackenzie surveyed the island group and its coasts in the period between 1744 and 1747, following this with a relatively brief survey of Lewis a year later. Two years after this, he published *Orcades, or, A Geographical and Hydrographical Survey* which included eight charts of the islands. Although the end result was less complete than Mackenzie originally intended, it impressed the Admiralty sufficiently for him to be commissioned, as a civilian, to prepare the first complete survey of the whole west coast, beginning with Scotland between 1751 and 1757, before carrying on to the rest of Britain and Ireland. The Royal Navy supplied Mackenzie with suitable vessels for the operation, first the smack *Culloden* and later the sloop *Bird*, and he worked his way steadily south down the coast from Cape Wrath.

It was only following his retiral from active fieldwork that Mackenzie had the resultant charts prepared for publishing and these appeared in the two-volume *Maritim Survey of Ireland and the West Coast of Scotland* in 1776, accompanied by two books of sailing directions and nautical descriptions. In his

Opposite. Detail of manuscript additions at Toward Point from Mackenzie's *The River Clyde*

discussion of the tides, rocks, shoals and anchoring-places of the Clyde between the Cumbraes and Glasgow, Mackenzie noted that 'no River whatever can be safer, or is better provided with spacious well-sheltered arms of the sea, of easy access, and capable of numerous fleets, than the Clyde is. In approaching it, there are neither rocks nor shoals, nor rappid tides to be feared.' However, in the succeeding description of the various harbours, he records that only lighters, or very small vessels, have sufficient water to carry them up to the quay at Glasgow. Similarly, Ayr, Irvine and Saltcoats were described as fit only for small vessels of less than 8 feet draught. Despite the width of the estuary, Mackenzie recorded the channel between Greenock and Port Glasgow as 'narrow and intricate, as far as Garvel Point; there being neither beacon, nor buoy, to direct vessels through it; therefore this part of the channel requires a pilot'. It was later stated that 'he who has McKenzie's charts . . . needs no pilot' and, in fact, his clear directions did have a serious impact on the piloting profession.

This chart of the Clyde was to appear in the second volume of the book, but the surveying of the estuary had been carried out nearly 20 years earlier, in 1757. In other words, Mackenzie was charting the river at about the same time that Smeaton, Barry and James Watt were engaged on their own surveys. It is accompanied by another map covering the Firth of Clyde which includes Arran, the Mull of Kintyre and Loch Ryan. As can be seen in comparison with later charts prepared by the naval officers employed by the Hydrographic Office, Mackenzie focused on sounding the known shipping routes of safe passage rather than producing a detailed description of the whole firth. Depths were taken by a hand lead during the operations, with positions determined by intersecting compass bearings to significant land stations. As a result of Mackenzie's method, the wealth of onshore information on significant coastal features recorded on the charts contrasts with the more limited marine detail but, given his restricted resources and the length of the coastline, the accurate record produced within the two decades of his employment is a reflection of his undoubted abilities.

While the textual description of the firth emphasises its relative safety, an inspection of the details shows the narrowness of the Clyde off Port Glasgow. This is the result of the constriction caused by Cockle Bank. The channel remains narrow right up to Glasgow, which is indicated in a markedly stylised manner, again underlining the focus on marine features. While Mackenzie indicates the recently constructed lighthouse on Little Cumbrae, subsequent manuscript additions to the sheet also mark a beacon at Toward Point and on Captain's Rock. Overall, the map shows the limited number of good havens in the upper firth for any vessel until it reaches Rothesay or Gourock. The chart was engraved in London by Thomas Kitchin, himself a noted cartographer and hydrographer to King George III.

Mackenzie's importance to British hydrography extended well beyond the drawing of the charts themselves, for he was the first to base his work on a rigid triangulation framework, having originally measured an onshore baseline on the Loch of Stenness when frozen and created a network of beacons on prominent points. In addition, his *Treatise of Maritim Surveying* introduced to a wider audience the station pointer as an instrument which improved the precision and speed of fixing the position of a survey vessel. This book was published in 1774, the year in which he was elected a Fellow of the Royal Society, and it was to remain a standard work for more than 50 years. Several of the conventions he introduced remain standard features of today's sea charts. Along with the surveys of his nephew, also named Murdoch Mackenzie, he raised the levels of accuracy of marine charts and contributed to the establishment of the Admiralty's Hydrographic Office.

Opposite. Murdoch Mackenzie, *The River Clyde* (1776)

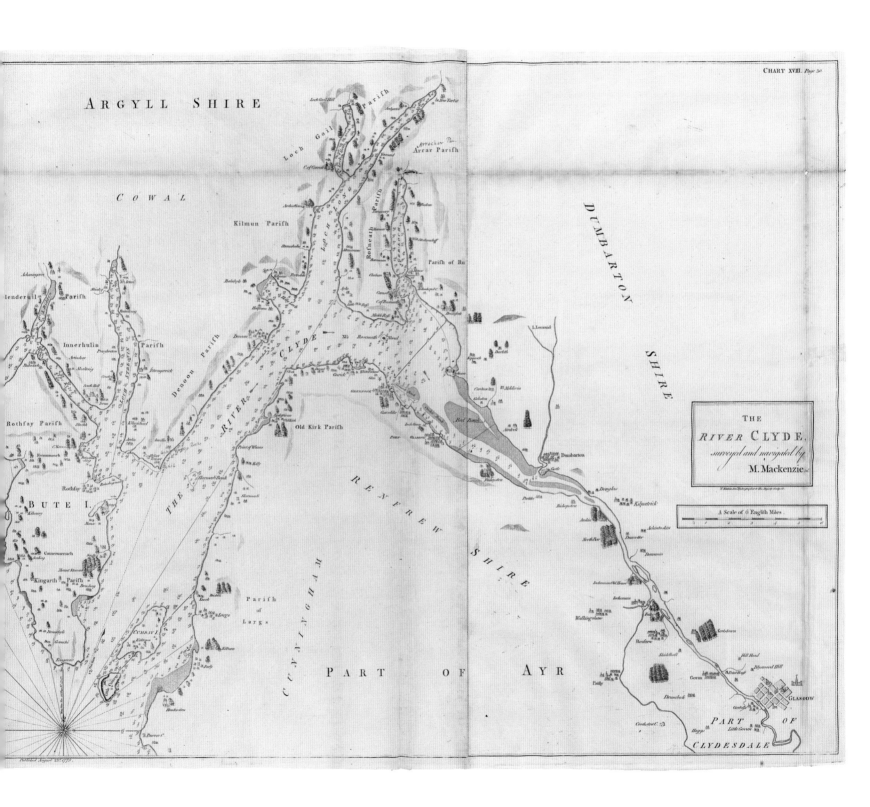

CHART XVIII. Page 30.

ARGYLL SHIRE

COWAL

DUMBARTON SHIRE

Kilmun Parifh

Rofneath Parifh

Parifh of Ru

Denoon Parifh

THE RIVER CLYDE

Glenderuil Parifh

Innerhulin Parifh

Rothfay Parifh

BUTE I.

Kingarth Parifh

Old Kirk Parifh

RENFREW SHIRE

CUNINGHAM

Parifh of Largs

CUMBRAY I.

PART OF AYR

Dumbarton

Kilpatrick

Renfrew

Paifly

GLASGOW

PART OF

CLYDESDALE

THE
RIVER CLYDE,
surveyed and navigated by
M. Mackenzie

A Scale of 6 Englifh Miles.

Publifhed Auguft 23.d 1775.

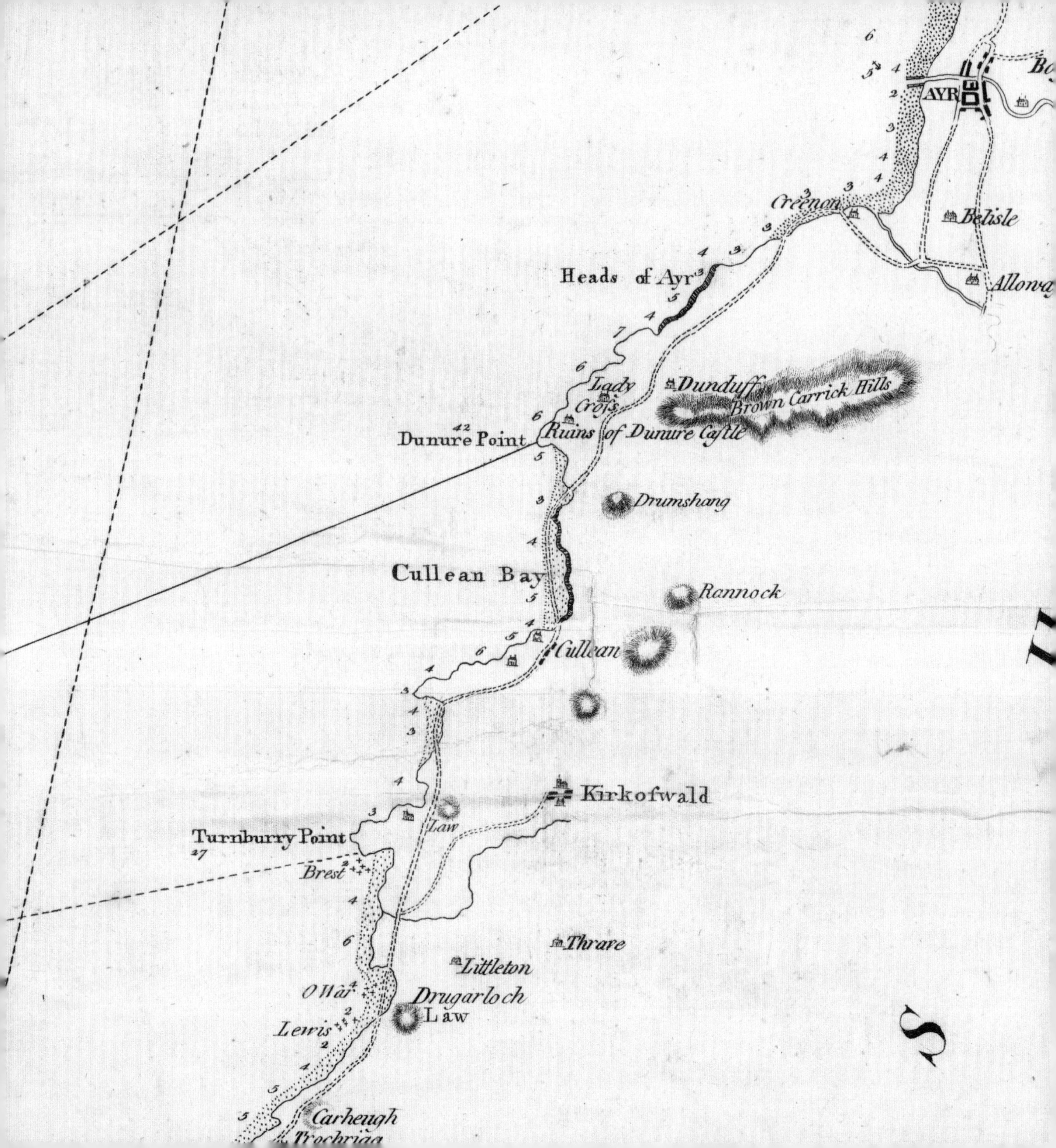

AYR

Brown Carrick Hills

Belisle

Creenon

Allowa

Heads of Ayr

Dunduff

Lady Cross

Dunure Point

Ruins of Dunure Castle

Drumshang

Cullean Bay

Rannock

Cullean

Kirkofwald

Turnburry Point

Law

Brest

Thrare

Littleton

Drugarloch Law

O War

Lewis

Carheugh Trochriaa

S

CHAPTER 16

The Firth of Clyde on Ainslie's chart of the west coast

On becoming a newly commissioned Crown employee, Robert Burns, subsequently the national bard, wrote to his close friend Robert Ainslie on 1 November 1789 informing him of his appointment as a customs officer. Burns had sought patronage through an appeal to the Earl of Glencairn but, more importantly, he also made use of a contact with Robert Graham of Fintry, Commissioner of Excise for Scotland, which opened up this change of career. Subsequently, Burns was to pen a sonnet to Fintry on receiving news of this appointment. In his own unique style of viewing the situation, he describes in his letter to Ainslie what might be seen as a rather unusual choice of employment thus, 'I know not how the word "exciseman", or still more opprobrious "gauger," will sound in your ears. I too have seen the day when my auditory nerves would have felt very delicately on this subject; but a wife and children are things which have a wonderful power in blunting these kind of sensations. Fifty pounds a year . . . you will allow is no bad settlement for a *poet*.' Burns was well aware of the unpopularity of customs officers, particularly in the countryside, where smuggling was often regarded as an alternative income for hard-pressed rural communities. Only three years later, he was to pen the darkly humorous 'The Deil's Awa Wi' Th'Exciseman', reflecting on a profession which put many beyond the pale and, possibly, on his own ambivalent attitude to such an occupation.

Burns was a man who was map literate, having been taught mathematics and surveying in his early years. Ainslie was the son of Robert Ainslie (1734–95), factor to Lord Douglas, and there are surviving plans which were probably drawn by the father as part of his duties. This chart of the west coast is, however, the work of another man with the same surname, John Ainslie, probably the leading Scottish cartographer and surveyor of the second half of the eighteenth century. The link, albeit somewhat tenuous, with the ploughman poet is that the map was engraved by Ainslie at the desire of the Commissioners of His Majesty's Customs and it is just possible that Burns used such a map in his work.

The chart covers the coast from Saltcoats to Whitehaven in Cumberland and includes the Isle of Arran. In a note on the map, Ainslie remarks that he had surveyed the coast to Fleet Bay in Kirkcudbrightshire but other stretches were copied from various surveys held by the Board of Customs. Subsequently, Ainslie would become familiar with the area on this map. He had surveyed the county of Wigtownshire in 1782 and was to complete a similar coverage of Kirkcudbright towards the end of the century, in addition to a very detailed mapping of the Eglinton estates, with over 170 separate plans which included the baronies of Kilwinning, Ardrossan and Dreghorn. Although undated, this chart forms part of a sequence prepared by Ainslie

Opposite. Extract showing coastal road across the sands at Culzean from Ainslie's *Chart of the west coast of Scotland*

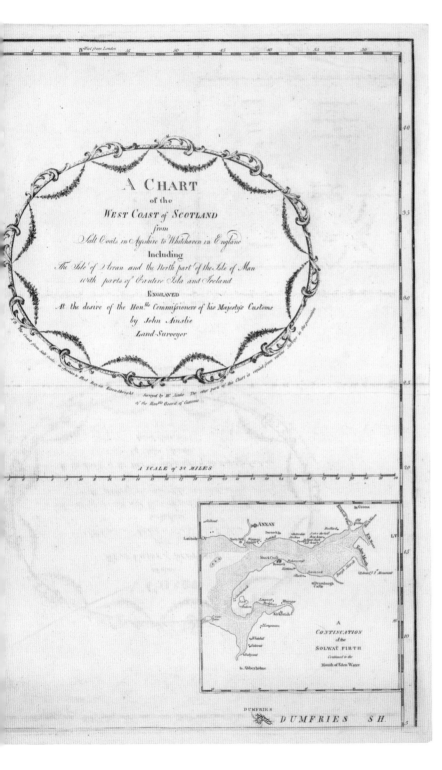

in the mid 1780s depicting the Scottish seaboard that also covered the east coast from Berwick to Duncansby Head in Caithness.

Drawn on six sheets at a scale of 2 miles to an inch, this is a markedly detailed record of the Clyde coast but, like the work of Mackenzie and others, it is not certain if the information was widely accessible to other users. While Ainslie is particular in describing himself as a land surveyor, the map displays many of the features expected of a maritime chart, such as rocks, soundings, anchorages and sandbanks, but one interesting feature is the delineation of the coastal roads running across the sands which were, no doubt, valued by those customs officers unfamiliar with the more intricate detail of the west coast along which they rode in patrol. Once again, the location of soundings and rocks emphasises a marked focus on the coast rather than the deeper waters of the firth, the figures showing just how shallow the immediate Ayrshire littoral was. The map also gives a good impression of the narrowness of the entries into the harbours of Irvine, Ayr and Saltcoats. The haven at Lamlash is marked, as are the two beacons on Lady Isle. Landward features include recognisable buildings and significant coastal hills, such as Brown Carrick and Dundonald, identified to aid navigation.

Some impression of the possible background to this chart can be seen in Robert Duncan's contribution to the *Statistical Account* for his own parish of Dundonald, published in 1793. Although it contains a homily on the evil effects of smuggling on the character, Duncan does point out that Troon 'was found to be a very convenient station for vessels employed in contra-band trade' during the time the Isle of Man retained distinct sovereignty but, with the British government's purchase of the feudal rights, the 'hostile traffic' had been 'nearly annihilated'. Whether or not Burns did consult such a map, the details of the coastline would have been invaluable for the crews of the customs cutters that would have patrolled the firth, particularly if they were unfamiliar with the estuary. Of equal importance is the area of coverage of the chart – a somewhat remote part of the south-west coast of Scotland, well away from the larger population centres and customs offices of the upper Clyde.

Opposite. John Ainslie, *Chart of the west coast of Scotland* (1784)

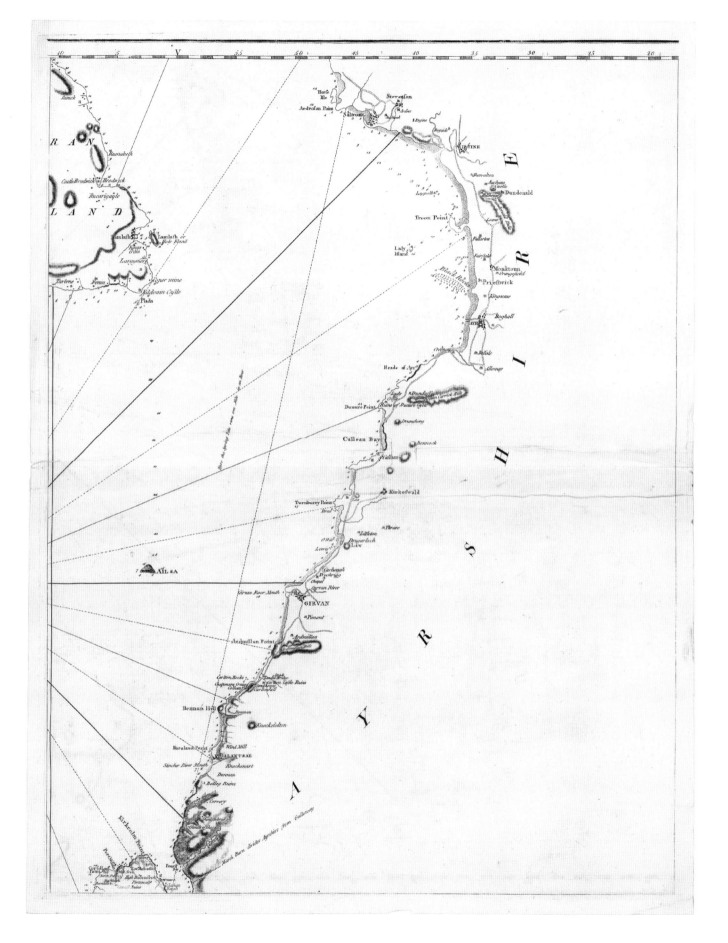

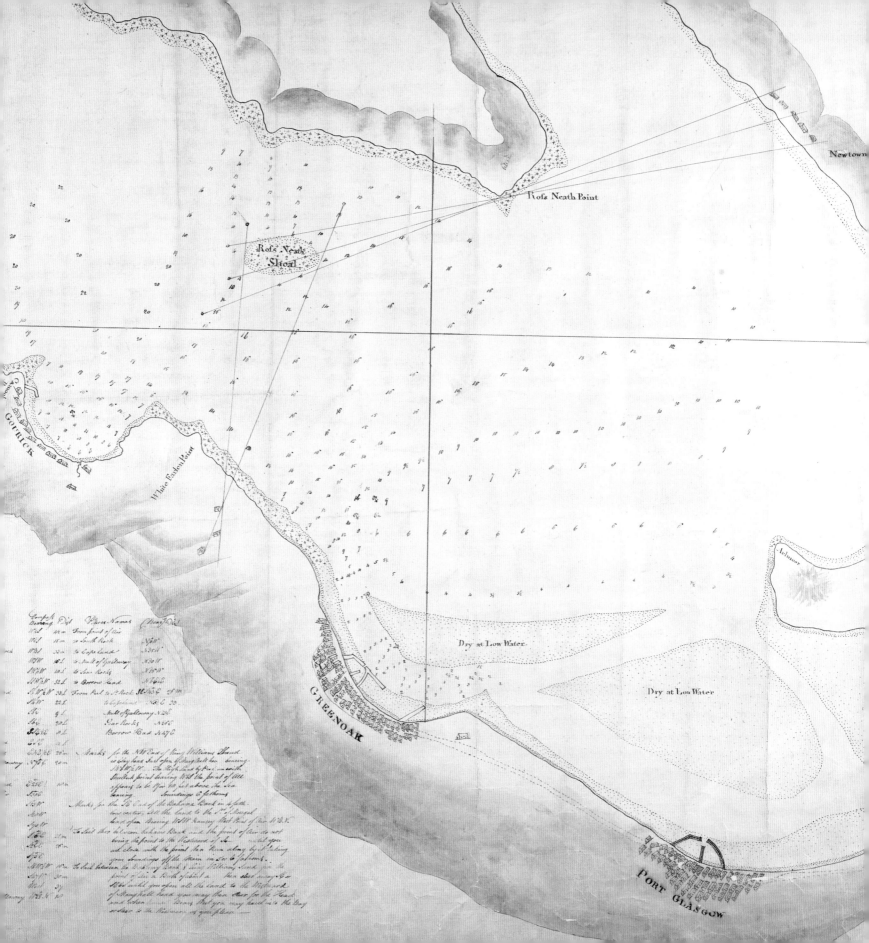

CHAPTER 17

A naval survey of the Clyde at the end of the eighteenth century

One of the major difficulties in any assessment of the charting of the Clyde is the tracing of just what plans and surveys were drawn for the varied requirements of a wide range of interests. As well as this, marine charts were working documents rarely designed for the library or for display and their survival could be affected by shipwreck, damage or disposal as more accurate versions were published. Like much of the cartography of this period, short print runs were very much the order of the day. When the Watt family first produced their map of the Clyde, only 450 impressions were made. However, as already discussed with the work of John Adair, not all marine cartography was published and the considerable body of surviving manuscript charts in various national archives remains a largely untapped resource for research. Several of these manuscripts formed the sources for printed Admiralty and other sea charts but many others remain as a unique record of the work of naval officers and other mariners.

These three depictions of different anchorages and stretches of the Clyde estuary are the work of George Thompson when he was based in the area between 1790 and 1792, soon after promotion to the post of master in the Royal Navy. They are part of the collection held at the Admiralty's Hydrographic Office Library at Taunton which includes many of the sketches and surveys made in the period before an independent surveying

department was created as part of the service. At that time, serving officers were encouraged, if not expected, to record as much information as they could about local tidal conditions, depths of navigable channels, the location of rocks and shoals and other such significant marine features. As part of their duties, they noted this information in their journals and often illustrated their annotations with coastal profiles, detailed surveys of safe harbours and charts of inshore waters. While the later charts of the Hydrographic Office were the work of officers commissioned by the Board of Admiralty, much of the marine cartography of the later eighteenth century was also carried out by the senior warrant officer aboard any of His Majesty's vessels, namely the master.

In 1790, the Admiralty issued the thirteenth edition of the *Regulations and Instructions Relating to His Majesty's Service at Sea* within which the various aspects of life on board and the duties of all the officers are explained. First published in 1734, this edition appeared in the same year as Thompson's earliest surviving surveys and it lists the master's responsibilities for a wide range of tasks. In particular, the navigation of the ship, including the setting of courses and the finding of the ship's position, was under his charge. Under the articles which specifically detail his duties, the master was 'to apply himself to observe the Appearance of Coasts, and how they shew them-

Opposite and overleaf. George Thompson, *Chart of Clyde off Greenock and Port Glasgow* (1792)

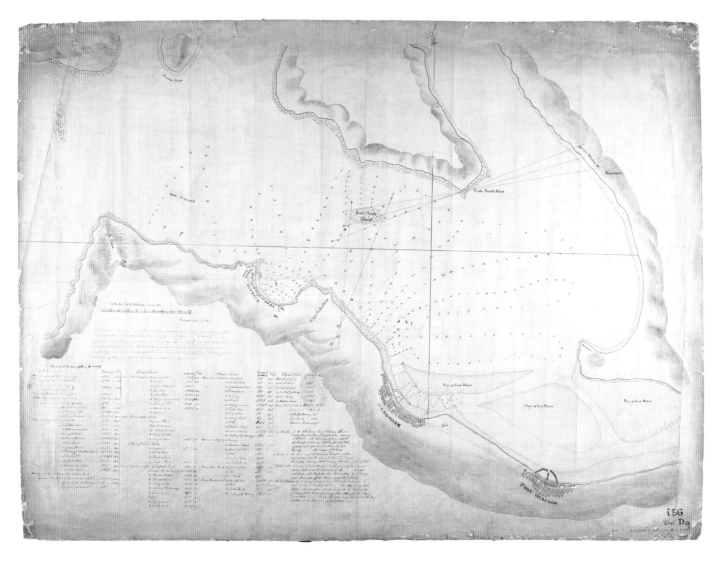

selves in different Points of View; and if he discovers any new Shoals or Rocks under Water, to note them down in his Journals, with their Bearings and Depth of Water'. The master on a navy vessel was in a category of his own, with frequently superior specialist knowledge and experience. He was partly responsible for supplying his own tools for the job and was expected 'to provide himself with the proper Instruments, Maps, and Books of Navigation, and to keep an exact and perfect Journal'. Frequently, the position of master could lead to a commissioned rank, as was the case for both James Cook and William Bligh.

Much of the chart production at this time was largely done by private enterprise. Some officers, such as Murdo Downie, the Aberdonian master of HMS *Champion*, were fortunate enough to have their work published for the benefit of other

Opposite. Gourock Bay (1792)

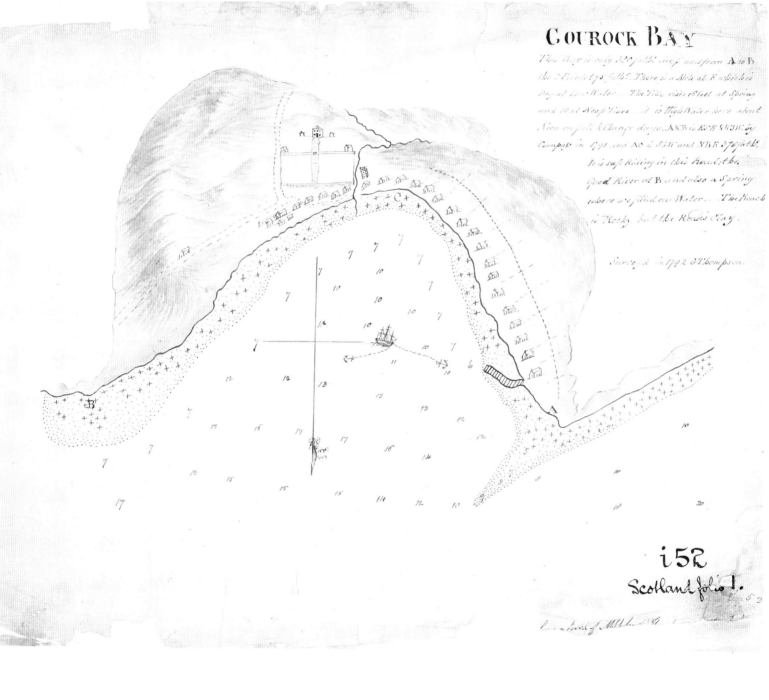

GOUROCK BAY

This Bay is only 320 yds. deep and from A to B
the 2 Points 875 faths. There is a Mole at E which is
dry at low Water. The Tide rises 10 feet at Spring
and 10 at Neap Tides. It is High Water here about
Noon on full & Change days. A & B is ENE & WSW by
Compass in 1791 and AC is SEbE and NWbE 376 faths.

It is safe Riding in this Road, the
Good River at B and also a Spring
where we filled our Water. The Beach
is Rocky but the Roads Clay.

Surveyed in 1792 by T. Thompson.

i52
Scotland folio 1.

mariners but many more carried out surveys for their own use and did not enjoy the financial return which might result from engraving or publication. Charts were probably circulated among fellow navigators and colleagues (or their mates) copied each other's work, allowing a slightly wider circulation of information. Their journals have recently been the subject of new research and provide a rich fund of information on the production, transfer and circulation of cartographic knowledge for the period. Certainly, Thompson's work deserved to be published – if only because these charts covered an important home estuary which was to remain without accurate charts until the work of Captain Charles Robinson in the late 1840s.

The largest and most detailed of this group of charts extends from Cloch Point to Port Glasgow – probably the section of the firth of most relevance to the Royal Navy – and, as with his other work, it was based on compass bearings with lines of soundings taken from the shore running out in right-angled sequences. Like the surveys prepared by Murdoch Mackenzie, Thompson's charts do not provide a systematic coverage of the whole seabed of the estuary but focus on the areas of greatest significance to sailing vessels. Much detail was recorded in his journals and sketched in from visual observation, often from the masthead which could often provide a better vantage point. The detail on these manuscripts and the related information was incorporated into later charts in use in the period before the Grand Survey of the British Isles inaugurated by Sir Francis Beaufort in the 1830s.

Both the Rothesay and Gourock Bay charts appear a little confusing to the landsman since the focus is markedly fixed on the marine features. Landward detail is mostly included to assist navigation and the seaward element of the coastline identifies shoals and rocks. Thompson subsequently surveyed several of the major Irish harbours in the period 1792–94 but seems to have finished his service by January 1801. His Remark Book has survived as a source for further study of one of the unsung heroes of British marine cartography.

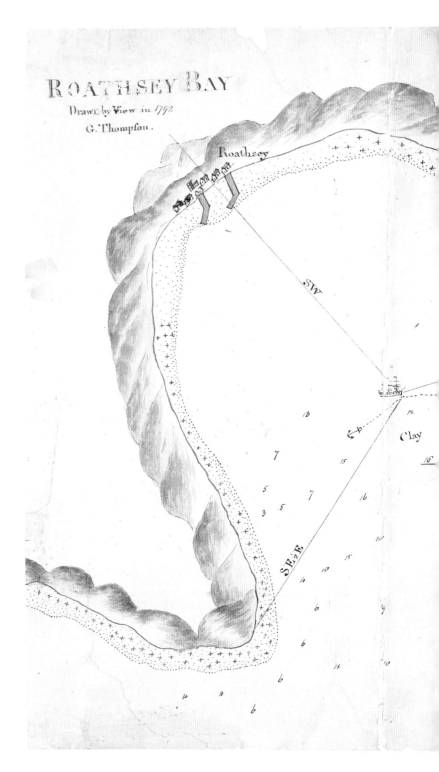

Details of bearings on George Thompson's chart of Rothesay Bay

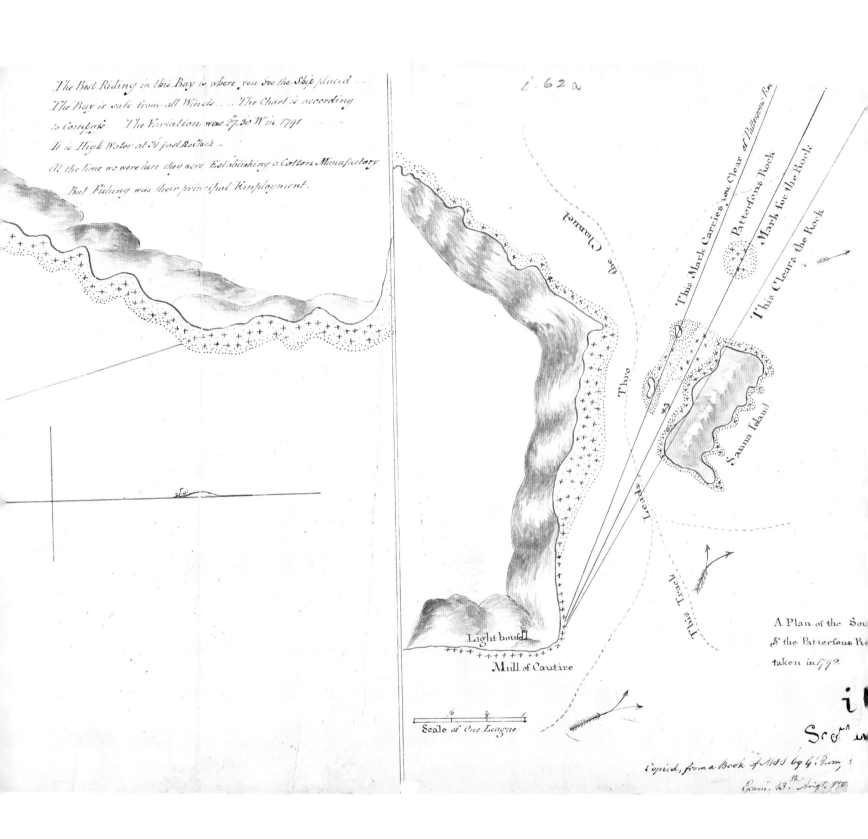

The Best Riding in this Bay is where you see the Ship placed —
The Bay is safe from all Winds. — The Chart is according
to Compass. The Variation was 27..30 W in 1791 ——
It is High Water at 3/4 past IIoClock —
All the time we were here they were Establishing a Cotton Manufactory
But Fishing was their principal Employment.

i. 62 a

the Channel

This Mark Carries you Clear of Patterson's Roc

Patterson's Rock

Mark for the Rock.

This Clears the Rock

Sanna Island

This Leads

This Track

Light house

Mull of Cantire

Scale of One League

A Plan of the So—
& the Patterson Ro—
taken in 1792.

i

Scotl

Copied from a Book of MSS by G. Thom
Exam: 13th Augt 1870

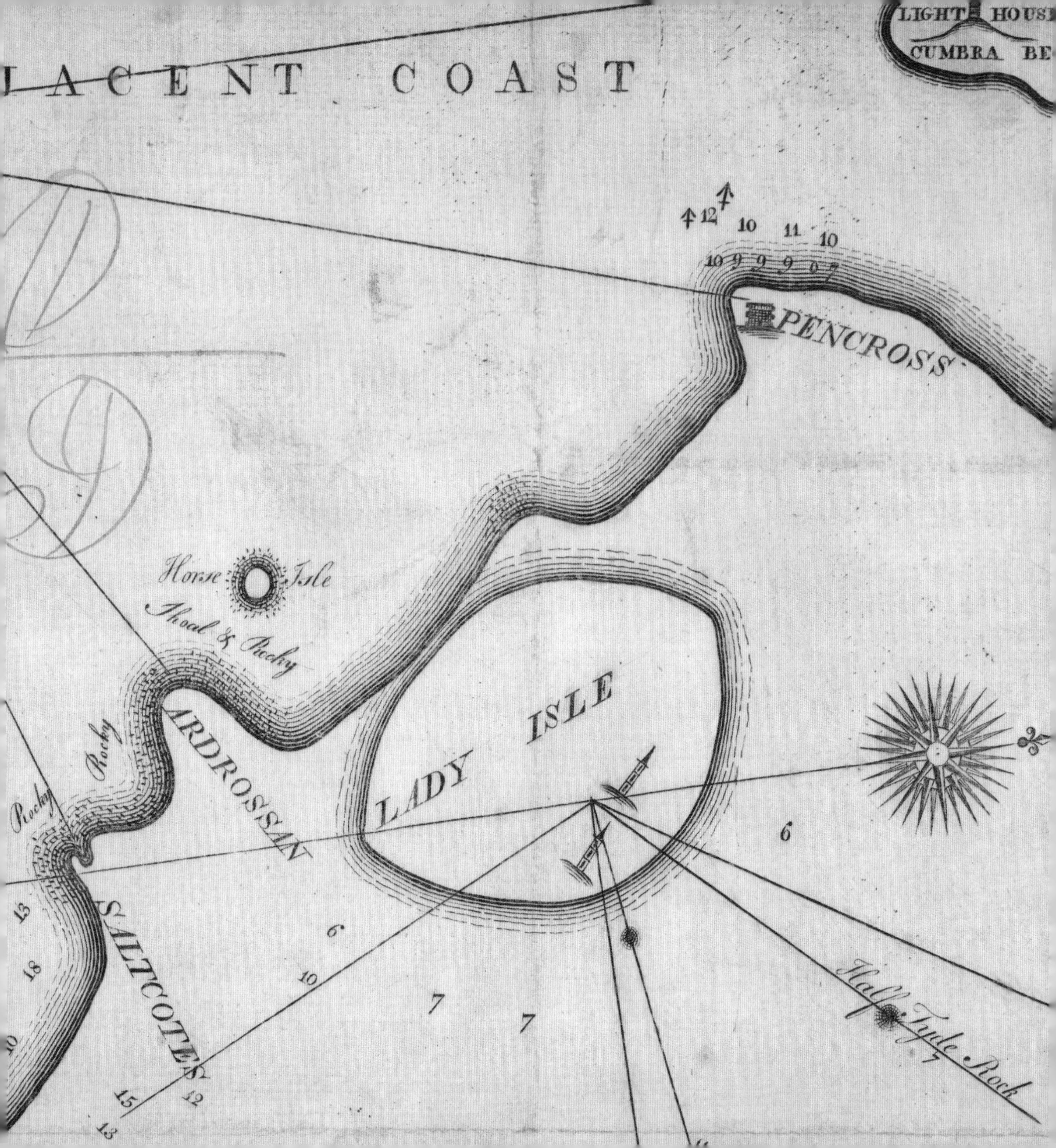

LACENT COAST

LIGHT HOUSE
CUMBRA BE

PENCROSS

12 10 11 10
10 9 9 9 9

Horse Isle

Shoal & Rocky

ARDROSSAN

Rocky   Rocky

Rocky

LADY ISLE

6

13

18

SALTCOTES

6

10

7

7

Half Tyle Rock

15   12

13

CHAPTER 18

Guiding the way: lighthouses and beacons on the Clyde

While there is a considerable literature on the work of various engineers to improve the navigability of the Clyde, comparatively little research has been carried out on the lights and beacons which were constructed and placed to ensure a safe passage for vessels entering the upper reaches of the estuary. Some of the early charts covering the firth indicate a safe route by the location of images of vessels at the appropriate parts of the channel but mariners were well aware of the problems faced in heavy seas when visibility was hampered by the bad weather somewhat typical of a Scottish west coast winter.

At about the same time that the merchants and magistrates were beginning to lobby for a more concentrated approach to dealing with the natural hazards of the river, action was also being taken to help mariners avoid the problems of the wider estuary. Again, the Glasgow burgh records provide valuable information on the range of work involved, particularly an entry for October 1748 indicating that the Dean of Guild was reimbursed for expenses and charges incurred 'in going to Ayr and Irvine in order to make a survey of the Lady Isles and the bays of Ayr and Irvine, for the benefite of shipping and navigating, and a chart to be drawn thereof'. Three years later, the minutes record similar survey work and sounding by him and William (more likely to be James) Barry carried out in 1750.

This activity was clearly part of a wider programme but specifically forms part of a process which was to result in a commission to build a lighthouse. In April 1756, parliament sanctioned the erection of such a light on the Little Cumbrae to indicate the narrow middle channel between it and the south end of Bute. Unlike its larger neighbour, the Wee Cumbrae is rough, rocky and has many cliffs, all of which necessitate its identification. The following year, legislation was enacted in which specific mention was made of the setting up of beacons, buoys and other marks to indicate such dangers. James Ewing constructed the first lighthouse on the summit of the island's highest point that year for the comparatively low cost of little more than £140. It was the second lighthouse to be built in Scotland and the original light comprised an open coal fire in a grate. This extremely rare but undated chart of Lady Isle and the adjacent coast is now assumed to be part of that surveying produced to support the safer navigation of the whole firth. As the title states, it was navigated and surveyed by James Barry and the area of coverage is remarkably similar to that mentioned in the 1748 council minute. More importantly, it indicates the newly built light on the Little Cumbrae and therefore is most likely to date from after 1757. It marks the various rocks, shoals and best anchorages on this stretch of the coast and is enhanced by a sequence of compass bearings. With its detailed description of the features of the immediate area, it acts in a similar fashion

Opposite and overleaf. James Barry, *Chart of Lady Isle and adjacent coast* (c.1760)

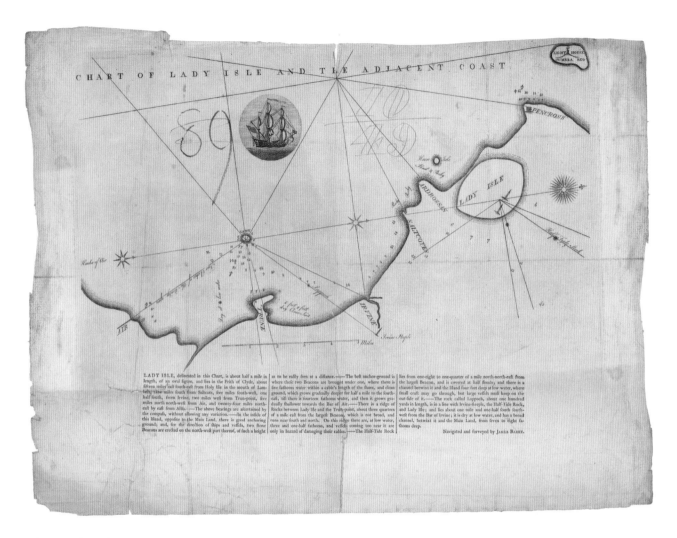

to a pilot's guide and emphasises that most shipping at this time was markedly coastal in focus. Unusually, an enlarged inset of the safe anchorage of Lady Isle, showing the two stone beacons built specifically to be seen at a distance, is located inland north of Ardrossan.

This document may be all that remains of Barry's surveying activity of the lower reaches of the estuary but surviving evidence from the Cumbrae Lighthouse Trust shows that he had been commissioned to draw a chart covering the whole of the mouth of the Clyde from the Mull of Galloway to the Mull of Kintyre and the River Clyde as far up as Glasgow and, in 1760, was paid the princely sum of £60 sterling for his efforts. One of the

more significant features of the historical record is the remarkably small number of names, mostly drawn from the ranks of the Glasgow mercantile community, which are recorded in the relevant documents of the various trusts and committees. It demonstrates that once an able practitioner like Barry had proved his worth, there were plenty of opportunities for him to be employed.

A clearer impression of the lighthouse and its situation on the summit of a small hill is given on this beautiful map of the Little Cumbrae which forms part of the book of estate plans prepared by John Ainslie for the Earl of Eglinton in 1789–90. More than 170 plans are included in the volume which depicts the various lands owned by the earl. Each illustration has a

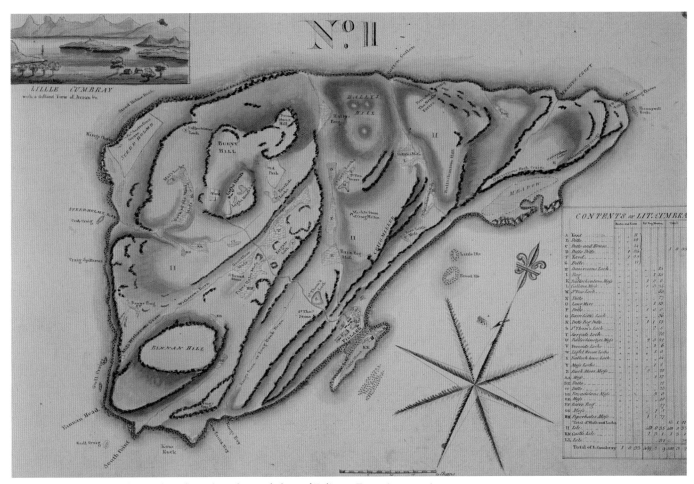

John Ainslie, *Plan of Little Cumbrae* from the volume of plans of Eglinton Estate (1789–90)

table of contents and an indication of land use. This plan shows the village, various tracks and the lighthouse yards, as well as including a coloured view of the island as an inset. Unfortunately, the inherent problems of illumination by a coal fire and the position of the tower at the top of the hill resulted in the light being frequently obscured by low cloud and fog, leading to its subsequent relocation. Today, the island provides a retreat based at Little Cumbrae House while the current Ordnance Survey maps continue to indicate Lighthouse Hill and the site of the original building.

As Murdoch Mackenzie noted, the inner waters of the Clyde are relatively safe, unlike other reaches of the Scottish coastline,

and they did not pose the same challenges to the great family of Scottish lighthouse builders, the Stevensons, as the Bell Rock or Skerryvore. Nonetheless, the Glasgow-born Robert Stevenson (1772–1850) took time away from his extensive duties as chief executive to the Northern Lighthouse Board to design the beacons illustrated in this third image which were proposed to be erected on the rocks of the Gantocks and Captain's Bridges in 1828. Both are termed beacons, otherwise unlit sea marks, are indicated in plan and section format, and are marked on small sketch plans of their immediate location. Interestingly, as beacons, neither appears to have been designed initially to carry a light. Stevenson had been involved previously in the recon-

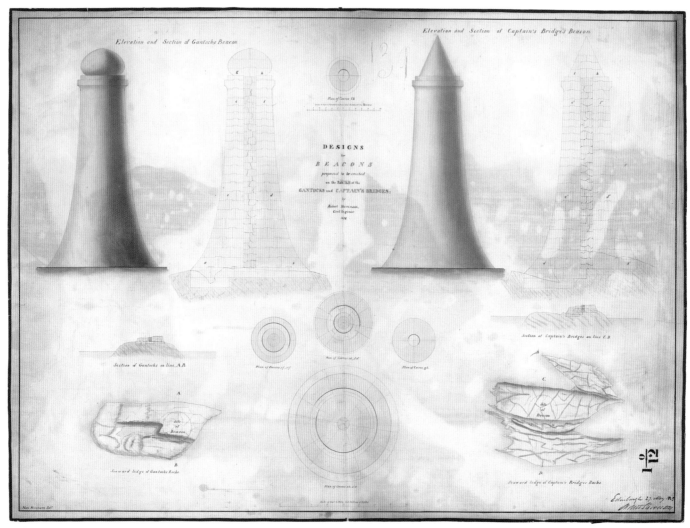

Robert Stevenson, *Design for beacons proposed to be erected on the rocks of Gantocks & Captain's Bridges* (1828)

struction and resiting of the Cumbrae lighthouse in 1793.

The Gantocks is a partially submerged igneous rock lying offshore from Dunoon Point, almost due west of Cloch Point. It is only covered at high-water spring tides and posed a significant hazard to local shipping and it was only in 1886 that a light was eventually located on the rocks. A subsequent guidebook to the Clyde describes the light as 'built of masonry, painted white, with lantern on top, showing 3 flashes in quick succession every 15 seconds'. Captain or Bridge Rock lies

offshore and south of Innellan and was listed in McKenzie's *Nautical Descriptions of the West Coast* as drying 'at two hours of ebb' tide. Recorded as being made of masonry, painted black, surmounted by a globe and, most importantly, to be avoided, it is known today as The Perch Beacon. Since the demolition of the prominent chimney of the Inverkip power station, it is now a more identifiable marker in the Clyde channel.

While such lights and beacons aided the negotiation of the firth's main channel, it was realised that the growth of shipping

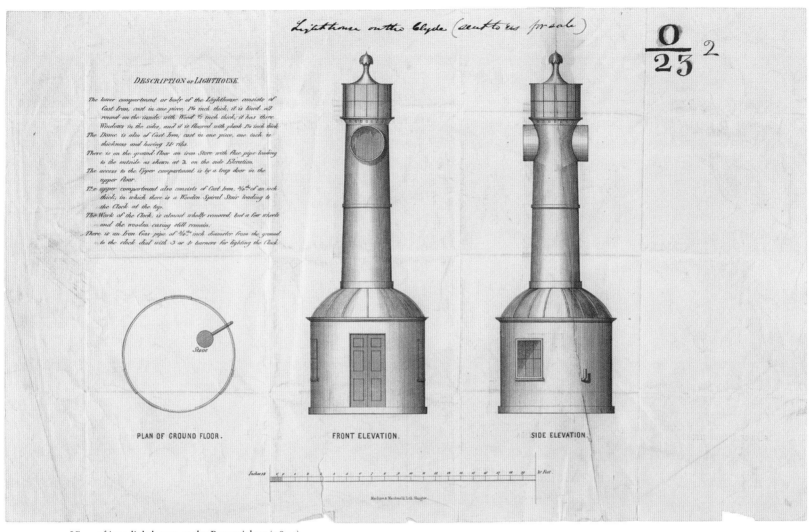

View of iron lighthouse at the Broomielaw (1824)

in the upper reaches of the Clyde could result in problems for vessels berthing at Glasgow. In 1824, the *Glasgow Mechanics' Magazine* carried an illustration of an experimental small iron lighthouse to be erected at the west end of the Broomielaw to prevent steamships from hitting the quayside at night. The proposed gas-lit lanterns facing both up- and downriver were found to be inadequate, largely due to problems experienced in balancing light and heat. By this date, David Brewster's experiments in zonal refracting lenses were being promoted to the

Northern Lighthouse Board as a more effective source of illumination. Nonetheless, the structure was erected and was illustrated in *The Glasgow Looking Glass* the following year. In 1842, George Martin located it to the west of York Street on his map of the city. It was subsequently offered for sale to the Stevensons. This sheet of elevations and plan from the family's cartographic archive replicates the original illustration and the description mirrors that in the magazine. Whether or not the firm purchased the construction is unknown but, given that it was offered without its original clock workings and the problems with the method of lighting, it may have been regarded as already out of date.

This final plan was prepared for the Cumbrae Lighthouse Trust by Andrew Duncan as part of his duties as engineer to the Clyde Navigation Trust. It accompanied a report he submitted in May 1865 regarding an improvement in the indication of the navigable channel at Skelmorlie Bank, a particularly notable and awkward feature in any approach to the upper firth. It lies almost midway between Toward Point and Skelmorlie, and at least two vessels have been recorded as foundering on or near the bank in the nineteenth century. Today it is identified on navigation charts by several lights. In addition to a plan of this stretch of the firth which marks the position of the proposed beacon on the hazard, Duncan supplied a sketch of the bank itself, as well as his design proposal for the construction and its foundations. Soundings are included and high- and low-water levels are marked. As an indication of the subsequent adoption of Duncan's scheme, it can be noted that reports on the loss of the *Toverus* in the channel in December 1875 mention its last location as being south-west of the light-buoy on the bank.

Duncan was originally from Moray and, earlier in his career, had worked with Alexander Gibb on harbour engineering projects in the north-east. In 1859, he succeeded John Ure as chief engineer to the newly established Clyde Navigation Trust and continued Ure's plans to establish docks, particularly at Windmillcroft. During his time in office, George Reith was appointed general manager of the Trust and, possibly recognising a kindred spirit in a fellow countryman, he was to give Duncan his support despite the latter's frail health. Thoroughly knowledgeable in the work of the Trust and the problems it faced, he oversaw the completion and opening of what became the Kingston Dock in October 1867 but died suddenly at home the following year. Among his many duties, he had sketched the Elderslie Rock, proposed the removal of the weir at Hutcheson Bridge, designed a patent pile-driver and investigated the accommodation for vessels in Rothesay harbour.

Opposite. Andrew Duncan, *Proposed beacon for Skelmorlie Bank* (1865)

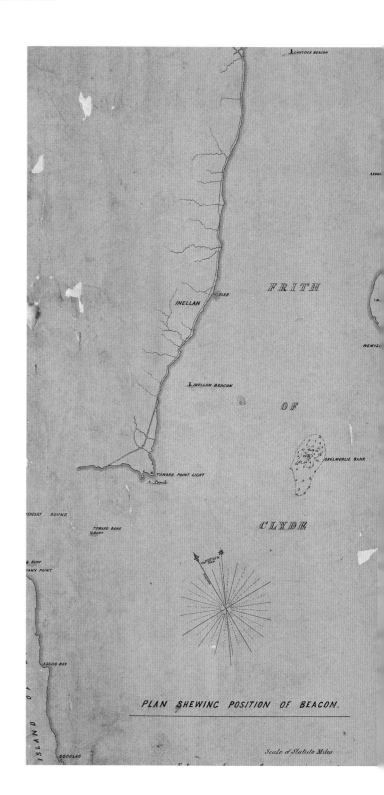

CUMBRAE LIGHT TRUST

PROPOSED BEACON FOR SKELMORLIE BANK.

Site of proposed Beacon or Tower shewn in Red on Plan

Plan referred to in Mr Duncan's Report dated 18th May 1865.

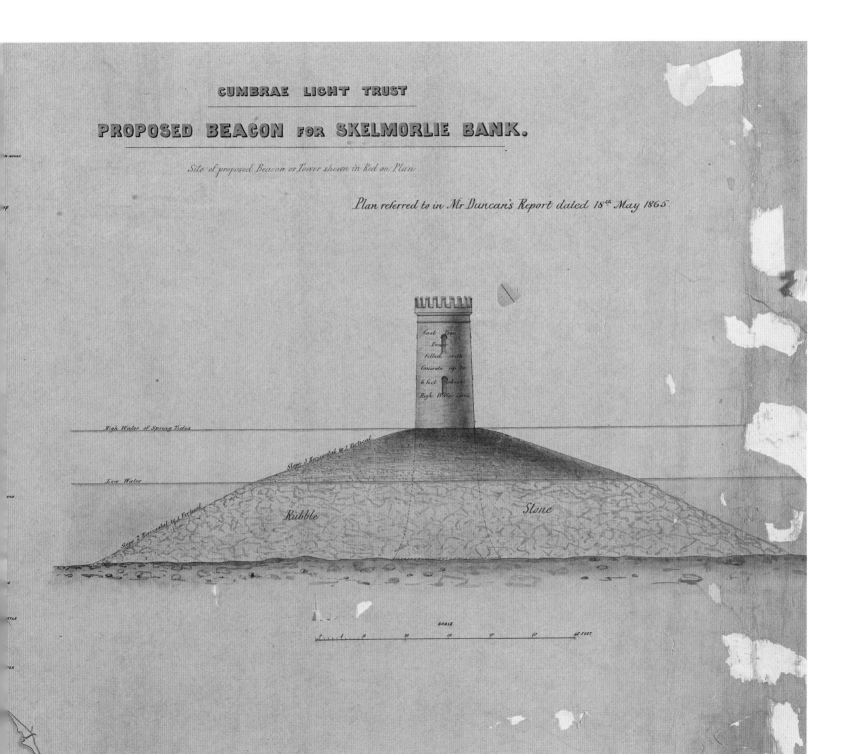

Cast Iron Tower filled with Concrete up to 6 feet above High Water level

High Water of Spring Tides

Low Water

Slope 3 Horizontal to 1 Vertical

Slope 2 Horizontal to 1 Vertical

Rubble

Stone

SCALE

The road from

Two & twenty houses
wet dock

B

872 by 154 feet

Dry dock

Anderstown

Anderstown's Water Engine

A Scale of 72 feet to the Inch

The New Quay at the Broomielaw

Coal quay Cotton Mill

CHAPTER 19

Glasgow's harbour begins to develop

Glasgow's first riverside quay was built on the Broomielaw in 1688, financed by Walter Gibson, at that time provost and one of the city's first merchants to trade with both Europe and the American colonies. While the many improvements to the navigability of the Clyde allowed larger vessels to reach that quay in the years of the following century, the demand for more extensive space for wharves, storage sheds and berths grew. It became increasingly apparent that Glasgow needed not only to focus on the river but also to invest in a programme which would extend and develop its harbour. Part of this consideration needed to take into account the side effect of the increased flow of water which was beginning to undercut both the Broomielaw quay and the new Jamaica Street Bridge. Another problem faced by the city was the increased incidence of flooding of properties close to the river, particularly on the north bank. At this time the south bank extended much further north into the river and was unsuitable for the construction of any proper wharf.

Initially, attention was paid to remedying these more immediate problems and, once more, the magistrates turned to one of the nation's leading practitioners – on this occasion, the Scottish civil engineer, John Rennie (1761–1821). His advice was sought in the summer of 1798 and it is clear from the records that, like his predecessors, he relied on maps and sections of the river prepared by local surveyors to enable him to make

any report. In this case, it was William Kyle who was authorised to provide an up-to-date plan of the river improvements. It was another two years before the magistrates took action on the subsequent report. Part of Rennie's solution to the flooding was to link the ends of the various jetties by training walls, combined with a programme of constant dredging. However, the council also consulted Thomas Telford (1757–1834), possibly the most celebrated of the early Scottish civil engineers, whose opinion was that the best results would be achieved by shaping the river bed to allow as much tidal water as possible to flow up to Glasgow.

Although these proposals were of equal importance, the first record of a petition to extend the quay only appears in 1804. Nonetheless, ideas and plans were being suggested by the end of the eighteenth century, as evinced by this undated plan which comes from the Clyde Navigation Trust archive. Given that the plan only shows what appear to be sailing craft, it is assumed that it dates from a period well before the developments of steam power. Prepared by one Alexander Farmer, this is an outline proposal extracted from a larger sketch of the harbour area from Partick to the new Glasgow Bridge. While naive in style and very much of its time, it is a uniquely informative document showing the river well before major changes were carried out. It indicates suggested wet and dry docks

Opposite. Alexander Farmer, *Plan of Glasgow Harbour from Partick to Glasgow Bridge* (n.d.)

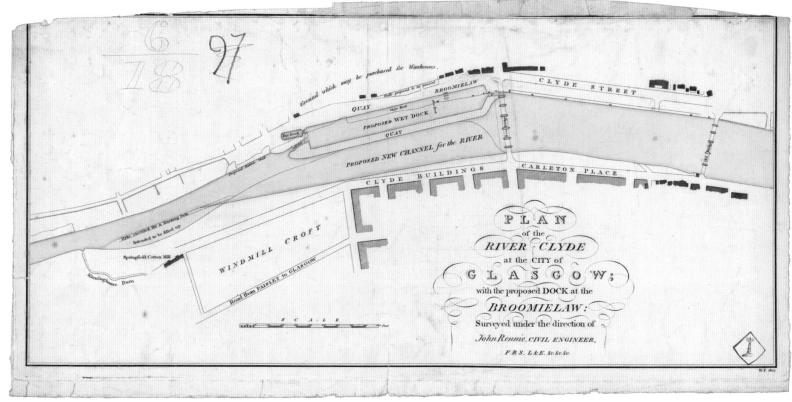

William Kyle, *Plan of the River Clyde* (1807), identifying John Rennie's proposed improvements

located east of Anderston and lying south of the road to Partick. One of three proposed jetties built out into the Clyde can be seen, in addition to a new stone-faced quay at the Broomielaw which is backed by a stylised but uniform design of stores and dwelling houses. This design also faces three sides of the wet dock. What appears to be the layout of a new street plan for Anderston is marked to the west. More importantly, the plan indicates features that were not part of the proposal but appear to be a true record of what existed at the time. These include a coal quay and cotton mill on the south bank, at what would eventually become Springfield Quay, lying to the west of Trades-ton. Such a coal quay had been established on the south bank by the late 1780s to facilitate shipments from the Govan coal pits. To the east of these, on the site of Windmillcroft, are marked a string of tenter frameworks used for drying fabrics, presumably cotton. Elsewhere on the plan, a dyeworks is located

east of the River Kelvin, which Farmer proposed to divert to flow into the Clyde downstream of the ferry at Partick. Significantly, there is no indication of a weir to protect the piers of the new bridge. On the other hand, it does identify the narrowing of the river immediately below the bridge where lands owned by the Trades House stretched towards the north bank.

Nothing is known of Farmer and no other plans by him have been traced. His somewhat amateur style suggests that he was neither a surveyor nor engineer. Much of the proposal hints at a lack of awareness of the practical requirements for the bulk handling and accommodation of goods. Neither wide doors nor hoist beams are marked on the buildings and this is not likely to have impressed the merchants. Far more importantly, the design of a dock at right angles to the river which would be entered through a narrow channel with a drawbridge and controlled by what appears to be lock gates reflects a limited

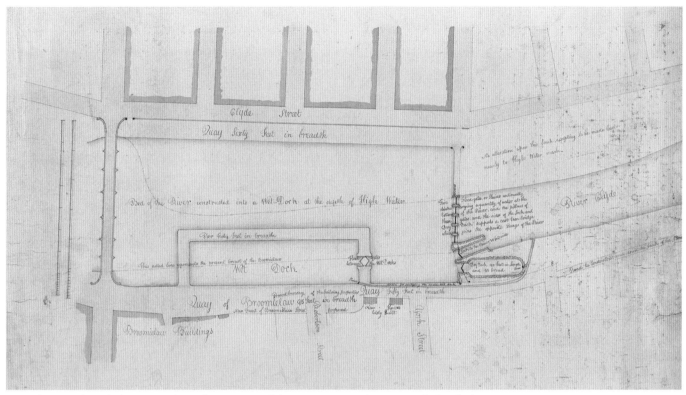

Peter Fleming, *Plan of Glasgow Harbour showing part of the river constructed into a wet dock at high water* (1806)

knowledge of the working of a vessel under sail in such a restricted channel as the Clyde at Glasgow. The proposal for lock gates at the entrance to a dock also betokens his unfamiliarity with, or at very least unawareness of, the range of the tide on this part of the Clyde. As it is far less than that at either London or Liverpool, there is less need for such features. Once again, a close scrutiny of a document pays dividends.

Both Rennie and Telford were aware of the problems facing the city in its needs for a better solution to harbour space. Following the initial approaches from the council, they extended their original remits beyond the mere investigation of the river to submit plans for the creation of a wet dock to provide improved facilities along the Broomielaw. They both considered this to be preferable to a reliance solely on the extension of quays, particularly as these would grow more distant from the city and eventually become more costly. Whether by chance or

collusion, the two men came up with a similar scheme to convert a section of the river bed into a dock, fed by a system of flood gates, and to create a new, straighter river channel immediately to the south. Their reports concur on several points, including a towing path for horses on the southern bank of the Clyde to assist becalmed vessels and the need for a dry dock as part of the improvement. Both men shrank from suggesting the cost of a scheme that would involve cutting back into the frontage of the Broomielaw Quay and recommended the less expensive alternative of converting part of the river bed instead. Rennie, however, offered the further option of a dock at Windmillcroft, which hints at a more far-sighted approach on his behalf.

Once again, local surveyors produced the plans on which their proposals were based. This 1807 version from the archive of the Stevenson family of civil engineers was drawn 'under the direction' of Rennie and it is most likely to have been prepared by William Kyle. Although it is not obvious from the design, it proposes a considerable change in the channel of the Clyde opposite the Broomielaw where the bank would be cleared, straightened and widened to make space for a dock on the north bank. Certain walls were to be removed and others built up, land was identified for warehouses and the proposed tracking path was included at Springfield, cutting across land reclaimed from the river. The second, manuscript plan depicted here was drawn by Peter Fleming in October 1806. At first sight, the differences between what it shows and what Telford proposed suggest that this is another version of Rennie's wet dock scheme, particularly regarding the north bank, but a closer investigation of the various reports indicates that this document was prepared two months before Rennie had an opportunity to inspect the site. It covers a similar area but has a different orientation, with south at the top of the sheet. Fleming had begun his career under Kyle's tuition and for a brief period in 1804 they formed a partnership. Much of his surviving work consists of engraved plans but this example shows his style of draftsmanship and his eye for detail.

Regardless of which proposed scheme Fleming's plan does represent, the drawing indicates the area under question and marks out a sequence of sluices, a wet dock enclosed by a pier and flood gates, a dry dock and the new bridge. No warehouses are marked but Fleming does show 'new houses lately built'. He identifies the line of where the existing quay wall ran and where the proposed new frontage of Broomielaw Street would be placed. However, of far greater importance is Fleming's astounding interpretation of the various suggestions put forward in the reports. What the plan shows has an echo of Smeaton's original idea of turning the river into a canal but in this case right at the heart of the city's harbour. A careful inspection shows that quays would be built on both banks of the river with a wall extending into the Clyde from the south to abut onto the sluice gates, thereby turning the whole breadth of the river downstream from the bridge into a far more sizeable wet dock. While bold and undoubtedly novel, this does not appear to reflect what either Telford or Rennie had considered and it is difficult to understand how such a concept would have

improved access for vessels, particularly given that Fleming also records that a cast iron bridge would link the dry dock and lock piers with both sides of the river. More importantly, such a basin would have been liable to considerable silting. The lock entry into this extended basin is set at only 30 feet wide which seems to imply that, in Fleming's mind, accommodation was intended to cater solely for smaller coasting craft.

A reading of the many debates and reports confirms that the Glasgow magistrates plainly put their money where they hoped it would bring mighty returns. Rennie was paid more than £270 in recognition of his services between 1800 and 1811, while Kyle was in receipt of nearly £100 solely for his 1802 river plan. What it seems the authorities were not prepared to do was finance the developments solely out of their own funds and the council certainly dragged its feet on any action. Part of this reticence was the continued recurrence of flooding along the banks of the Clyde and the awareness that such proposals would fail to resolve the vulnerability of the quays to inundation at exceptionally high tides. Neither of the plans was adopted and nothing further was discussed until the idea was raised again in 1820. Slowly, the quays were extended downstream of the bridge, leading to considerable overcrowding whenever a prevailing westerly wind facilitated the passage of vessels up to Glasgow. There are frequent references to ships being berthed three and four abreast in the congested harbour and this situation continued until 1867 when the first proper tidal dock was opened on land at Windmillcroft. By this date, most of the immediate area beside the river had been built upon.

Prior to this, William Simpson (1823–99) recorded some of the changes taking place here in this coloured drawing of the new quay being constructed on the south bank. Based on a sketch originally produced in 1848, the image was worked up into this attractive watercolour almost 50 years later. It depicts the work associated with the widening of the Clyde in preparation for the eventual building of the General Terminus Quay, completed in 1849, and shows the operations being carried out downriver from Windmillcroft. These included the massive foundations for a large riverside crane. This work, begun in 1837, was not completed fully until 1858. By removing

William Simpson, *New quay on south bank* (1848)

a considerable swathe of land at this point, the width of the river increased from 145 to 400 feet, thereby providing more space for ships to berth. The painting clearly highlights the scale of such an engineering project.

Simpson had been born in Carrick Street in Anderston ten years before David Tod and John Macgregor began their engineering business there. Subsequently, they established the Clyde Foundry slightly downriver. Their company purchased land in 1839 at what is now known to be Newhall on the south side of the river, where they opened what is frequently claimed to be the first iron-shipbuilding yard on the Clyde. This land was cleared during the quay construction project and the shipyard moved further downriver to Meadowside as part of the gradual process of separating the shipbuilding businesses from the harbour proper. In the background to his drawing, Simpson shows a ruined building identified as Tod & Macgregor's works which was, in fact, one of the ranges facing the company's Newhall yard. This location is confirmed on George Martin's 1842 map of the city. During the excavations, a temporary wooden wharf was erected and Simpson's sketch identifies two steamships berthed there.

CLYDE NAVIGATION.

...CTION OF THE RIVER CLYDE SHEWING THE CREATEST DEP...

...THE YEARS 1758, 1824, 1839, 1853, 1861, AND 1871, RESPEC...

1871.

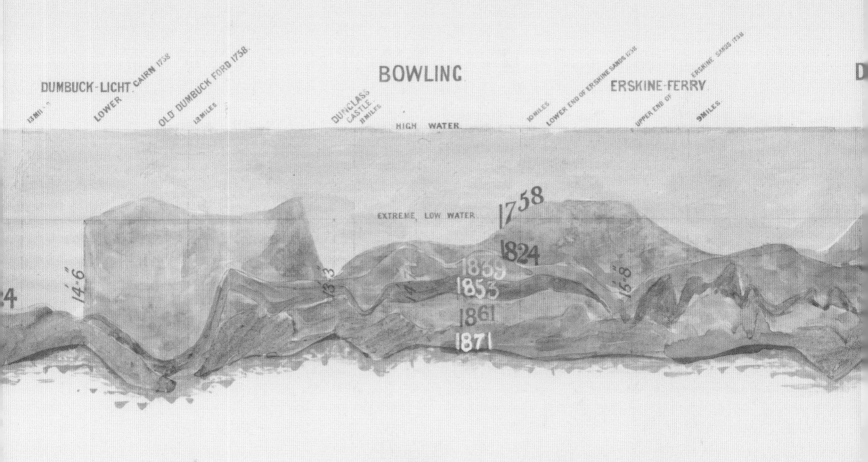

DUMBUCK-LICHT CAIRN 1758.

LOWER

OLD DUMBUCK FORD 1758.

13 MILES

BOWLING

DUNGLASS CASTLE
11 MILES

ERSKINE-FERRY

LOWER END OF ERSKINE SANDS 1758

ERSKINE SANDS 1758

UPPER END OF

9 MILES

D...

HIGH WATER.

EXTREME LOW WATER.

1758

1824

1839
1853
1861
1871

14·6

13·3

15·8

CHAPTER 20

The work of James Deas

While the names of Smeaton, Golborne, Watt, Rennie and Telford are rightly celebrated for their involvement with developing the Clyde, it could be argued that their efforts only paved the way for the major changes to the harbour facilities at Glasgow which turned the river into the industrial powerhouse it became in the second half of the nineteenth century. If the credit for such growth can be given to any one person, the man with the highest claim would be, arguably, James Deas (1827–99), who was appointed resident engineer to the Clyde Navigation Trust in 1869, following the early death of Andrew Duncan. Deas held the post until his own sudden death in 1899. Regrettably, his name does not appear in any of the great national biographies, but his 30 years of service to the Trust is a record of impressive achievement.

Born in Edinburgh, he trained in the offices of John Miller, the great engineer of the early Scottish railway network, before succeeding his father as chief engineer to the Edinburgh and Glasgow Railway Company. At the age of 42, he took up the Clyde Trust post and the scale of the operations carried out under his direction gives some idea of the energy in Glasgow at that period. Described as a man of vision and imagination,

with an outstanding capacity for work, this can be best exemplified by the growth of the harbour. When he was appointed, the quay length stretched for only a little over 3 miles and the water area amounted to 76 acres but, by the time of his death, the landing area had been extended to 18.5 miles and the dock space to over 200 acres.

Deas benefitted from the establishment of the Navigation Trust in 1858 as this enabled a more holistic approach to the considerations concerning the deepening of the channel. Despite the structural work to constrict the river's flow, it was the persistent dredging that ensured a sufficient depth of channel up to the city's quays. This fascinating and colourful profile of the various depths at six different dates identifies the level of the challenges faced in the various efforts to improve the navigation. What is most striking is the amount of shoaling that existed at extreme low water in 1758, particularly in the stretch between Dalmuir and Glasgow Bridge, and how much of that had been removed by 1824. The section also shows the deep channel immediately off Port Glasgow which seems to endorse the magistrates' wisdom in selecting it as the original site for a harbour. Steam-powered dredging and the use of hopper barges

Opposite and overleaf. James Deas, *Longitudinal section of the River Clyde showing the greatest depths of the channel in the years 1758, 1824, 1839, 1853, 1861 and 1871* (1871). Note the Elderslie Rock bar

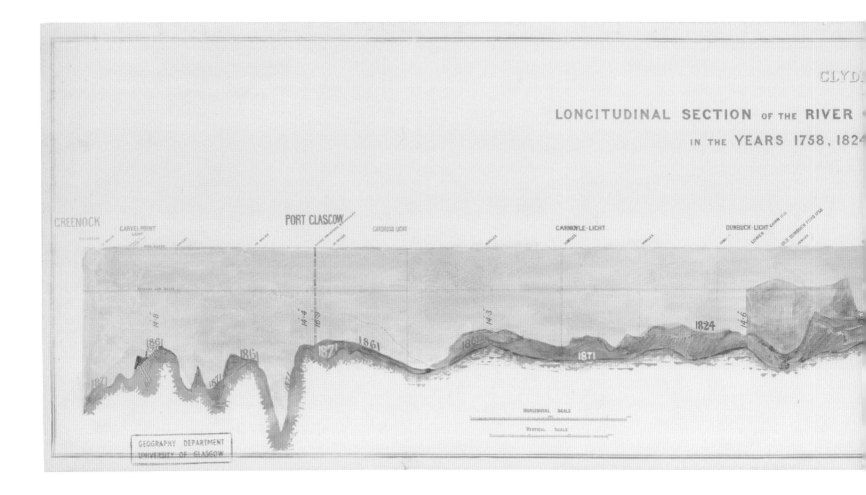

continued to be required to ensure a suitable depth of channel but, significantly, the profile identifies the Elderslie Rock as a major feature of the river bed. Deas is credited with the engineering project which eventually helped dispose of this natural obstacle – a hard whinstone intrusion extending across the Clyde and presenting a considerable hazard to shipping. This profile is dated 1871 and it would be another 15 years before the project was completed. To give some impression of the scale of this work, 76,000 pounds of explosives were used and 110,000 tons of rock removed to clear the channel.

Deas undoubtedly took pride in the achievements of the Trust and was a significant promoter of its success. His several papers on the Clyde and its improvements were frequently accompanied by detailed plans, including this sequence of profiles, dating from 1875, which depict the river from the confluence with the Kelvin to the Old Bridge, buildings along its banks and the harbour for three separate years. The 1800 image clearly emphasises the lack of any significant development of the riverbank but does indicate the weir built to protect the piers of the Jamaica Street Bridge, as well as the narrowness of the channel at the Broomielaw, the Springfield cotton mill and the fishing draught at the Govan ferry. Forty years later, there are marked changes to the whole shape of the Clyde as it flows through the city. By this date, Telford's proposals to create a

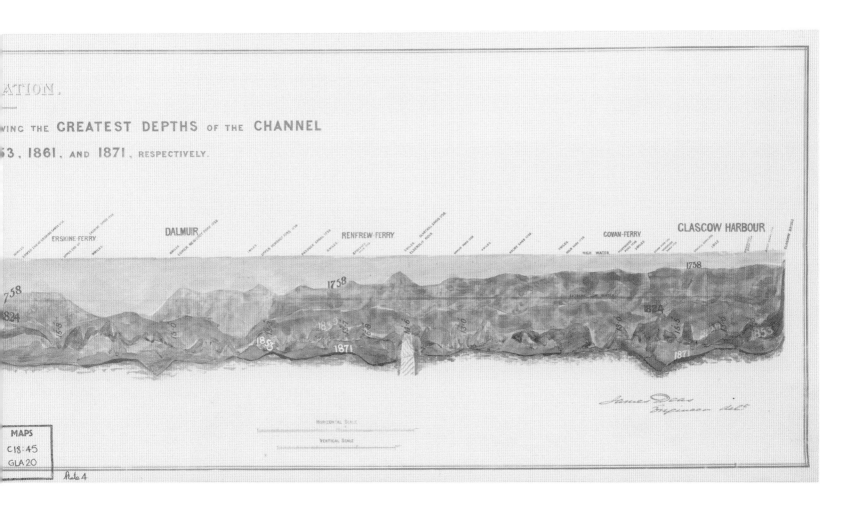

more uniform width can be seen where the banks have been considerably smoothed. John Barclay's slip-dock is identified on the north bank at Stobcross, in addition to the location of Robert Napier's Lancefield and Tod & McGregor's engine works. Immediately upriver is Steamboat Quay and, of course, this underlines a major reason for much of the alteration.

The third plan is dated 1875 and is unique in showing the vessels berthed in the harbour on one particular day, namely 10 May. The congestion caused by the lack of adequate docking facilities can be clearly seen by the number of ships lying abreast of each other at Glasgow Bridge. This situation had been well captured on Thomas Sulman's panoramic view of the city in 1864 where the crowded nature of the quays downstream of the Broomielaw is obvious. However, Deas also shows the Kingston Dock and the various wharves extending westward along both banks. These include Anderston, Springfield, Mavisbank and Plantation Quays. Stobcross Dock is marked as under construction and the several cranes indicated give an impression

Overleaf. James Deas, *Plans of the harbour at Glasgow* (1800, 1840 and 1875)

CLYD[

PLAN of th[

N

VILLAGE of MEICKLE GOVAN

RIVER KELVIN

GOVAN FERRY HOUSE

FERRY

FISHING DRAUGHT

SCALE of FEET

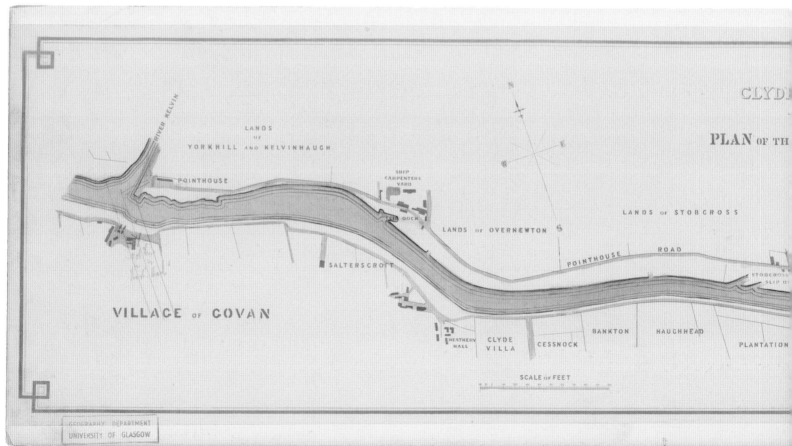

CLYD[

PLAN of th[

N

RIVER KELVIN

LANDS
OF
YORKHILL AND KELVINHAUGH

POINTHOUSE

SHIP
CARPENTERS
YARD

DOCK

LANDS of STOBCROSS

LANDS of OVERNEWTON

POINTHOUSE   ROAD

SALTERSCROFT

STOBCROSS
SLIP D[

VILLAGE of GOVAN

HEATHERY
HALL

CLYDE
VILLA

CESSNOCK

BANKTON

HAUGHHEAD

PLANTATION

SCALE of FEET

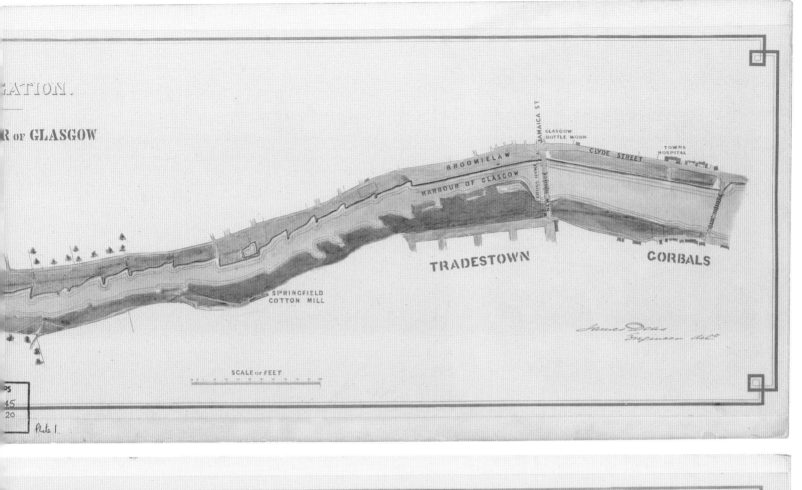

ATION.

R of GLASGOW

BROOMIELAW

HARBOUR OF GLASGOW

JAMAICA ST

GLASGOW BOTTLE WORK

CLYDE STREET

TOWNS HOSPITAL

TRADESTOWN

CORBALS

SPRINGFIELD COTTON MILL

SCALE of FEET

Plate 1.

45
20

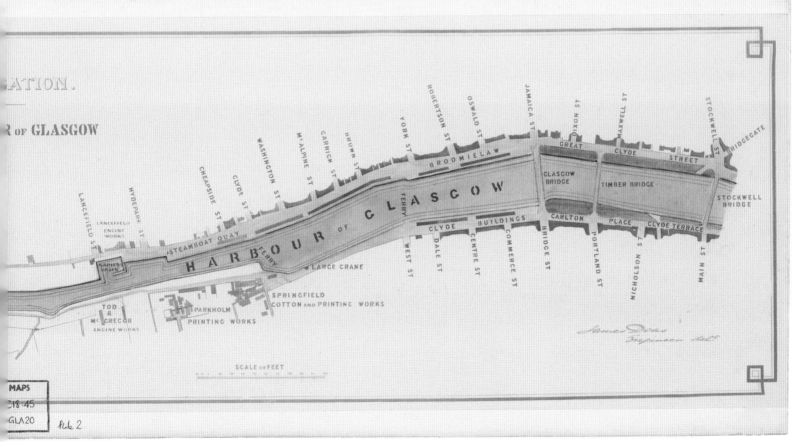

ATION.

R of GLASGOW

LANCEFIELD ST

LANCEFIELD ENGINE WORKS

HYDEPARK ST

CHEAPSIDE ST

CLYDE ST

WASHINGTON ST

McALPINE ST

CARRICK ST

BROWN ST

YORK ST

ROBERTSON ST

OSWALD ST

JAMAICA ST

DIXON ST

MAXWELL ST

STOCKWELL ST

BRIDGEGATE

GREAT

CLYDE

STREET

GLASGOW BRIDGE

TIMBER BRIDGE

STOCKWELL BRIDGE

BROOMIELAW

HARBOUR OF GLASGOW

FERRY

CLYDE BUILDINGS

CARLTON

PLACE

CLYDE TERRACE

STEAMBOAT QUAY

FERRY

LARGE CRANE

WEST ST

DALE ST

CENTRE ST

COMMERCE ST

BRIDGE ST

PORTLAND ST

NICHOLSON ST

MAIN ST

NAPIERS BASIN

TOD & McGREGOR ENGINE WORKS

PARKHOLM PRINTING WORKS

SPRINGFIELD COTTON and PRINTING WORKS

SCALE of FEET

MAPS

C18 45

GLA20

Plate 2

of the size of the operations underway. However, what is possibly more significant is the beginning of a demarcation in the location of industry along the river, with the shipbuilding yards now moving downstream to an area around the mouth of the Kelvin. There are few images of the Clyde which make such an immediate impression of change as these three plans.

During his period of office, the Queen's Dock was opened at Stobcross in 1877. At that time, it was stated to be the largest of its kind in the British Isles and consisted of two parallel basins. It was followed by the construction of two public graving docks. However, his greatest achievement is regarded as the building of the Prince's Dock on the south bank, completed in 1897. In both docks he devised a successful system of hollow concrete cylinders as foundations for the quay walls. In addition to overseeing the establishment of passenger wharves at Govan and a cattle depot at Shieldhall, he was also largely responsible for developing the Clutha ferry service. In an amazingly confident but turgid address to the Glasgow meeting of the Institution of Naval Architects in 1882, he praised the city as the chief seaport of the west of Scotland (although, in truth, it faced little competition), rising from a second-rate inland provincial town to the 'Second City of the Empire'. This dramatic change over less than a century he asserted was based on the local epigram that 'Glasgow made the Clyde, and the Clyde has made Glasgow'.

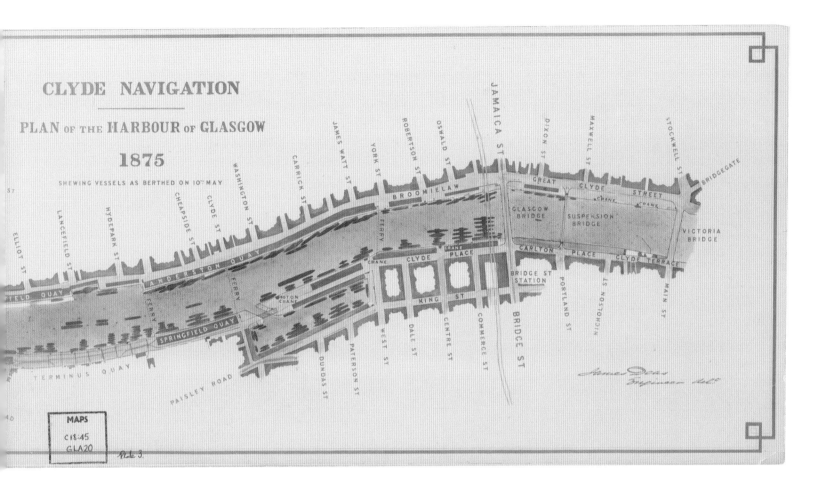

This *New Map of the River and Firth of Clyde* was produced in 1899 by the Newcastle firm of printers and publishers, Andrew Reid and Co. but is based on work by Deas and, given its date, it stands as an appropriate epitaph to him. Apart from the details of the shoals and banks, it also indicates the main channel, buoys, lights and beacons on the upper river, in addition to the Lang Dyke and various ferries. The limit of the Navigation Trust's jurisdiction is defined but this does not result in any diminution of the impressive record of industries, shipyards and other works identified on either bank. Individual firm names are recorded in an accompanying index to the map and this underlines the variety of businesses having a close connection

with the river. As the map depicts the river downstream from Carmyle to Gourock, it covers the very heart of Clydeside. Although there is less information on the individual berths in the various docks than appears on the plan that Deas himself produced in the same year, it is the detail of riverside firms which is striking. Over 30 separate shipbuilders and yards are named. Additionally, the information on the many other ancillary trades, such as rope works, sailmakers, boilermakers, timber ponds and other engineering services brings home the sheer scale of enterprise on the Clyde at the turn of the century. Nor is this an image frozen in time, for three proposed docks are shown downriver from Whiteinch, again reflecting the gradual

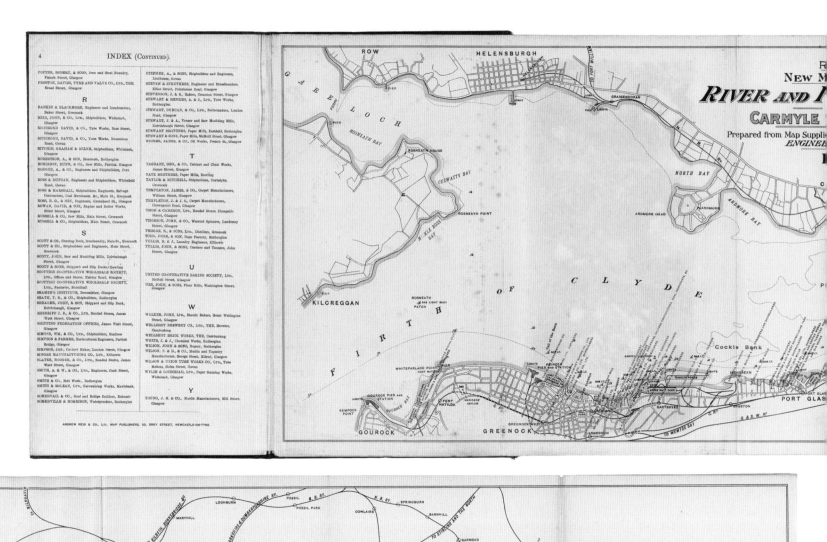

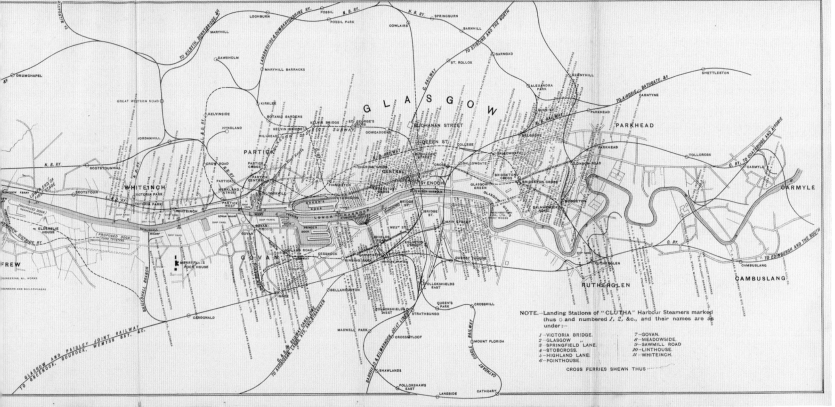

NOTE.—Landing Stations of "CLUTHA" Harbour Steamers marked thus ○ and numbered 1, 2, &c., and their names are as under:—

1—VICTORIA BRIDGE.
2—GLASGOW "
3—SPRINGFIELD LANE.
4—STOBCROSS.
5—HIGHLAND LANE.
6—POINTHOUSE.
7—GOVAN.
8—MEADOWSIDE.
9—SAWMILL ROAD.
10—LINTHOUSE.
11—WHITEINCH.

CROSS FERRIES SHEWN THUS

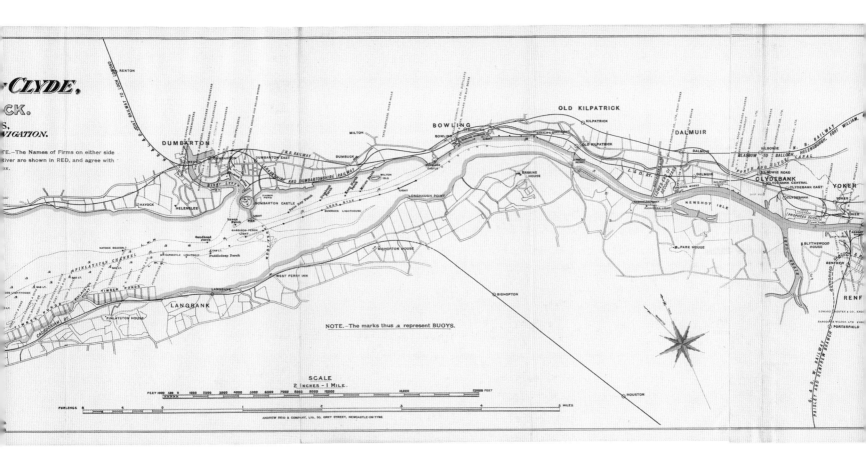

movement downriver of several of the major yards to Mead-owside, Scotstoun and Clydebank as the extensions to the harbour quays absorbed land. Railway links are marked and one interesting feature is the identification of both the landing stations of the Clutha river ferries and the newly opened Subway system. Such changes in the city's transport network, particularly the advent of the electric tram system, would soon put many of the ferry services out of business.

Since the time of Deas, the Clyde at Glasgow has undergone considerable and quite rapid change. The Queen's Dock has been infilled and is now the site of the Scottish Exhibition and Conference Centre, while the eastern half of the Prince's Dock became the site for the 1988 Garden Festival. Part of the Festival site was subsequently redeveloped for the Glasgow Science Centre and as Pacific Quay, now a media centre occupied by the radio station Capital Scotland and the headquarters of both BBC Scotland and Scottish Television. It remains to be seen what will happen to the three graving docks lying immediately downriver from these significant additions to the riverside scene.

Opposite. Andrew Reid, *Reid's new map of the river and Firth of Clyde* (1899)
(based on the work of James Deas) showing extract of the accompanying index

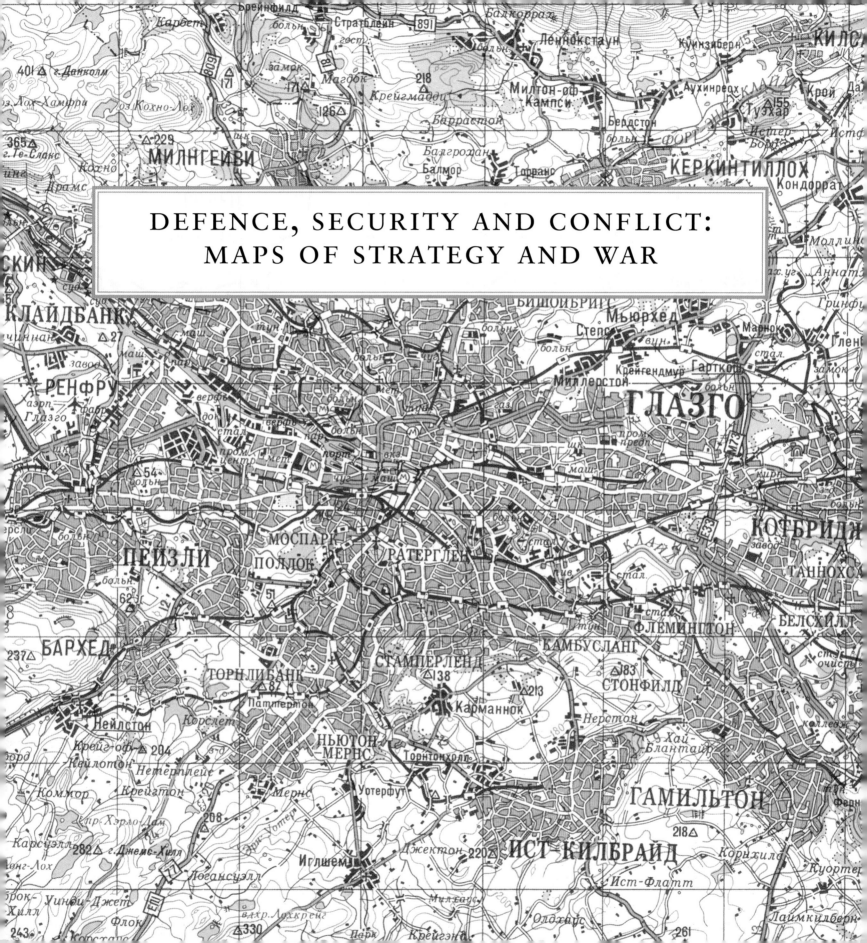

DEFENCE, SECURITY AND CONFLICT: MAPS OF STRATEGY AND WAR

Prospectus Arcis Regiæ BRITANNODUNENSIS *ab Occidente.* *Their Maties Castle of* DUMBRITTON *from the West*

4

CHAPTER 21

John Slezer's depictions of Dumbarton Castle in the 1690s

Sitting on a volcanic plug of basalt rock, Dumbarton Castle has a longer recorded history as a stronghold than any other place in Scotland. Of all the many fortified sites that have been built beside or near the Clyde, it is possibly the most strategically important – a fact recognised by its being the seat of the kingdom of Strathclyde from at least the fifth century. It commands not only the entrance to the River Leven and, hence, access to Loch Lomond and the Southern Highlands but is also situated at the point where the channel of the River Clyde really begins to narrow. The first mention of a fortress located here in the medieval period is in the charter of King Alexander II (1198–1249) founding a burgh at his new castle of Dumbarton in July 1222. During the Middle Ages, it was an important royal stronghold and was used as both a prison and base for the Scottish navy.

In March 1639, it was seized by forces loyal to the Covenant and a sketch map of the Clyde coast, showing the castle and the entry to the Clyde, within the papers of James Butler, first Duke of Ormond (1610–88) and now held in the University of Oxford, was prepared as part of the planning of a relief expedition which never set out, largely as the castle was restored to the monarch under the terms of the Treaty of Berwick later that year. Records show that little was spent on improving the defences until the later 1680s when the likelihood of conflict

between the recently established Protestant monarchy of William and Mary and the supporters of the Stuarts was realised at the battle of Killiecrankie. Although Dumbarton was never to be affected directly by the campaigns of the various Jacobite uprisings in the first half of the eighteenth century, the confidence of the governments of both Queen Anne and the early Hanoverian kings was sufficiently shaken that a renewed building programme was inaugurated at many of the royal castles in Scotland. Like other similar fortresses, Dumbarton was to be used as a place of detention for captured Jacobite prisoners.

This prospect of the castle taken from the west is one of three depictions included in John Slezer's *Theatrum Scotiae*, published in 1693 at the time when improvements were being carried out. Through the influence of certain leading Scottish noblemen and his own abilities as a skilled draftsman, Slezer had been appointed chief engineer in Scotland in 1671. As part of his duties, he was instructed to carry out a survey of the nation's defences and, about the year 1678, he formulated a plan to produce a work to illustrate many of the significant towns and buildings throughout Scotland. This was to be the first pictorial survey to cover the whole of the country and was accompanied by descriptive texts prepared by Sir Robert Sibbald, Geographer Royal for Scotland.

The relationship between Slezer's duties and this end product

Opposite. John Slezer, Dumbarton Castle: the prospect of ye castle of Dumbritton from ye West in Theatrum Scotiae (1693)

Detail of poor sketching of building at summit of hill and the figures below from Slezer's Dumbarton Castle from the east

Major George Grant, in 1677–79. Slezer's plan may well be related to a detailed description of the castle made in April 1696 by Major Francis Montgomerie, subsequently officer in command of the fortress.

Within the structure of Slezer's book, the plates that depict Dumbarton Castle follow immediately after the opening two views of Edinburgh but before his illustrations of Stirling and its castle and those of Glasgow. It is doubtful if this is an indication of the castle's perceived importance as its situation, and limited space were to restrict its value as an important military base. While Slezer's use of a camera obscura in the production process has been discussed elsewhere, the three images of Dumbarton do not seem to correspond easily with each other, particularly in the representation of the rock itself. They do, however, show the site's excellent natural defences. What the second image of the castle viewed from the east also displays is the rather crude fashion in which some of the building detail has been engraved, as can be seen in the linework on the summit of the right-hand mound and the almost incomplete depiction of figures at the foot of this rock.

Although Slezer had obtained financial support and the grant of a royal licence for this work, the first of a projected series of volumes of views, he was to be dogged by the same lack of publishing success as his contemporary, the cartographer John Adair, with whom he competed for sufficient funding from the Scottish Parliament. His business relationship with Sibbald was seriously damaged when he had Sibbald's Latin descriptions translated into English without acknowledging him in the text. He died in 1717, leaving debts which were not settled until six years later. On the other hand, the *Theatrum Scotiae* was to reappear in at least another five 'editions' up to 1814, and Slezer's initial foundation of topographical drawings of significant country houses was to be carried on later in the century by such figures as the surveyor John Elphinstone and the artist Paul Sandby.

is clearly seen in his work at Dumbarton for a surviving plan of the castle, drawn by him in 1696 and held in the Board of Ordnance papers at the National Archives, which is surmounted by a prospect of the castle as seen from the side of the town. Apart from certain minor changes of detail in the foreground, this is the same image as appears in the published *Theatrum* as this view from the west. Slezer's description is a little confusing since the town lies to the north of the castle. The plan itself indicates the new entry and the reconstructed southern defences, which had been carried out under the garrison commander,

Opposite. John Slezer, *Dumbarton Castle: the prospect of ye castle of Dumbritton from ye East* in *Theatrum Scotiae* (1693)

Facies Arcis BRITANNODUNENSIS *ab Oriente.* *The Prospect of y͏ͤ Castle of* DUMBRITTON *from y͏ͤ East.*

5.

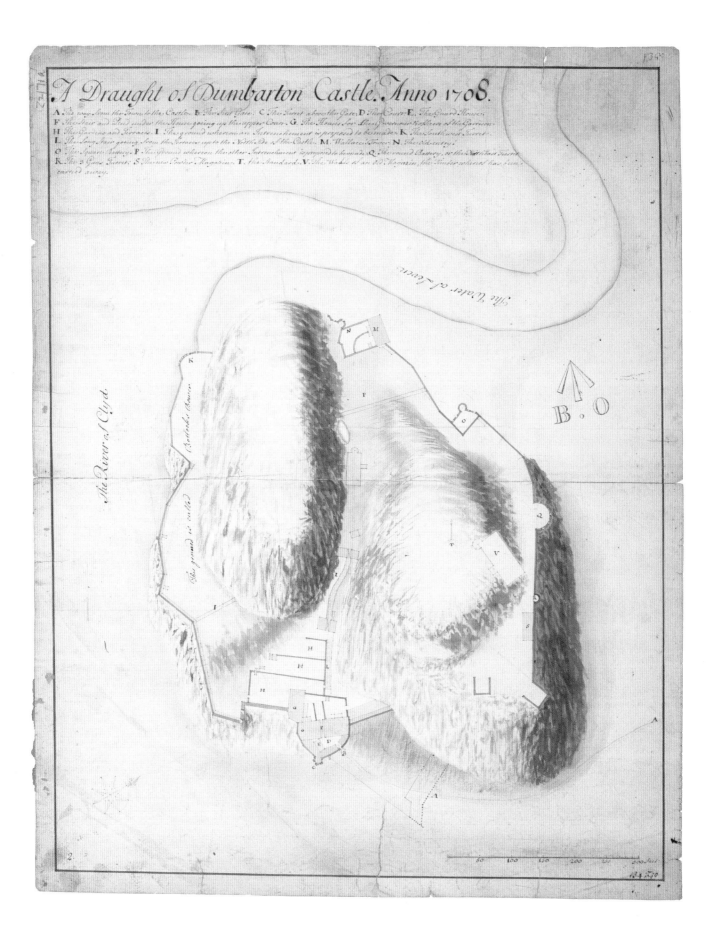

A Draught of Dumbarton Castle. Anno 1708.

A. The way from the Town to the Castle. B. The first Gate. C. The Turret above the Gate. D. The Court. E. The Guard House.
F. The Stair and Shed under the House going up the upper Court. G. The House for Stores, Armour &c kitchen of the Garison.
H. The Barracs and Terrace. I. The ground whereon an Intrenchment is proposed to be made. K. The South and Turret.
L. The Long Stair going from the Terrace up to the North Side of the Castle. M. Wallace's Tower. N. The Sentry.
O. The Square Battery. P. The Ground whereon the other Intrenchment is proposed to be made. Q. The round Battery, or the White's Turret.
R. The 2 Gune Turret. S. The new Powder Magazine. T. The Standard. V. The Works of an old Magazin, the Timber whereof has been carried away.

The Water of Leven

The River of Clyd.

B. O

CHAPTER 22

The Board of Ordnance
returns to Dumbarton

Despite the interest paid to Dumbarton Castle by John Slezer and Major Montgomerie's description, the military authorities appear to have been more concerned in dealing with any threat of trouble in the Highlands nearer its source. In many ways, Dumbarton was a little too distant from those areas occupied by the clans who might support any Stuart claimant to the throne. Although improvements were made, the castle was of far less importance in the scheme of national defence, particularly at a time when the British army was more heavily involved in the theatres of war in Europe. By the year 1704, the garrison was listed as only 40 men, but an unsuccessful French invasion attempt in support of a Jacobite rising in 1708 highlighted a need for better preparations. Significantly, a report submitted to the Board of Ordnance in February 1710 questioned the value of investing any large sums of money on Dumbarton's defences, and it is worthwhile noting that, although troops were housed in a block referred to as the French Prison, none of the surviving plans show any suggestion of a barracks building to house a large number of soldiers.

These two manuscript plans, drawn by Theodore Dury and John O'Brien in 1708–09, come from a collection of military cartography held in the National Library and may relate to this investigation of Dumbarton's condition as a stronghold. They are part of a programme to improve the army's overall knowl-edge of Scotland which was to result in the active involvement of a considerable number of military engineers in mapping the country's roads, forts and general topography. This was directed under the authority of the Board of Ordnance, a department of state and forerunner of the Ordnance Survey which, by the early 1680s, had responsibility not only for the construction of fortifications and barracks but also for the production of maps and plans. Several foreign engineers played a significant role in the early stages of the development of British military cartography, reflecting the technical advances in Europe under the influence of such figures as Sébastien Le Prestre, Marquis de Vauban. It is believed that Slezer may have come from the upper Rhineland and Dury was French, while another French-man, the Huguenot Lewis Petit, was to be appointed chief engi-neer in Scotland in 1715.

These plans reflect the standard practice of the day in their design and it is possibly an indication of the relative lack of attention paid to the castle that, whereas the number of surviving plans for Edinburgh Castle, Fort William and Fort Augustus total 46, 31 and 47 respectively, only 8 cover Dumbarton. Being produced for the army, none of the plans give any detail of either the shoals or channels of the Leven or the Clyde. Dury had been appointed chief engineer in Scotland in about 1690, joining Slezer in that office, and was to be posted subsequently

Opposite. Theodore Dury, *A draught of Dumbarton castle* (1708)

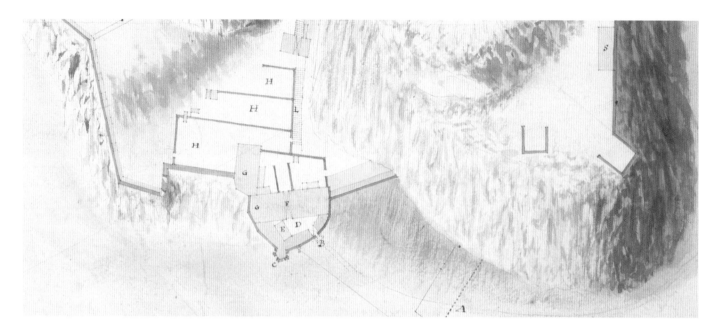

to Stirling Castle as engineer in 1707. Captain O'Brien was later involved in a survey of harbours along both sides of the Firth of Forth in 1714, working in association with John Adair.

There are subtle differences both between these two plans and from Slezer's draft of more than a decade earlier. Dury shows a new square battery and two suggested entrenchments within the perimeter of the outer wall which are not shown on O'Brien's design. O'Brien's suggestions, drawn with a different orientation, include a new governor's house and passage cut through the rock, as well as a new wall to enclose a parade ground considered 'mightily wanting in the Castle'. O'Brien had objected to Dury's design for Edinburgh and it may be that Dumbarton was another case where differing opinions produced different designs. It was generally considered that Dury's proposals for improved defences at Edinburgh and Stirling were too ambitious. This was particularly the case as the army's policy moved towards having a greater military presence in the Highlands, combined with the growing acceptance that such inherited medieval structures as Dumbarton had ceased to be defensively effective.

Possibly, the castle's most significant role at this time was during the Malt Tax riots in Glasgow during the summer of 1725 when two infantry companies retreated from an angry mob of protesting citizens behind its walls until the agitation was suppressed by a more sizeable force under the direct command of Lieutenant General George Wade, Commander-in-Chief of the army in Scotland. On visiting the castle later that year, he was to see for himself the weakness of the garrison and only two years after this he ordered a large-scale reconstruction of the defences. This refortification can be seen in King George's Battery and the Governor's House, built in the 1730s to designs by Captain John Romer, one of the Board of Ordnance's finest engineers. He was to work closely with Wade in the creation of barracks, bridges and roads to assist in controlling Scotland. While there are several surviving military plans by Romer dating from between 1719 and 1732 and depicting Inverness, Fort William and Fort Augustus, there is nothing in his hand covering Dumbarton.

Opposite. John O'Brien, *A plan of the castle of Dumbarton and the repairs ...* (1709)

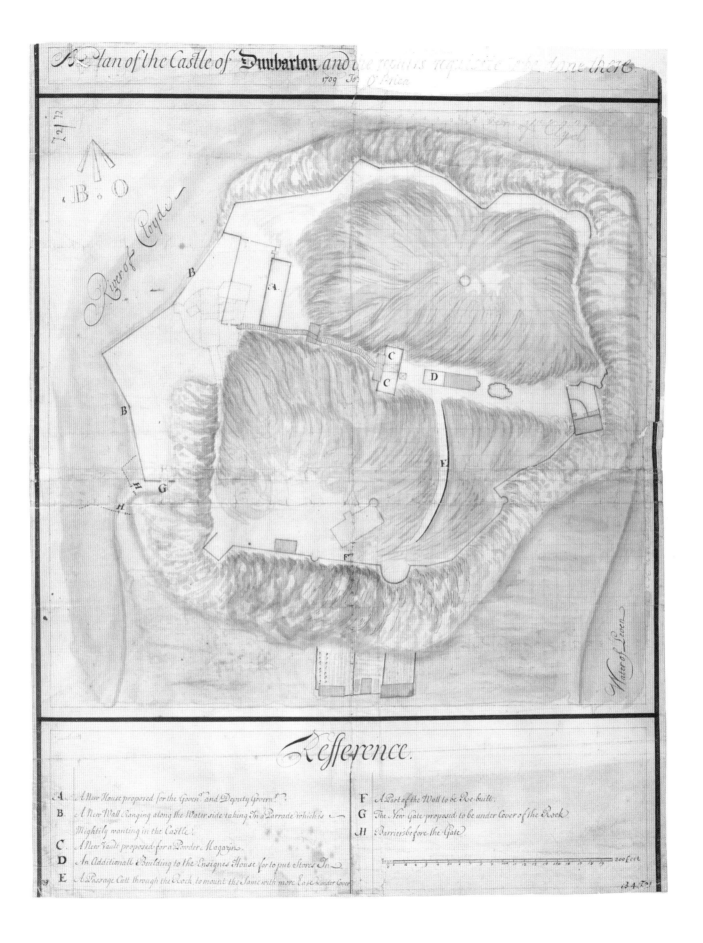

A Plan of the Castle of Dunbarton and the repairs requisite to be done there.
1709 Jo. O'Brien

River of Clyde

Water of Leven

Refference.

A   A New House proposed for the Govern'. and Deputy Govern'.
B   A New Wall Ranging along the Water side taking In a Parrade which is Mightily wanting in the Castle.
C   A New Vault proposed for a Powder Magazin.
D   An Additionall Building to the Ensignes House for to put Stores In.
E   A Passage Cutt through the Rock to mount the same with more Ease & under Cover

F   A Part of the Wall to be Re-built.
G   The New Gate proposed to be under Cover of the Rock
H   Barriers before the Gate

200 feet

CHAPTER 23

William Roy on home ground:
Clydesdale on the Military Survey, 1753–54

In spite of the efforts of the military establishment to secure a degree of peace in Scotland, Hanoverian troops stationed in the Highlands found themselves greatly hampered by the marked lack of detailed topographical knowledge of the country during the Jacobite Rising of 1745–46. Following the battle of Culloden, Lieutenant Colonel David Watson, then Deputy Quartermaster General in north Britain, convinced the Duke of Cumberland of the need for a proper map to ensure the pacification of the 'disaffected' areas and, as a result, it was resolved to make 'a compleat and accurate Survey of Scotland, and of the Coasts, Creeks, Rivers, Islands, &c, thereof'. The resulting Military Survey of Scotland, which was carried out between 1747 and 1755, is a uniquely impressive picture of the whole of the mainland at a time before many rural areas were radically altered through the process of agricultural improvement.

At one time, the Great Map, as it was then called, was also referred to as the 'Roy Map', reflecting the key role that William Roy had in its production. Roy was born in 1726 at Miltonhead, near Carluke, the son of the estate factor to the local laird, Sir William Gordon, at Hallcraig. Through the close social and family networks of the period, he came to the attention of Watson who appointed him, at the age of 21, as civilian director of the entire operation, possibly influenced by the innate talent

Roy had shown in some early sketch maps of Culloden. Certainly, Watson must have been impressed, for he paid Roy's salary out of his own pocket throughout the Survey and, for the first three years, Roy was its sole surveyor.

Given the scope of the whole undertaking and its limited equipment, it is not surprising that the work was based on a series of chain traverses taken along the courses of the major rivers and their tributaries, lochs and the principal roads. Intervening detail was sketched in from individual survey stations. As Roy himself was later to write, the map 'is rather to be considered as a magnificent military sketch than a very accurate map of a country'. However, this comment continues to be taken at face value and overlooks the key fact that the Survey actually consists of two parts. The mapping of the Lowlands was undertaken as a second phase from 1752 onwards. More importantly, it benefitted from an increased staff and much healthier funding, largely through the intervention of the Dundas family of Arniston, whose members were influential advisers to the government and significant patrons of the Survey itself.

The motivation for such an extension to cover the rest of the country beyond the Highlands is less apparent, particularly given the availability of contemporary mapping of the Lothians (based on the surveys of John Adair) by fellow engineer, John

Opposite. Military Survey of Scotland, extract
showing the area around Hallcraig and Milton

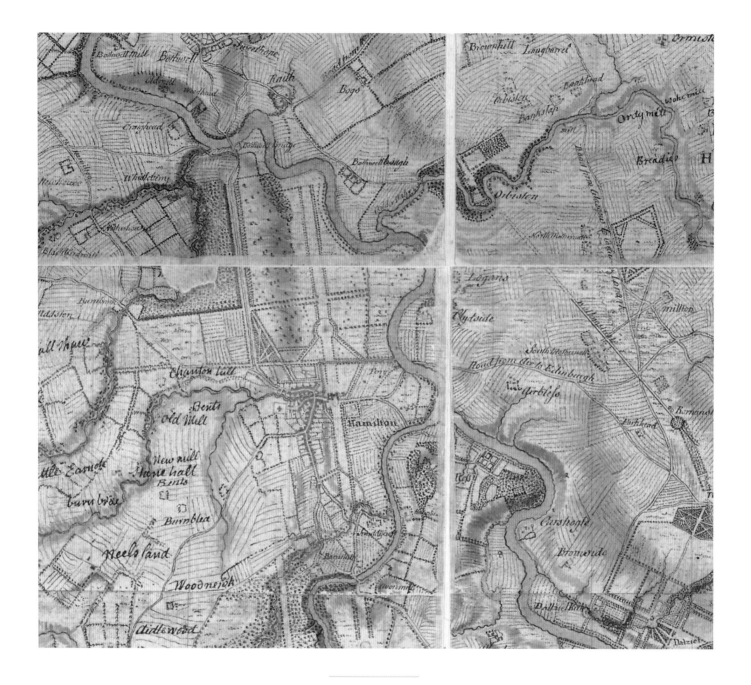

Above. Extract of Military Survey showing the layout of the policies at Hamilton Palace

Opposite. Comparative images of the Fair Copy of the Highlands and the
Lowlands map of the Clyde showing the river between Old Kilpatrick and Greenock

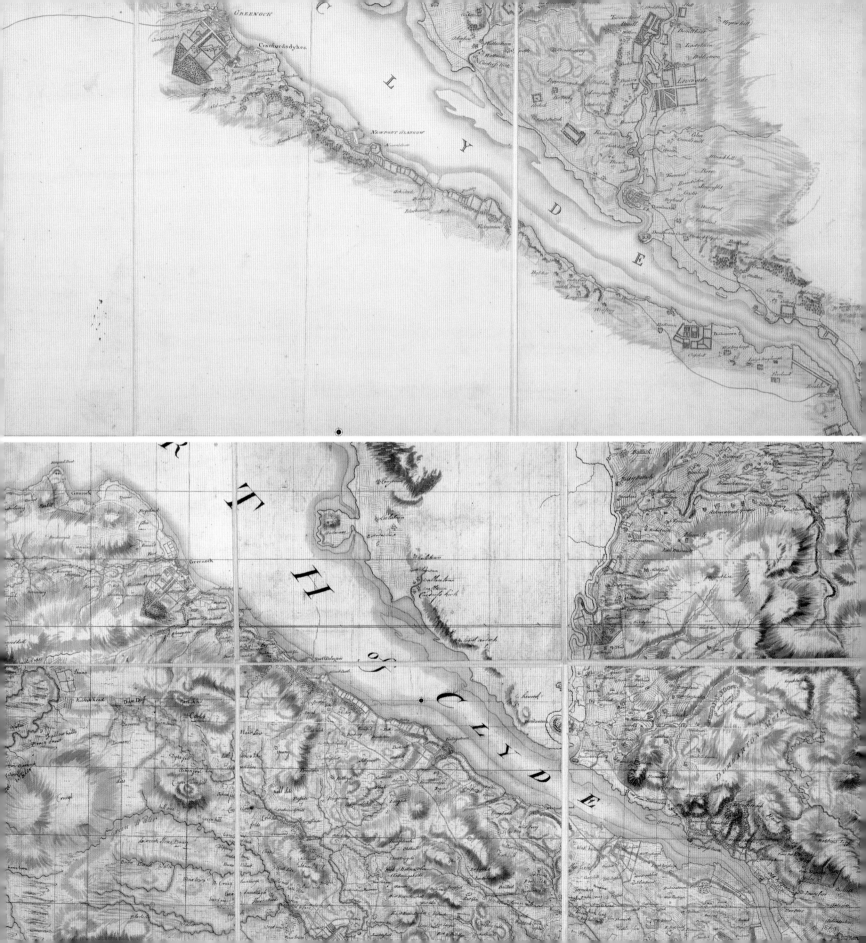

Elphinstone published in 1744 and Tweeddale by William Edgar in 1741, but may have had much to do with the symbolic representation of Scotland being brought together as one united whole. Given the relatively better road system, the greater density of settlements and the number of improved estates south of the Midland Valley, combined with the interests of many more landowners loyal to the Hanoverian monarchy, it is tempting to assume a greater accuracy for this phase of the Survey. Certainly, Roy was very familiar with this area and, by this date, the men under his direction would be well practised in their procedures.

Southern Scotland was mapped by two teams working north from the border and, given that Roy was responsible for surveying the western section, we can see his own elegant hand in the mapping of Clydesdale and of his birthplace. Attention to local detail is impressive. The area around Hallcraig carries as many place names as the depiction of the lands immediately surrounding Glasgow, while several local estate policies are indicated (e.g. Milton itself, Bonnington, Carmichael and Lockharthill). A careful study of the detail of the river emphasises how significant a barrier it was to local transport communications at that time. From Crawford to Glasgow, there are only three bridges marked crossing the Clyde – one just west of Wandel, with others at Bothwell and Lanark. In addition, the surveyors have provided a very careful representation of the bends and meanders of the Clyde and its tributaries (e.g. the two Calder Waters and Medwin Water).

Possibly of greater significance to anyone using the Survey as a historical record is the fact that a fair copy of the Lowland section of the map was never made and the coverage here consists of the original survey drawings. There are a few sheets in the Central Belt where the mapping of the Highlands meets that of the southern survey. These provide a valuable opportunity to compare the differences in depiction between what is described as the Fair Copy of the 'Original Protraction' and the rougher-looking but less edited version of the map of the Lowlands. Much of the preparation of the Fair Copy was in the hands of Paul Sandby, acknowledged as the leading English watercolour artist of the period. He introduced a wider range of colour but also a rather stylised representation of arable fields based on the contemporary standard military practice. Although the Fair Copy coverage of the Clyde focuses very much on the river itself, with little of the hinterland shown, comparison of the two depictions between Stobcross and Greenock gives an indication of some of the variation, as shown in the layout of Scotstoun.

One final point of interest in the mapping of the Clyde area is that the islands of Bute and Great Cumbrae provide the exception to a much-repeated comment of the map's focus on the mainland alone. Such coverage is the only example in accord with the original resolution to map the islands but it provides a fascinating insight not only into settlement on these islands themselves but also of the influence of another Stuart, the third Earl of Bute.

Opposite. Detail of the Isle of Bute

PLAN of the ROMAN STATION called CASTLE DYKES, near CARSTAIRS,———1753.

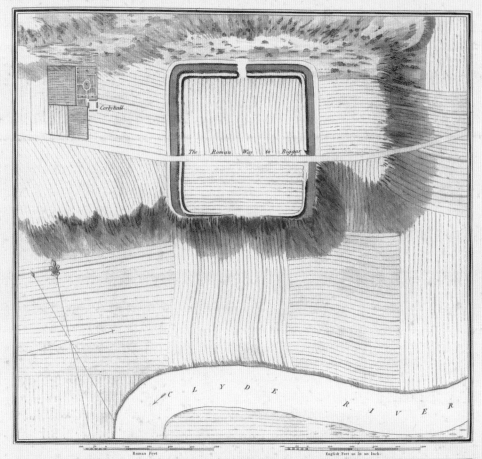

Roman Feet

English Feet 60 in 80 an Inch:

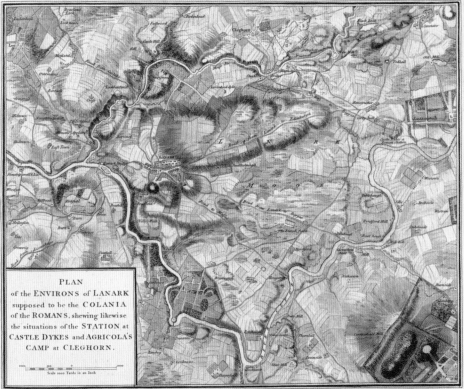

PLAN
of the ENVIRONS of LANARK
supposed to be the COLANIA
of the ROMANS, shewing likewise
the situations of the STATION at
CASTLE DYKES and AGRICOLA'S
CAMP at CLEGHORN.

Scale 1000 Yards in an Inch

CHAPTER 24

The Military Survey in print:
Roy's *Military Antiquities of the Romans in Britain*

The impending outbreak of what became the Seven Years War terminated work on the Military Survey and clearly had an impact on the quality of its final stages. David Watson retained the map sheets until his death in 1761 and these eventually passed into the Royal Library before being transferred to the British Museum. In consequence, the Survey itself appears to have had little influence on either the subsequent cartography of Scotland or on military strategy north of the border. In 1805, the London cartographer, Aaron Arrowsmith was to consult it when preparing his map of Scotland for the Commissioners for Making Roads and Building Bridges in the Highlands, finding its detail and accuracy superior to the existing road surveys. Otherwise, it would seem that only Roy himself was to make use of the Survey maps.

However, of far greater impact to subsequent mapping was the experience that the Survey gave to both Watson and Roy. In 1755, Watson was appointed a Commissioner for the Forfeited Estates, part of the government scheme to remove the causes of dissent in the Highlands and, at the first meeting of the Board that June, he tabled a paper entitled 'Instructions to the surveyors to be employed in surveying . . .' based on what had been learnt on the Great Map. This was to influence land surveying throughout Scotland for much of the rest of the century. That same year,

Roy, still a civilian, along with his army colleagues, was ordered south to survey areas that might be under threat of invasion. It was only at that time that he was appointed a practitioner engineer and, very soon after, received a commission as a lieutenant in the 51st Regiment of Foot.

His ability and experience as a military cartographer had been recognised by now and he was promoted steadily until he reached the rank of major general in 1781. Twenty years earlier, he had been appointed Deputy Quartermaster General and during the 1760s he became a strong advocate of the value of a national survey for the whole of Great Britain, based on his experiences both at home and on the continent. Although he did not live to see it, the year following his death saw the founding of what was to become the Ordnance Survey and he is rightly credited as its 'father'.

While surveying southern Scotland, Roy developed a strong interest in Roman antiquities. A letter of his addressed to Watson in September 1752 contains several references to military matters of an earlier period, particularly relating to the Roman occupation of the area. His subsequent military career kept him from home until 1764 when, on a visit to his mother in Lanark, he was able to further his researches and augment his sketch plans of Roman sites. Finding himself with a degree of relative leisure, he began

Opposite. William Roy, Plan of the Environs of Lanark from *The Military Antiquities of the Romans in Britain* (1793)

Ordnance Survey triangulation station on the site of William Roy's birthplace at Miltonhead near Carluke

Although the bulk of Roy's archaeological sketches are of other parts of the Lowlands, at least one site, the Roman camp west of Lockharthill, is clearly indicated on the Military Survey covering Clydesdale and it reappears in the *Military Antiquities* as a published plate (plate 27), described as a 'Plan of the Roman Station called Castle Dykes, near Carstairs'. There are certain differences between the manuscript and the printed versions. On the Military Survey, the camp is shown lying between Ravenstruther and Lockharthill whereas the printed copy indicates the camp lying east of Corbyhall and having a Roman road running through its centre. Regardless of the variance, Roy's work shows an extensive enclosure bounded by an escarpment overlooking the flood plain of the Clyde, emphasising the site's strategic importance. Although published in 1793, the plan is clearly dated 1753 and confirms Roy's presence in the area that year.

Of possibly greater value is the detailed 'Plan of the Environs of Lanark' lying in the lower half of the same plate. This is an almost exact replication of the detail appearing on the original Survey sheets and, unlike them, benefits from not being dissected. As such, it provides an extremely rare, if uncoloured, example of the Survey in print. The title notes that this is the supposed site of the Roman settlement Colania and that the plan indicates both the station at Castle Dykes and the camp at Cleghorn. In the prefatory introduction to the book, Roy rather coyly mentions that in the autumn of 1764 an Agricolan marching camp was 'very accidentally found at Cleghorn', thus reigniting his interest. Although there is no indication of the discoverer, there can be little doubt that it was Roy himself, particularly as a second illustration (plate 9) detailing the camp's layout commanding an adjacent river crossing is dated September 7th 1764. Surprisingly, although the ramparts are suggested, Cleghorn is not named on either the Lanark environs plan or the Military Survey itself, suggesting that Roy's updating of information on the Survey sheets was selective.

to compile what was to become his magnum opus, *The Military Antiquities of the Romans in Britain*. Sadly, Roy died before seeing the work in print but he did bequeath a manuscript copy to the Society of Antiquaries of London, which had elected him a Fellow in 1776, and they published the work in 1793. In a time when antiquarianism was flourishing, Roy was strongly influenced by the work of contemporary writers, including the notorious *De Situ Britanniae*, the literary forgery which appeared in 1757. Nonetheless, his carefully drawn plans are a reliable record of the layout of many important sites, several surveyed for the first time and, like the Military Survey itself, they have an important historical significance in detailing locations subsequently destroyed by later development.

Opposite. William Roy, detail of the
environs of Lanark from the Military Survey

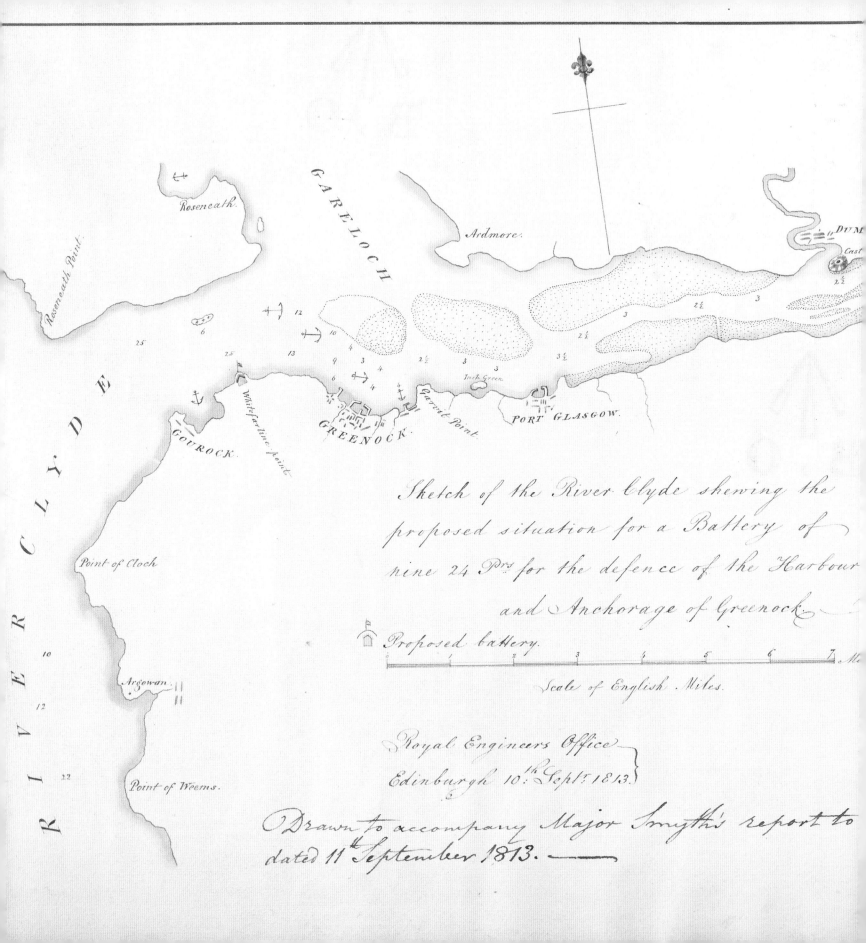

GARELOCH

Roseneath.

Roseneath Point.

Ardmore.

DUM

Cast

2½

25

25

12

6

25

10

13

9

4

4

3

6

4

4

4

Inch Green.

2½

3

3

2½

3½

2½

3

3

GOUROCK.

Whitefarline point.

GREENOCK.

Garvil Point.

PORT GLASGOW.

Point of Cloch

R I V E R   C L Y D E

10

12

12

Argowan.

Point of Weems.

Sketch of the River Clyde shewing the
proposed situation for a Battery of
nine 24 Pr.s for the defence of the Harbour
and Anchorage of Greenock.

Proposed battery.

0   1   2   3   4   5   6   7   Mi

Scale of English Miles.

Royal Engineers Office
Edinburgh 10.th Sept.r 1813.

Drawn to accompany Major Smyth's report to
dated 11th September 1813.

CHAPTER 25

Later defence preparations for the Clyde

While the field of Culloden saw the last major battle fought on British soil, the threat to the defence of the country through invasion or bombardment did not go away, particularly during the Napoleonic Wars at the end of the eighteenth century. Although the large collection of Board of Ordnance plans held at the National Library date mainly from the period prior to 1760, it also contains a small number of works prepared to safeguard against the possibility of French or American attack. Government officials saw the Firth of Clyde as one area in need of protection, particularly following the failed invasion of French troops at Fishguard in early 1797. While policy was strongly influenced by confidence in the vigilance of the Royal Navy, this was strengthened by the location of fortifications and gun batteries at strategic points along the coast.

This composite document, drawn in September 1813, consists of a map of the Clyde covering the Tail of the Bank and a detailed plan of the location of a battery, both surmounted by plans and sections of the separate buildings of its stores, guardhouse and magazine. It reflects a concern for the unprotected state of an estuary of particular importance to Britain's international commerce. The Clyde map specifically identifies the proposed position of a battery of nine 24-pounder guns to defend the harbour at Greenock but also marks soundings, sandbanks and shoals between Gourock and Dumbarton, as well as selected anchorages, particularly off Greenock. The heavy calibre 24-pounder long gun was a favoured weapon of the Royal Navy and the location sited at Whiteforeland Point would develop into Fort Matilda between 1814 and 1819, subsequently becoming a coastal battery during the Great War.

While the map is very much a locational sketch, the large-scale plan of the battery bears all the appearance of the contemporary military style of mapping in its choice of colouring and the combination of building cross sections with a detailed layout. The plan itself was prepared in the Royal Engineers Office in Edinburgh and is not dissimilar from the style of the later Ordnance Survey large-scale surveys. It was prepared for Lieutenant General Gother Mann, colonel commandant of the Corps of Royal Engineers by the engineer officer, Major James Carmichael-Smyth, who had served in Spain under Sir John Moore and would command the Corps of Engineers and Sappers at the battle of Waterloo. At the time this document was drawn, Mann was Inspector-General of Fortifications but he had previously served under Hugh Debbeig, one of the officers who had been employed on the Military Survey of Scotland, and had submitted a report on the state of defences along the east coast. In other words, these men knew what they were about and work by Smyth elsewhere shows his attention to vertical measurements and the need to protect any battery from gunfire

Opposite and overleaf. Sketch of the river Clyde (1813)

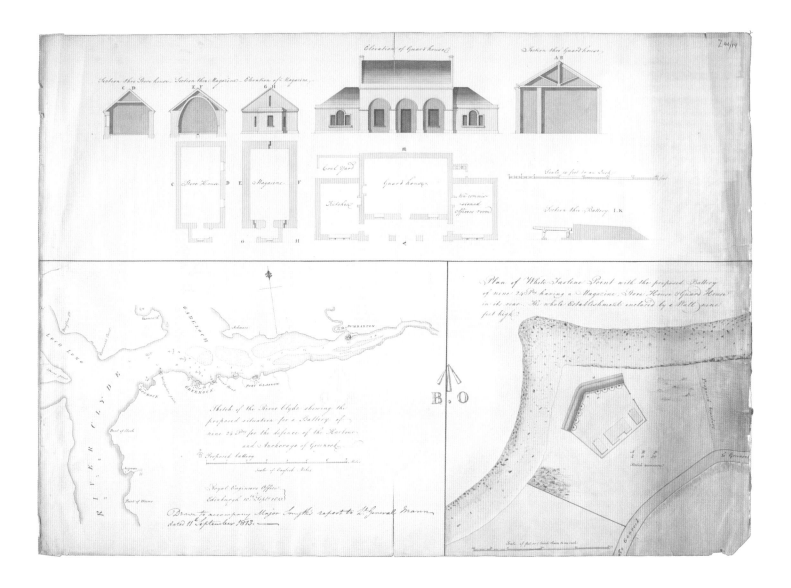

either from the sea or from a surprise landward attack. In this case, the buildings were to have an enclosing wall 9 feet high.

Like many other military plans, this was only one in a sequence of suggestions for the defence of the Clyde. In 1795, another Royal Engineer officer, William Gravatt, drew a small sketch of a suggested 12-gun battery to be sited west of Greenock. Gravatt was subsequently appointed Assistant Inspector of the Military Academy at Woolwich and was influential in continuing the style of the chief drawing master of his student days, Paul Sandby. Ten years before Smyth's proposals, Lieutenant General Richard Vyse had commented on the unprotected state of the Clyde at the same time that Major General William Wemyss and Captain Henry Evatt of the Royal Engineers carried out a survey of the river up to Greenock to accompany a report on the geography of the area and the best location for a battery.

Following Napoleon's defeat and abdication in 1815 and

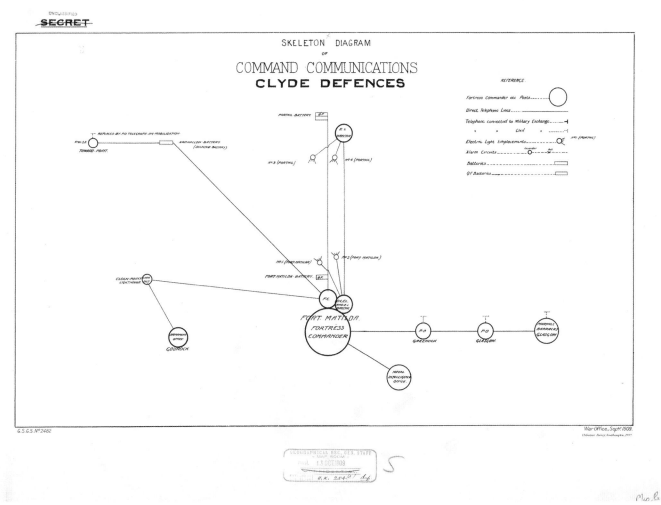

Maps to accompany the Scottish coast defence scheme: GSGS2020 (1907–09)

the Treaty of Paris, the Board of Ordnance's focus turned elsewhere and, by the end of the nineteenth century, the build-up of the Imperial German Navy under Admiral Alfred von Tirpitz resulted in a growing focus on the east coast, particularly in the development of naval bases at Scapa Flow and Rosyth. Nonetheless, the Clyde remained an important seaway for British trade and needed to be defended in time of conflict. This set of three images comes from a collection of maps prepared by the Geographical Section of the War Office's General Staff as part of a scheme for Scotland's defence concentrated on the estuaries of the Forth, Clyde and Tay, as well as Aberdeen. Each set included a general map of the particular area at a scale of 4 miles to an inch, one at a more detailed scale and a skeleton diagram of the command communications. These were prepared between 1907 and 1909 and show that forward planning was, as ever, part of the military strategy for defence.

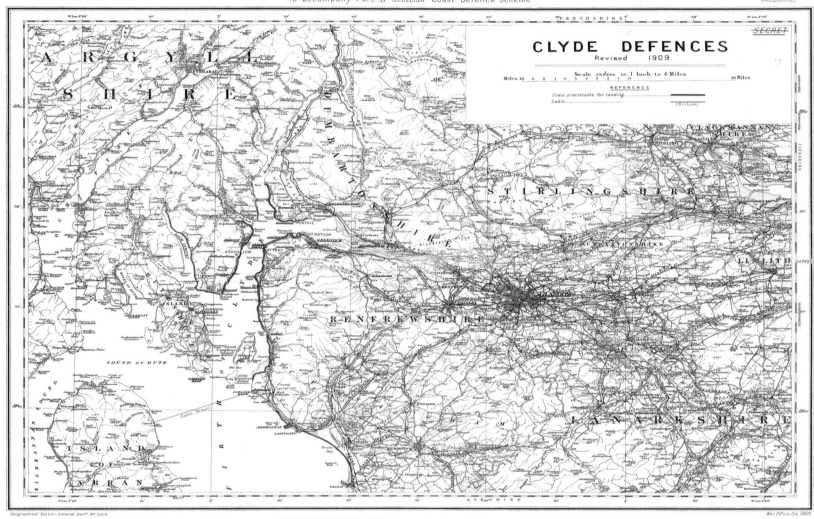

Maps to accompany the Scottish coast defence
scheme: 2341 (above), 2482 (opposite) (1907–09)

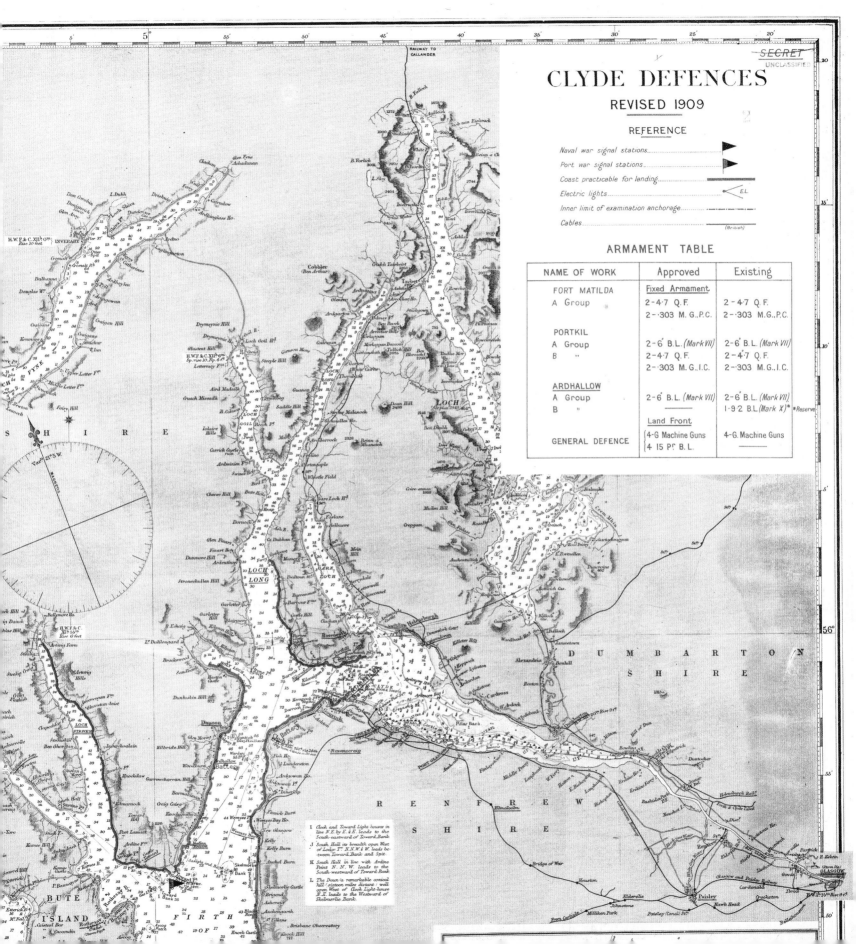

CLYDE DEFENCES
REVISED 1909

REFERENCE

Naval war signal stations	▶
Port war signal stations	▶
Coast practicable for landing	——
Electric lights	◄ E.L.
Inner limit of examination anchorage	————
Cables	———— (British)

ARMAMENT TABLE

NAME OF WORK	Approved	Existing
FORT MATILDA	*Fixed Armament*	
A Group	2 - 4·7 Q.F.	2 - 4·7 Q.F.
	2 - ·303 M.G.P.C.	2 - ·303 M.G.P.C.
PORTKIL		
A Group	2 - 6ʺ B.L. (Mark VII)	2 - 6ʺ B.L. (Mark VII)
B ,,	2 - 4·7 Q.F.	2 - 4·7 Q.F.
	2 - ·303 M.G.I.C.	2 - ·303 M.G.I.C.
ARDHALLOW		
A Group	2 - 6ʺ B.L. (Mark VII)	2 - 6ʺ B.L. (Mark VII)
B ,,		1 - 9·2 B.L. (Mark X)*
	Land Front	
GENERAL DEFENCE	4 - G Machine Guns	4 - G. Machine Guns
	4 15 Pr. B.L.	

*Reserve

I *Cloch and Toward Light-houses in line N.E. by E. ¾ E. leads to the South-eastward of Toward Bank.*

J *South Hall its breadth open West of Lodge Tⁿ N.N.W ¼ W. leads between Toward Bank and Spit.*

K *South Hall in line with Ardine Point N.N.W. leads to the South-westward of Toward Bank.*

L *The Down a remarkable conical hill (sixteen miles distant) well open West of Cloch Light-house N.E. leads to the Westward of Skelmorlie Bank.*

The area map is based on the relevant Ordnance Survey coverage and marks the stretches of coastline which were regarded as practicable for the landing of invading troops, which included most of the south Cowal peninsula and almost the whole seaboard from Fort Matilda to Troon. Also delineated is the cable laid between Corrie on Arran and Portincross which would act as a defence boom and deterrent against U-boat infiltration. Contemporaneously with these documents, Fort Matilda was rearmed with modern guns, a territorial artillery garrison and searchlight was established at Ardhallow between Dunoon and Innellan, and further batteries sited at Portkil and Cloch Point, all of which are shown on the Clyde defences map. Inevitably, gun practice clashed with the enjoyment of the river by the Glasgow holiday-makers going 'doon the watter' and, in the peaceful days of the Edwardian summer, local MPs were to challenge the Secretary of State for War on the timing of such events.

Interestingly, on the slightly more detailed chart of the Clyde prepared in the War Office in 1909, the cable only runs out into deep water from Fairland Head. This chart is clearly an amended version of the Admiralty chart of the whole of the Firth of Clyde first prepared by Robinson between 1846 and 1849. It would appear that the defence plan was to force any potential naval threat into the channel between Bute and the Cumbraes where any intruder would come within the range of the coastal batteries. These are all indicated on the plan, as are two separate signal stations and the arcs of the electric lights. Of possibly greater value to the military historian is the appended armament table, which lists the individual batteries, in addition to their existing and approved weaponry. At this stage, Cloch Point is not yet recorded but, overall, the relatively small number of guns appears remarkable for an estuary of such importance, particularly when contrasted with the images of the subsequent battles on the Western Front which the Great War calls to mind. Looking at the map and the location of defensive positions, it is quite striking that no consideration is given to the defence of more remote parts of the coastline. While the Jacobite Rising had underlined the possibility of remote landings, later military strategy clearly focused on the more immediate threats to important centres of shipbuilding and industry.

While the first image from this trio can hardly be described as a map, it provides visual information on the communications network and command structure behind the defence planning. In some ways, it is redolent of some of the earlier-discussed mapping in the way in which relative location is more important than accuracy. The diagram indicates the direct telephone links to various points, including the lookout at Cloch Point lighthouse and the Maryhill Barracks in Glasgow, giving an impression of just how information would be transferred following any potential attack.

During the Great War, additional batteries were to be located at Cloch Point and Ardeer, the latter to protect the strategically important Nobel Company's explosive works on the Ayrshire coast. This final map of the Cloch Point Battery identifies the boundary of the establishment, as well as the location of the guns, defence electric lights and their arcs of coverage. Again drawn by Royal Engineer draftsmen, this map is a record of what was built rather than what was proposed. What is clear from the surviving documents is that both Admiralty charts and Ordnance Survey maps were used as the cartographic bases for a variety of purposes and were supplemented by drawings of individual batteries and their associated buildings. In the case of the battery at Cloch Point, it covered the eastern side of the anti-submarine boom and worked in tandem with searchlights located at the opposite end at Dunoon designed to illuminate any potential night targets for the Cloch guns.

Opposite. War Office, Cloch Point gun battery and electric light establishment produced by the Royal Engineers based on Ordnance Survey 1:2500 map of Renfrewshire (1915)

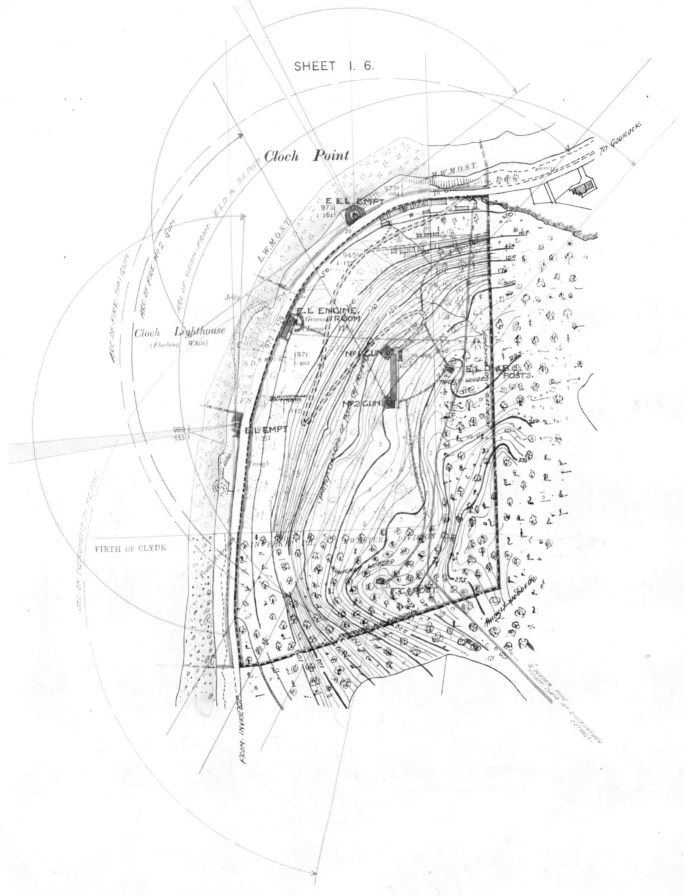

SHEET I. 6.

Cloch Point

To Gourock

Cloch Lighthouse
(Flashing White)

E.E.L EMPT

E.L ENGINE ROOM

No 1 GUN

No 2 GUN

E.L D.L.B.O. POSTS.

E.L EMPT

FIRTH OF CLYDE

NOTE: PROPOSED. W.D. BOUNDARY. EDGED. IN. RED. THUS.

Glasgow-Clydebank
Schiffswerft John Brown und Co.

Karte 1:100 000 1:63 360
Blatt Blatt
Sch. 26 Sch. 72

Kriegsaufnahme:
596 R 109

Länge(westl.Greenw.): 4° 23' 0˝ Breite: 55° 55' 0˝ (Bildmitte)
Mißweisung: -14° 10' (Mitte 1938)

Nachträge:
2.10.39.

500   0   500   1000 m

Maßstab etwa 1: 15 000   (1cm ═ 150 m)

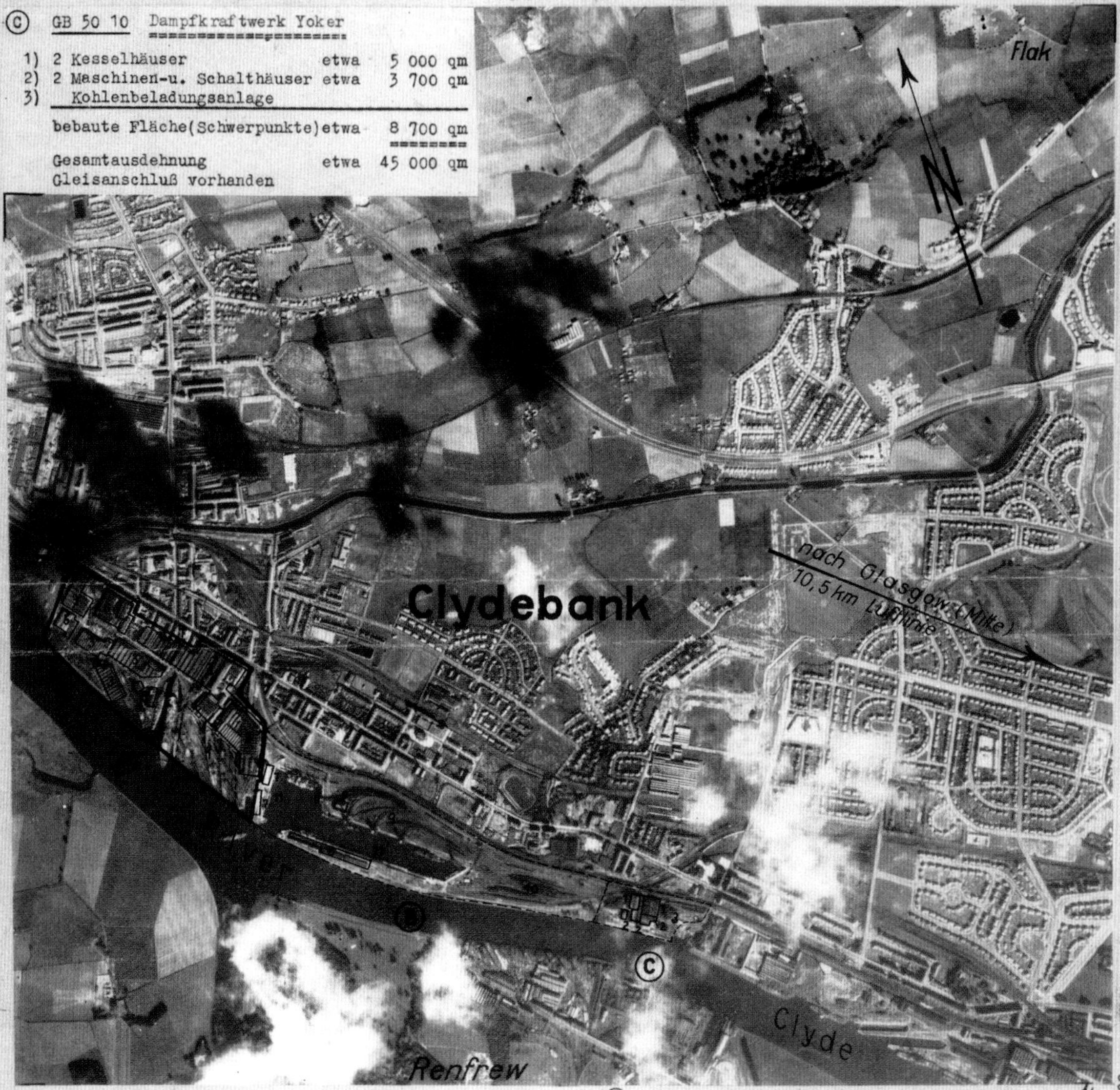

Ⓒ GB 50 10 Dampfkraftwerk Yoker

1)	2 Kesselhäuser	etwa	5 000 qm
2)	2 Maschinen-u. Schalthäuser	etwa	3 700 qm
3)	Kohlenbeladungsanlage		

bebaute Fläche(Schwerpunkte)etwa   8 700 qm

Gesamtausdehnung   etwa 45 000 qm
Gleisanschluß vorhanden

Flak

N

Clydebank

nach Glasgow (Mitte)
10,5 km (Luftlinie)

Clyde

Renfrew

308

Ⓐ GB 83 22 Schiffswerft John Brown & Co.

1)	Hellinge		
2)	1 Baubassin		
3)	Werft u. Maschinenbau-Halle	etwa	98 000 qm
4)	2 Maschinenhäuser	etwa	5 000 qm
5)	1 Lagerhalle	etwa	3 500 qm
6)	1 Kesselschmiede	etwa	9 500 qm

bebaute Fläche(Schwerpunkte)etwa 116 000 qm

Gesamtausdehnung   etwa 290 000 qm
Gleisanschluß vorhanden.

Ⓑ GB 45 45 Rothesay - Dock

6)	3 Umschlagschuppen	etwa	6 300 qm
7)	2 Lagerschuppen	etwa	3 300 qm
8)	1 Betriebsgeb. f. Entlade-kräne	etwa	1 400 qm
9)	4 Entlade-Aufzüge		
10)	Gleisanlagen		
11)	Verladekais m. fahrbaren Kränen		

bebaute Fläche (Schwerpunkte)etwa 11 000 qm

Gleisanschluß vorhanden.

CHAPTER 26

War comes to the Clyde

While the defence preparations for the Firth of Clyde appear extremely effective, the strength of the Royal Navy and its success in bottling up the German High Seas Fleet in their bases at Wilhelmshaven and Kiel, particularly after the battle of Jutland, ensured that the threat of naval bombardment of the British coast was averted during the Great War. Only two decades after the scuttling of almost the entire German fleet at Scapa Flow, Great Britain and Germany were again at war. However, by this date strategy had been fundamentally and radically changed by the realisation of the significance of air power in the ability of enemy forces to inflict damage by bombing raids. While there had been attacks on London and other parts of England by German Zeppelin airships and bombers from 1915 onwards, the problems of weather conditions and navigation made any accuracy in hitting targets difficult. Nonetheless, these were a harbinger of a new kind of warfare where the front line could be in the citizen's home.

Senior members of the German Naval Staff had first made proposals to bomb Britain soon after the outbreak of the Great War. This tactic was regarded as having the potential to diminish the enemy's determination to prosecute the war. However, by the time of the Second World War there was a strong thread in the Luftwaffe's doctrine against the use of 'terror bombing' of non-military targets, it being seen as a diversion away from the more strategic policy of destroying an enemy's military forces. Regardless of this and of any legal considerations, aerial bombing was to be a major characteristic of the Second World War and underlined the significant fact that air power became the decisive factor in combat.

In its preparations for any hostile air attacks, the British government was acutely aware of the concentration of major industries in particular parts of the country and the experience of German bombing raids on Guernica in the Spanish Civil War, as well as on Warsaw and Rotterdam in the early months of the conflict, only underlined the need for air superiority. With the occupation of Denmark in April 1940 and the fall of France and Norway two months later, Germany acquired various naval and air bases which made its ability to strike at potential industrial targets less logistically problematic. Basing strategic decisions on an enemy's principal target being military, the naval bases at Scapa Flow and Rosyth on the east coast of Scotland were seen as potentially under most threat, but the concentrations of heavy industry in the Clydeside area were equally vulnerable – in particular, the shipbuilding yards along the river, the Rolls Royce aero-engine plant at Hillington and various explosive and engineering ordnance factories at Bishopton, Irvine and Dalmuir.

Opposite. German Luftwaffe, Frame SC445483 covering Clydebank and indicating the John Brown shipyard, Rothesay Dock and the Yoker electricity power station (1939)

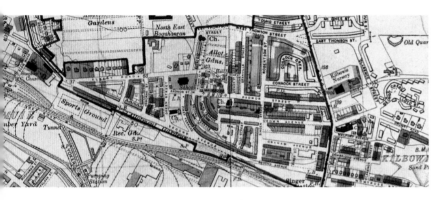

By September 1940, what came to be known as the 'Blitz' began in earnest with a change in German strategy away from attacking Royal Air Force bases to a focus on the bombing of major British cities, in particular London. In preparation for such attacks, aerial photograph reconnaissance surveys had flown over much of Britain early in the war and this survey was supplied to the bomber pilots to assist in locating specific shipyards and other industrial targets. The Clydebank image shown here was photographed on 2 October 1939, less than a month after the declaration of war, and is one of a sequence covering strategically significant locations on or near the Clyde. It was prepared at a scale of 1:100,000 and is notated as a 'War Record'. Aerial photography was an ideal medium for enemy pilots since there was none of the selectivity that often affects what is depicted on maps. On this photograph, three places are highlighted as strategically important: the John Brown shipyards at Clydebank, the Rothesay Dock and the electrical power station at Yoker. During the war, John Brown's yards built, among other vessels, the battleships, *Duke of York* and *Vanguard* and the aircraft carrier, *Indefatigable*.

The photograph is annotated with detailed intelligence information on the individual sites. For the shipyards, it lists slipways and the construction basin, along with the floor space of machine rooms, warehouse and boiler shop, while the dock notes cover such features as railway tracks and storage sheds. Looking at the photograph shows that each feature has been numbered

and delineated by a heavy black line to emphasise the exact location. More significantly, the newly constructed liner *Queen Elizabeth* can be identified sitting at the fitting-out dock in the shipyard before it was dispatched to New York to clear the berth for warship construction. Clydebank's distance from Glasgow is also indicated. Although the image has been affected by a small amount of cloud cover, the main targets are very clear. What is evident from the photograph is the large number of new suburban housing developments lying north of the river but also the considerable area of green space on either side of the Forth and Clyde Canal.

While there was a sequence of relatively small attacks on Glasgow after its first air raid in July 1940, Clydeside saw little in the way of aerial bombing until the March of the following year, when two devastating raids by Heinkel 111 and Junkers 88 bombers flying from airfields in western France attacked and largely destroyed Clydebank. While the main thrust of these attacks, which took place over successive nights, were the shipyards and docks, the Dalmuir ordnance factory and the Admiralty oil fuel depot at Dalnottar, they were not a military success. The strategic targets were not seriously damaged and the raids did little to hinder production. On the other hand, the loss of life and the degree of damage to the burgh's housing stock brought home the grim reality of modern warfare to the whole of Scotland. More than 500 people were killed and only seven of Clydebank's 12,000 houses remained undamaged. However, rather than terrorising the morale of the local population, it had the counter-effect of strengthening the determination 'to see it through'.

Glasgow also suffered serious damage during the Clydebank raids, with more than 600 people being killed. Subsequent raids on Greenock over two nights in May 1941 caused in excess of 300 fatalities. Such high casualties in relatively small local populations were partly due to the proximity of housing to many of the factories and works but also to the large number of incendiary bombs dropped. These raids flew over much of central

Opposite. Plan showing the central area of extensive war damage in Clydebank burgh (1945)

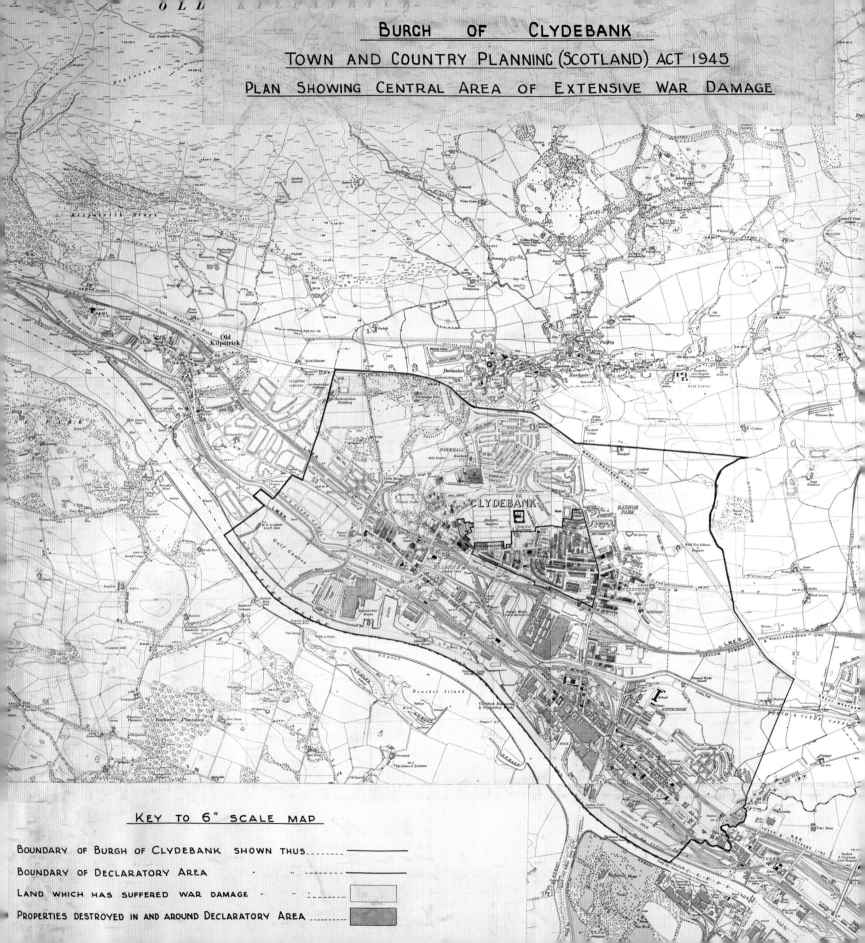

BURGH OF CLYDEBANK

TOWN AND COUNTRY PLANNING (SCOTLAND) ACT 1945

PLAN SHOWING CENTRAL AREA OF EXTENSIVE WAR DAMAGE

KEY TO 6" SCALE MAP

BOUNDARY OF BURGH OF CLYDEBANK SHOWN THUS

BOUNDARY OF DECLARATORY AREA

LAND WHICH HAS SUFFERED WAR DAMAGE

PROPERTIES DESTROYED IN AND AROUND DECLARATORY AREA

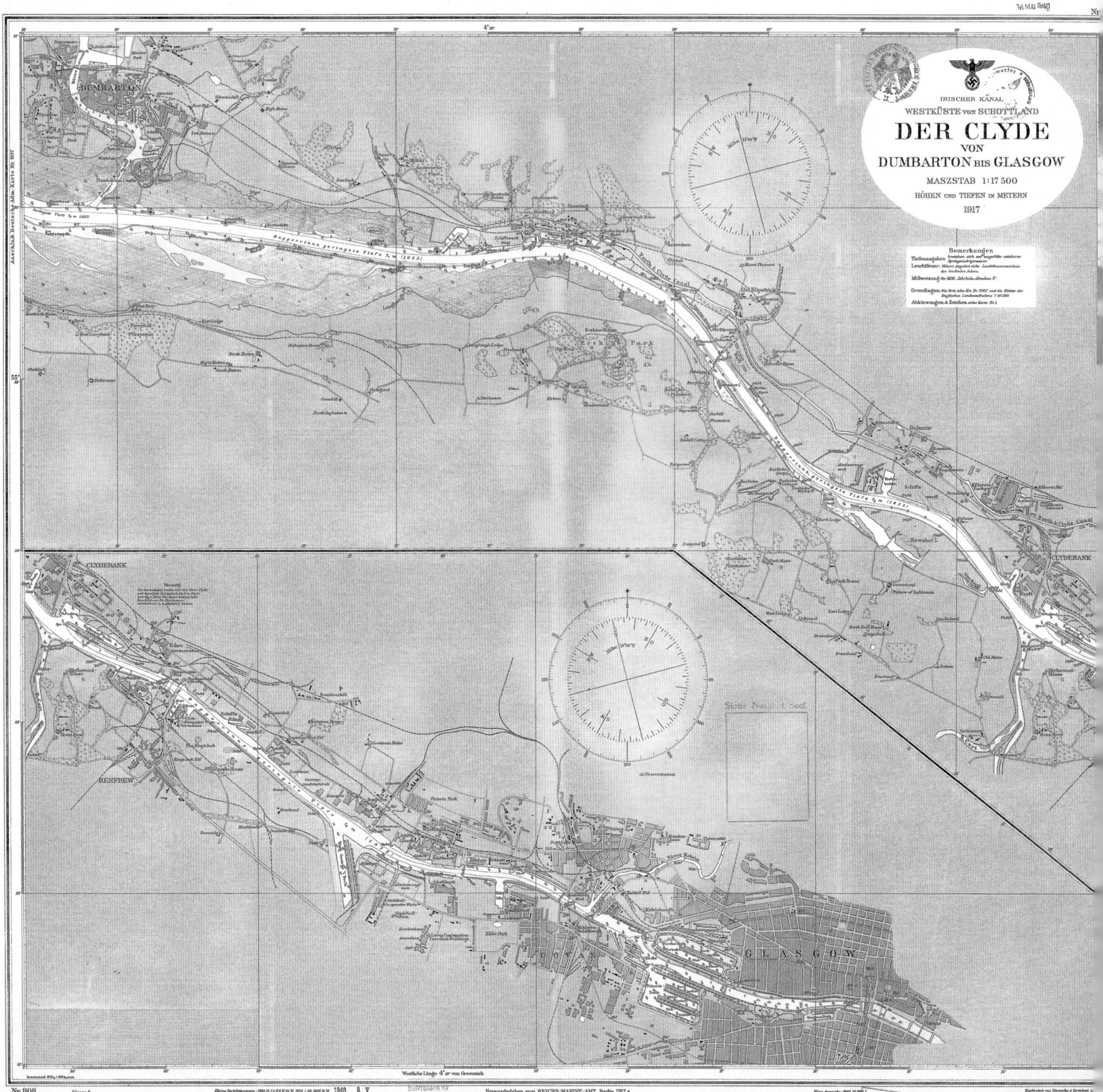

IRISCHER KANAL
WESTKÜSTE VON SCHOTTLAND
DER CLYDE
VON
DUMBARTON BIS GLASGOW
MASZSTAB 1:17 500
HÖHEN UND TIEFEN IN METERN
1917

Bemerkungen

DUMBARTON

CLYDEBANK

CLYDEBANK

RENFREW

GLASGOW

Westliche Länge 4° 20' von Greenwich

Nr. 808   Klasse 6.   Herausgegeben vom REICHS-MARINE-AMT, Berlin 1917.
1940. 9. V.

Scotland which would be well aware of the attacks by the constant drone of aero-engines followed later by the lurid glow in the sky to the west. However, lack of co-ordination in the Luftwaffe's High Command and the diversion of attention to the invasion of the Soviet Union in June 1941 saw the effective ending of major raids on Scotland.

This plan produced in 1945 (p. 133) shows the central area of extensive damage to Clydebank and comes from a series of development plans prepared by the Scottish Office Development Department. It was accompanied by an extensive array of supporting reports, written statements and compulsory purchase orders gathered between the period immediately after the raids and 1976 while the mapping is, unsurprisingly, based on the relevant Ordnance Survey 6-inch coverage, revised up to 1938. Most importantly, it marks in a separate colour those properties destroyed in and around the area defined in the Town and Country Planning (Scotland) Act of 1945. This appears as a comparatively small area north of the Singer sewing machine works and the scale of the destruction is obvious. What is also clear is the minimal impact that the bombing had on the engineering works, docks and shipyards beside the river.

The anti-submarine boom installed to protect the natural anchorage of the Tail of the Bank was to be equally effective during the Second World War despite the shocking torpedo attack in Scapa Flow which resulted in the sinking of the outdated battleship *Royal Oak* in October 1939. Partly as a result of this, the Clyde was made the base for the Home Fleet during the early months of the war and it was the one link to the sea to remain open to the Atlantic supply convoys and, subsequently, troopships throughout the conflict. While the German army's General Staff (*Generalstab des Heeres*) had been prevented from gathering intelligence information on Great Britain prior to 1937, the Kriegsmarine, the navy of Nazi Germany did not have the same difficulties concerning contemporary naval mapping. This was largely due to the trend of reissuing Admiralty charts with updated details concerning

beacons, wrecks and changes to lights. This chart of the Clyde from Dumbarton to Glasgow was published in 1917 by the interwar Reichsmarine. Although so dated, the sheet has been stamped above the map with the authority of the Naval High Command (*Oberkommando der Kriegsmarine*) and given a date of May 1940. This is repeated in the chart's supplementary notes regarding minor amendments. In addition, the title is surmounted by the Command's insignia of a swastika surmounted by an eagle.

Engraved by the printing firm of Giesecke & Devrient, which had premises in Leipzig and Berlin, it is a direct copy of the British Admiralty chart of the Clyde, numbered 2007 and drawn at a scale of 1:17,500. Additional comments indicate that information was also drawn from the relevant Ordnance Survey 6-inch map of the area and supply details on tides, lights and compass declination. The chart bears all the traits of the original work prepared by the Admiralty – in particular, the grey shading of the landward areas – but is also an interesting mix of two languages. For example, many of the features of most interest to military forces have been translated into German, while others remain as they appear on the original, leading to such anomalies as Shieldhall Co-operative works lying to the south of *Holzlager* (timber storage). Beacons have been coloured (red for the north bank and yellow for the south) to help identify the channel.

Combined with the aerial photography use by the Luftwaffe and the Special Edition maps of the *Abteilung für Kriegskarten und Vermessungswesen* produced for the Wehrmacht, charts such as this coverage of the river emphasise the wealth of information gathered by different branches of the German military. In truth, the Kriegsmarine's attention during much of the war was focused on the Battle of the Atlantic and on attacking the transatlantic convoys which were to keep Britain's population fed and its war effort supplied. Nonetheless, had there been a serious U-boat attack on shipping in the Clyde, such cartography would have been essential to such a policy.

Opposite. Kriegsmarine Oberkommando, *Abteilung Seekriegsleitung der Clyde* (prepared in May 1940)

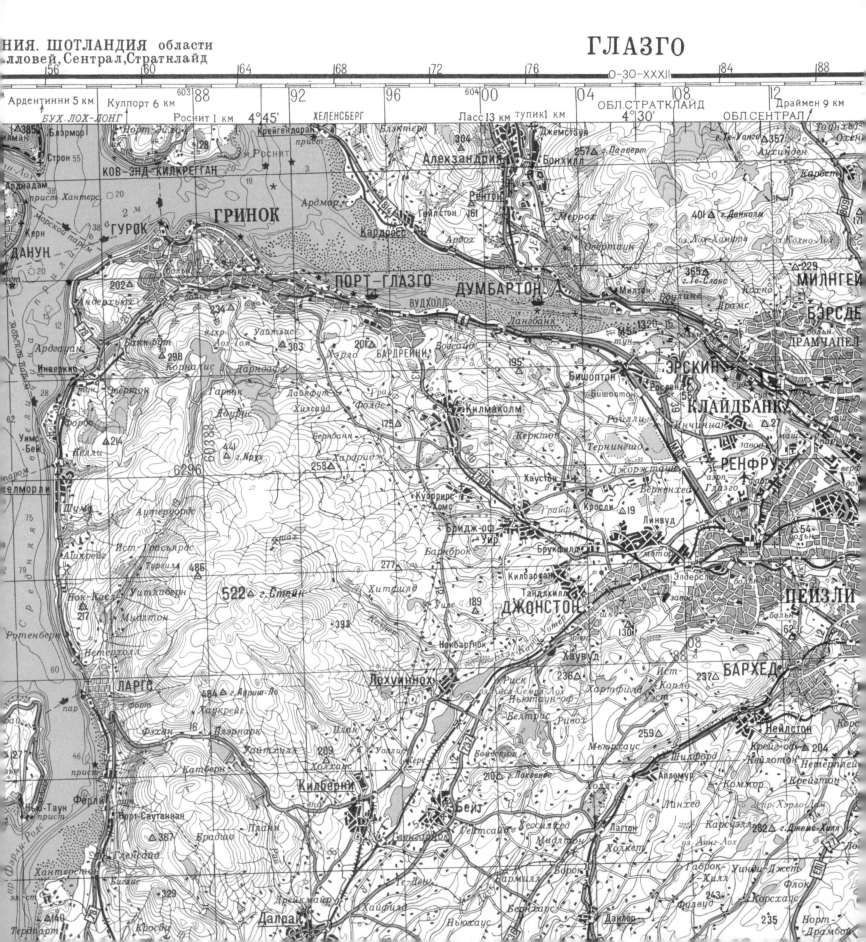

CHAPTER 27

Cold War mapping
by the Red Army

These two colourful maps of the Clyde area are part of a fascinating archive of maps covering practically every country in the world and produced by the Soviet military authorities for over 50 years before, during and after the Cold War. Such a programme was possibly the largest conducted by any one survey organisation. Maps were published at a variety of scales and these examples come from the 1:200,000 series coverage of Great Britain and from the more detailed 1:10,000 plans of selected towns and cities. This was a massive programme of production, employing something in the region of 35,000 staff in the Military Topographic Directorate (*Voyenno Topografischeskogo Upravleniya*) of the Soviet Army General Staff, with factories in several of the former Soviet satellite states. Following the break-up of the USSR in the 1990s, these maps became available in the West for the first time and the staggeringly impressive detail brought to light the high levels of intelligence available to military commanders 'behind the Iron Curtain'. Inevitably, their existence fuelled a considerable debate over Soviet military strategy and whether these plans were produced for a specifically hostile attack or were merely part of a wider scheme to map the world by a major world power.

It appears that the earliest maps were based on the host country's own mapping, combined with additional information gleaned from a variety of resources, which may have included 'local knowledge', but from the early 1960s onwards, photographic technology became the preferred means of production – in other words, using satellite and high-altitude aeroplanes. This illustration of the general sheet of the Clyde estuary comes from the British 1:200,000 series, although coverage was also produced at scales of 1:1,000,000, 1:500,000 and 1:100,000. It is titled *Glasgow* and was produced in 1985. Like all the small-scale maps published in this programme, the sheet numbering system is based on that adopted by the International Map of the World where the globe is divided into equal-sized zones based on degrees of latitude and longitude, with each grid square divided into 36 sheets and numbered accordingly. This standardisation, along with a similar approach to colouring, choice of names and features identified, allowed for a high level of consistency which would have been of great benefit in any military operation.

Certain apparent occasional lapses in the depiction of railways (for example, the omission from this sheet of Rutherglen station which closed in 1964), emphasise that the maps frequently show more recent developments than their contemporary Ordnance Survey counterparts. When compared with the Seventh Series 1-inch map, the lack of colouring to indicate minor roads on the Soviet versions seems to suggest a focus on major routes. This is strengthened by annotations on the width,

Opposite. Soviet Army General Staff, 1:200,000 sheet N-30-II covering Glasgow and the lower Clyde (1985)

ВЕЛИКОБРИТАНИЯ. ШОТЛАНДИЯ области
Дамфрис-энд-Галловей, Сентрал, Стратклайд

ГЛАЗГО

14-30-02   N-30-II

Состояние местности на 1972-1975 гг.   Издание 1985 г.

ГРИНОК
ГУРОК
ДАНУН
ПОРТ-ГЛАЗГО
ДУМБАРТОН
МИЛНГЕЙВИ
БЭРСДЕН
КЕРКИНТИЛЛОХ
КИЛСАЙТ
КЛАЙДБАНК
РЕНФРУ
ГЛАЗГО
КОТБРИДЖ
ПЕЙЗЛИ
ДЖОНСТОН
БАРХЕД
КАМБУСЛАНГ
СТОНФИЛД
ГАМИЛЬТОН
ИСТ-КИЛБРАЙД
ЛАРГС
ДАЛРИ
МИЛПОРТ
СТЮАРТОН
ФЕНИК
СТАРТХЕЙВЕН
СТИВЕНСТОН
КИЛУИННИНГ
АРДРОССАН
СОЛТКОТС
ЭРВИН
КИЛМАРНОК
НЬЮМИЛНС
ДАРВЕЛ
ГАЛСТОН
ГРИНХОЛМ
КЕРФОРД
ТРУН
МОХЛАЙН
МЬЮРКЕРК
ПРЕСТУИК
КАМНОК
ХОЛМХЕД
ДАЛМЕЛЛИНГТОН
МЕЙБОЛ
КЕРКМАЙКЛ

1:200 000

в 1 сантиметре 2 километра

км 4 2 0   4   8   12 км

Сплошные горизонтали проведены через 20 метров

clearance and carrying capacity of bridges. There are examples of the road numbering system being different from our own and, more significantly, distances between locations are indicated for main routes. Additionally, this Russian map has a much better indication of ferry routes, such as Ardrossan to Brodick. Place-name addicts will be delighted to see that Moscow in East Ayrshire has been included on the sheet. Like others in this series, a detailed description of the area covered appears on the verso of the Glasgow map. This is an extended commentary on population, topography, the transport network, local climatic conditions and, in this case, includes a small map indicating four separate categories of land use.

If anything, it is the vast number of street plans produced during this period which truly highlights the levels of information-gathering behind the programme. It is only in very recent years that research into this remarkable resource has taken place, hampered by the piecemeal way in which the maps have been released. However, it is increasingly considered more likely that these plans were intended for civil administration following a successful invasion rather than for any planned attack. These plans are the one exception to the standardised sheet numbering system and are positioned to cover the urban areas regardless of the grid. In total, plans of 91 British and Irish towns and cities were produced. Of these, only seven cover locations in Scotland, namely Aberdeen (1981), Dundee (1992), Dunfermline (1979), Edinburgh (1983), Glasgow and Paisley (1981), Greenock (1979) and Kilmarnock (1958). Undoubtedly, Dunfermline was chosen because of its proximity to the naval dockyard at Rosyth.

This example shows Port Glasgow, forming part of the two-sheet plan of the Greenock area. As is standard with this series, they are labelled as secret (*CEKPETHO*) but it has been suggested that a higher level of 'top secret' mapping may have existed for more sensitive information. In a way similar to the maps prepared for the Germany army in the Second World War, buildings have been colour coded to identify their different purposes: administrative, which includes prisons, are shown in purple, housing (brown), locations of military importance (green) and industry (black). Ten separate colours were used overall in the printing. Streets are frequently named and, although not immediately obvious, the contour interval for these plans is 2.5 metres, while spot heights are shown to tenths of a metre, emphasising the high level of information-gathering behind their production.

Apart from the care in providing such comprehensive detail on the plans themselves, the sheets also include alphabetical lists of important sites and street names, as well as detailed descriptions of the immediate locality. These again incorporated a record of population, terrain and significant industries. Elsewhere, more practical details would include whether local rivers would freeze in winter. Despite the Ordnance Survey claim that all Soviet mapping of Great Britain was based on its own products, research has confirmed that not only did the large-scale plans of British towns and cities include material derived from several other sources but also that much of the material which was based on OS mapping was well over 50 years old. In fact, it is clear that the plans are not merely copies but were freshly created and tailored to suit specific needs.

As one recent commentator has stated 'the Soviet plans offer a very different view of a familiar landscape'. They bring back a reminder of the days of the Cuban missile crisis when the world held its breath. They also remind us of the secrecy and high levels of detailed knowledge behind intelligence in today's global environment.

Opposite. Soviet Army General Staff, 1:200,000 sheet
N-30-II covering Glasgow and the lower Clyde (1985)

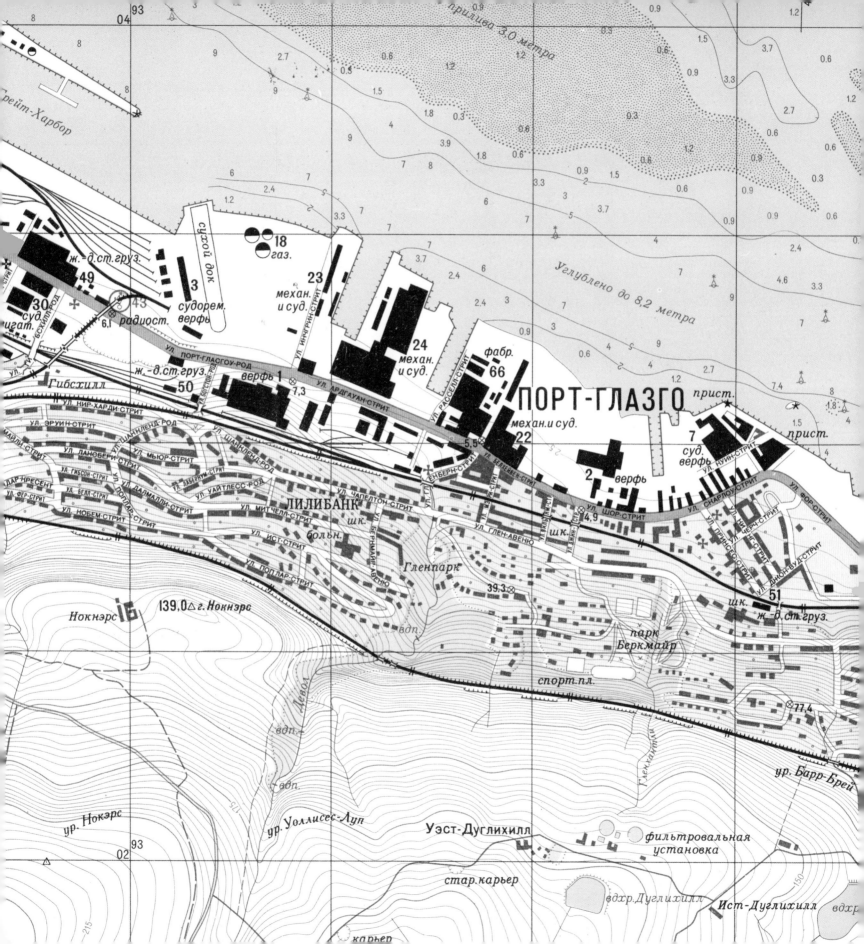

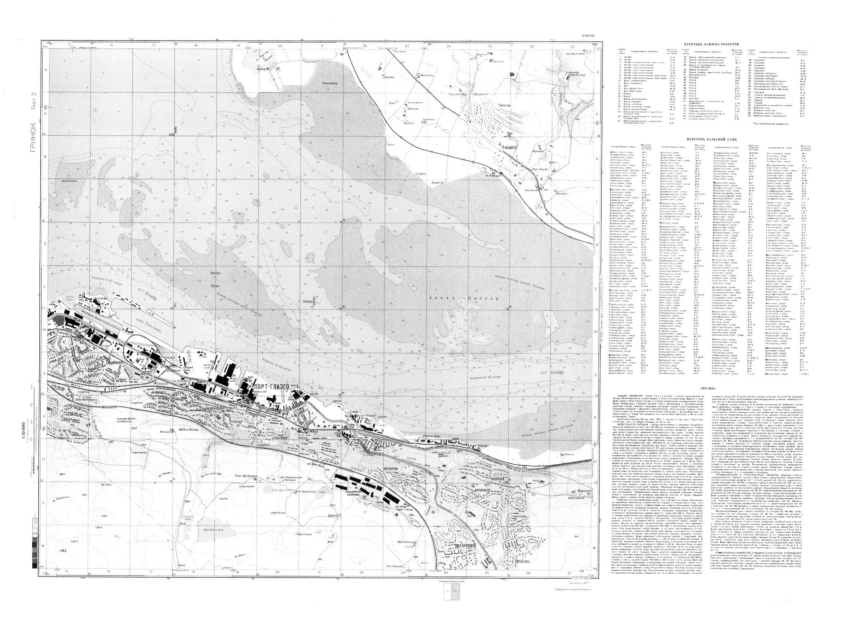

Opposite and above. Town plan of Greenock
sheet 2 showing Port Glasgow (1977)

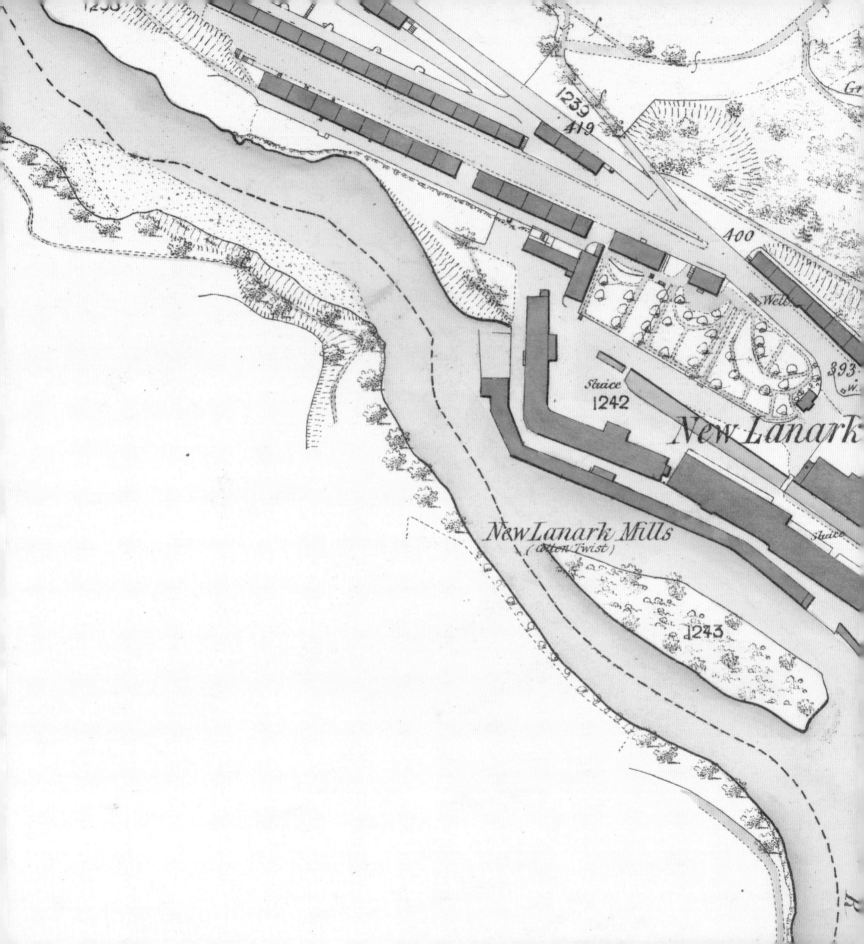

New Lanark

New Lanark Mills
(Cotton Twist)

Sluice
1242

1243

Well

400

393

419

1239

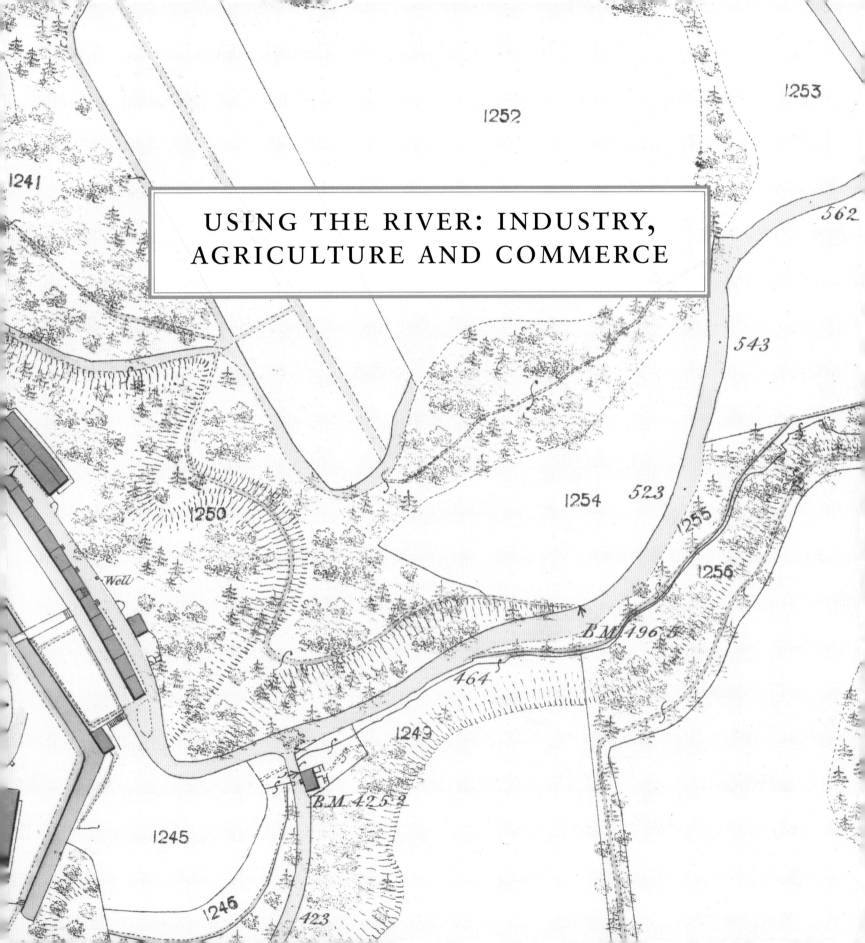

USING THE RIVER: INDUSTRY, AGRICULTURE AND COMMERCE

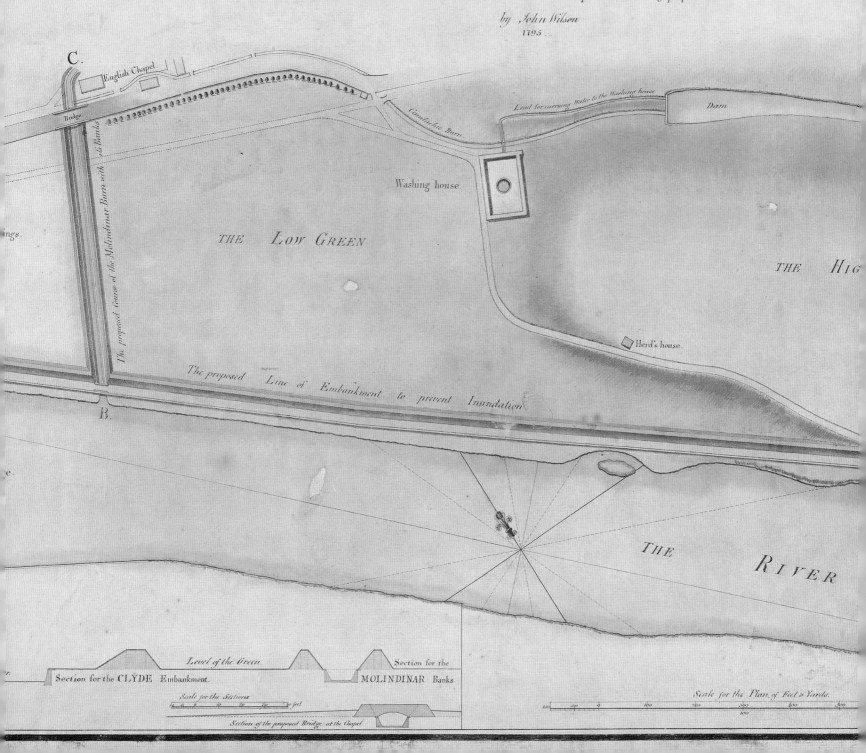

Banking, drainage and washing: Glasgow Green at the turn of the eighteenth century

These plans of Glasgow Green provide some indication of how the city of Glasgow attempted to use the waters of the Clyde for a variety of purposes at the dawn of the nineteenth century – a time before the major changes which were to alter its whole relationship with the river. John Wilson's 1795 depiction reflects efforts by the burgh authorities to resolve some of the problems it faced as a result of a burgeoning population. It is estimated that by 1801 this had reached 77,000 and certain indications of the impact of this growth on services were already being realised. One difficulty residents faced was the flooding of low-lying areas beside the river during times of high water. Such inundation not only affected the lands of the Low and High Greens, as well as their bleachfields and washing greens, but also caused the waters of the Molendinar Burn to back up into the backlands at the foot of the Saltmarket and Bridgegate. As many of the sewers in this part of the city emptied directly into the Molendinar, this caused the noisome effluent to be washed back into the streets.

In May 1794, a council committee was to investigate proposals for a new street to Glasgow Green and to alter the course of the Burn. Wilson was to develop this further with a realignment of the outflow of the drainage to carry the waste into the Clyde itself. In addition, the bottom of the Burn was to be raised, with the straightened channel flowing directly south from the English chapel to the Clyde. A tunnel passing under the Molendinar would take waters flowing from the east. Wilson's plan also notes that such a tunnel would be insufficient to cope with water from the Camlachie Burn, which was to be diverted well to the east of the High Green. On inspection of the plan, this proposal seems to run counter to his indication of a dam and lead designed to supply water from the Camlachie to the Green's washing-house. The embankment suggested for the Low Green and a cross section indicating various levels are also marked.

More than ten years earlier, the council had approved the building of a dyke on the south side of the New Green but, in a forewarning of what has been experienced in more recent times, this work between the bottom of the Saltmarket and Hutcheson Bridge was to be cited as a major cause of increased flooding on 18 November 1795. That flood was also to destroy the nearly completed first Hutcheson Bridge. Work on it had begun the previous year and its inclusion by Wilson provides a fascinating snapshot in time. Designed to improve access to the south bank of the river, the bridge was an impressive structure of five stone arches, as depicted here, and built at a cost of £6,000, funded partly by the patrons of Hutcheson's Hospital. As remuneration for his work on this and other plans of the Green, Wilson was to receive the considerable sum of £25 and 4 shillings in the following March.

Opposite and overleaf. John Wilson, *Plan of the Low Green of Glasgow* (1795)

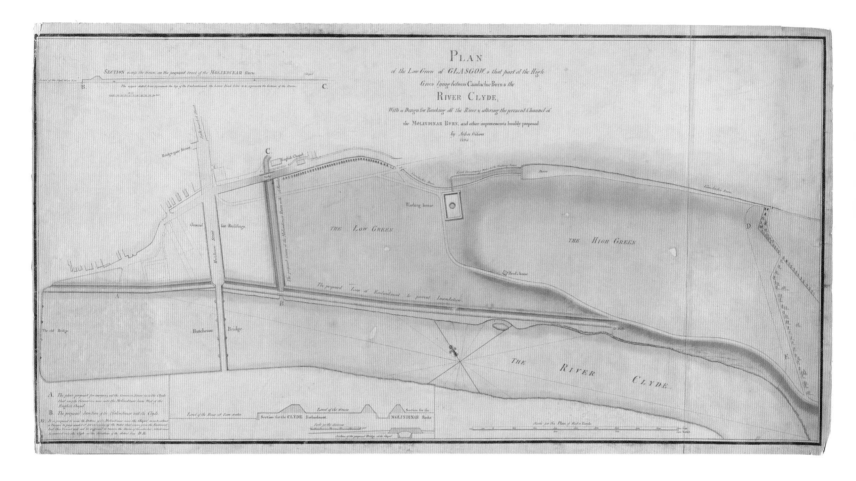

William Kyle's plan shows a new design for improvements on the Green suggested by James Cleland and dates from 1813. By this period, Cleland had been appointed city treasurer and the year after this plan was published, he became superintendent of public works for the city, a post he was to hold for two decades. While celebrated as a leading statistician in his day, it was in his involvement with improvements to such public works that he made his greatest contributions to Glasgow. The plan accompanies Cleland's report, which also discusses the raising of a water supply from the river, removing the Camlachie which 'frequently sends forth an offensive effluvia' and creating walks on the Green in order that the citizens can enjoy 'its beautiful situation on the banks of the Clyde'. As part of the 'gentrification' design, Cleland proposed the removal of the communal washing-house to a less intrusive site beside the bleaching green but further from the homes of those who used it.

Although this second plan ties in well with the earlier depiction, there are noticeable differences reflecting the background to each. Kyle's survey indicates the pipes which will supply pure water from the river to the bleaching fields, as well as the trees

Opposite and overleaf. William Kyle, *Plan of the Green of Glasgow exhibiting a design by James Cleland for sundry proposed improvements* (1813)

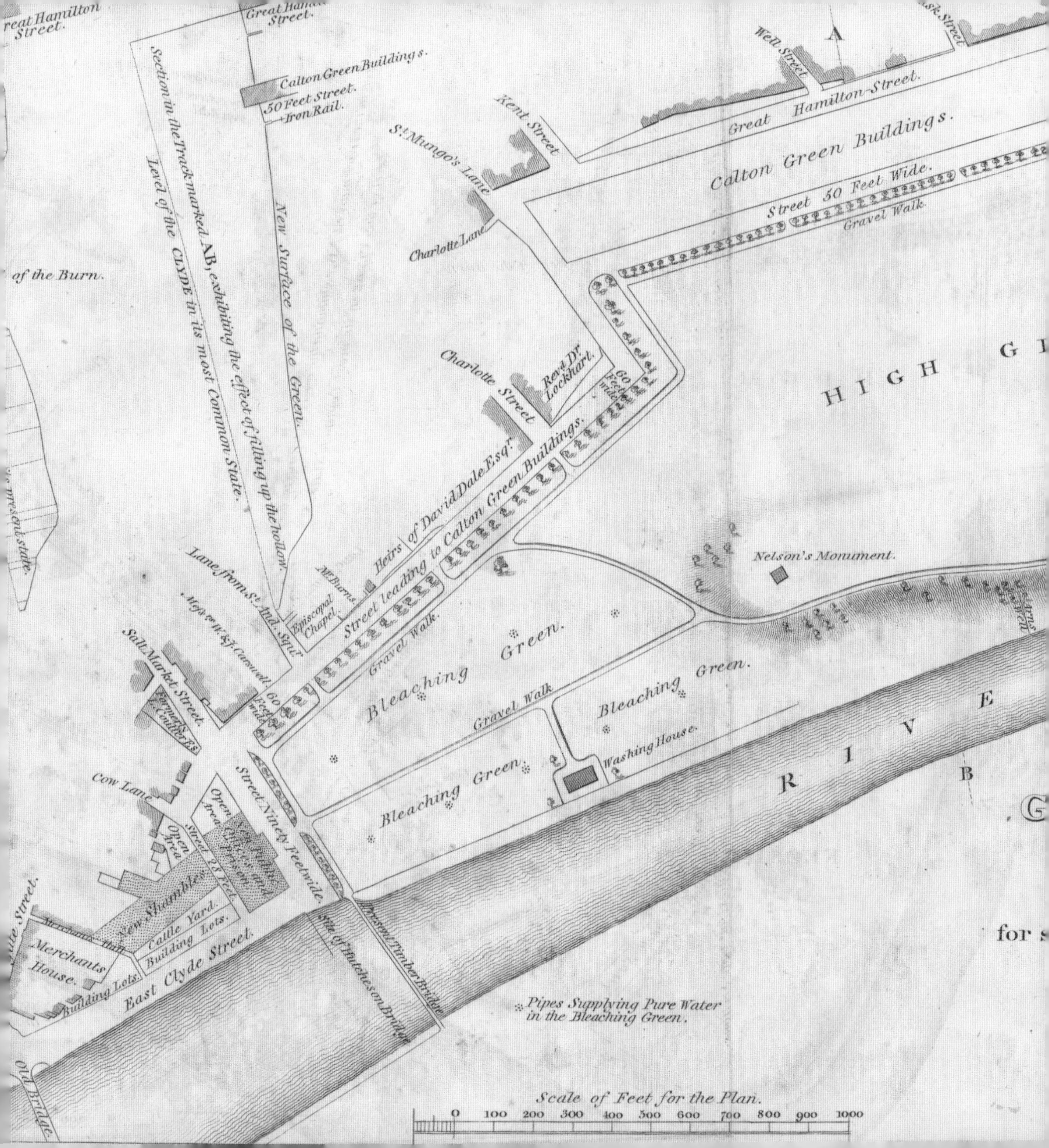

reat Hamilton Street.

Great Hamilton Street.

Calton Green Buildings.

50 Feet Street.

Iron Rail.

A

Well Street.

usk Street.

Kent Street.

St Mungo's Lane.

Great Hamilton Street.

Calton Green Buildings.

Charlotte Lane.

Street 50 Feet Wide.

Gravel Walk.

Section in the Track marked AB, exhibiting the effect of filling up the hollow.

Level of the CLYDE in its most Common State.

New Surface of the Green.

of the Burn.

present state.

Charlotte Street.

Revd Dr Lockhart.

60 Feet wide.

HIGH G

Lane from St And. Sqre.

Mrs W. & F. Clanwall.

Heirs of David Dale Esqr.

Street leading to Calton Green Buildings.

Mr Burn's.

Nelson's Monument.

Salt Market Street.

Episcopal Chapel.

Gravel Walk.

60 Feet wide.

Bleaching Green.

James Street.

Bleaching Green.

Cow Lane.

Street Ninety Feet wide.

Gravel Walk.

Bleaching Green.

Gravel Walk.

Bleaching Green.

Washing House.

R I V E

B

Merchants's Hall.

New Shambles.

Open Area.

Cattle Yard.

Street 28 Feet.

Open Area.

Building Lots.

Bleaching Green.

G

for s

Hute Street.

Merchants House.

Building Lots.

East Clyde Street.

Site of Hutcheson Bridge.

Proposed Timber Bridge.

* Pipes Supplying Pure Water in the Bleaching Green.

Old Bridge.

Scale of Feet for the Plan.

0   100   200   300   400   500   600   700   800   900   1000

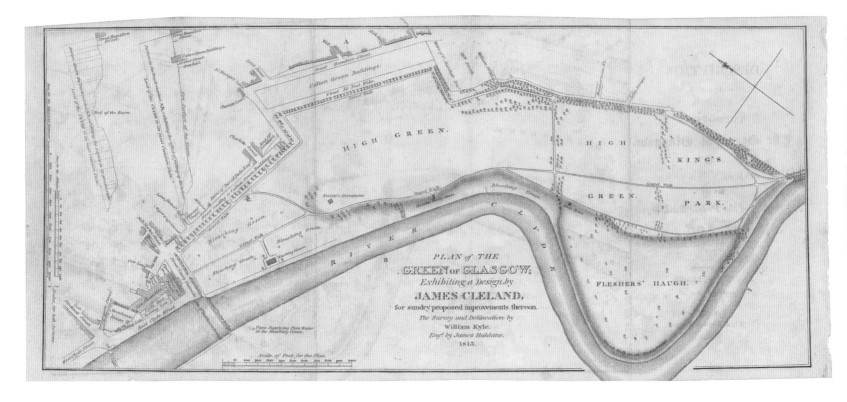

to be part of an amenity planting scheme to enhance the enjoyment of the riparian location. One significant addition of particular relevance to the river is the identification of the Glasgow
Humane Society's boathouse on the later plan. Founded in
1790, the society's employed officers have been responsible for
saving the lives of several thousands of residents and visitors
for over two centuries and continue its work of prevention,
rescue and recovery today.

Cleland was experienced in drawing his own plans but
employed Kyle, the leading surveyor in Glasgow at that time,
believing that 'the name of this Surveyor is justly allowed to be
a sufficient certificate'. Both plans also indicate the building on
the High Green which had been occupied by the town's cowherd,
responsible for over 120 head grazing on the rich grass beside
the river. Subsequently, this building was to be the location of a
house for Glasgow Golf Club, founded in 1787 and resident
on the Green until 1835. As the first golf club in the west of
Scotland, its original home beside the Clyde was to be a precursor

of many courses which enjoy a view of the river or its estuary.

This watercolour of the river as it approaches the city provides
an excellent image of activities on Glasgow Green. Produced
by the landscape painter Hugh William Williams (1773–1829),
it indicates washerwomen at work on both banks, laying out
large sheets to dry on the Green. The painting also provides a
very good impression of the Old Bridge and its humped construction, as well as the low-lying nature of the ground on the north
bank. It is likely that the building depicted on the far right is
the Humane Society house, thereby helping to date the work to
the late 1790s. By 1793 the artist was advertising a drawing
academy in the city but by the end of the century he had moved
to Edinburgh. Later known as 'Grecian' Williams, he had previously produced an illustration of the Forth and Clyde Canal in
1792 and followed this up with views of the city's Cathedral
and Infirmary, the Clyde from Dalnottar and of Dumbarton,
again all as topographic records of various scenes to meet a
growing demand for illustrations of Scottish locations.

Hugh William Williams, *The city of Glasgow* (c.1800)

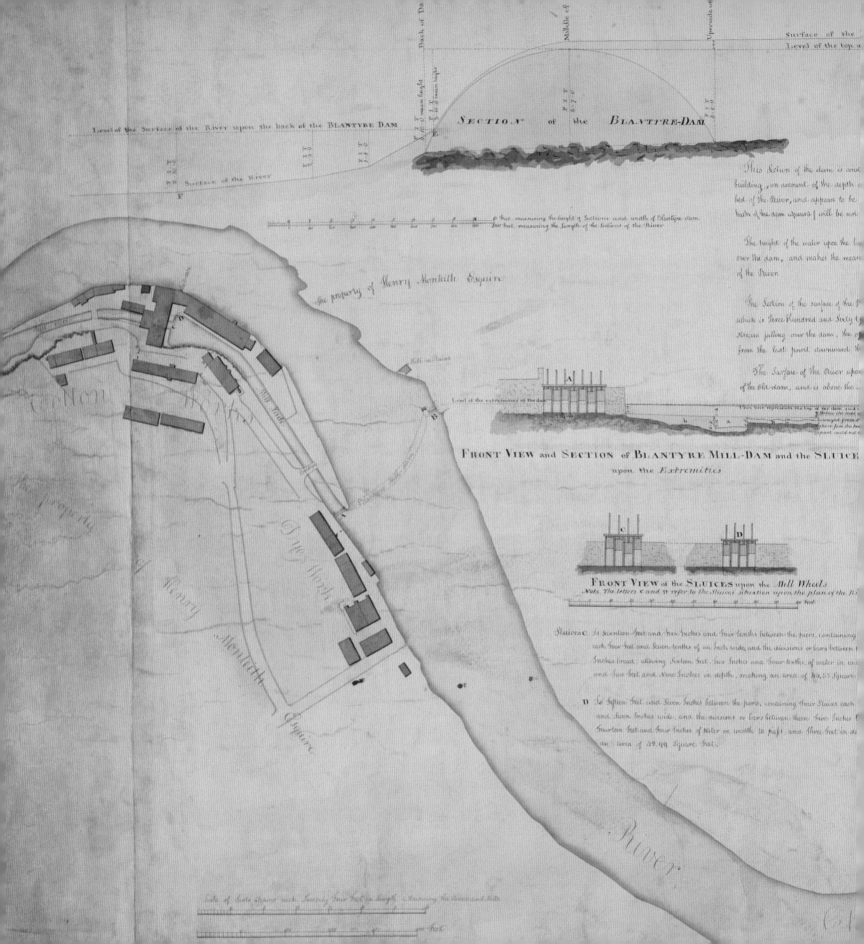

SECTION of the BLANTYRE-DAM

Level of the Surface of the River upon the back of the BLANTYRE DAM

Surface of the River

This Section of the dam is const
building, on account of the depth o
bed of the River, and appears to be
back of the dam upward will be not

The height of the water upon the ba
over the dam, and makes the mean
of the River.

The Section of the surface of the S
which is Three Hundred and Sixty s
stream falling over the dam, the o
from the last point downward th

The Surface of the River upo
of the old dam, and is above the

FRONT VIEW and SECTION of BLANTYRE MILL-DAM and the SLUICE
upon the Extremities

The property of Henry Monteith Esquire

Level of the extremities of the dam

FRONT VIEW of the SLUICES upon the Mill Wheels
Note. The letters C and D refer to the Sluices situation upon the plan of the Fi

Sluice C is seventeen Feet and Six Inches and Four Tenths between the piers, containing
each Four Feet and Seven tenths of an Inch wide, and the divisions or bars between
Inches broad; allowing Sixteen Feet, Two Inches and Four tenths of water in wi
and Two Feet and Nine Inches in depth, making an area of 44,55 Square

D is Fifteen Feet and Seven Inches between the piers, containing Four Sluices each
and Seven Inches wide, and the divisions or bars between them Five Inches
Fourteen Feet and Four Inches of water in width to pass, and Three Feet in de
an area of 42,99 Square Feet.

Scale of Beds of about each Twenty Four Feet in length Showing the Islands and Falls

CHAPTER 29

Cotton mills on the Clyde

For many people, the mention of cotton mills on the River Clyde calls up an immediate vision of the World Heritage site at New Lanark, possibly Scotland's best preserved and most celebrated industrial tourist attraction. However, the village of Blantyre had also been chosen by David Dale as the site for a similar mill on the Clyde in 1785. Influenced by the work of Richard Arkwright in the use of water power to spin a kind of cotton described as water-twist, Dale, one of Glasgow's leading merchants and financiers and his partner James Monteith began manufacturing two years later and, by 1791, the mill was employing more than 350 people. In the same year, a second mill was erected and by the time of the *New Statistical Account*, written in 1845, the local minister provided a considerably detailed description of the impact of the mills on the parish.

A weaving factory with more than 450 looms had been added in 1813 and work was subsequently diversified into turkey-red dyeing. By 1816, the Blantyre Cotton Works was the second largest employer among the more than 40 cotton manufacturing firms in Scotland. In total, more than 900 people made up the workforce of the various processes, with those employed having a working week of 69 hours. However, with a similar approach to that at New Lanark, Dale was concerned for those he employed and most were housed in a specifically designed village which included a church, public washing-house,

water pumps, drying green and library. In a tone very redolent of its time, the parish minister closed his account by stating that 'the people of Blantyre have reason to congratulate themselves on the rapid strides they have already made, and are still making'.

Gilbert Innes of Stow, a director of the Royal Bank of Scotland and an associate of Dale, visited the mills in September 1790 and described them as 'infinitely cleaner and the machinery greatly superior to Pennycuik'. Monteith bought Dale out and became sole proprietor in early 1793 at about the time that France declared war on Great Britain. He successfully averted financial disaster by moving to sell his cloth by public auction but was to die in 1802. His youngest son Henry took over the family business. Four years later, he was involved in the first of several legal disputes with the Duke of Hamilton and others over the location of his Clyde mills and the impact that the dam at the Blantyre Works was having on the river's salmon fishing. This process, raised in the Court of Session, required the preparation of plans to indicate the layout of the mills, sluices and dams. On this occasion, the Duke employed Peter Fleming to produce this plan over the winter of 1806–07, following a report he had commissioned on the dam earlier that year. Fleming had trained under William Kyle and was to publish a detailed large-scale plan of Glasgow soon after finishing this

Opposite and overleaf. Peter Fleming, *Plan of the River Clyde from and including the Blantyre Cotton Works* (1806–07)

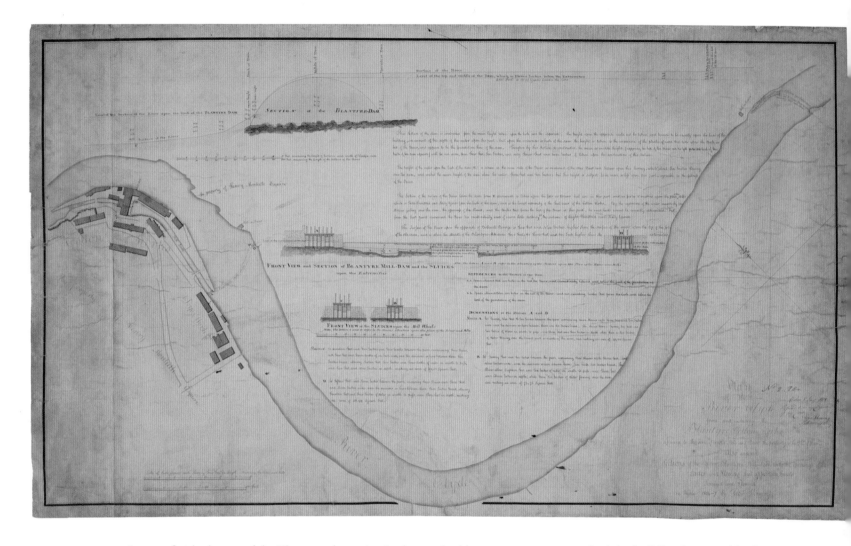

survey. A more finished copy of the Blantyre plan exists in the family papers housed in Hamilton Town House Library, while accompanying legal documents detail the action against Monteith compelling him to remove or lower his dam dyke. This litigation was to carry on well into the 1820s and Neil Robson was to prepare another plan and section of the dam in 1849.

Fleming's working manuscript depiction of the works is a valuable contemporary record of the building layout of both the cotton and dye works. It indicates that earlier mills had been established on the opposite bank of the river and that an older dam had been constructed upstream. However, it is the detail of the sectional views of the sluices and mill dam which captures the attention of anyone consulting it. In fact, the mapping of the river appears as more of a framework to the text. Not only does this underline the precision employed in

Opposite. Detail of cotton mills at New Lanark from William Forrest, *The county of Lanark* (1816)

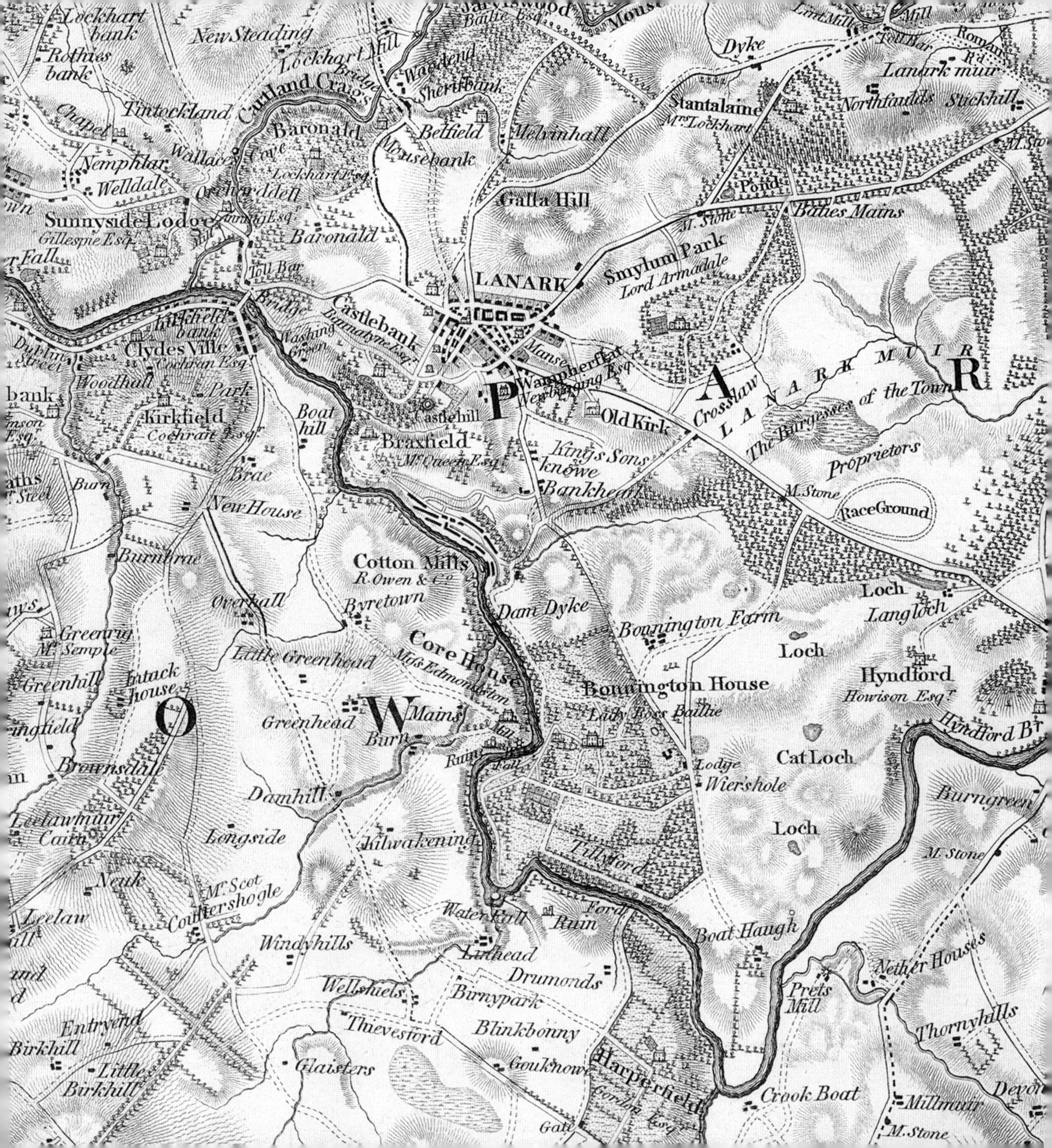

Lockhart bank

New Steading

Lockhart Hill

Rothes bank

Mill

Romana Rd

Tollbar

Dyke

Lanark muir

Cartland Craigs

Wandend

Sheriffbank

Stantalaine
Mr Lockhart

Northfaulds

Slickhill

Tintockland

Baronald

Belfield

Melvinhall

Chapel

Mousebank

Pond

Bathes Mains

Nemphlar

Welldale

Galla Hill

M. Stone

Sunnyside Lodge
Gillespie Esq.

Baronald

LANARK

Smylum Park
Lord Armadale

Orchardleh
Innis Esq.

Fall

Toll Bar

Bridge

Castlebank

Castlebank
Bannatyne Esq.

Manse

Wampherflat

A

Crosslaw

LANARK MUIR

Litchetbank

Clydes Ville
Cochran Esq.

Washing Green

P

Newbigging Esq.

The Burgesses of the Town

Dublin Street

bank

Woodhall

Park

Boat hill

Castlehill

Old Kirk

Proprietors

kirkfield
Cochran Esq.

Braxfield
Mc Queen Esq.

King's Sons

M. Stone

RaceGround

Brae

Icnowe

ths Steel

Burn

New House

Bankhead

Burnbrae

Cotton Mills
R. Owen & Co

Loch

Langloch

Overhall

Byretown

Dam Dyke

Bonnington Farm

Greenrig
Mr Semple

Little Greenhead

Core House
Miss Edmondstoun

Loch

Hyndford
Howison Esq.

Greenhall

Intack house

Mains

Bonnington House

O

W

Greenhead
Burn

Lady Ross Baillie

Cat Loch

Hyndford Br

Brownsdale

Lodge

Wiershole

Burngreen

Damhill

Ruin

Hall

Loch

Leelawmuir Cairn

Longside

Kilwakening

Tillyford

M. Stone

Neuk

Mr Scot

Water Fall

Ford

Ruin

Coultershogle

Boat Haugh

Leelaw

Windyhills

Linhead

Nether Houses

Entryend

Wellshiels

Drumonds

Prets Mill

Birkhill

Thievestord

Birnypark

Blinkbonny

Harperfield
Gordon Esq.

Thornyhills

Little Birkhill

Glaisters

Goukhow

Crook Boat

Millmuir

Gate

M. Stone

Devon

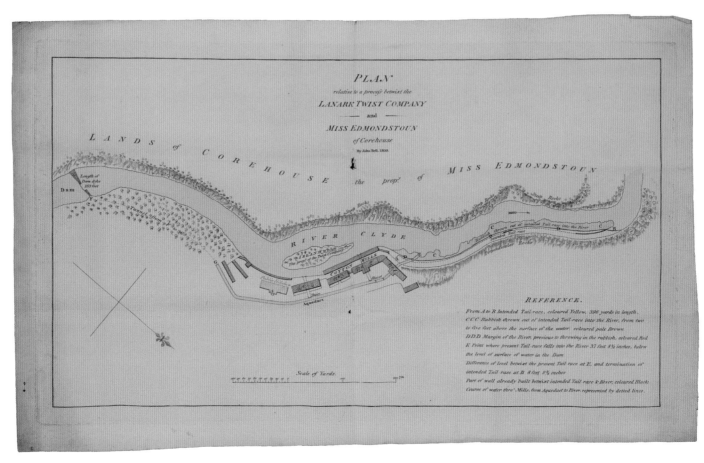

measuring the structural elements required for water power but it also reflects the gradual change in what was expected from a surveyor. The profession was moving away from a mere recording of land and entering the sphere of what was increasingly regarded as civil engineering. Fleming himself was subsequently to emigrate to Canada where he developed a career as a railway and road surveyor.

It is worthwhile noting that Blantyre's most famous son, the nineteenth-century missionary and explorer of central Africa David Livingstone (1813–73) was employed in the cotton mill at the Blantyre Works from the age of ten, along with his brother John, as a 'piecer', tying broken threads back on the spinning machines. In their early years, both men would have been very familiar with the river and the mills, dams and sluices depicted on this plan. The mills continued in operation until Monteith's company went into liquidation in 1904 and most of the buildings fell into disrepair. Little remains of the village other than Shuttle Row, Livingstone's birthplace, now listed as a national memorial and operated by the National Trust for Scotland.

Although the mill and village complex at New Lanark is better known, there are surprisingly few early plans of the area which identify the works in any detail. Although William

Above and opposite. John Bell, *Plan of mills at New Lanark relating to a Court of Session process between the Lanark Twist Company and Miss Edmondstoun* (1809)

PLAN

relative to a procefs betwixt the

LANARK TWIST COMPANY

—— and ——

MISS EDMONDSTOUN

of Corehouse

By John Bell, 1809.

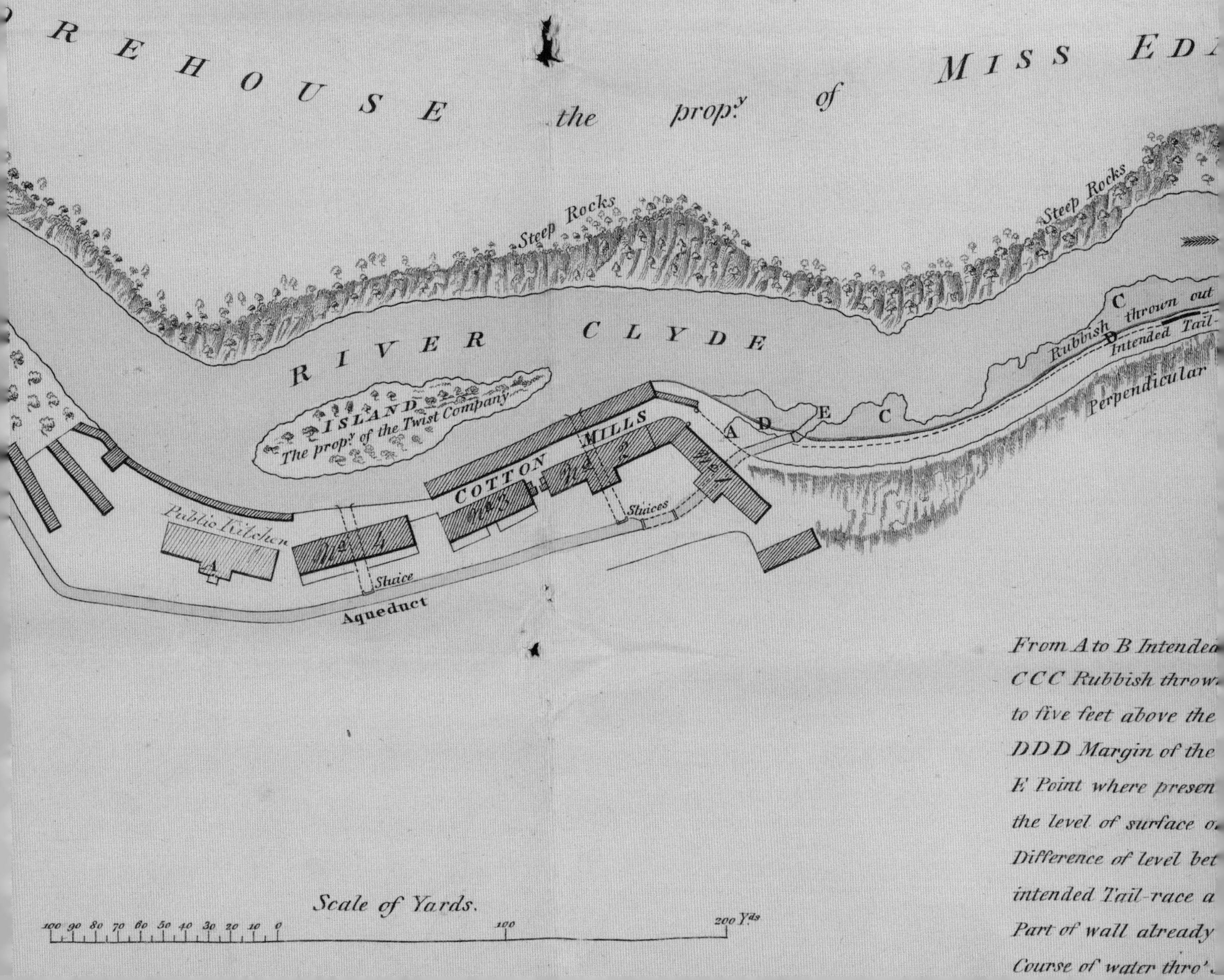

OREHOUSE   the   prop.y   of   MISS EDI

Steep Rocks

Steep Rocks

Rubbish thrown out

C

Intended Tail-

Perpendicular

RIVER   CLYDE

ISLAND
The prop.y of the Twist Company.

D

E

C

COTTON MILLS

Sluices

Public Kitchen

A

Sluice

Aqueduct

From A to B Intended

CCC Rubbish throw

to five feet above the

DDD Margin of the

E Point where presen

the level of surface o.

Difference of level bet

intended Tail-race a

Part of wall already

Course of water thro'

Scale of Yards.

100 90 80 70 60 50 40 30 20 10 0   100   200 Y.ds

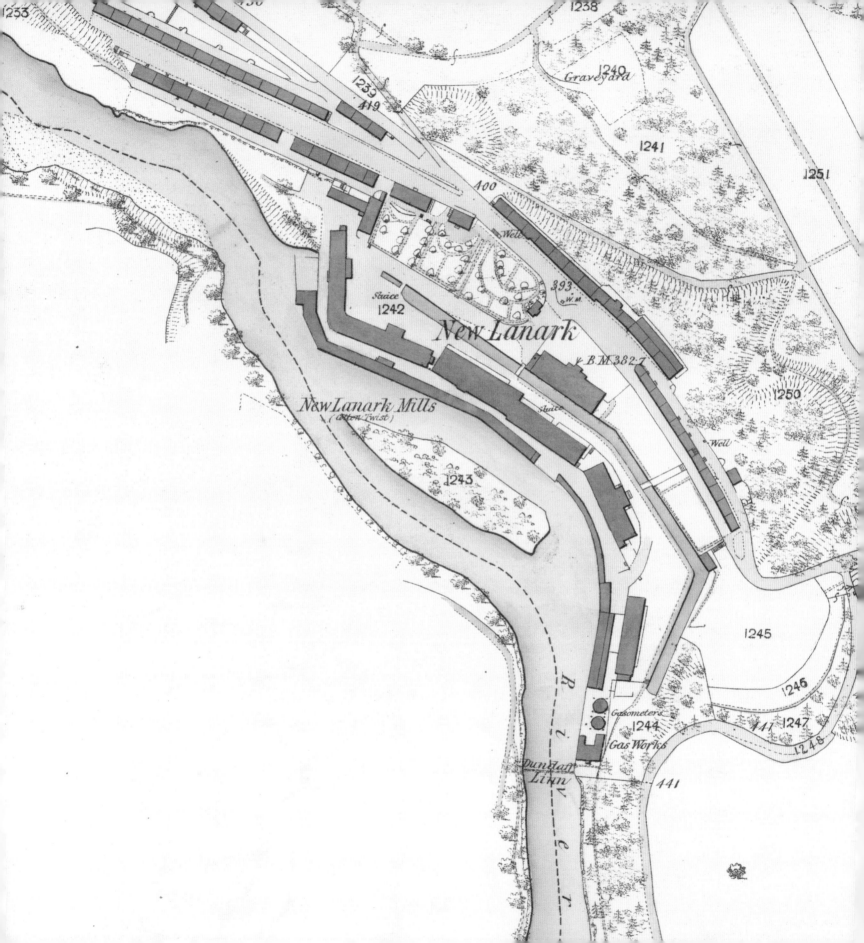

Forrest's map of Lanarkshire does provide a clear image of the general layout of the terraced housing and the main sluice, it cannot compare with Fleming's Blantyre plan as a source of information. As the extract shows, the county map does mark the dam dyke and that the mills were owned by Robert Owen and his company. However, this more detailed depiction of the mills, sluices and their situation in relation to the Clyde and the neighbouring estate of Corehouse does provide an illustration of the site in its formative years. The plan was prepared by John Bell, standing in for John Ainslie, in 1809 for the Corehouse owners, the Edmondstones, with whom Owen had a long-running dispute over the construction of a dam, trespass and the impact of the mills on their property. Bell was an experienced and able substitute for Ainslie and in the same year was to produce a detailed survey of the Tay. Disagreement over the original dam at New Lanark had led to Owen seeking an alternative solution in the extension of the tail race further downstream but, as the plan indicates, the excavation of material and subsequent deposition into the river had narrowed the channel. This affected the banks on the Corehouse side, resulting in a Court of Session process. Interestingly, a manuscript addition to the depiction indicates a 'public kitchen' where Owen's school building was located. Rarely an easy man to do business with, Owen failed to convince the court, compensation was awarded to the Edmondstones and the extended sluice was never finished.

Like many Ordnance Survey large-scale plans of the mid nineteenth century, the first edition 25-inch coverage of New Lanark is only indicated on the relevant Lanark parish sheet. This has no mapping of the Corehouse estate, situated in neighbouring Lesmahagow, because the maps were produced on a parish-by-parish basis. Nonetheless, the relevant plan, surveyed in 1858 and published six years later, records definitively the individual buildings of the cotton mills, the main sluice, the gas works and gasometers, Dundaff Linn and the mill dam further upstream. What comes through quite clearly even in this rather

Working dress uniforms of Sappers and Miners, 1854 from T.W.J. Connolly, *The History of the Corps of Royal Sappers and Miners* (1855)

restricted record of the settlement is its position in a predominantly rural setting and emphasises a degree of remoteness which can still be experienced today.

This final illustration is of the contemporary working dress uniform of the men who prepared such plans and comes from the standard history of the Corps of Royal Sappers and Miners written only three years before this plan was surveyed. It shows the instruments used in such work – in particular a brass transit theodolite – and a Royal Engineer officer (in black coat) with his field book in hand. Significantly, all three visible cap badges carry the same grenade motif, indicating that both officers and other ranks were all part of the one unit.

Opposite. Detail from the Ordnance Survey, *25-inch Lanarkshire, First Edition, Sheet 32.3* showing New Lanark (1864)

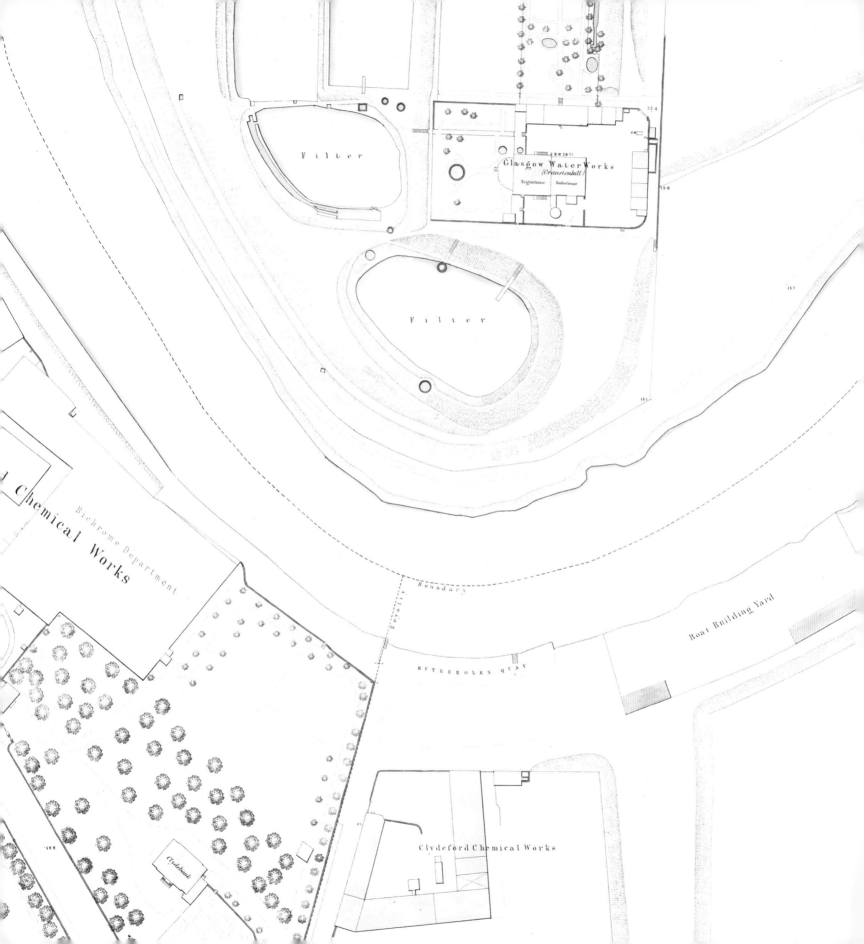

F i l t e r

22 4

Glasgow Water Works
(Cranstonhill)

Enginehouse   Boilerhouse

19 6

F i l t e r

157

151

d Chemical Works

Bichrome Department

Chemical Works

Boundary

Boat Building Yard

Royalty

RUTHERGLEN QUAY

Clydebank

598

Clydeford Chemical Works

CHAPTER 30

Shipbuilding and the river at Rutherglen

While Rutherglen developed initially as a weaving and mining community, it changed to a more industrialised landscape during the nineteenth century as manufacturing spread outwards from the east end of Glasgow. Being located on the Clyde, it was well placed for the location of a boatbuilding business and in 1856 Thomas Bollen Seath (1820–1903) established a small yard close to the former ferry crossing at Rutherglen Quay. Seath had been born in Prestonpans in East Lothian but the family moved to Glasgow while he was still a boy. His father worked for a coastal shipping company and Thomas was to follow him, showing an early aptitude and commitment despite a childhood injury to his spine. Described as 'a shrewd and practical Scot, keen in business', he had first begun shipbuilding beside the mouth of the Kelvin, on the west bank to the north of Tod and Macgregor's Meadowside yard.

From here, he launched the passenger ferry *Artizan* which commenced its service on Queen Victoria's birthday in 1856 by carrying 800 passengers from Rutherglen to the old weir at Glasgow Green. At this pre-railway date, there was no alternative means of carrying large numbers of people, and in one four-month period the vessel carried no fewer than 36,000 passengers. Immediately after its launch, Seath moved his business to Rutherglen and, in recognition of its new home, one of the first craft

built was named *Royal Burgh*, as a replacement for *Artizan*. For more than 40 years, a remarkable marine enterprise flourished here, producing a wide range of over 260 tugs, barges, coasters, ferry boats, and paddle and screw steamers constructed on what is a very constricted part of the river.

Seath's yard is possibly best known for the celebrated *Clutha* ferry boats, basically shallow draught omnibuses built for the Clyde Navigation Trust and employed in transporting commuters up and down the Clyde. Six were delivered in 1884 and, by 1896 twelve ferries were conveying in the region of 2.5 million customers each year. These vessels could carry 200–350 passengers and a regular half-hour service plied between Victoria Bridge and Whiteinch. However, the opening of an established service on the Glasgow Subway in 1897 and, more immediately, the development of the electric tram network resulted in the withdrawal of the ferry service in 1903.

Interestingly, in 1890 Seath himself had built five electrically propelled passenger vessels specifically for the River Seine and the success of the yard was based on his innovative designs for small vessels, influenced by direct experience, attention to detail and a high standard of workmanship. The quality of the vessels was best defined by the long life of several Seath craft. At least one steamer, *Enterprize*, was sold for assembly in Singapore and

Opposite and overleaf. Sequence of two editions of Ordnance Survey, *1:500 Glasgow town plan, Sheet X.3.10* (1857–58, 1892–94) and three *Lanarkshire 25-inch editions, Sheet X.3* (1895, 1913 and 1935) to indicate boatbuilding at Rutherglen

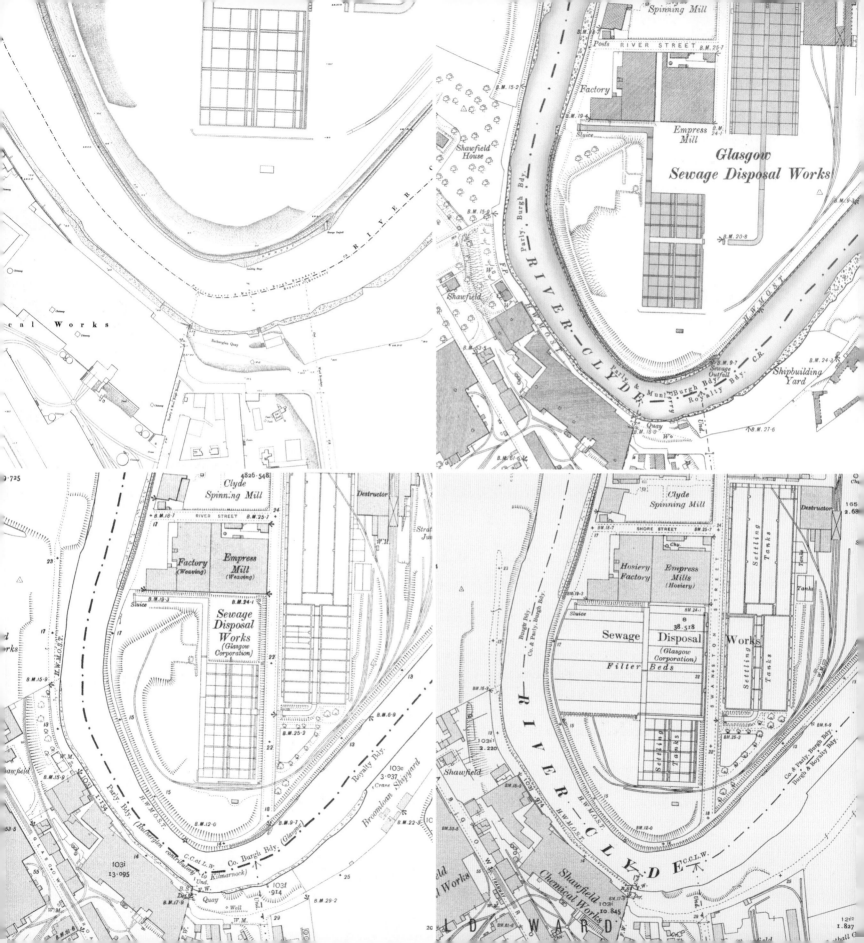

J. Millar, *Paddle steamer 'Bonnie Princess'* (1882) built at the Seath shipyard, Rutherglen

the motor vessel *Nelcebee,* launched in 1883 and reassembled at Port Adelaide, survives today as the only nineteenth-century sea-going commercial steamship extant in Australia, forming part of the South Australia Maritime Museum collection.

When steamers were required for passenger services in the Lake District, the company successfully developed the transportation of vessels in sections for rebuilding and launching where required. The oldest boat on Lloyd's Yacht Register, *Esperance,* was one such. Built for H.W. Schneider, chairman of Barrow steelworks, this steam yacht became best known as Captain Flint's houseboat in Arthur Ransome's classic children's novel *Swallows and Amazons* and was later used as such by the BBC in their film adaptation. Other surviving vessels include the Ullswater steamers, *Raven* and *Lady of the Lake.* Customers included King Mongkut of Siam, who ordered *Little Eastern,* William Robertson, William Buchanan, James Steel & Sons, and Patrick Henderson through whom Seath built several smacks for the Scottish-owned Irrawaddy Flotilla Company.

Seath died in 1903 and is buried in the city's Southern Necropolis, not far from the site where he introduced shipbuilding as an industry. Vessels continued to be produced in the area. Prior to moving to Clynder on the Rosneath peninsula in 1901, E. & G. McGruer built a number of sailing yachts at Rutherglen for private Scottish owners, mostly to designs by Alfred Mylne. The Rutherglen yard was taken over by William Chalmers & Co. who continued to construct coasting steamers

and barges, as well as a string of naval auxiliary boom defences up until 1920. By this time, it was also called Broomloan shipyard. Records indicate that the last firm to occupy the yard was Rennie, Ritchie & Newport. Today the site is occupied by a small industrial estate and, upstream, the Rutherglen Cruising Club has a jetty still in use, accessed at the end of the appropriately named Seath Road.

This sequence of Ordnance Survey maps emphasises how much industry was being carried on along the banks of the Clyde in this area but, surprisingly, the depiction of the boatyard is much less detailed than that of many other buildings. The maps cover the period 1864 to 1935, by which time a yard is no longer marked, and show the gradual encroachment of works, railways and business premises on land once occupied by country houses such as Clydebank. Across the river from the Seath yard were the filter beds and engine house of the Cranstonhill Water Works, which pumped water filtered through sand to the east end of the city, while lying to the west were James and John White's extensive Shawfield Chemical Works, at one time the largest of their kind in the world.

What these maps do not show is the major obstacle for any sizeable vessel using the Clyde in the Rutherglen area – namely, the tidal weir across the river which maintains a deep, wide channel of water through Glasgow Green. Passage is only possible at high tide which restricts vessel access to only about seven or eight instances each month.

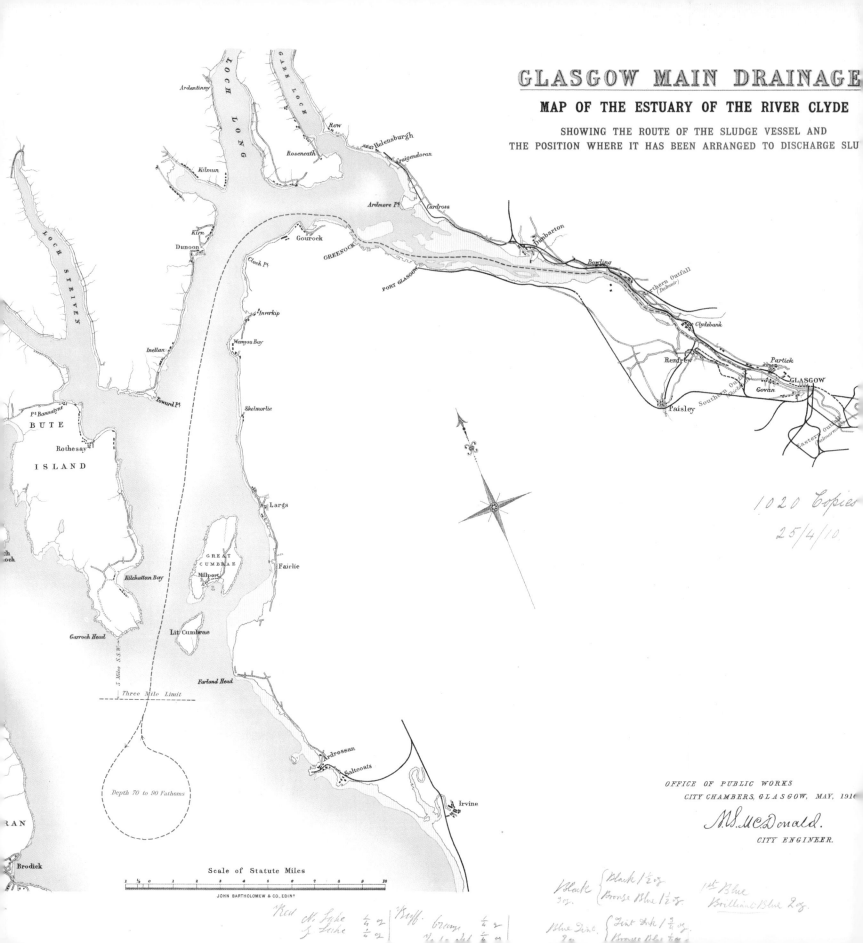

GLASGOW MAIN DRAINAGE

MAP OF THE ESTUARY OF THE RIVER CLYDE

SHOWING THE ROUTE OF THE SLUDGE VESSEL AND
THE POSITION WHERE IT HAS BEEN ARRANGED TO DISCHARGE SLU

1020 Copies
25/4/10

OFFICE OF PUBLIC WORKS
CITY CHAMBERS, GLASGOW, MAY, 1910

M.S. McDonald
CITY ENGINEER.

Scale of Statute Miles

JOHN BARTHOLOMEW & CO. EDIN.

CHAPTER 31

Dealing with the side effects of a growing population: plans for sewage disposal

Today, there are many aspects of life which we take for granted. Nowhere is this more evident than in the provision of fresh and clean water in our homes and the removal of waste. These benefits have been hard won. Like many other parts of Great Britain, the impact of a rapidly expanding industrial base combined with an exponential population growth during the mid nineteenth century in several towns in Clydesdale had serious implications for public health and hygiene. As the largest urban area, this was most noticeable in Glasgow itself. During the 1840s in particular, a series of major epidemics raised public awareness of the need for better housing conditions and the appropriate disposal of human waste. As was noted at the time, 'dunghills lie in the vicinity of dwellings, and from the extremely defective sewerage filth of every kind constantly accumulates'.

James Pagan, avid historian of the city's history and subsequently editor of the *Glasgow Herald*, highlighted the impact on the purity of the Clyde. He recorded in 1851 'we laid down just as many drains and sewers as would carry our night-soil to the nearest stream – and thus, instead of poisoning the air that we breathed, we poisoned the water that we drank. The effect of some thousands of water-closets pouring their contents into the Clyde cannot but be odious in the extreme; and every one may have felt that in summer days, after a long drought,

the river, from this cause, literally sweats abomination, and we have more than once seen people sickened from it on board the steamers.' The condition of the river was lampooned in the final verse of a popular song published in 1875. In a style somewhat akin to the poetry of William Topaz McGonagall (1825–1902), 'Bonnie Banks of Clyde' contains these lines:

> At length we reach the city, where the Clyde runs not so clear,
> And the awful smell arising makes a fellow feel quite queer,
> Especially at Jamaica Bridge it would make your spirits droop,
> To see the water here as thick as Cooking Depot soup.

The damage to what James Deas described as the character of the river's salubrity from both industrial pollution and domestic waste was obvious and, despite the improvement in the provision of clean water as a result of John Frederick Bateman's Loch Katrine scheme, improvements in sanitation, drains and the treatment of sewage only properly came into place at the end of the nineteenth century.

The construction of underground railway lines in the city resulted in a need to reconstruct Glasgow's sewers and the main drainage scheme was divided into three areas, each with its own treatment works. The extensive Dalmarnock sewage works which occupies a loop enclosed by the River Clyde in southern

Opposite. John Bartholomew, *Map of the Estuary of the River Clyde showing the route of the sludge vessel and the position where it has been arranged to discharge sludge* (1910)

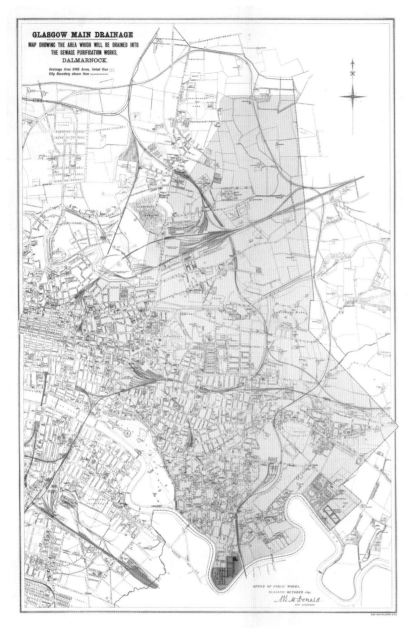

John Bartholomew, *Glasgow Main Drainage. Map showing the area which will be drained into the sewage purification works, Dalmarnock* (1895)

Glasgow was mapped in detail. When opened in 1894, it was Scotland's first large-scale site designed to deal with untreated waste and continues in operation today. In 1904, a second works was opened at Dalmuir, followed by another plant at Shieldhall in 1910. The Dalmarnock works were designed by Gustav Alsing (1836–96), a Dane who had settled in England and who was a leading expert in chemical precipitation. He introduced several improvements in the method of disposal and was retained by the city authorities as consulting engineer. The plan was prepared by the Edinburgh cartographic firm of John Bartholomew who were contracted to provide a wide range of work for the city authorities from the late 1880s onwards. They seem to have worked closely with Alexander Beith McDonald (1847–1915), city engineer and surveyor from 1890 to 1914, and the firm's archive has several examples of Glasgow plans covering street improvements, parks and gardens, all with McDonald's name appended. This depiction is no exception and dates from August 1903 when more than 2,000 copies were printed. It indicates the various precipitation tanks and filter beds of the works but also marks the effluent channel and its outflow immediately opposite Shawfield House, in addition to the various railway sidings of the Caledonian Railway where wagons were filled with solid waste for disposal. Like many other large-scale Bartholomew maps of this period, it has been based on the Ordnance Survey 6-inch map but, more importantly, it provides an image of the industrial development of the east end of Glasgow.

In association with the overall scheme to handle Glasgow's waste, Bartholomew's also prepared this general map for the city's Office of Public Works one year after the opening of the Dalmarnock works to identify the area which would drain into its purification tanks. It highlights in light red the 3,465-acre drainage area in the east of the city, as well as the plant itself. Although this covers a considerable area, much of the land in the northern portion of the map is noticeably devoid of housing, particularly north-east of the railway engineering works at Cowlairs and St Rollox. The drainage area does extend to part of Blythswood but omits most of the city centre south of George Square and that part of the old town immediately east of Salt-

John Bartholomew, *Glasgow Main Drainage. Plan of Dalmarnock sewage works* (1903)

Detail of the discharge area of the sludge vessel

market. The map is markedly similar in style to another document commissioned by McDonald two years later for the City Improvement Trust where various lands to be acquired for clearance were highlighted as part of the scheme to reduce overcrowding and improve the living conditions in the older part of the city. Such plans as these emphasise the growing involvement by local government in a wide range of social, health and other civic elements of urban life.

By the use of settlement tanks at Dalmarnock, solid waste could be pressed and subsequently sold as sludge cake, marketed as agricultural fertiliser. However, not all by-products could be so utilised and, by the early twentieth century, surplus sludge was pumped into purpose-built boats which transported the material downriver on a daily basis and discharged it into the main channel of the Firth of Clyde off Garroch Head. It was only in 1998 that a European Commission Directive, designed to combat adverse effects on the environment, prevented such dumping. The third map in this sequence shows the estuary, the route of the sludge vessel and the location in the firth where it had been designated that material could be discharged, as agreed with the Board of Trade. Several versions of this map

were produced with various dates starting in 1898. Interestingly, these earlier versions do not identify the Dalmarnock works and had very short print runs. Later printings of over 1,000 copies were to be published. As the map shows, discharge could only take place more than 3 miles south of Garroch Head and where the channel depth was between 70 and 90 fathoms. It also indicates the points of outfall from the three sewage works but, due to the inaccessibility of Dalmarnock, other steps had to be taken. In consequence, in 1914 a pipeline nearly 10 kilometres long was laid beneath the city's streets to connect with Shieldhall, facilitating the pumping of untreated material there for subsequent marine disposal.

Over the twentieth century, Glasgow Corporation employed a sequence of seven vessels specifically designed to transport the waste downriver, including the *Gardyloo* on charter from Lothian Regional Council in the 1970s. To more delicate constitutions, it may come as a surprise that there was a tradition of carrying organised groups of passengers on board during the summer months. Only the *Shieldhall*, built by Lobnitz of Renfrew in 1954, survives in British waters, now preserved and frequently used for excursions in the Solent.

Mess.rs Charles Tennant & Comp.y, St. Rollox.

see Appendix.

Singeing by Gas.

Mess.rs Hall's Singeing Work, West Bath Street.

up Dock.

CHAPTER 32

The Hammers 'Ding-Dong': shipbuilding at Glasgow

The story of the Clyde has been inextricably linked with ship-building for nearly 200 years and has been discussed in depth by many authors in a range of studies covering yards, vessels and shipping companies. These describe the achievements, the highs and the lows of an industry that gave the world the term 'Clyde-built' and has seared its place into an inherited vision of west central Scotland to this day. While there is little need for a reiteration of the history of this relationship, some discussion of the mapping of the Glasgow shipyards may be valuable in supplementing the descriptions of the improvements to the channel of the Clyde.

The first shipyard to be established on the upper reaches of the Clyde at Glasgow was that of John Barclay, opened in 1818 at Stobcross on the north bank a little more than a mile west of the Broomielaw. This site was an ideal location where a gentle slope ran down to the river at a point with sufficient depth for the launching of larger ships. His son Robert subsequently added slipways to the facilities thereby enabling the hulls of vessels to be inspected. This was particularly valuable at a time when there were no dry docks available. This image by an unknown artist illustrates the slip-dock of the Stobcross yard and appears within a manuscript account of the Barony parish prepared by James Hopkirk of Dalbeth. Containing an important and unique collection of ink drawings of the city, Hopkirk's 1827 account provides a valuable record of the changes he had seen over the previous 40 years. Unlike other illustrations of docks, which tend to display crowds celebrating the launch of a ship, this small sketch provides a very clear picture of several significant features relating to local craft and the river at this period.

Initially, much of Barclay's business was involved in ship repair and it is likely that this vignette illustrates teams of men working on the hull of what is a comparatively small sailing vessel constructed in wood, possibly in the process of careening – a procedure during which barnacles could be removed to lessen their impact on navigation – or repairs to any damage or rot could be made below the water line. The latter is more likely as the workforce seem to be in the middle of either removing from or placing against the hull a sequence of wooden frames while a larger party may be in the process of hauling the ship. Given the detail of the vessel's superstructure, it does not appear to be under construction. Although materials would change and steam-boats would increasingly dominate work on the Clyde, wooden-built craft would continue to need attention for a considerable time to come. In addition, the size of the particular boat once again emphasises that much of the early construction and repair

Opposite. Sketch of Stobcross slip-dock from James Hopkirk's manuscript Statistical Account of the Barony Parish of Glasgow (1827)

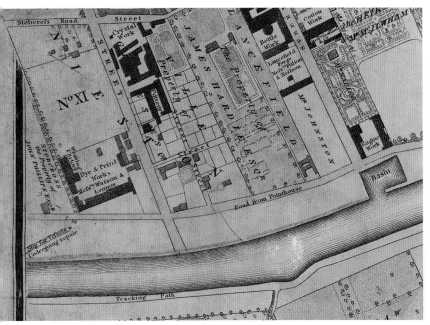

Detail from David Smith's *Plan of the City of Glasgow and its Environs* (1828) showing Napier's engine work and basin and slip-dock (at edge of map)

business concerned vessels with a smaller tonnage involved in the coasting trade. One other feature of the drawing is the comparative narrowness of the river itself, indicating that it was drawn before the works of the later century which considerably widened the channel. Elsewhere in the volume, Hopkirk included an illustration of David Napier's fitting-out basin at Lancefield Quay occupied by two paddle steamers.

This first map extract indicates the north bank of the river and is taken from David Smith's 1828 single-sheet reduction of his earlier plan of Glasgow. It is one of the very few contemporary maps to show any detail of the emerging signs of shipbuilding in Glasgow but clearly indicates the single slipway for ship repair at Stobcross and Napier's basin lying beside his engineering works at Lancefield. By this date, Napier had begun shipbuilding, but what is most striking about the map is the relatively suburban location of these original industries, surrounded as they are by parks and gardens. In fact, all of the neighbouring businesses springing up in the area appear to be

decidedly small-scale. The map also indicates an early ferry crossing at Springfield linked to Tod's cotton works, as well as the delineation of the west end of the harbour which brings to focus the subsequent difficulties created by the juxtaposition of the shipyards with the harbour quays.

Over the following decades, many plans were prepared to indicate the river and the industries which grew up along its banks, but relatively few have survived to show the various shipyards towards the end of their heyday. This unique manuscript draft of the harbour of Glasgow in 1955 was prepared by Henry Alan Moisley, a member of the Department of Geography at the University of Glasgow, and a version was included in the Glasgow volume of the *Third Statistical Account of Scotland*, published in 1958. It is considerably larger than the black and white figure indicating riverside land use which eventually accompanied the *Account's* extensive text on shipbuilding and marine engineering. The later reduction was drawn by Ian Kinniburgh, another Glasgow geographer and, while faithful to the original, its size reduced the clarity of Moisley's original.

The immediate impression of the plan is the complete occupation of both banks downstream from the Broomielaw by various shipbuilding and engineering industries, particularly on the north bank. In addition, the density and concentration of businesses within what was no more than a 6-mile stretch is clearly seen. Slipways and graving docks are identified but, more importantly, the larger size gives a greater impression of the scale of operations in the harbour, as well as the segregation between the industrial and the port facilities. All the major yards are named, from Harland and Wolff at Govan to John Brown's at Clydebank, while companies involved in engineering are identified with their product, such as Bull's metal propeller foundry at Yoker. The Geography Department was subsequently to develop an international reputation for teaching cartography but Moisley's earlier cartography provides a concise image of the Clyde at Glasgow when it was still an important artery.

University staff from several disciplines made a considerable contribution to the *Third Statistical Account* of the city but, apart from a brief mention of air service competition, a perusal of the discussion of the industries on the river written by Andrew

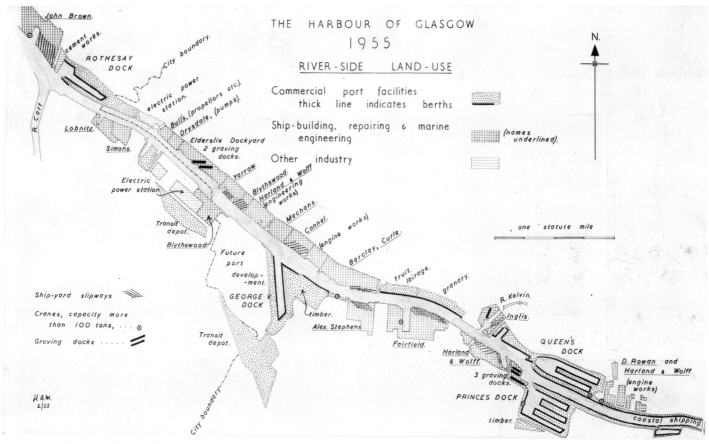

H.A. Moisley, *Map of River Clyde showing shipyards, docks and other engineering works* (1955)

M. Robb, emeritus professor of naval architecture, and other chapters gives little impression of the radical and devastating changes which Clydeside would face in the following two decades. In that same year, the British Association for the Advancement of Science met in the city and again the bulk of the text for the associated survey produced for the occasion, *The Glasgow Region*, was written by university staff. Moisley wrote a chapter on the city's spheres of influence and was also partly responsible for an excursion leaflet of notes on the port installations and industries along the Clyde which contained graphs on the river's depth, in addition to details of various ships' engines and vessels launched. He was also the co-author of the *Third Statistical Account* volume covering the counties of Renfrew and Bute and subsequently became professor in the Geography Department at Ahmadu Bello University in Nigeria in 1963.

Today, there is something of an ambivalent attitude to the river as it flows through the reaches once occupied by those docks and shipyards. While much riparian redevelopment has taken place, vestiges of the river's former industrial heritage remain, most notably the derelict but nationally unique Govan graving docks, now the subject of a vocal preservation campaign for retention as a maritime heritage park. Regardless of the outcome of this particular issue, the integration of the river into the lives of those citizens who live on its banks remains markedly more tentative than in many other European cities.

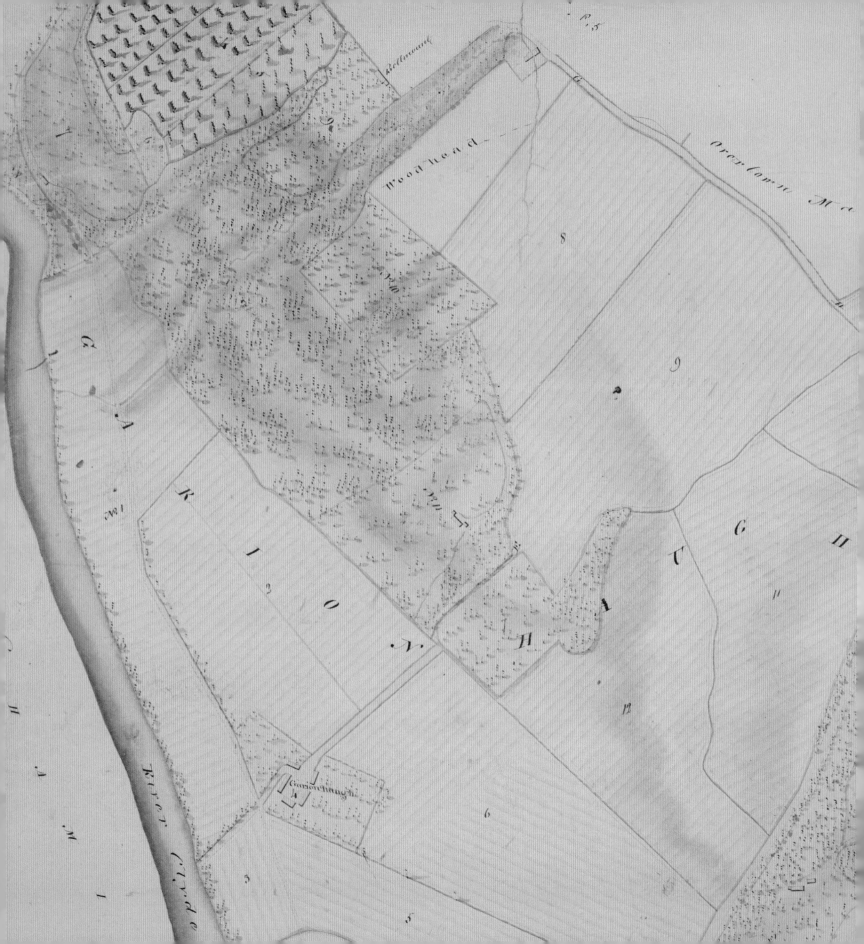

CHAPTER 33

'It borders the orchards of Lanark so fair'

During much of the twentieth century, that part of Clydesdale lying between Lanark and Hamilton was celebrated for its fruit growing, nurseries and orchards, continuing a type of land use which, according to accounts, may go as far back as the fifth century. Glasgow's orchards were mentioned in the text of the Blaeu atlas and it is no coincidence that the title cartouches of both atlas maps covering the Lanarkshire wards display figures carrying baskets of fruit.

John Naismith devoted a short chapter on gardens and orchards in his 1806 work, *General View of the Agriculture of the County of Clydesdale* in which he emphasised the importance of the local markets to the cultivation of vegetables before discussing the range of fruit produced in the Clydesdale orchards. Although the bulk of these were relatively small, they focused on growing apples, pears and plums. By this date, he estimated that over 340 acres were devoted to fruit trees but warned that late frosts frequently affected the crop. The Napoleonic Wars appear to have stimulated a new interest in horticulture leading to the establishment of the Clydesdale Fruit Merchants' Corporation in 1809. The benefits of a well-drained sunny slope were also touched on by various contributors to the *New Statistical Account of Scotland* where the development beyond the large gardens of country houses indicated an extension to more commercial ventures. However, even at that date, Revd James

Clason commented on the impact of foreign imports, albeit from England and Ireland, on the value of local orchards. In a telling subsequent comment, the writer observes that 'orchards if neglected in regard to culture soon die out, and any fruit they produce is small and destitute of flavour'. The precarious nature of the market worked against a more widespread cultivation. Nonetheless, in the general observations on Lanarkshire written for the *Account* in 1845, the charm of the area is highlighted thus, 'From Lanark to Hamilton is one continued orchard; and when the fruit-trees are in blossom, the drive through is one of the most delightful that can be enjoyed.'

This attractive plan of the farms of Garrion-haugh and Garrion Mill dates from the beginning of the nineteenth century and was originally part of the Coltness House archive. Although undated and showing no indication of the surveyor, it identifies a ford across the Clyde at this point, suggesting that it was drawn before the completion of Garrion Bridge in 1817 as part of the Ayr–Edinburgh turnpike road. While much of the plan is coloured to indicate various land uses, the title specifically mentions orchards and it delineates several others, including Pathhead and Bellmount on the south-facing slope of the valley. The regularity of the fruit tree plantings contrasts with the mapping of natural woodland. Regardless of such identification, the accompanying table of contents clearly shows that the

Opposite. Plan of the Garrion-haugh and Garrion Mill Farms (c.1810)

acreage of land under orchard was comparatively small.

Fruit tended to be sold by auction, generally for the Glasgow or other nearby markets, and during the second half of the nineteenth century the growing urbanisation of west central Scotland created a demand which led to a growth in the distribution of fruit production in the valley. In 1879–80, Robert and William Scott set up the Clydesdale Preserve Works in Carluke, originally to preserve the excess fruit produced by their Orchard Estate. By the beginning of the twentieth century, Clydesdale was considered to be Scotland's principal fruit-growing area, with the cultivation of strawberries, gooseberries and currants exceeding even that of Perthshire. By 1908, over 2,250 acres were devoted to soft fruit with another 765 acres under orchards.

This unusually coloured map of the central Clyde valley comes from sheet 73 of the Land Utilisation Survey of Britain, which was the first national systematic assessment of land cover and use. This survey was compiled between 1931 and 1935 under the direction of L. Dudley Stamp, subsequently professor of geography at the London School of Economics and one of the most significant British geographers of the twentieth century. Based on the contemporary Ordnance Survey Popular Edition sheets, this map covers an area entitled 'Falkirk and Motherwell' and includes the important fruit-growing stretch of the Clyde between Hazelbank and Hamilton. Most of the surveying was carried out by volunteers, in particular schoolchildren and students, under the direction of County Directors of Education, in the case of Lanarkshire, R.C.T. Mair. Fieldwork was based on 6-inch sheets as these could be used to identify individual fields and the detail was subsequently reduced to a 1-inch map. Stamp's vision was to use the exercise not only as a valuable educational experience for children and a useful training in a sense of wider responsibility but also to be independent of any central government involvement. Despite the perennial problems associated with financing such a project, the surveying itself was remarkably successful, with 90 per cent of the work being completed within three years. The intervention of war in 1939 delayed publication and there were major losses when the premises of G.W. Bacon, one of the publishers, were completely destroyed by enemy bombing. Eventually, 34 of the Scottish maps covering much of the lowland areas were published by the beginning of the 1950s and these were to prove of value in post-war planning.

The colour scheme of the survey was quite simple: light green for meadow and permanent grass, brown for arable, yellow for heath or hill pasture, dark green for woodland, purple for gardens and red for urban or agriculturally unproductive areas. Within this system, individual categories were further subdivided by the use of symbols; for example, gardens were classified as being either sufficiently large enough to produce fruit, vegetables and flowers, or nurseries or orchards. The map clearly indicates an extensive purple ribbon of such horticultural areas running south-east from Crossford, around Dalserf and Rosebank, and on the south-facing slopes on either side of Horsley Brae. This density of specialisation is even more noticeable on the relevant Ordnance Survey series mapping of the period. Although the Survey's policy was to publish new sheets based on the National Grid from 1945, updated county mapping continued to be issued for certain areas. This extract from the 25-inch survey of Lanarkshire revised in 1940 was not published until 1946 but indicates a considerable acreage of land under orchards and glasshouses in the area immediately surrounding Crossford. The regularity of the tree symbols indicating fruit growing contrasts with the natural woodland of, for example, the valley of the Braidwood Burn.

In many respects, this map marked the end of the period of significant local fruit growing. Since the 1950s, the impact of competition from global markets, the growing domination of the food retail industry by supermarkets and the cheap provision of fruit from overseas growers have combined to undermine what was a relatively small-scale local production. The successors of the Scott preserve business no longer grow their own fruit for factory processing and the focus of production and ownership has changed. Poor orchard management, a lack of financial incentive or resources, the loss of land to property development and the decline in local horticulture have made considerable changes to the local landscape. While far less dramatic than the decline in shipbuilding and engineering downriver, this

Land Utilisation Survey, *Sheet 73 Falkirk and Motherwell* (1945)
showing details of orchards at Crossford running south-east

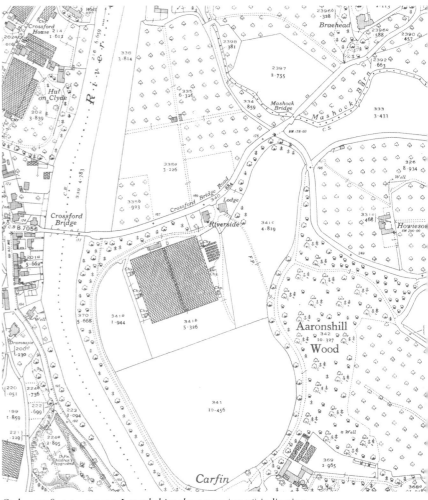

Ordnance Survey, *1:2500 Lanarkshire sheet 25.5* (1946) indicating
orchards and greenhouses

change has also had a considerable impact on what was certainly
a distinctive feature of Clydesdale.

Today, the Clyde valley landscape is one of garden centres,
operating more as retail outlets for local day-trippers and
frequently reliant on imported plants, as well as some farming
and forestry. The few fragments of commercially unviable fruit
growing tend to reflect its marked decline at the end of the
twentieth century, with only eight sites recorded in the most
recent survey with orchards of more than 100 trees. Soft fruit
is no longer grown commercially. The area remains Scotland's
best example of valley orchard land use and efforts are being
made to reverse what appears to be a terminal decline, largely
through the activities of the Clyde Valley Orchards Cooperative
which seeks to preserve this important element of a nationally
historic environment at a time when biodiversity and sustain-
ability, as characterised by local produce and varieties, have
become topics of international concern.

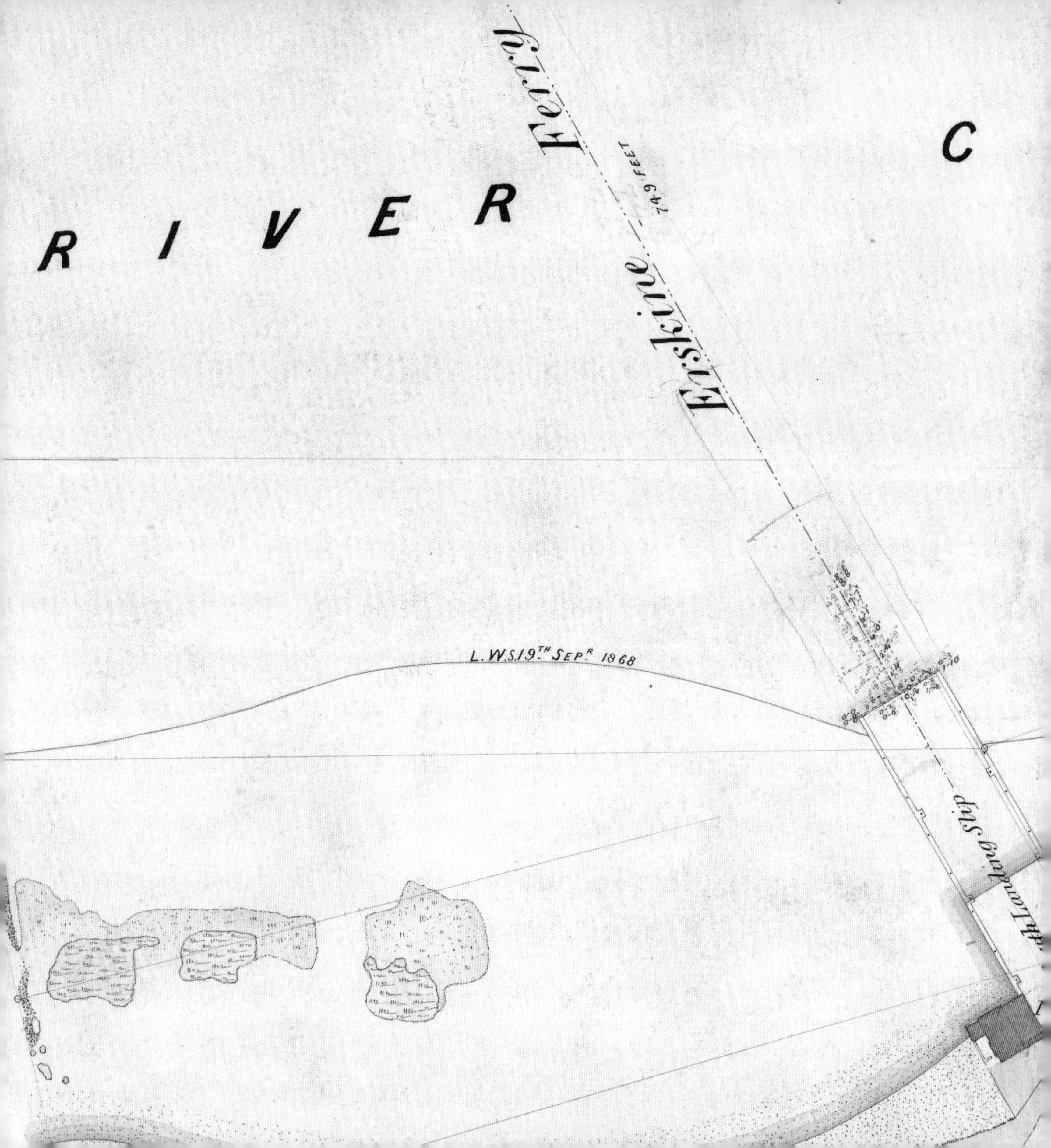

R I V E R

C

Erskine Ferry

749 FEET

L.W.S.19TH SEPR 1868

Landing Slip

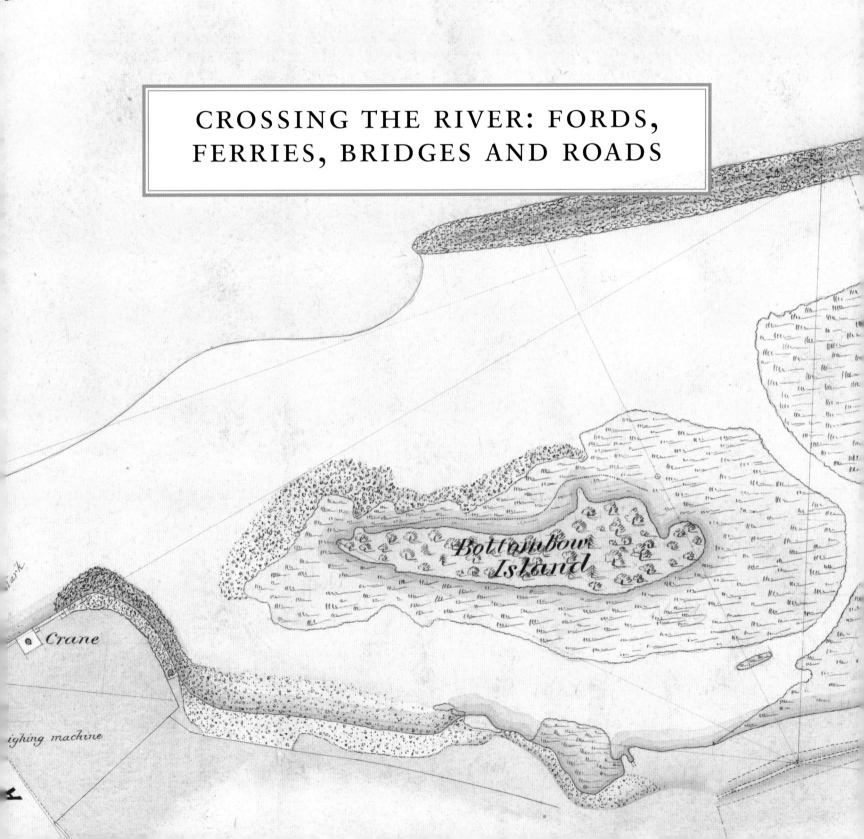

CROSSING THE RIVER: FORDS, FERRIES, BRIDGES AND ROADS

Y D E

Bottombow Island

Crane

ighing machine

CHAPTER 34

Early river crossings
around Glasgow

When the first edition of the Geological Survey of Scotland's 6-inch coverage of the Glasgow area was published in 1870, the map, somewhat unusually, indicated the location of a number of sites where Neolithic dug-out canoes had been discovered. These had been found not only on the river's banks but also at Glasgow Cross and near Drygate. Whether or not this indicates a considerably wider area of flooding or a marked variation in the channel in prehistoric times, it does show that the river was navigated from the earliest times and that it required some method to negotiate a crossing. Presently, there are about 72 bridges of different types of construction which cater for a variety of means of transport crossing the Clyde on its 176-kilometre journey to the estuary. This chapter considers the range of crossings displayed on a selection of maps over time. The earlier discussion of the Pont manuscript map of Lanarkshire drawn at the end of the sixteenth century highlighted the comparatively small number of bridges which crossed the Clyde, but the map omits any indication of the considerable number of fords which were undoubtedly in use. Many of these may have been seasonally dependent on water levels in the river but, given its length and the density of population suggested by the number of place names, these would have been a significant means of crossing a body of water which probably posed more

challenges to transport than provided a useful means of communication, particularly upriver from Glasgow.

This unsigned plan is most likely to be the earliest detailed depiction of a sizeable part of Glasgow and shows the original Old Bridge, the city's crossing for more than 400 years. Constructed in stone by the authority of William Rae, Bishop of Glasgow from 1339 to 1367, it linked the growing town with the barony of Gorbals and replaced an earlier wooden structure. For its day, it must have been an impressive sight, being a little over 400 feet long with a gentle hump. Unlike some later illustrations, the plan is a faithful record of its original eight arches. Over time, its structure was altered as the weight of traffic increased. The two northern arches were infilled in the 1770s and, in 1821, Thomas Telford was commissioned to widen it. Eventually, scouring by the river had so eroded the supporting piers that it was replaced 30 years later by the present Victoria Bridge, designed by James Walker and now the city's oldest surviving road bridge. Of possibly greater interest is the depiction on the plan of both a horse ford lying to the east of the bridge and the city's Water Port at its north end. The presence of the ford is another indication of the shallow nature of the Clyde at this time and, interestingly, it is shown leading directly to a cattle enclosure on the north bank, suggesting it may have

Opposite and overleaf. Plan of part of the city of Glasgow (1764)
showing Glasgow Bridge and the horse ford

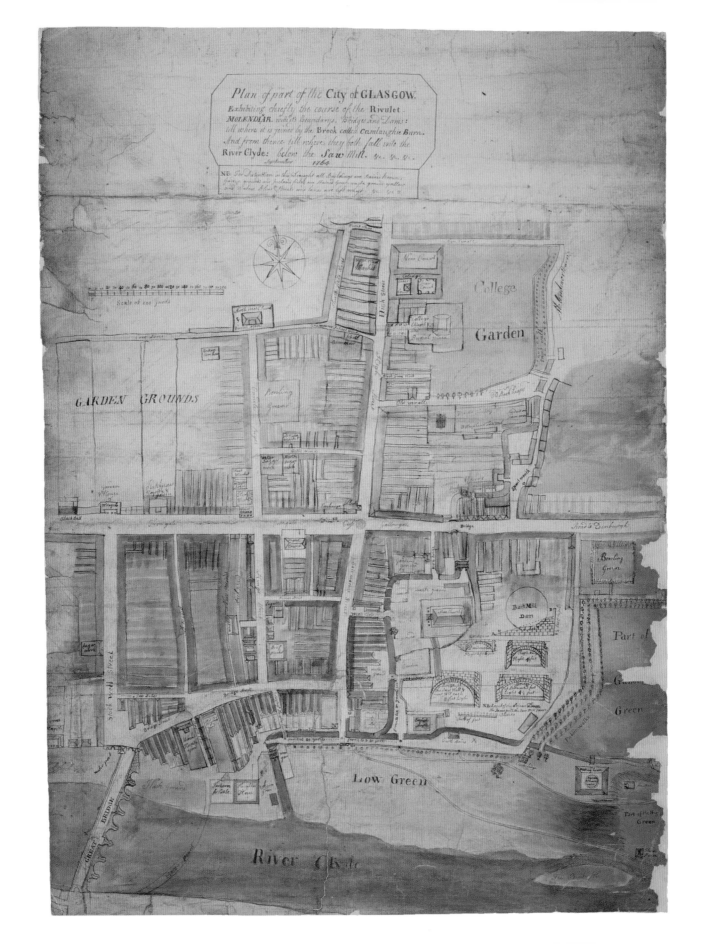

Plan of part of the City of GLASGOW.
Exhibiting chiefly the course of the Rivulet
MOLENDAR. with it's boundarys, Bridges and Dams:
till where it is joined by the Brook called Camlaughie Burn.
And from thence till where, they both fall into the
River Clyde: below the Saw Mill. &c. &c. &c.
September 1764.

College Garden

GARDEN GROUNDS

Back Mill Dam

Part of

Green

Low Green

River Clyde

Part of the Green

William Simpson, *The Auld Brig* (1846)

been used by drovers. The plan was prepared for a legal case relating to mills on the Molendinar Burn and its detail may be based on a survey by James Barry commissioned for the city magistrates.

A better impression of the Old Bridge is provided by this watercolour produced by the Glasgow-born artist, William Simpson. From 1840, he served an apprenticeship in the city's leading lithographic firm, Allen and Ferguson. During his time there, he was commissioned to produce a series of sketches of Glasgow's older buildings which appeared as monochrome illustrations in 1848 in Robert Stuart's *Views and Notices of Glasgow in Former Times*. These were subsequently turned into watercolours painted between 1893 and 1898. Dated 1846, this image provides a unique picture of the alterations to the bridge which is now depicted with only six arches as well as the changes effected by Telford prior to its subsequent demolition. More importantly, it also gives an impression of the river at low water showing horses fording there. Upriver, Simpson also records the five arches of Robert Stevenson's Hutcheson Bridge, completed in 1833. More famous as a war artist and journalist, his career working partly for the *Illustrated London News* is a record of travel and adventure which included sketch-

ing the tomb of Omar Khayyám, accompanying the Afghan Boundary Commission in 1884–85 and being present at the opening of the Suez Canal.

Further upriver, another ford had long existed linking the lands of Farme with Dalmarnock on the north bank, as indicated on the engraved estate plan dated to about 1790 and surveyed by the Edinburgh-based surveyor, William Bell. Bell had a long, and presumably successful, career preparing a wide range of surveys throughout Scotland between 1760 and 1813 but this appears to have been his only commission in Lanarkshire. He is additionally listed in the Edinburgh directories as an engraver, optician and natural philosopher. The plan very clearly indicates how the river meanders on the relatively flat lands of its middle course. This ford connecting Rutherglen with Glasgow was not the safest of crossings and the local newspaper recorded one fatality 16 years before this plan was prepared. Such incidences of drowning occurred at several other crossings on the river, particularly north of Abington where it is characterised by a broad and deep current and at Clydesholm, which had the added danger of the proximity of Stonebyres Linn immediately downstream.

Like several of the other plans of this period, it identifies

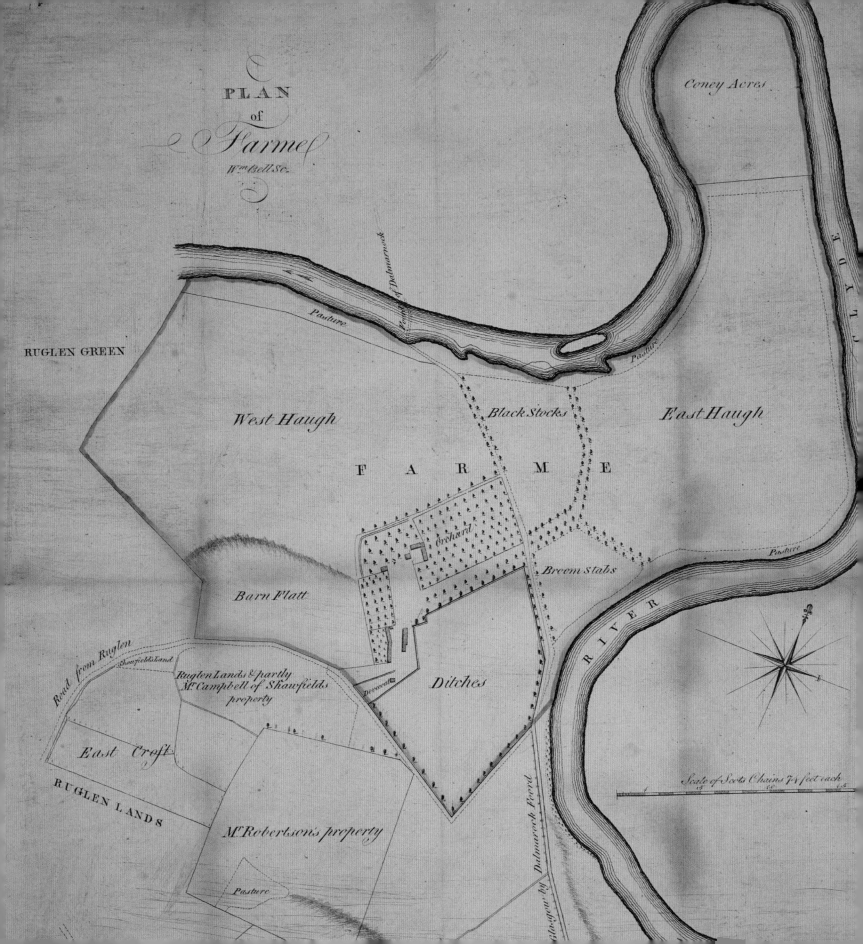

PLAN
of
Farme
Wm Bell Sc.

Coney Acres

LYDE

RUGLEN GREEN

Pasture

West Haugh

Black Stocks

East Haugh

F A R M E

Orchard

Broom Stabs

Pasture

Barn Flatt

RIVER

Road from Ruglen

Shawfields land

Ruglen Lands & partly
Mr Campbell of Shawfields
property

Dovecoat

Ditches

East Croft

R U G L E N   L A N D S

Mr Robertson's property

Pasture

Scale of Scots Chains 74 feet each

not only the estate lands but also a drying green beside the river where local weavers could wash and bleach their manufactures. The proprietors of the Farme estate, the Fairie family, retained an understandable interest in the navigation of the upper river and, in 1813, James Fairie corresponded with the road surveyor, Bryce Macquisten, regarding the restoring of the Clyde's navigability above the Broomielaw Bridge. The ford was subsequently superseded by a timber bridge strong enough to carry loaded carts and wagons. It was constructed in 1820–21 by the turnpike road trustees who also erected a tollhouse on the north bank. This rare contemporary illustration of the original structure comes from the manuscript collection which forms part of the personal library of David Murray (1842–1928), a leading Glasgow solicitor, historian and bibliographer. A second wooden bridge replaced this crossing in 1848 and this was subsequently superseded by the present five-span iron and steel bridge in 1891.

What is clear from earlier writings is the effect of the weir at Glasgow Bridge on both traffic and the negotiation of the upper river. About the year 1745, craft were said to have sailed as far as Westthorn near Dalbeth but the *New Statistical Account* for Rutherglen set the burgh as the upper limit and noted there were no vessels plying above Glasgow Bridge, thereby strengthening the argument that the river was more a hindrance to, than an effective means of, connections between places along its banks. This is very much the case where the Clyde flows through the more populous parts of the Nether Ward of Lanarkshire where various roads linking Edinburgh with Ayr and Lanarkshire, as well as Hamilton with Galashiels and, of course, Glasgow with Dumfries and Carlisle cross it. These significant routes required safe and secure means of negotiating the Clyde but were frequently seen as 'hilly, steep and inconvenient'. Before the development of turnpike trust roads in the latter half of the eighteenth century, a series of fords and ferries grew up. In fact, the incidence of place names such as Hyndford, Howford and Tillieford is a clear indication of their frequency.

Opposite. William Bell, *Plan of Farme* (c.1790) which indicates the ford at Dalmarnock

Above. Sketch of Dalmarnock Bridge from James Hopkirk's manuscript
Statistical Account of the Barony Parish of Glasgow (1827)

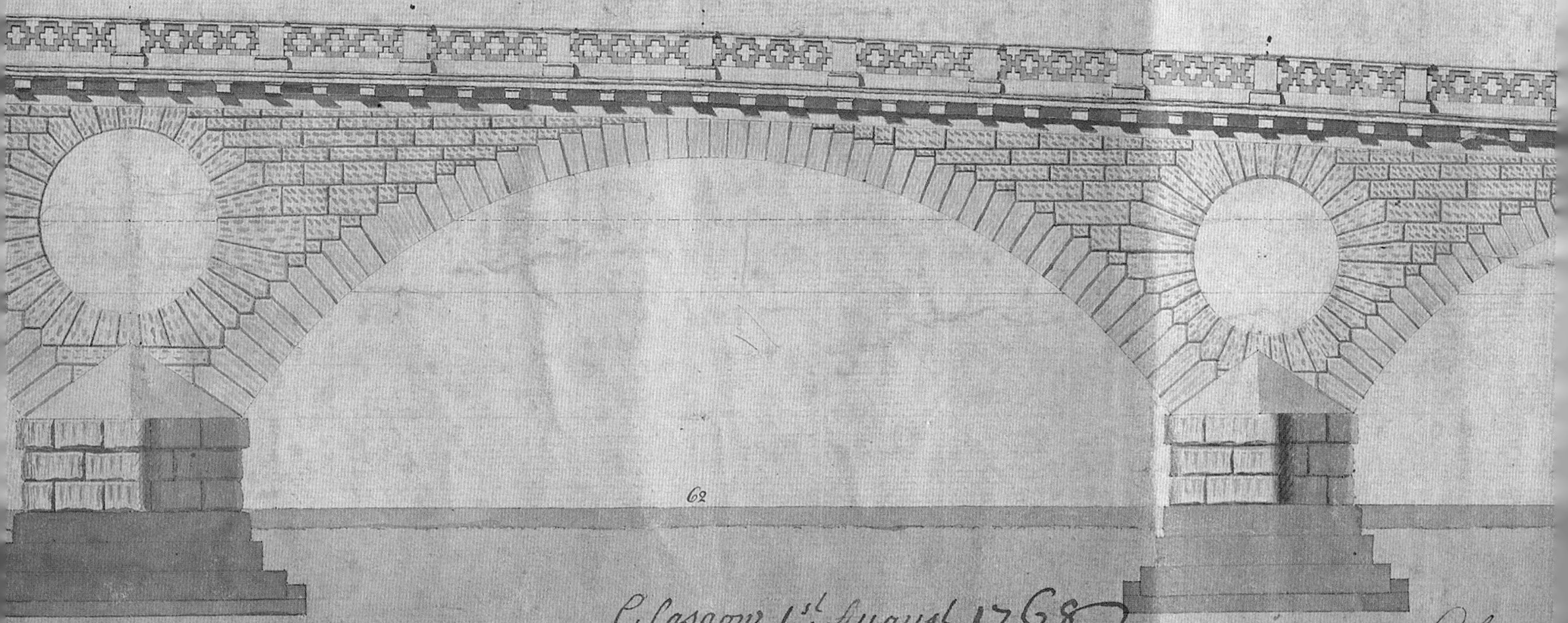

Glasgow 1st August 1768

George Murdoch

John Adam

100 Feet

62

Glasgow
The 6
in the
Provost
Councell
Buchan
Relative

CHAPTER 35

Two early Glasgow bridges

When parliament passed the act to initiate the improvements in the Clyde in 1759, its terms also provided for the building of a bridge to link Glasgow and the village of Gorbals. This recognised not only the inadequacy of the Old Bridge but also the impact that Smeaton's plans for a lock and dam would have on the local fords crossing the Clyde. This was to be no mean piece of work and the council was authorised to borrow £20,000 to fund its construction. While engaged on his survey, John Smeaton had also been asked to investigate the best site for the proposed bridge. He reported his findings in October 1760. As with his other work, the engineer made a thorough investigation of several potential locations, measuring and sounding at least seven alternatives between Jamaica Street and Glasgow Green. Consideration was given to the width of approach roads, the necessary span required, the slope and height of the two banks and the qualities of the soil in the river bed. At this date, little of the land on either bank had been occupied and there was less concern about interference with existing buildings or gardens.

Regardless of what has been written subsequently of Smeaton's involvement with what became known as the Broomielaw Bridge, his recommendation was for a shorter crossing at or near the middle of Ducat Green. In fact, he prepared a plan and elevation for such a proposal at this site which survive within his papers at the Royal Society. It is instruc-tive to read his opinion of the Jamaica Street alternative which states that 'the bottom is the worst of all, and the water deepest, nor does the line of this street produced cut the stream at right angles, which is a disadvantage that ought always to be avoided'. His comments expand on it being too near the present wharf and too far from the bulk of the inhabitants, but he saves his strongest criticism for the impact of an increased velocity on the river bed between the proposed piers which 'may produce fatal consequences upon the adjoining piers'. Clearly, Smeaton did have the expertise to anticipate this immediate consequence but did not have the wider vision to foresee how rapidly the city would grow in the next three decades, but it is perhaps fortunate that this recommendation was similarly shelved in preference for a subsequent proposal.

Eight years later, this report was resurrected by the then provost George Murdoch as part of the lobbying process for additional parliamentary consent. Smeaton, however, refused the commission and that summer the council received a second report from two surveyors detailed to determine the best location for the bridge. One of these was John Laurie, an experienced Edinburgh practitioner who subsequently became Land Surveyor to the Forth and Clyde Navigation and employed John Ainslie early in his career. The other man just happened to be James Barry, the bridge commissioners' choice for the job and by now

Opposite and overleaf. William Mylne, *Plan of Jamaica Street Bridge* (1768)

the council's preferred employee for any major commission. Their report reflects the care they paid to inspecting the river bottom at both the Jamaica Street location and at the foot of the Saltmarket, as well as inspecting the roads leading to the individual sites. In conclusion, they found the former 'the most proper fitt & commodious place . . . in point of situation but also in respect of the bed or bottom of the said river'.

Less than two months later, in August 1768, William Mylne, an Edinburgh architect then working on the capital's North Bridge, presented the magistrates with this design, which consisted of seven arches supported by piers well sunk into the river bed and with circular roundels above to allow the clear passage of any floodwater. The plan specifically marks the level of both high and low water. In appreciation of his work, Mylne was offered the freedom of the city while Barry was appointed to oversee the project for the first year. He so impressed the authorities by his 'most punctuall and constant attendance' and his attention to detail that they doubled his salary over the period of construction. The bridge was finished in 1772 but, unfortunately, it was of its time and was slightly arched, resulting in difficulties for heavier loaded carts. There was also concern about the strength of its foundations which was resolved by the construction of a weir soon after completion. This, however, created a major obstruction to the passage of any vessels. In reality, the authorities were faced with a paradoxical situation where they wanted a deeper channel but the consequences were greater scouring and flooding by the river. By 1778, sand and gravel to depth of up to 7 feet had been washed away from the foundations and when John Golborne revisited the city in 1781, he expressed his concern about the impact of the bridge on the

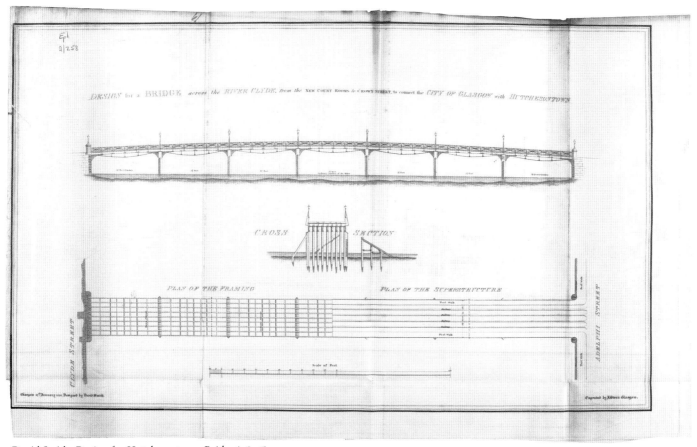

David Smith, *Design for Hutchesontown Bridge* (1826)

upper river navigation. He suggested cutting down certain piles and removing other obstructions in the three largest arches. Mylne's bridge was subsequently replaced in 1836 by one designed by Telford which retained the seven arches of the original design.

As Glasgow began to grow and developments south of the river led to a demand for easier links with the town centre, the city authorities considered additional bridges. Slightly upstream from the Broomielaw, a further crossing was proposed to link the old town with the developing community in Hutchesontown by a bridge near the foot of the Saltmarket. Begun in 1794, it was almost completed when it was washed away in the serious flooding in the following autumn. Both John Wilson in his plan of the Low Green and Thomas Richardson in his *Map of the Town of Glasgow & Country Seven Miles Round* of the same

year identify the site of the bridge's all-too-brief existence. Funded partly by the heritors of Hutcheson's Hospital, the original bridge at over 400 feet long must have reflected the city's growing self-confidence but the level of damage was so great that it proved impossible to rebuild. At the beginning of the new century, a replacement footbridge was erected on a site just upriver. This was built of timber and, while described as elegant, it was always going to have a relatively short life in the climate of the west of Scotland and proved inadequate for the number of people crossing it every day.

The two elevations illustrated here show designs presented by two separate engineers for a stone replacement of the original Hutcheson Bridge. David Smith, a leading Glasgow surveyor, submitted a proposal in 1826 which included an elevation, cross section and overall plan. Smith was responsible for some of the

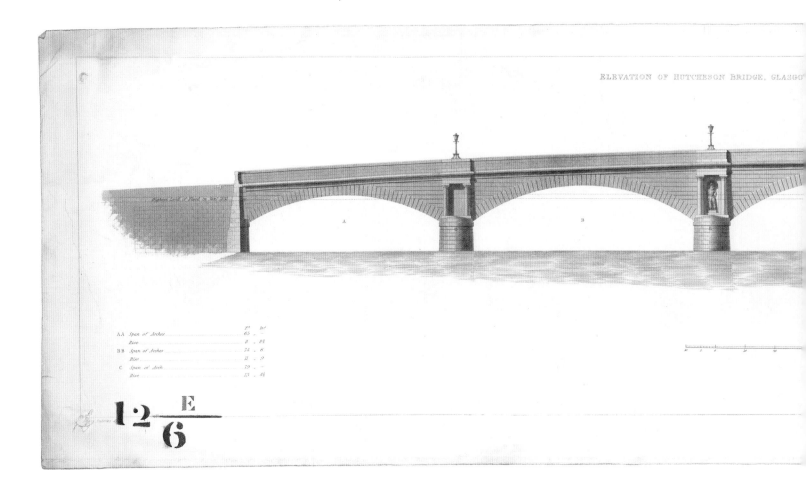

AA *Span of Arches* — 65 . —
Rise — 8 . 8¼
BB *Span of Arches* — 74 . 6
Rise — 11 . 9
C *Span of Arch* — 79 . —
Rise — 13 . 4½

12 E/6

finest maps of the city at this period and he enjoyed a career in surveying and engineering which lasted for 50 years. His design reflects the need for a more level bridge surface with the increasing amount of traffic within the city. It also indicates the lighting thought necessary to illuminate the structure. In comparison with Mylne's plan for the Broomielaw Bridge, this appears a much lighter and possibly more elegant work. With the changes in building design, the arch spans are considerably wider and the piers less solid. Smith's suggestion indicates footwalks on either side of the main thoroughfare and the design of the framing of the structure. His cross section gives a very good impression of the way in which the roadway sat above the bridge's framework. The plan was no mean piece of work and was prepared by Glasgow's leading engraver of the day, Joseph Swan.

Like many other contemporary surveyors, Smith branched into civil engineering as the century progressed. In 1823 he was working with Thomas Telford on the Crinan Canal and his output of plans covering locations throughout western Scotland is an impressive record of what a successful figure could achieve. Although the local man, Smith's proposal was not successful and this second illustration shows the accepted design as suggested by Robert Stevenson. Having been born in the city, Stevenson knew the background to, and some of the problems posed by, the Clyde flooding. At the time of his submission, he was serving as engineer to the Northern Lighthouse Board, a post he held for 34 years, but his commissions extended well beyond the building of lighthouses to the design of roads, canals and railways at a time when such skills were in heavy demand.

In comparison with Smith's design, Stevenson's bridge seems a sturdier structure, possibly reflecting the concerns many may

PLATE VI.

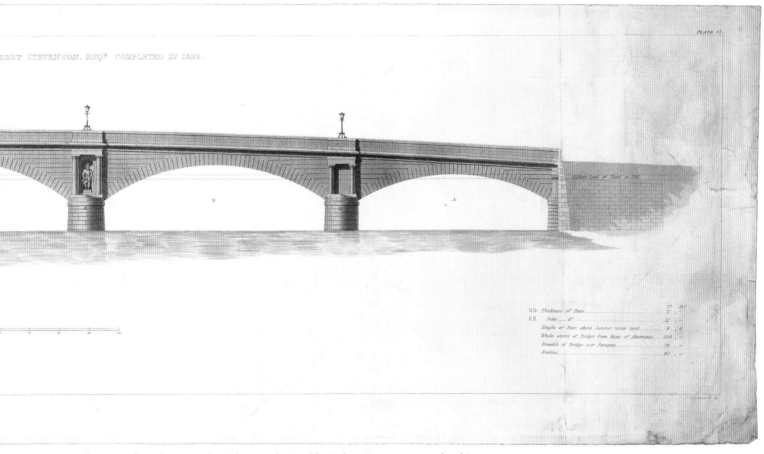

BERT STEVENSON. ESQ^R COMPLETED IN 1832.

DD Thickness of Piers
EE Ditto   d°
    Height of Piers above Summer water level
    Whole extent of Bridge from faces of Abutments
    Breadth of Bridge over Parapets
    Radius

Elevation of Hutcheson Bridge, Glasgow, designed by Robert Stevenson, completed in 1832

have had following the destruction of the first bridge. The engineer has reduced the number of spans to five and the enclosed parapets give the structure a sense of solidity. More importantly, the illustration provides greater information on the dimensions of the bridge, with details of the length and rise of the individual spans, the thickness of the piers, its height above summer water levels and the breadth of the structure. Gas lamps are also identified in the design. Tellingly, Stevenson also includes an indication of the high-water level of floods in 1782 and January 1831 – a feature noticeably missing from Smith's design. One distinctive feature of his bridge was the addition of figures in the niches above the central piers. Built between 1829 and 1833, it had a relatively short life for by 1868 it too had become unsafe. Although frequently this has been argued as the result of the deepening of the river, it was more to do with a design

weakness since the bridge could not support the increased weight of traffic. It was demolished that year and replaced by the Albert Bridge, opened in 1871. This image of Stevenson's proposal was produced by John Hawksworth, a little-known architectural engraver, who also specialised in portraits, working in London between about 1819 and 1848. Two other names are associated with the design. A note indicates that it came from the architectural library of John Weale, a London publisher of popular architectural and scientific work. As Weale had purchased the library in High Holborn in 1834, this illustration clearly is a record of the completed bridge design rather than the original submission. It was drawn by James Andrews who may have been employed as an artist with the Lighthouse Board since examples of his work showing the Skerryvore and Ardnamurchan lighthouses survive.

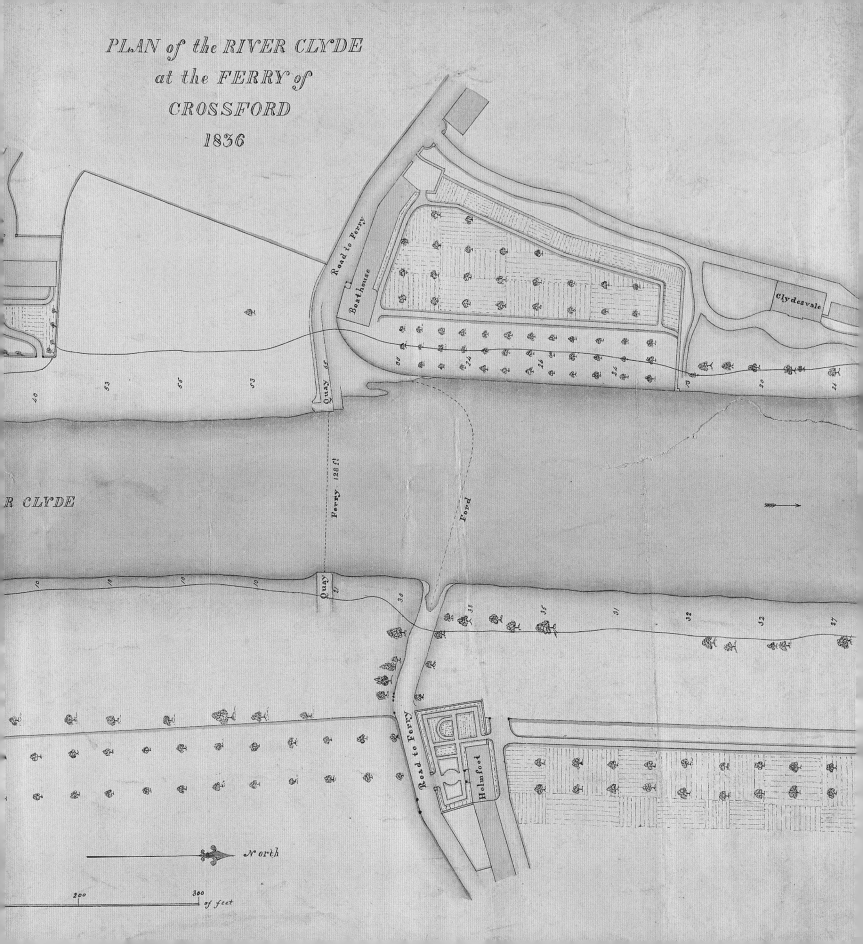

PLAN of the RIVER CLYDE
at the FERRY of
CROSSFORD
1836

Clydesvale

Road to Ferry

Boathouse

Quay 65

Ferry 126 ft

Ford

R CLYDE

Quay

Road to Ferry

Holmfoot

North

200   300
                    of feet

CHAPTER 36

Crossford Ferry

Upriver from Glasgow, one established ferry crossing of importance was at Crossford, lying on a more direct route between Lanark and Hamilton and operating well into the nineteenth century. This line avoided the steeper ground of the valley overlooking Stonebyres Linn and provided a safer passage because of the greater breadth of the river here. It was the source of considerable litigation regarding fishing rights and the charges imposed by the local ferryman, Archibald Martin. He had acquired the ferry rights in 1809 and sought to re-establish a service after a 30-year gap. Taylor and Skinner indicated 'Crossford Boat' on the delineation of the road from Lanark to Hamilton in their *Survey and Maps of the Roads of North Britain* of 1776 but, while most sources date a bridge to 1793, the location of a ferry alone at this point on the river on Forrest's county map would appear to challenge these assertions.

One of the several local Acts of Parliament relating to turnpike trusts which received royal assent in 1834 was that concerned with maintaining and repairing certain roads in Lanarkshire and with the construction of a bridge over the Clyde at Crossford. This was only the most recent legislation relating to roads and bridges in the county and it is highly unlikely that any bridge would have been considered if one was already in place. Proprietors who contributed £50 towards construction were entitled to become trustees, the money being recouped by the imposition of pontage rates on those using the crossing. These rates varied between 3d for a coach to ½d for anyone on foot. Apart from various sections discussing the routes of the roads, tolls and properties affected by the building of the road and bridge, the act also gave power to the trustees to destroy or shut up any fords and discontinue any ferries crossing the river up to a distance of half a mile from the bridge. Compensation to the ferry owner was stipulated but this turned out to have similar legal wrangles because of Martin's intransigence.

James Wilson drew this plan of the Clyde at the Crossford ferry in 1836 as part of a sequence of maps prepared for the trustees from 1833 onwards which included the approach roads to the crossing. As can be seen, both the ferry and a ford are indicated, as well as a boathouse, which is still indicated on the present Ordnance Survey maps. However, there is no image of the bridge itself, which was situated well upstream. Little is known of Wilson other than that he appears to have been a local man based in Lanark between 1837 and 1843 and working mostly on estate plans. The artistry and neatness of his drawing style, particularly on his manuscript drafts of the proposed roads to the ford, suggest that he was already an experienced draftsman by this date. Despite extensive searching, no surviving

Opposite and overleaf. James Wilson, *Plan of the River Clyde at the Ferry of Crossford* (1836)

plan of the bridge has been traced. It is a reminder that what survives from the past is frequently partial and its use requires caution in any subsequent assumptions based on such evidence alone. By September 1835, construction of the bridge was virtually complete and, eventually, it was opened in 1836, having cost in total £2,650. The monies raised from the tolls helped pay off the original investment by 1859 but income from the dues were badly affected by the development of the local railway network, resulting in the abolition of turnpikes and their tolls in the second half of the nineteenth century. Today, Crossford Bridge tends to be bypassed by most traffic travelling along the A72 between the M74 and Lanark.

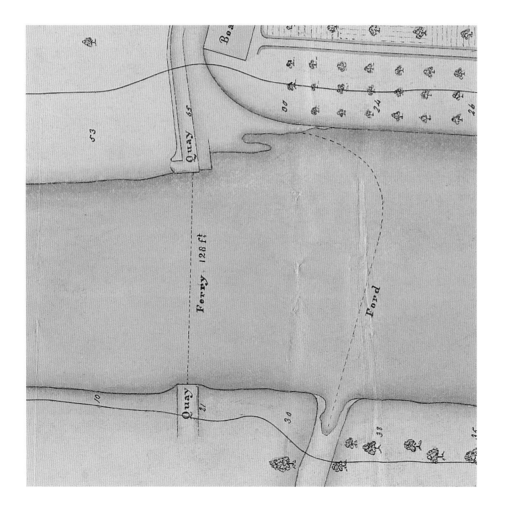

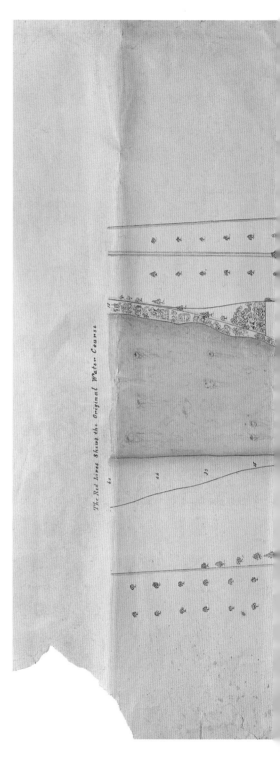

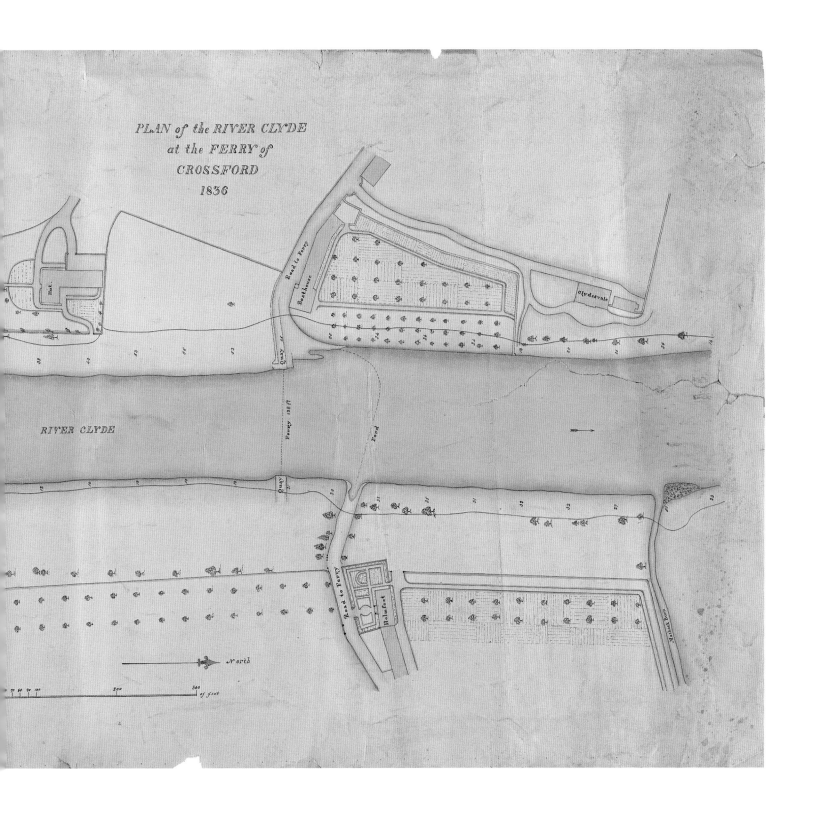

PLAN of the RIVER CLYDE
at the FERRY of
CROSSFORD
1836

RIVER CLYDE

North

of feet

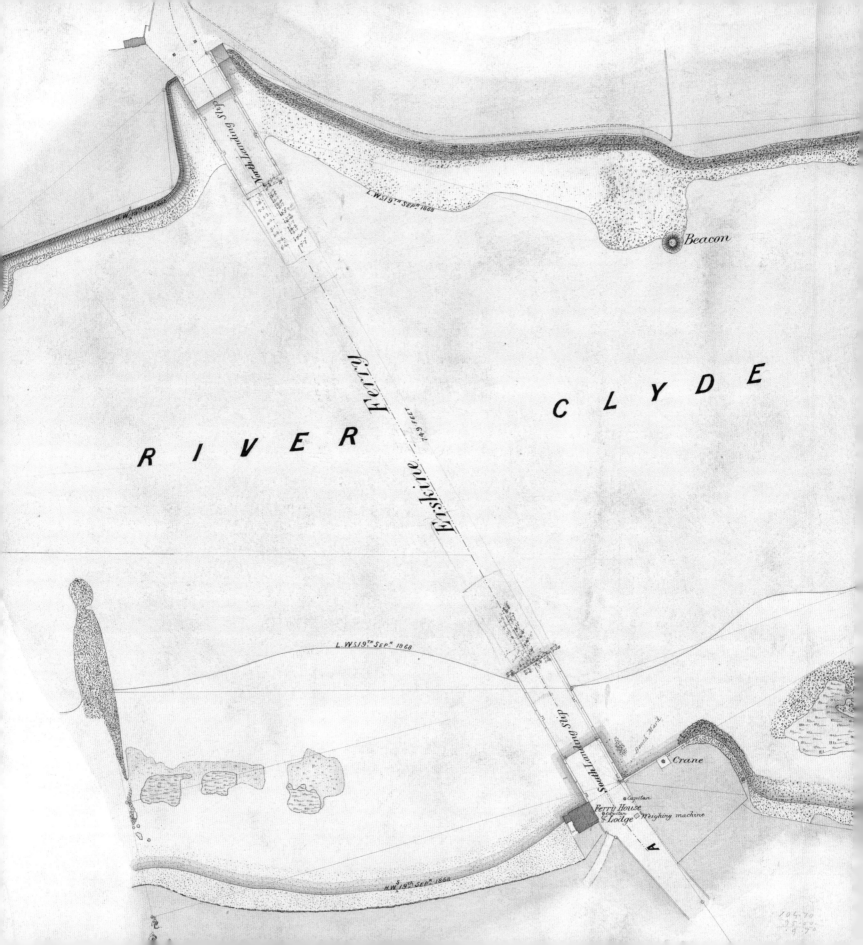

RIVER CLYDE

Beacon

North Landing Slip

Erskine Ferry   74.9 FEET

L.W.S 19ᵗʰ SEPᵗ 1868

L.W.S 19ᵗʰ SEPᵗ 1868

South Landing Slip

Bench Mark

Crane

Capstan

Ferry House

Capstan

S. Lodge

Weighing machine

H.W.S 19ᵗʰ SEPᵗ 1868

CHAPTER 37

The river crossing at Erskine

Although much closer to the mouth of the Clyde, a ferry crossing at Erskine seems to have been in use here from an early date, largely as the river was sufficiently shallow to ford on foot or by horse and, at this point in its course, the Clyde is less than a quarter of a mile wide. Also known as the East Ferry to differentiate it from another downriver at Dumbuck, it linked an ancient route from Paisley to Old Kilpatrick. With the engineering works carried out to deepen the channel, a ferry was established in 1777 to transport horses and vehicles, as well as pedestrians, while the West Ferry was operated chiefly for foot passengers. Stone for the quays, described as 'abundantly commodious', was taken from quarries owned by Lord Blantyre. However, further work to improve the Clyde's navigation suggested by Golborne, which included the construction of two jetties close to the south quay of the crossing, began to have a detrimental effect on the efficiency of its operations. In 1783, Blantyre presented a complaint to the Glasgow magistrates that these jetties projected further into the river than the quays on both banks, causing them to fill up with silt and resulting in them only being accessible at or near high water. This particular situation re-emphasises the difficulties created by the various jetties in the condition of the channel. These frequently caused swirls and eddies, which inevitably resulted in the deposition of mud, silt and sand in their lee.

Blantyre demanded that the river bed be reconfigured in the area of the ferry by the deposition of quantities of stone and the council awarded him £40 damages. In consequence, new quays were built, but the continued improvements to the channel led to further problems for Blantyre, particularly regarding the effect of walls and dykes on the view over the river from his home at Erskine House. While both Ainslie's map of Renfrewshire and Charles Ross's estate plan of Erskine clearly name the Erskine Ferry, neither appears to identify the contentious jetties which were the source of the problems nor is there any clear sign of the West Ferry. By the 1840s, this lower ferry had declined in usage and, although there were plans to build quays and develop a communication with Dumbarton, little appears to have been done. This left Erskine as the lowest crossing on the Clyde and its importance extended beyond the merely local. It served a considerable traffic from the Western Highlands and the freight charges provided a useful income to the family. However, the river continued to be a source of contention between them and the city. In 1875, further compensation of £12,500 was awarded in response to subsequent claims, and the matter was only resolved when the Clyde Navigation Trust purchased the ferry rights in the 1890s.

As various steamboat services developed, passengers could embark at Erskine, where a neat and comfortable inn, a favourite

Opposite and overleaf. David Stevenson, *Plan and section of part of the River Clyde at Erskine Ferry* (1868)

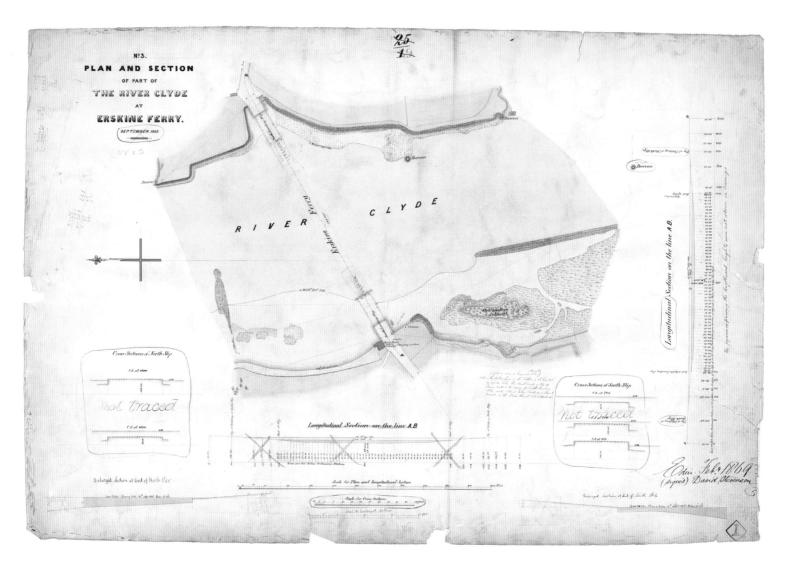

resort for dinner parties from Glasgow, had been established. Despite its popularity and significance, there are surprisingly few surviving references to the ferry here. Prior to 1832, much of the bed of the river channel remained sufficiently shallow for the operation of a punt pushed by large poles. As the channel deepened, however, a more reliable means of propulsion was deemed necessary and a chain ferry replacement was introduced. In 1833, the Dumbarton-based shipbuilding company William Denny and Son tendered for a vessel for the crossing for the sum of £110 while Blantyre is recorded as inviting later tenders in 1855. This depiction of the ferry site comes from a set of folios which forms part of the Stevenson family archive and

Opposite and overleaf. Freeman, Fox and Partners, *Erskine Bridge plan showing position of bridge piers* (1967) and *General layout of the approach road system on the north side of the Erskine Bridge* (1967)

FORTH & CLYDE CANAL

STATION ROAD

GREAT

PLOT 18
Area to include
Site offices

North
Abutment

Abutm

DUMBARTON ROAD

Pier 9   Pier 14

Pier 11   Pier 12   Pier 13

Pier 10

FORTH & CLYDE CANAL

Pier 7   Pier 8

R I V E R

Pier 6

C L Y D E

MUD

H.W. M.O.S.T.

ST. PATRICKS
STONE

240 ft   Bridge

Generally deck width ~ 40'-0"

Pier 5

ERSKINE FERRY

DUMBARTON ROAD

Mooring area

Pier 4

Pier 3

Abutment wall

350 ft

Pier 1 Pier 2

Any land required in this area must
be negotiated direct with the
Hospital authorities

South Abutment

Access road available
throughout contract.

Course of ANTONINE WALL

BRAES ROAD

Diversion of Dalnottar Burn.

Farm Track

North Dalnottar

5+00

10+00

15+00

20+00

25+00

30+00

35+00

SLIP ROAD 1

SLIP ROAD 2

SLIP ROAD 4

SLIP ROAD 5

SLIP ROAD 3

Dalnottar Cemetery

STATION ROAD

Bowling Green

Recreation Ground

Tennis Courts

Old Kilpatrick Station

Bus Stop

Bus Stop

Footpath

Track

Dalnottar Burn

140+00

ERSKINE BRIDGE

Church

Dumbarton Road

LIMIT OF CONTRACT

Dalnottar Burn.

Forth & Clyde Canal

illustrates a detailed report on the river and the crossings both at Erskine and at the West Ferry. Prepared by David Stevenson (1815–86) in September 1868, it shows the crossing and refers to a steam ferry-boat track. By the date of this plan, Stevenson was the managing partner of the family business, overseeing various navigational and harbour works throughout the British Isles, as well as continuing the family connection with the Northern Lighthouse Board. The plan was accompanied by several cross sections and extensive tables of low-water measurements, several of which were calculated by the Glasgow surveyor, Thomas Kyle. It does not appear to have any connection with the introduction of a chain haulage system and the only line marked relates to a cross section of the river bed. Beacons, capstans and the ferry house are identified, as is the entrance to Erskine harbour which marked Boden Boo (Bottom Bow) Island. What is possibly most noticeable is the necessity for the land slipways to extend a considerable way into the river to clear the silted banks.

Following the sinking of the ferry, a steam-powered vessel was introduced on the service and, with a crossing time of only five minutes, it continued to serve a valuable purpose well into the twentieth century. The third (and last) steamer was launched in 1936 from the Fleming and Ferguson yard and it was used eventually as a relief vessel for the Renfrew Ferry. In fact, the last boat in service at Erskine was slightly older but was converted in 1962 to take more cars. It operated until the ferry closed in 1971. By the early 1960s, the growth in car ownership and the increase in road transport led to a decision to build a number of road bridges in Scotland. Initial priority was given to the Tay Road Bridge as there were concerns about the siting and cost at Erskine, particularly regarding the clearance required to allow naval vessels to continue to have unrestricted access to the upper river and for newly constructed ships to be able to reach the open sea from the Clyde shipyards. In 1964, consulting engineers were appointed and a clearance height of 160 feet above the water level was selected as acceptable. Work began in 1967 on what was then the biggest single span bridge of its type and it was officially opened in July 1971. Government policy at the outset was to levy tolls to recover the construction

costs within about 20 years but insufficient weight was given to the impact of tolls on its use. In retrospect, the bridge was built before traffic flows justified its construction and it was soon realised that such charges would never recoup the monies involved. By 1981–82, the accumulated operating deficiency had reached nearly £25 million, which was more than double the original cost of construction. However, it was not until March 2006 that tolls were eventually abolished.

The bridge was designed by Dr William Brown of Freeman, Fox and Partners and carries the A898 as a link between the M8 and the A82. Daily traffic flows remain comparatively light, at about 35,000 vehicles per day, which is less than 25 per cent of the figure for the Kingston Bridge in the centre of Glasgow. Today, it provides an important access route to Loch Lomond, the Trossachs and the Highlands for visitors arriving at Glasgow Airport. These two images come from of a sequence of folio designs for the bridge produced for the Scottish Development Department. Drawn in late 1967, before construction began, they indicate the bridge and the proposed road interchange layout at Dalnottar. Considerable attention is given to the parcels of land accessible only during the time of building, including the site offices and access road. The bridge's 14 stanchions are marked and, when compared with the size of the actual river crossing between pillars five and six, the scale of the whole work necessary to provide sufficient clearance is apparent. Moreover, the difficulties faced by those involved in building the bridge may be realised in the limited turning movements indicated on the approach roads. In addition, the extent of mud siltation, particularly on the south bank, and the rather restricted road access to the ferry itself emphasises the limitations of the crossing. The second image of the bridge's northern approaches gives an excellent impression of the complications faced by modern road construction, particularly where an earlier pattern already exists. It also indicates such further elements as the diversion of water courses and landscaping involved in this work, while the general notes emphasise the precision required for working documents like these. Today, both ferry jetties have survived but, unlike the harbour at Bottom Bow which has reverted to a natural habitat, they have an air of unkempt neglect.

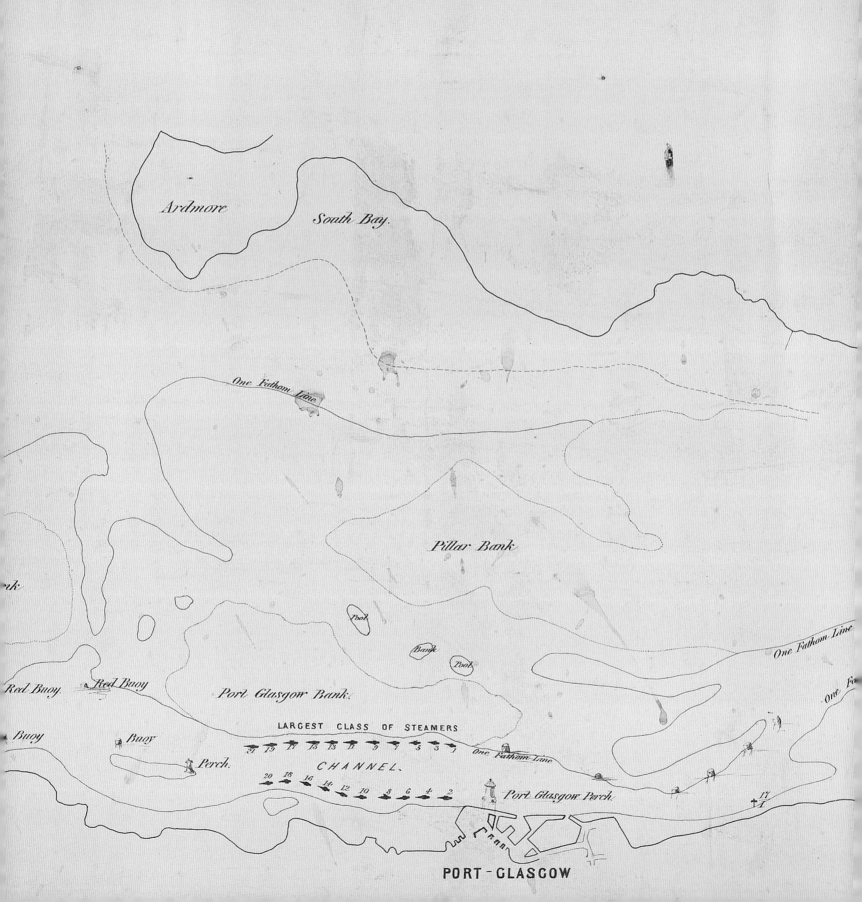

Ardmore

South Bay.

One Fathom Line

One Fathom Line

One Fathom Line

One Fo

Pillar Bank

Pool

Bank

Pool

Red Buoy

Red Buoy

Buoy

Port Glasgow Bank.

Buoy

Perch.

LARGEST CLASS OF STEAMERS

One Fathom Line

CHANNEL.

Port Glasgow Perch

PORT-GLASGOW

HER MAJESTY'S VISIT TO THE CLYDE.

CHART

SHEWING THE PROPOSED

TOURISM, LEISURE AND RECREATION

ARRANGEMENT OF THE CLYDE STEAMERS

BELOW GARMOYLE LIGHT.

AUGUST, 1847.

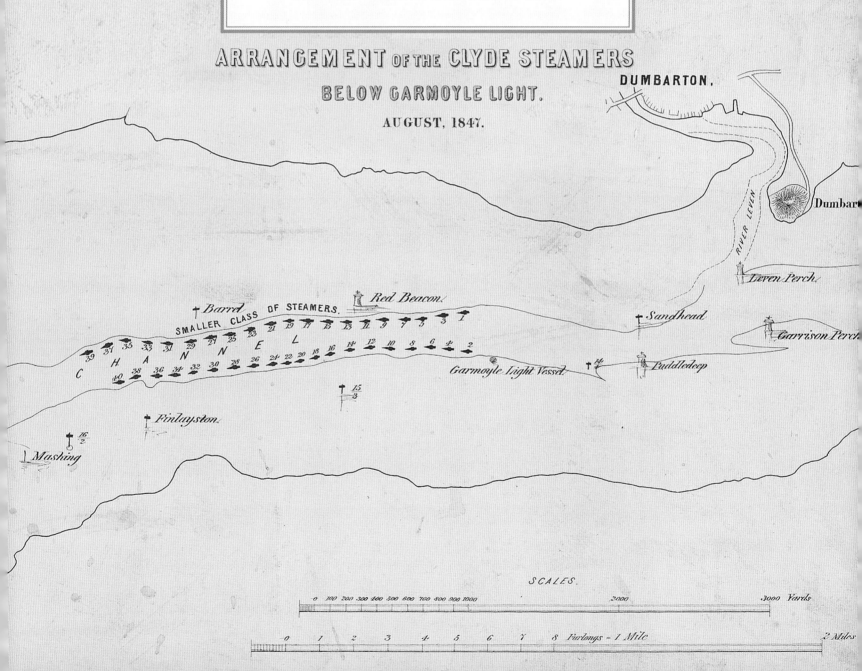

SCALES.

0 100 200 300 400 500 600 700 800 900 1000   2000   3000 Yards

0   1   2   3   4   5   6   7   8 Furlongs - 1 Mile   2 Miles

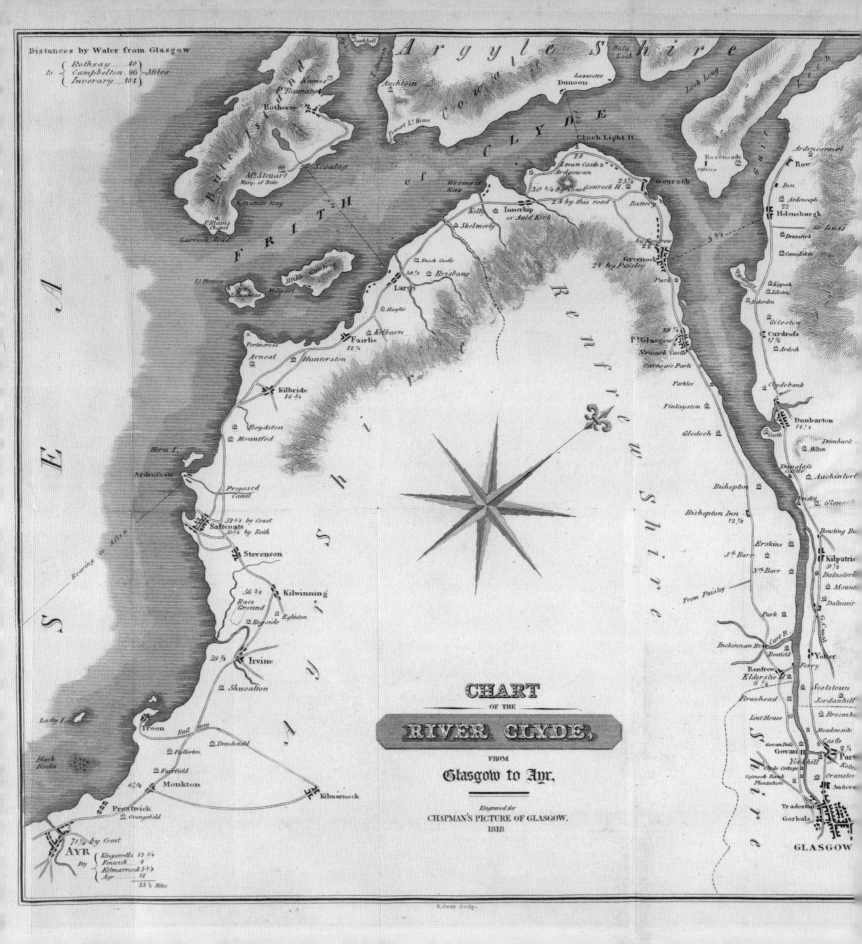

CHART
OF THE
RIVER CLYDE,
FROM
Glasgow to Ayr,

Engraved for
CHAPMAN'S PICTURE OF GLASGOW.
1818

Distances by Water from Glasgow

to
{ Rothsay 40
{ Campbelton .. 96 } Miles
{ Inverary 104

GLASGOW

71½ by Coast
AYR
By
Kingswells 13¾
Fenwick 4
Kilmarnock 5¾
Ayr 12
─────
35½ Miles

Argyle Shire
Cowal
FRITH of CLYDE
Bute Island
Renfrew Shire
AYR SHIRE

R. Gray Sculp.

CHAPTER 38

Clyde maps for
the early tourist

Although Henry Bell failed to follow up his initial success in steam navigation in the years subsequent to the launch of his vessel *Comet*, several other entrepreneurs took up the challenge and rapidly developed an extensive range of passenger services to many locations on the Clyde coast and beyond. Destinations which once involved long and sometimes arduous travel by coach were now more easily accessible to a growing section of the travelling public as part of a burgeoning tourist industry. With this came a healthy growth in the production of guide-books, itineraries and other 'tourist' literature. Towards the end of the eighteenth century, local publishers began to meet a demand from visitors to the area for works describing its local history, as well as discussing important buildings and features.

The Paisley surveyor, Charles Ross produced a *Traveller's Guide to Lochlomond and its Environs* in 1792 but not every venture in this particular field of publishing met with success. Five years later, James Denholm's *Historical Account and Topographical Description of the City of Glasgow and Suburbs* appeared, following a failed project to produce a history of the parish and town of Lanark. At about the same time, he had similarly unsuccessful plans for a work covering the Clyde valley while a scheme by Thomas Richardson, the Glasgow-based surveyor, to prepare a map of Lanarkshire met with equal failure.

Regardless of this, Richardson had more success with his *Guide to Loch Lomond*, which first came out in 1798, illustrated with maps from actual surveys. A second edition which included details of a trip to the Falls of Clyde came out the following year.

With Glasgow well placed as an access point for Loch Lomond, the Trossachs, the Clyde coast and 'the Land of Burns', guidebooks grew to incorporate descriptions of a wider range of places within reach of the city. As the coverage extended, it was natural to include maps to illustrate the routes and places of interest discussed. Some of the earlier accompanying maps were rather basic. A good example of this is the map which first appeared in the third edition of Robert Chapman's *Picture of Glasgow; or, Strangers' Guide* which, confusingly, has imprint dates of 1818, 1820 and 1822. Chapman had first issued the book in 1806 and a second edition followed six years later, but it is a reflection of the speed of the growing market that this chart of the Clyde was to appear only six years after Bell's *Comet* made its maiden voyage.

Possibly the most attractive and detailed of the early tourist maps to show the estuary is that which accompanied the earlier editions of James Lumsden and Son's *Steam-Boat Companion; and Stranger's Guide to the Western Islands*. This first appeared in 1820 and was produced in several editions up to 1839. The

Opposite. Chart of the River Clyde from Glasgow to Ayr, engraved
by Robert Gray for Robert Chapman's *Picture of Glasgow* (1818)

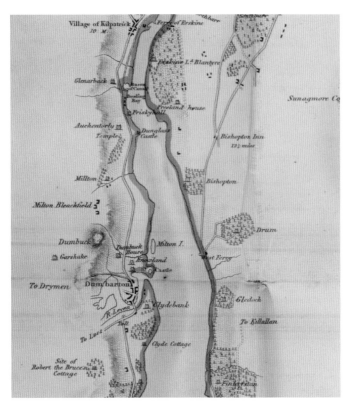

channel, such as the Botanic Garden at Sandyford and the site of Robert the Bruce's cottage. Ferries and distances from Glasgow are marked on both depictions and the coverage includes the coast of Northern Ireland, underlining a significant destination for much of the local steamer trade. Overall, this is a markedly superior map to several of its contemporary competitors – most notably that which accompanied Pigot's *Commercial Directory of Scotland*.

It was engraved by William Home Lizars (1788–1859), one of Edinburgh's leading engravers and, as the title indicates, was 'constructed from the best authorities' that may have partially included the Lizars firm's own *Travelling Map of Scotland*. Interestingly, Lizars employed two significant Glasgow artists, Horatio McCulloch and Daniel MacNee, in their early careers, to hand-colour prints for the family firm. McNee had worked for Lumsden while a teenager and both painters were encouraged by him in later life. Like Lizars, Lumsden began his career apprenticed to his father, before succeeding him in his family's engraving and publishing business in 1820. James Lumsden senior had been responsible for engraving John McArthur's 1778 plan of Glasgow, but his son appears to have focused more on the publication of diaries, almanacs and guidebooks, later employing Hugh Wilson to engrave maps. Lumsden had accompanied Bell on that first trip of the *Comet* in 1812 and, as a board member of the Clyde Trust he played a significant role in improving the navigability of the river. He was elected Lord Provost in 1843 and, in more than 50 years of public service to Glasgow, was involved in many social and philanthropic concerns, including the promotion of the first model lodging houses. A founder of the Clydesdale Bank, he was also involved briefly in running river steamers and was to be vocal in his concern for Henry Bell in his later years. Six years after his death, a bronze statue of Lumsden was erected in the city's Cathedral Square but, more significantly, his support and inspiration resulted in the raising of a monumental obelisk beside Dunglass Castle in 1838 commemorating Bell's achievement.

map itself was available separately for 3s. As an indication of the rapid development of services in the firth, the 1820 edition listed 23 steamers serving the west coast, while only eight years later this figure had increased to 59 vessels employed in a trade which ran between such ports as Liverpool, Belfast, Greenock and Helensburgh.

The similarity in the parent work's subtitle suggests that Lumsden's work succeeded that of Chapman, but of greater interest is the map's design, which is akin to the 1759 Watt map in the way it depicts both the river and firth. Although not having the same credentials as the earlier work and presumably designed for a different audience, Lumsden's provides a clear, informative and less clumsy illustration. On the river, the map identifies key properties and features on both sides of the

Opposite and above. James Lumsden, *Map of the Frith of Clyde* (1830)

MAP of the RIVER CLYDE Laid down on a LARGER SCALE.

ARDGOWAR · LOCHABER · APPIN

MAP of the FRITH of CLYDE and Western Highlands of SCOTLAND Constructed from the best Authorities for the Strangers Guide and STEAM BOAT COMPANION

PUBLISHED BY J. LUMSDEN & SON GLASGOW.

HER MAJESTY'S VISIT TO THE CLYDE.

CHART
SHEWING THE PROPOSED
ARRANGEMENT OF THE CLYDE STEAMERS
BELOW GARMOYLE LIGHT.

AUGUST, 1847.

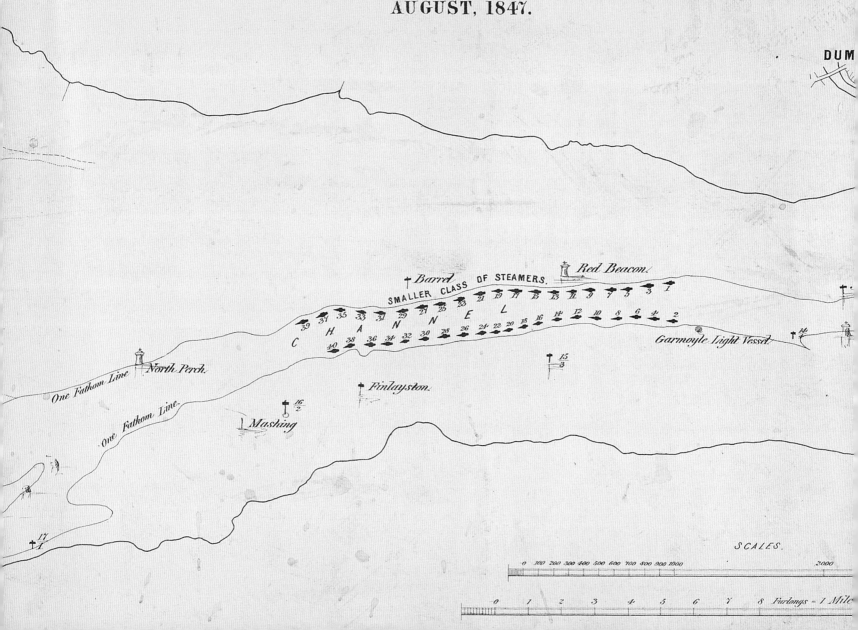

DUM

Barrel
SMALLER CLASS OF STEAMERS.
Red Beacon.

Garmoyle Light Vessel

One Fathom Line   North Perch.

One Fathom Line.

Finlayston.

Mashing

SCALES.

0 100 200 300 400 500 600 700 800 900 1000   2000

0   1   2   3   4   5   6   7   8   Furlongs = 1 Mile

CHAPTER 39

'We are all up on tiptoe here':
Queen Victoria's visit to the Clyde in August 1847

So wrote the *Glasgow Herald* correspondent just prior to the arrival of the monarch on the Clyde in the late summer of 1847. Queen Victoria's visit to the area was probably the first royal presence in the estuary since the circumnavigation of Scotland by James V to subdue the lords of the Western Isles in 1540 under the guidance of his pilot, Alexander Lyndsay. On that occasion, the King left his fleet at Dumbarton and rode back to Edinburgh. The Queen's visit appears to have been more of a pleasure trip for her, the Prince Consort and their two eldest children. Preparations for the journey had been based on guidance provided by the Glasgow shipowner, James Burns and his clerk, David Hutcheson. Accompanied by a squadron of naval vessels, the royal party left from Osborne House, the family's new residence on the Isle of Wight, on Thursday 11 August on the yacht *Victoria and Albert* and entered the firth six days later.

In her journal, the Queen noted: 'between 12 & 1, we reached Greenock, which is the port of Glasgow, & both the shore and ships were covered with myriads of people. No less than 39 steamers all overcrowded, followed us. Such a scene was never seen before. Added to these, boats & ships of all kinds, were going about in all directions & not getting out of the way. We however got safe in board the *Fairy* & steamed up the Clyde.' After visiting Dumbarton Castle, the royal visitors returned to Greenock, escorted by a flotilla of steamers, before sailing into Loch Long and subsequently visiting Rothesay, Oban Bay, Staffa, Iona and Fort William. As part of the tour, the Queen also inspected the Crinan Canal and travelled along it in a barge provided by Burns himself.

This Clyde Navigation Trust plan shows the positioning of the river steamers on either side of the channel between Port Glasgow Bank and Dumbarton Castle. These would have accommodated many of those wanting a closer view of the royal visitors and underlines the potential hazards of a crowded waterway. The royal yacht itself had a greater draught than the usual depth at Dumbarton, hence the use of the tender *Fairy*. In preparation, advertisements had appeared in the local press offering the best vantage points for viewing the progress of the vessels. Departures from the Broomielaw began at 3 a.m. and large crowds also made use of the Greenock Railway to reach the most advantageous spots. Among the many vessels in this flotilla was the recently built cross-channel steamer *Thetis*, also owned by Burns, with the Lord Provost and magistrates and representatives of the River Improvement Trust among its passengers.

Prepared by the Glasgow firm of draftsmen and lithographers, Maclure & Macdonald, the plan includes the various

Opposite. Detail of Clyde River Trust, *Her Majesty's visit to the Clyde* (1847). Chart showing proposed arrangement of the Clyde steamers below Garmoyle Light, 1847. See p. 198–99 for full map

navigational beacons and buoys which the Trust maintained to safeguard passage in the lower river, but it also emphasises just how narrow the Clyde was as a navigable channel. It also shows the level of planning that went into ensuring that the visit was a success, particularly as there was an underlying concern to foster the sovereign's fondness for Scotland. The event was also captured in an oil painting by the Greenock marine artist, William Clark, a member of the Royal Northern Yacht Club. His eye for precise detail not only provides an impressive record of the ships involved but also highlights the congestion caused by an enthusiastic public.

This excursion was taken against a background of political unrest both at home and abroad. The Great Famine which had ravaged Ireland was also affecting the Highlands and it was a time of growing social upheaval in much of Europe. Despite this, there was a genuine excitement about the visit and the enthusiastic displays of loyalty towards the party can be seen in both the press and journal coverage of the day. Among the naval officers who attended the royal party was the commander of HMSV *Shearwater*, Captain Charles Gepp Robinson, who

was actively involved in charting the Clyde area at that time for the Hydrographic Office as part of a complete survey of the coastal waters of the United Kingdom. Coverage of the Clyde was only completed in 1849 and Robinson's expertise would have been invaluable, particularly in an area rarely visited by the fleet. His chart of the mouth of the Clyde underlines the rapid shallowing of the river off the Tail of the Bank and shows the many shoals and sandbanks lying between Greenock and Ardmore Point.

The interest taken in the Queen's visit by so many of her subjects resulted in a considerable tourism boom for the area and the trip proved a real coup for local shipping interests, particularly for Burns himself, who went on to achieve a virtual monopoly of the steamer connections to the Western Highlands and Islands. This was later passed on to his nephew, David MacBrayne. With a good eye for business promotion, the West Highland steamer service was being advertised as the 'Royal Route' soon after the event. While Queen Victoria and Prince Albert may not have been the first tourists on the Clyde, they were certainly two of the most influential.

Above. William Clark, *The Queen's visit to the Clyde* (1847)

Opposite. Admiralty chart, *The Clyde, Loch Fyne, &c. 2159* (1849)

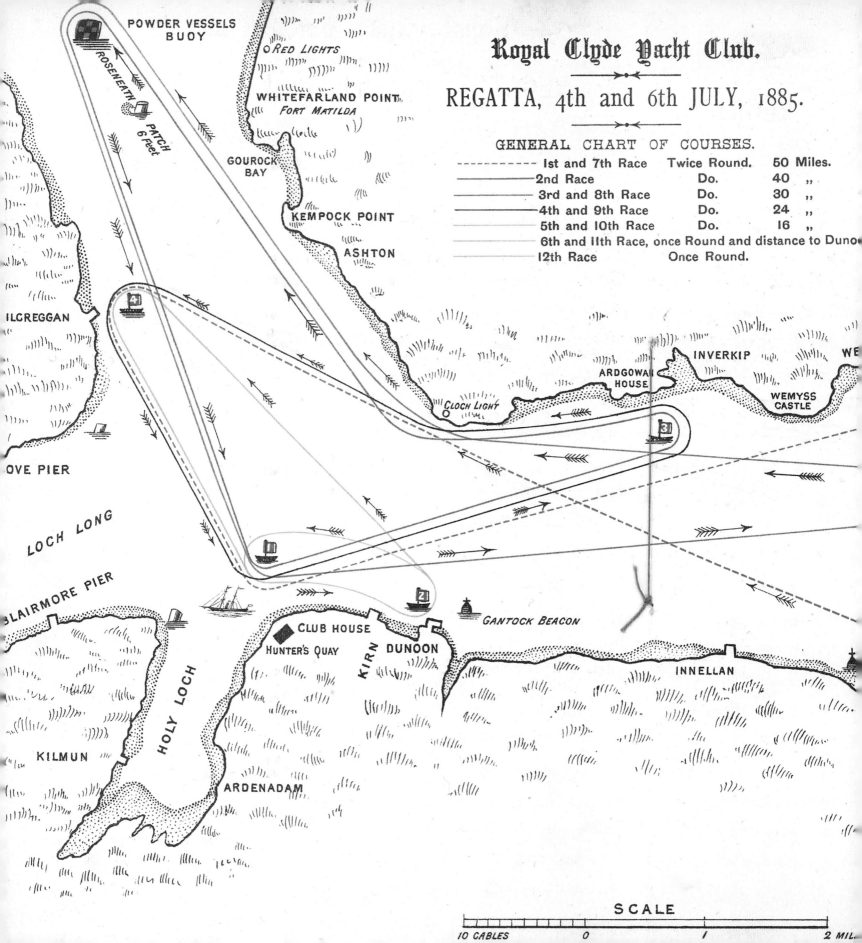

Royal Clyde Yacht Club.

REGATTA, 4th and 6th JULY, 1885.

GENERAL CHART OF COURSES.

1st and 7th Race	Twice Round.	50 Miles.
2nd Race	Do.	40 ,,
3rd and 8th Race	Do.	30 ,,
4th and 9th Race	Do.	24 ,,
5th and 10th Race	Do.	16 ,,
6th and 11th Race, once Round and distance to Duno[on]
12th Race	Once Round.

POWDER VESSELS BUOY

RED LIGHTS

WHITEFARLAND POINT
Fort Matilda

ROSENEATH

PATCH 6 Feet

GOUROCK BAY

KEMPOCK POINT

ASHTON

KILCREGGAN

INVERKIP

ARDGOWAN HOUSE

WEMYSS CASTLE

WE[MYSS]

CLOCH LIGHT

OVE PIER

LOCH LONG

BLAIRMORE PIER

GANTOCK BEACON

CLUB HOUSE

HUNTER'S QUAY

KIRN

DUNOON

INNELLAN

HOLY LOCH

KILMUN

ARDENADAM

SCALE

10 CABLES   0   1   2 MIL[ES]

CHAPTER 40

On yachts, yachting and regattas

Earlier sections in this book have considered vessels involved in the commercial transportation of either goods or people or naval defence within the estuary. However, the Clyde also offers ideal opportunities for enjoyment through the pleasures of sailing. The history of the Greenock shipbuilding firm founded by John Scott in 1711 records that they constructed the first Clyde vessel to be recognised as a racing yacht. This was a 45-ton cutter for Colonel John Campbell, MP for Ayr Burghs, which was launched by his wife, Lady Charlotte in 1803. From that time onwards the Scotts became closely identified with the production of such craft, including the cutters *Hawk* and *Hope* but in the early years of the nineteenth century the pastime was largely the sport of the aristocracy and the well-to-do.

Although it had its origin in Northern Ireland, the first yacht club to be founded on the Clyde was the Royal Northern Yacht Club (RNYC) in 1824. It is Scotland's oldest such club and throughout much of the nineteenth century its list of commodores was filled by members of the Scottish nobility, including two dukes and two earls. One other early enthusiast was James Smith of Jordanhill, considered by some as the father of Clyde yachting. An enthusiastic sailor, he was the first commodore of the Royal Clyde Yacht Club, founded in 1856 and based at Hunter's Quay. As provost of Helensburgh, he

frequently entertained fellow yachtsmen at the Baths Hotel, which he had purchased from Henry Bell's widow. From its earliest days, the RNYC organised regattas at almost every suitable port in the immediate area, particularly Lamlash, Largs and Rothesay. When Queen Victoria visited the Clyde in 1847, the yachts of the club sailed out in fleet to meet her off the Cloch Lighthouse. In 1878 the RNYC opened a clubhouse at Rothesay, from which many of its races and regattas commenced.

As the surviving charts show, many of the earliest races were over basically square courses designed for the larger yachts owned by wealthy Glasgow industrialists. Gradually, the number of venues increased along with the number of clubs as the sport grew in popularity, especially encouraged by the changes in design to include smaller craft. By the turn of the century, the Clyde was second only to Cowes on the Isle of Wight in terms of yacht building, sailing and racing. In fact, it was chosen as the venue for the 12-metre class 1908 Olympics sailing event, which was won by the Dumbarton-built *Hera*, crewed entirely by members of the Royal Clyde Yacht Club. This attractive chart which appeared on its regatta programme for July 1885 marks the routes of the various courses to be raced over that weekend – although there was no sailing on the Sunday! Distances ranged from 16 to 50 miles for the major events and

Opposite and overleaf. Royal Clyde Yacht Club,
General chart of the course for regatta, July 1885

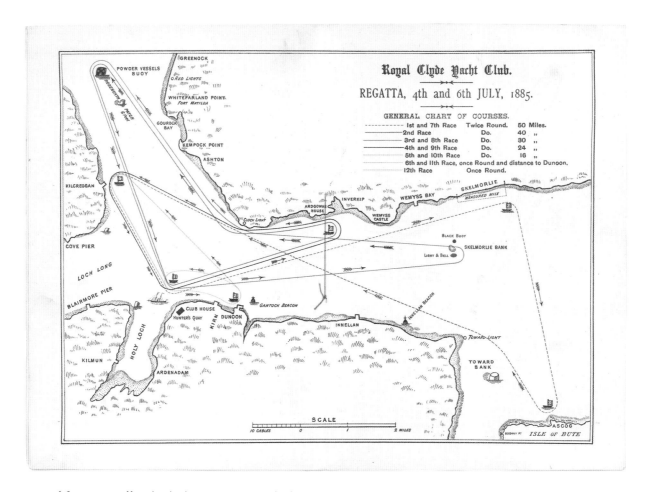

a top prize of £100 was offered. The longest course, which was twice round, headed for the more open waters between Skelmorlie and the Isle of Bute before turning north for Kilcreggan. Piers, buoys and beacons are identified, as are the marker boats but, being a chart for those well versed in navigation, the publisher saw no need to include a north point. Races were organised according to various classes with craft ranging from under 3 tons to the considerably larger 125-ton *Wendur*. This was owned by John Clark of Largs, one of the Clarks of Paisley, and constructed by Hendersons at their Meadowside yard only two years earlier. A shorter race was also set out for pleasure boats no longer than 19 feet.

Eleven years later, the RNYC's Rothesay regatta attracted entries from both the Prince of Wales (*Britannia*) and his nephew,

the Kaiser Wilhelm II (*Meteor*). Both men raced yachts built at the Henderson shipyard and designed by the Scottish naval architect, George Lennox Watson (1851–1904), whose clients also included the Coats family of Paisley, the Vanderbilts and Sir Thomas Lipton. By this date, such events had become popular as spectator events and the paddle steamer *Duchess of Hamilton* ran special cruises for those wishing to view the races. The programme for that event was also decorated with illustrations of the racing flags of the individual yachts entered for the event. This illustration gives a sense of how colourful such occasions must have been.

The second racing chart illustrated indicates a more extensive course and accompanied a special regatta programme issued in 1897 to celebrate the Diamond Jubilee of Queen Victoria.

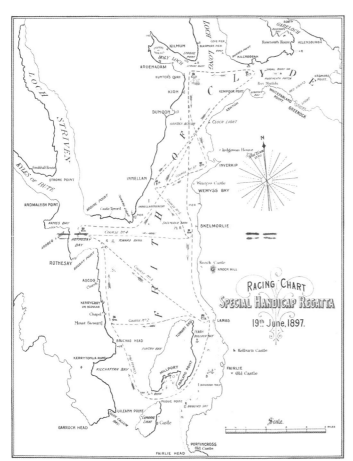

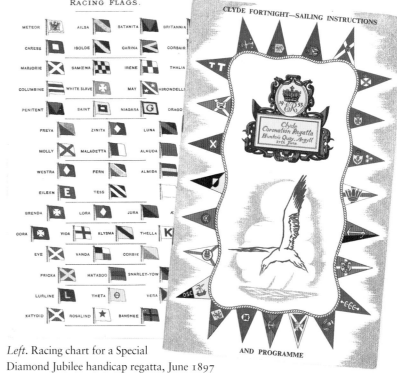

Left. Racing chart for a Special
Diamond Jubilee handicap regatta, June 1897

Above left. Racing flags illustrated in the Royal
Northern Yacht Club's Rothesay regatta, 1896

Above right. Cover of the Clyde Fortnight
Coronation Regatta programme, 1953

Being half a century after her visit to Greenock, she did not visit the Clyde on this occasion. Again, the chart identifies the routes, piers, marker boats and other important features of the channel, but in this case it also indicates the shoaling between Largs and Fairlie Head, along with selected soundings. Unlike the earlier Maclure and Macdonald depiction, on this occasion the printer William Lyon did include a detailed compass rose on the chart but he also failed to number the courses correctly.

Britannia did not race on the Clyde that year but continued to serve both Edward VII and his son, King George V, winning 231 races in her career, including all seven races for her class on the French Riviera and beating the 1893 America's Cup defender. When it passed into history, its demise marked the end of big-yacht racing in Europe as smaller and more affordable class yachts gained popularity. Following the end of the Second World War, the Clyde yacht clubs did much to promote international competition, and in late July 1947 the International Clyde Fortnight, the main yachting event of the year, witnessed the RNYC's unsuccessful attempt to regain the Seawanhaka Cup for smaller craft. Given that a gathering of the Home Fleet off Greenock coincided with the second half of the Fortnight, the estuary must have been a very crowded place. This final image of the cover of the 1953 Coronation Regatta programme is decorated by the burgees of the various participating sailing clubs over that fortnight. Something of the spectacle of such events can still be seen in the present-day regattas at Helensburgh, Gourock, Inverkip and Rhu.

however the Salmon have in a g

the Clyde, owing to the public

Boats.

Canals

CHAPTER 41

Fishing, salmon
and the Clyde

The first recorded foreign commerce of Glasgow concerned the curing and exporting of Clyde salmon and, as is well known, the salmon (or 'the fish that never swam') forms part of the coat of arms of both the city and the university. These emblems can be traced back to the seals of the Bishops of Glasgow, the salmon first appearing on Bishop William Wyschard's seal in 1270. Walter Gibson, one of the leading early mercantile entrepreneurs in Glasgow, is also recorded as exporting barrels of herring at the end of the seventeenth century. Such trade was confirmed in Revd Peter Brown's description of the parish of Rutherglen for the *New Statistical Account* of 1845 which recorded that there had been a considerable commerce in salmon with France, with brandy being traded in exchange. However, by the end of the eighteenth century, there were already ominous signs of the impact of the growing occupation of the river banks on fishing. In July 1798, the Glasgow merchant David Tod was identified as having interrupted the town's salmon fishing opposite his property on the river.

This image comes from the manuscript Statistical Account of the Barony Parish drawn up by James Hopkirk in 1827 and indicates the nets and boats engaged in fishing on the river at that time. His narrative records that, on a single day following a flood, 140 fish were caught in the short stretch between Dalbeth and Westthorn. Nonetheless, the situation deteriorated and in 1872 a Royal Commission report identified the Clyde as one of the most heavily polluted rivers in Britain. Four years later, James Deas attributed the complete destruction of the salmon fishery to the combined impact of the river improvements and the emptying of sewage into it. At that date, the River Trustees were still paying more than £200 each year to the burgh of Renfrew in recognition of the damage.

These two associated plans form part of the documentation prepared for a Court of Session process between Daniel Campbell of Shawfield (*c.*1737–77) and the Heritors of the Lands of Dalmarnock. Campbell was the grandson of his more famous namesake who was a leading merchant and represented the Glasgow Burghs as a Member of Parliament from 1716 to 1734. In 1707 he had purchased the estate of Shawfield, located on the south bank of the river close to Rutherglen. The elder Campbell died in 1753 and the process was raised three years later.

Looking at what is depicted on the plans might lead to the presumption that they were drawn solely to illustrate a dispute over fishing rights on the river. At this date, no major improvement of the channel had yet been taken and the salmon fishery was still of considerable importance to communities along its banks, being part of the assets of any property. Both depictions

Opposite. Illustration of salmon fishing on the Clyde from James Hopkirk's
manuscript Statistical Account of the Barony Parish of Glasgow (1827)

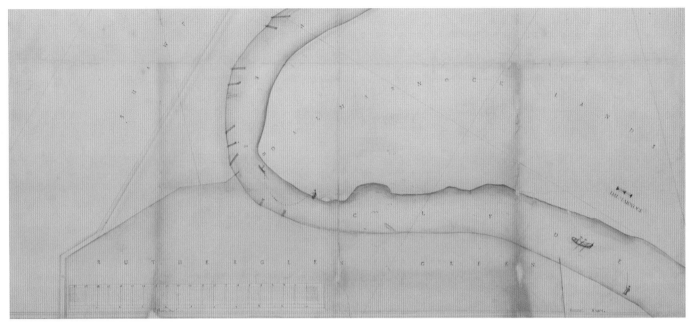

James Barry, *Plan of the River Clyde at Shawfield* (1756)

show the bend in the river at Rutherglen Green but, more importantly, they identify a sequence of bulwarks built out from the Shawfield bank. These were claimed to have affected the Dalmarnock fishing, although Campbell dismissed this as 'altogether trifling and cannot be the real motive of this opposition'. The more stylish of the two was prepared for the Dalmarnock Heritors by James Barry. While it shows all the signs of an accomplished surveyor in its neat linework, elegant compasses and accurate scale bar, it is a much less informative document than the work prepared to support Shawfield's position. In their memorial, the major Dalmarnock heritors describe Campbell's plan as 'far from being accurate and seems to be done by some unskilled and prejudiced hand and no body from looking at it can properly guess it to have been designed to represent the thing which is intended by it'.

Unskilled it may be, but it is in the explanation which appears on this second depiction that the central argument of the case can be discerned, namely the loss of land on the Shawfield side by the river's encroachment. Understandably, Campbell was concerned about the damage to his property. Earlier bulwarks

constructed to protect the banks had been swept away in previous years and a farmhouse, garden and cornfield had been lost earlier by the undercutting of the bank. He had a growing concern that the river would eventually create a new course and damage his property further. His version identifies a parcel of land amounting to 4.5 acres which had been deposited as silt and sand over the previous half century, thereby extending the Dalmarnock property while the Clyde slowly eroded his own land at Shawfield Brae. As the river cut into this bank, it became deeper and this restricted the ability to draw any fishing nets. Two sandbanks which are stated to have caused further encroachment are also marked. Eventually the process fell asleep but the plans bear witness to the effect of erosion on an unprotected riverbank.

Whether or not he was a fisherman himself, James Barry included sketches of men fishing either from the banks or from boats in the river in several of his Clyde plans. As can be seen in this small extract from the Barry version, this plan was no exception. Given the style of dress of the solitary figure, this may show a recreational angler enjoying a day on the river. Barry was to return to Dalmarnock in 1773 to prepare a plan

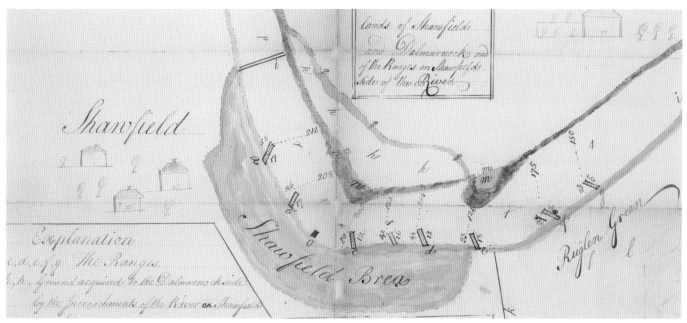

View of the River Clyde and its banks at Shawfield (1756)

of the surviving properties in the village for yet another legal dispute.

While there is neither salmon nor sea trout fishing available in the upper reaches of the river because these species cannot pass the falls at Stonebyres, conditions have improved greatly over recent years, aided by the construction of a fish ladder at Blantyre. Catches of 20-pound salmon are once more being recorded on the middle stretches of the river. Several associations seek to maintain, develop and improve fishing and good angling practice. This simple yet clear map of the various pools and flats of the Clyde between the Roberton Burn and Thankerton was prepared for the website of the Lamington and District Angling Improvement Association and was once displayed on their permits. The club leases 9 miles of the Clyde where clear water runs on a good gravel bottom through open country. Twelve specific locations are identified, as well as additional information on access roads and recommended parking places. More valuably, the plan is a further example of well-designed contemporary mapping meeting a specific purpose and is widely available on the Internet.

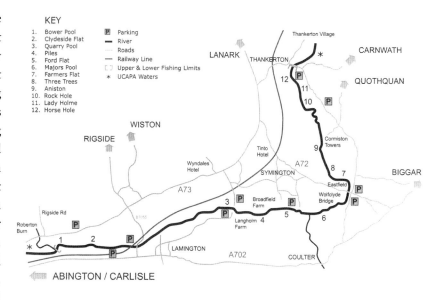

Map of the fishing pools, flats and holes on the River Clyde at Lamington

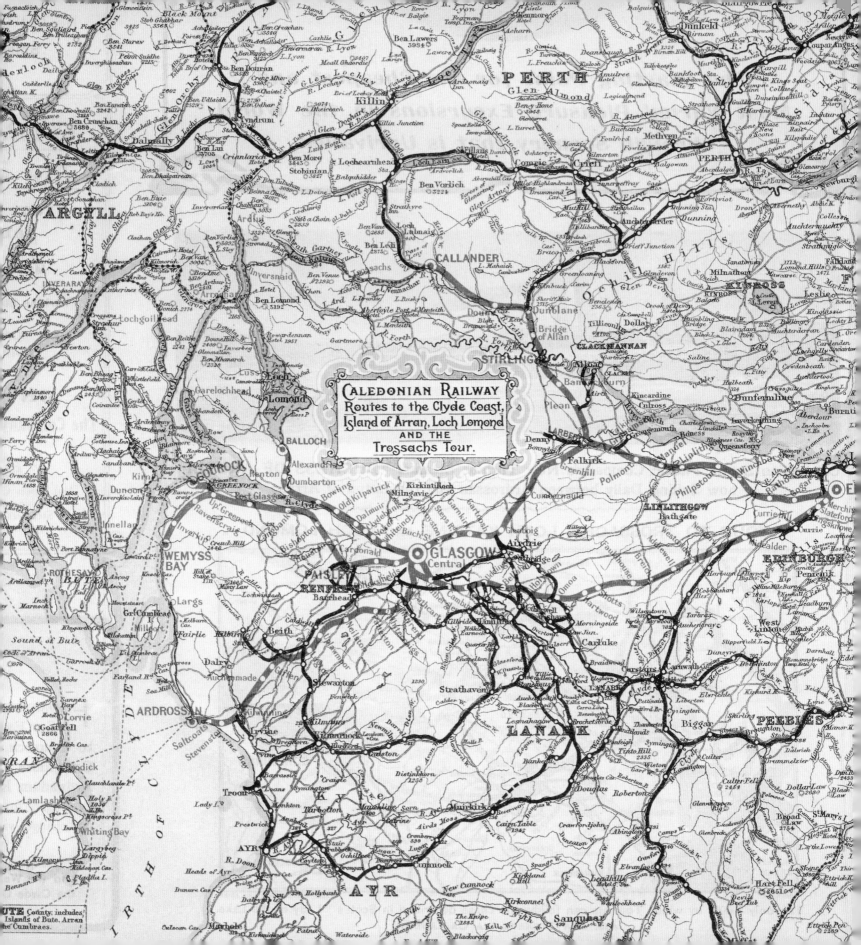

CALEDONIAN RAILWAY
Routes to the Clyde Coast,
Island of Arran, Loch Lomond
AND THE
Trossachs Tour.

CHAPTER 42

The birthplace of the Open: golf by the Clyde

While the existence of a golf course on Glasgow Green at the end of the eighteenth century has been mentioned earlier, for many people the association of golf with the Clyde calls to mind images of the strikingly attractive greens of the Ayrshire coast. From West Kilbride southwards, more than a dozen courses lie on a coastal stretch of less than 50 miles. Predominantly links courses, these include a group of six that encircles the town of Troon, as well as Prestwick Golf Club which inaugurated the first Open Championship in 1860 and was to host the first ten competitions. Three Open Championship courses can be found in this area and, with convenient transport links by rail, air, ferry and road, in addition to majestic scenery, the area markets itself successfully as one the best golf destinations in the world, as well as being the home of the Open Championship. As the Scottish leisure industry grows and develops, such a commercial approach to the sport makes a considerable contribution to the national economy. Assessments of the economic impact suggest that the game contributes over £1 billion in revenue and supports nearly 20,000 jobs.

Golf in Scotland has a long history but, in many ways, its growth, particularly away from the major urban areas, was undoubtedly aided by the development of the railway system. It is estimated that between 1870 and 1914, something in the region of 200 courses were opened, including Prestwick St Nicholas (1877), what is now Royal Troon (1878), Kilmarnock Barassie (1887) and Western Gailes (1897). The association between the game and the train is well seen in this tourist map produced by John Bartholomew for the Caledonian Railway Company in 1906. Although the small cover illustration in this instance indicates a train passing the east coast course at Stonehaven, it accompanies a map which specifically highlights routes to the Clyde coast and Arran resorts, with the added emphasis that 'the pleasure sailing on the Clyde is the finest and cheapest in the world'. Steamboat routes with key destinations are delineated on what is very much a standard Bartholomew map of Scotland for this period. This particular version does not indicate golf courses but, nine years later, the Bartholomew firm was to issue this more specific map of Scottish golf courses which could be reached by the Caledonian Railway and its connecting lines. It was printed as four images to a sheet and a note on the surviving proof shows that 20,500 copies were ordered for the February of 1915.

Sport historians may take an interest in noting the number and range of both nine- and eighteen-hole courses marked on the map but, regardless of its title, it is a real conundrum for anyone wanting to consider the promotion of golf in Scotland

Opposite and overleaf. John Bartholomew, *Caledonian Railway tourist map* (1906) and image of golf course and train passing

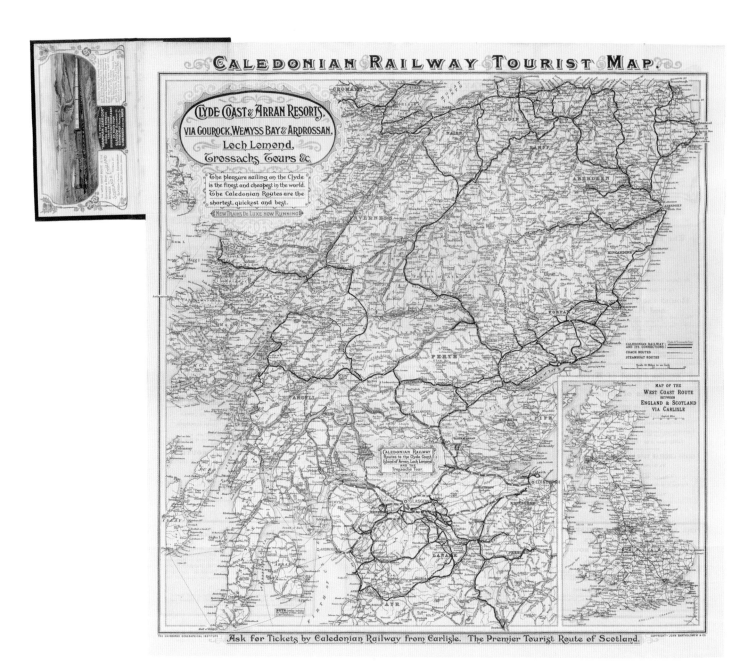

CLYDE-COAST & ARRAN RESORTS,
VIA GOUROCK, WEMYSS BAY & ARDROSSAN,
Loch Lomond,
Trossachs Tours &c.

The pleasure sailing on the Clyde
is the finest and cheapest in the world.
The Caledonian Routes are the
shortest, quickest and best.
NEW TRAINS DE LUXE NOW RUNNING.

MAP OF THE
WEST COAST ROUTE
BETWEEN
ENGLAND & SCOTLAND
VIA CARLISLE

Ask for Tickets by Caledonian Railway from Carlisle. The Premier Tourist Route of Scotland.

in the early years of the twentieth century. While the courses at Dornoch, Gleneagles, Carnoustie and, even, Stonehaven are all identified, the map provides no indication of those at Muirfield, St Andrews or, indeed, any of the many other Fife courses. While it might be argued that these are not served by a direct connection to the Caledonian Railway itself, this cannot justify the omission of the important courses at Prestwick, Troon or Turnberry, particularly when the ten Arran courses are clearly identified. It is evident that the Caledonian Railway map contract was an important and lucrative one for Bartholomew, helping

Opposite and overleaf. Bartholomew, *Golf courses of Scotland reached by the Caledonian Railway* (1915)

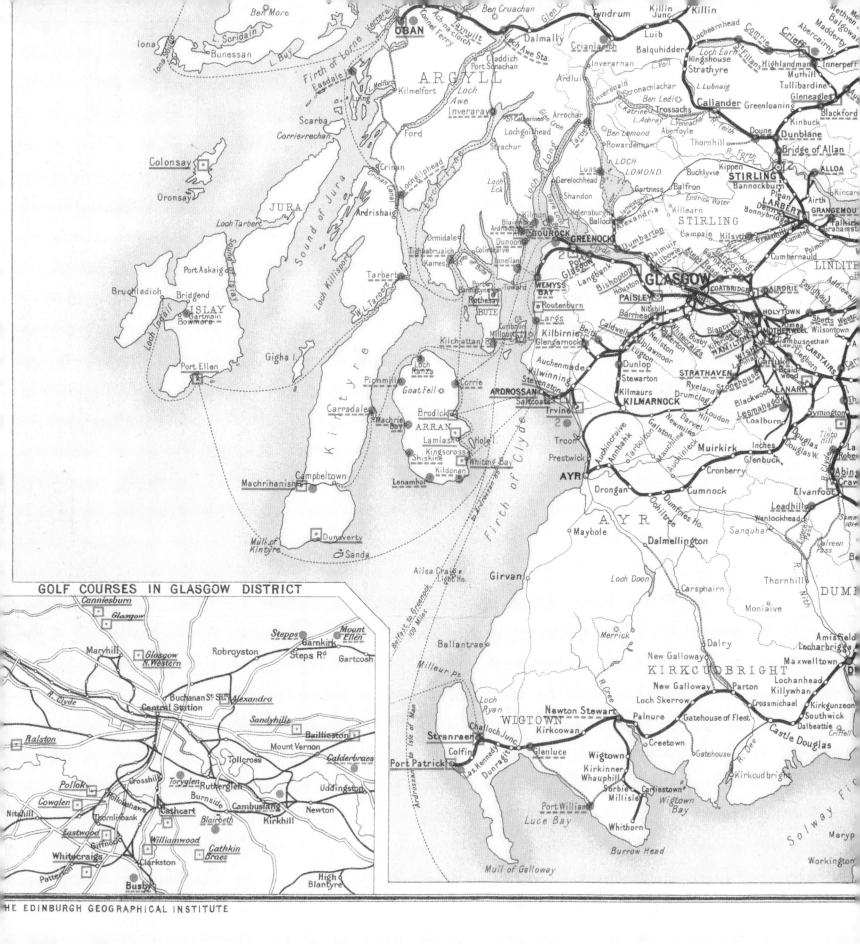

Ben More
Ben Cruachan
Glen
Killin
Killin
Killin
Loch
L. Scridain
Kerrera
Ach-na-cloich
Taynuilt
Tyndrum
Junc
Lochearnhead
Comrie
Iona
Bunessan
OBAN
Connel Ferry
Dalmally
Luib
Strathyre
Comrie
Crieff
Abercairny
Iona Sound
L. Buy
Firth of Lorne
Loch Awe Sta.
Crianlarich
Kingshouse
Loch Earn
St Fillans
Highlandman
Innerpeff
Easdale
Lochgoilhead
ARGYLL
Balquhidder
L. Voil
Strathyre
Muthill
Tullibardine
Colonsay
Scarba
Kilmelfort
Loch
Awe
Inverarnan
L. Lubnaig
Gleneagles
Oronsay
Corrievrechan
Ford
INVERARAY
St Catherines
Arrochar
Ben Ledi
Trossachs
L. Katrine
Callander
Greenloaning
Blackford
Loch
Eck
Crinan
Ardrishaig
Lochgilphead
Strachur
Stronachlachar
L. Achray
L.Vennachar
Doune
Kinbuck
Dunblane
JURA
Loch Tarbert
Crinan Canal
Loch Goil
Ben Lomond
Aberfoyle
Thornhill
R. Forth
Bridge of Allan
Ormidale
Kilmun
LOCH
Rowardennan
Kippen
STIRLING
Ardrishaig
Blairmore
Helensburgh
Luss
LOMOND
Buchlyvie
ALLOA
Port Askaig
Tighnabruaich
Dunoon
Garelochhead
Balloch
Jamestown
Gartness
Balfron
Airth
GRANGEMOU
Bruichladdich
Bridgend
Kames
Shandon
Alexandria
Killearn
Endrick Water
LARBERT
ISLAY
Gartmain
Kyles
GOUROCK
GREENOCK
Dumbarton
Campsie
Kilsyth
Denny
Falkirk
Bowmore
Rothesay
Toward
Dalmuir
Milngavie
Bonnybridge
Loch Indaal
BUTE
Colintraive
WEMYSS
Port
Glasgow
Langbank
Bishopton
Houston
GLASGOW
COATBRIDGE
AIRDRIE
LINLITH
Port Ellen
Gigha I.
Gt.
Cumbrae
BAY
Largs
Routenburn
PAISLEY
Nitshill
Cumbernauld
Kilchattan Bay
Millport
Kilbirnie
Beith
Caldwell
Barrhead
Busby
Whitecraigs
Blantyre
HOLYTOWN
Shotts
West
Pirnmill
Loch
Ranza
Glengarnock
Neilston
Uplawmoor
MOTHERWELL
Wilsontown
Corrie
Kilwinning
Auchenmade
Stewarton
Dunlop
Eaglesham
HAMILTON
WISHAW
CARSTAIRS
Carradale
Goat Fell
ARDROSSAN
Stevenston
Kilmaurs
Drumclog
STRATHAVEN
Stonehouse
CARLUKE
Braid
Machrie
Bay
Brodick
Saltcoats
KILMARNOCK
Ryeland
Law Jun.
wood
ARRAN
Irvine
Darvel
Loudon
Hill
Blackwood
LANARK
Lamlash
Troon
Auchincruive
Annbank
Galston
Newmilns
Lesmahagow
Symington
Kingscross
Prestwick
Tarbolton
Mauchline
Coalburn
Douglas
Tinto Hill
Shiskine
Holy I.
Auchinleck
Muirkirk
Inches
Douglas W.
Abin
Kildonan
Whiting Bay
AYR
Glenbuck
Crav
Machrihanish
Lenamhor
Drongan
Cronberry
Elvanfoot
Campbeltown
Cumnock
Leadhills
Maybole
Ochiltree
Wanlockhead
Mull of
Kintyre
Dunaverty
Sanda
Ailsa Craig
Light Ho.
Girvan
AYR
Dalmellington
Loch Doon
Sanquhar
DUM
Thornhill
Carsphairn
Moniaive

Canniesburn
Maryhill
Glasgow
Stepps
Barnkirk
Mount
Ellen
Glasgow
N. Western
Steps Rd.
Gartcosh
Robroyston
Merrick
Dalry
Amisfield
Lochairbriggs
Buchanan St Stn.
Alexandra
Maxwelltown
D
New Galloway
Central Station
Ralston
Sandyhills
KIRKCUDBRIGHT
R. Clyde
Baillieston
New Galloway
Parton
Lochanhead
Killywhan
Mount Vernon
Loch Skerrow
Crossmichael
Kirkgunzeon
Pollok
Loch
Ryan
Newton Stewart
Palnure
Gatehouse of Fleet
Southwick
Crosshill
Torglen
Rutherglen
Uddingston
WIGTOWN
Creetown
R. Dee
Dalbeattie
Cowglen
Burnside
Challoch Junc.
Kirkcowan
Cathcart
Cambuslang
Newton
Gatehouse
Castle
Douglas
Nitshill
Thornliebank
Stranraer
Wigtown
Criffel
Eastwood
Williamwood
Blairbeth
Kirkhill
Colfin
Glenluce
Kirkinner
Carsluith
Giffnock
Cathkin
Braes
Wha011hill
Kirkcudbright
Whitecraigs
Clarkston
Sorbie
Garliestown
Wigtown
Bay
Patterton
Port Patrick
Las Kennedy
Dunragit
Millisle
Busby
High
Blantyre
Port William
Whithorn
Maryp
Luce Bay
Burrow Head
Solway Fir
Mull of Galloway
Workington

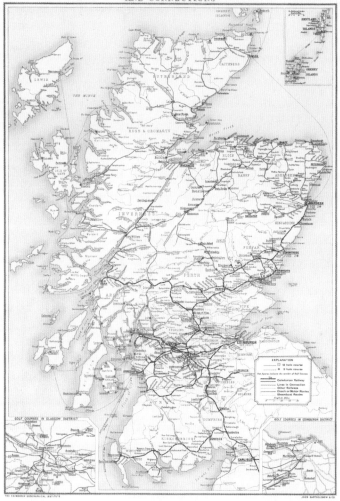

to maintain the company's domination of tourist mapping in Scotland for much of the twentieth century.

Of slightly greater relevance to the development of what might be called 'sports cartography' is this plan of Troon Golf Links prepared in 1888. It was produced by the leading Glasgow firm of lithographers, Maclure, Macdonald and Co. and published ten years after the first meeting to establish Troon Golf Club, held in the Portland Arms Hotel. Part of the promo-

tion of the course was to attract people to the area and develop the village. It is known that the surveyors advised the club that clearing land on the links between the Gyaws and Pow Burns would be too expensive and, as an alternative, they suggested a reduction to a six-hole course lying west of Gyaws as a canny compromise. Subsequently, extensions to 12, then 15 and, eventually, 18 holes were planned. Unfortunately, there is no clear indication of who was responsible for the plan's preparation but it appears that it was drawn out by the members themselves. Credit for laying out the original course, however, goes to Charlie Hunter, keeper of the green at Prestwick. He had learnt his trade under the watchful eye of Thomas Mitchell Morris, otherwise known as Old Tom, who won three of the first five Open Championships.

The Old Course at Royal Troon now has the longest and shortest holes in Open Championship golf and today's detailed plans of the individual holes on major courses are frequently accompanied by video flyovers with information on the direction for each stroke. While apparently more basic, the original plan gives a far greater flavour of what the course looked like when opened. It identifies the various sand dunes, walls and woods which would have proved a challenge to any players of the day and the distances are only given in approximation. More significantly, bounding the course on the east is the all-important railway line. In 1978 the club was awarded royal status to celebrate its centenary and in 2016 Royal Troon hosted the 145th Open Championship, the ninth occasion that it was played there.

While the final illustration is more modern, it is an interpretation of the original 18-hole course laid out for the third Marquis of Ailsa at Turnberry, which was opened in July 1901. An earlier plan of the ground had been prepared by John Eaglesham, a civil engineer based in Ayr, but it took another eight years before the idea came to fruition. Troon had its part to play in this later development, the course being laid out and its construction supervised by William Fernie, the Troon professional. Turnberry Golf Club was established in 1902 and, after a couple of false starts, the growing commercial interest in developing the immediate area by providing public rail transport

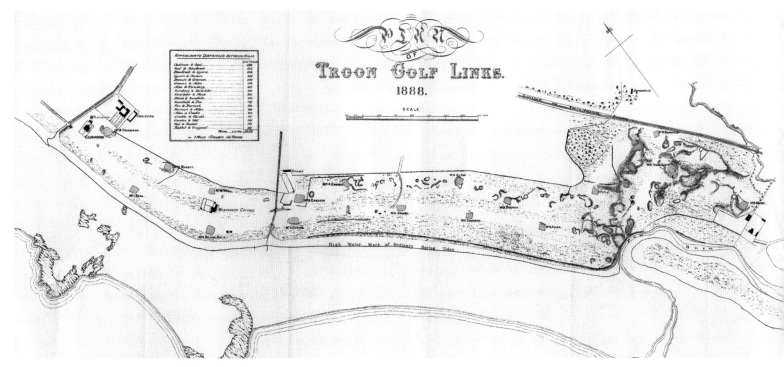

and hotel accommodation led to an agreement between the Glasgow and South Western Railway Company and Lord Ailsa. Once again, the creation of a golf course was seen as an enhancement to the value of the local estate, but in this instance the landowner also happened to be a director of the railway company and a keen golfer. Ailsa understood the benefits of good rail connections to what was a markedly remote rural community and had seen the effect on communities further up the Ayrshire coast. In May 1906, the hotel and line opened, and at that point the railway company took over the sole right to manage and maintain the course.

No plans survive to show Fernie's original layout of the course and, in a certain way, this modern re-creation of the original design is part of the 'heritage' industry prevalent in many aspects of life today. Over time, the course has been developed and improved. Today, Turnberry is an international golfing resort and spa linked to its famous hotel. What have not changed are the spectacular and commanding views over the Firth of Clyde.

No.	Yards	No.	Yards
1	300	10	450
2	350	11	500
3	370	12	360
4	280	13	280
5	400	14	260
6	200	15	370
7	160	16	240
8	290	17	570
9	360	18	300
	2710		3330

Total 6040 Yards

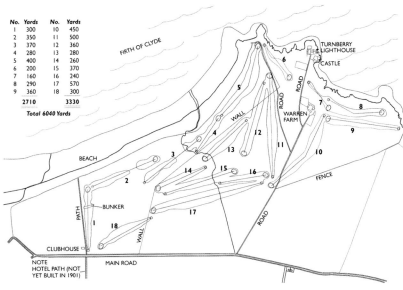

Top. Plan of Troon Golf Links (1888)

Above. Reproduction of plan of the original 18-hole course at Turnberry based on plan laid out by Willie Fernie, opened in July 1901

221

CHAPTER 43

Tourist maps for
the general public

Surprisingly, despite the increased interest in Ordnance Survey maps from collectors and researchers, comparatively little has been written on the organisation's early tourist maps produced in the interwar years. This is all the more unusual because the designs of both their covers and content reflect a major change in the way in which the Survey approached its mapping, moving it away from a heavily scientific-based body to a more commercially minded producer of cartography for a much wider audience. Despite the introduction of colour to the third edition of the 1-inch maps at the start of the twentieth century, there were serious concerns about the low sales of Survey maps in comparison to those of its competitors, particularly the *Reduced Ordnance Survey* maps produced by George Philip and John Bartholomew. This poor performance was set against a background of a growing popularity in walking, cycling and motoring as leisure pursuits. Hampered by government authorisation, the Survey did not regard itself as part of a popular map market – in fact, there was a strand of opinion which saw its job as making maps, not selling them.

In 1911, Colonel Charles Close was appointed its Director General and, only three years later, he served on a Departmental Committee set up to investigate sales of small-scale maps in particular. He was determined to produce a new style of map, revolutionising the appeal of the 1-inch series by changing its appearance. A coloured Glasgow District map produced in 1914 can be seen as a sign of things to come. The confidential findings of the Committee's investigation confirmed the lack of any mechanism whereby the Survey could compete in the commercial world. Two recommendations were proposed to meet the problem head on, namely that advertising material should be prepared and that map covers should be printed with more attractive designs. Other proposals included the setting up of local agents to sell the maps and the publication of maps of tourist districts. As one commentator has observed, 'If the maps themselves were masterpieces of the cartographer's art, the dowdy covers did everything to conceal the fact.'

The outbreak of war in August 1914 prevented any major improvement in the situation but, following the Armistice, the implementation of a policy to improve the image of the map product was greatly enhanced by the appointment, as artist and designer, of a young, newly demobilised Royal Engineer, Ellis Martin (1881–1977), who almost single-handedly turned the sales figures round in a year. His influence is best seen in the cover designs for a series of new tourist maps which usually depicted a scene from the immediate area of coverage. However, he was not alone in producing attractive images to sell Survey maps.

The two stylish covers here illustrated are the work of Arthur

Opposite. Ordnance Survey, *Rothesay and Firth of Clyde tourist map* (1920)

Palmer, who worked for a time as Martin's assistant during his 44 years of service. Published in 1922 and 1921 respectively, they are the two maps to cover parts of the Clyde area. The map *Rothesay & Firth of Clyde* was also sold as *Dunoon and the Clyde*, thus highlighting the two most popular resorts of the estuary. This image shows the watercolour cover design illustrating a scene of the Cowal peninsula backed by hills and with a sailing yacht in the foreground. Ellis Martin himself was to design an alternative illustration for the *Dunoon and the Clyde* map but, in this case, it was a stylised design of a party in an open tourer using the map to try and find their way before the sun sets. The Auld Brig at Ayr features in an evocatively misty and contrasting style for Palmer's *Burns' Country* cover. While possibly not portraying the town in an ideal fashion for a tourist map, it is still a memorable image and, perhaps, conjures up some of the poet's own directness. In fact, Palmer was responsible for most of the Scottish tourist maps published up to 1935 but, unlike their English counterparts, only one, Invergordon to Loch Ness, from 1933, shows the familiar hiker resting against a wall. Palmer's talent for landscape illustration can be clearly seen and these covers bear the hallmarks of his art, notably their art-nouveau design and limpid calligraphy. His illustrations have been described as recalling a past atmosphere and it is certainly true that part of their appeal is based on nostalgia.

Turning to the maps themselves, it is rewarding to compare the contents of both with the information contained in the sheets of the newly available *Popular Edition* 1-inch maps which began to appear at about the same time. Both maps, however, were based on earlier revisions from 1902–04. One of the most striking differences is in the way relief is indicated, with the tourist maps using a combination of hachuring, contours and layer colouring but without any hill shading. This colouring seems to be unique to individual maps, since the Cowal map has a slightly more yellow tinge on the higher ground compared with the somewhat orange tone of the *Burns' Country* map. Some grading of roads based on their width is also added. While they are described as tourist maps, it is difficult to see what additional information or enhancements have been added to set them apart. Certainly, they have been centred on areas of interest and lie outside the standard sheet framework of the contemporary 1-inch maps, but readers familiar with the plethora of signs and information on modern tourist maps would possibly find these quite ordinary. The Cowal map does not identify ferries or hotels and even omits Largs railway station while its Ayrshire counterpart is similarly lacking in highlighting features which may be of interest to the visitor. Certainly, both Burns's Cottage and the Old Brig o' Doon are marked, but one would really need to know where to look to find them. More prominent is an unusual indication of 'Roman trenches' east of Tarbolton. While such tourist maps mark a change in direction, the Survey still had a long way to go in catering for the holiday-making market.

Both Martin and Palmer gave these maps style and flair, while Close's influence was fundamental in changing methods as well as attitudes both within the Survey and among the map-buying public. His period as Director General is frequently viewed as a high point in the organisation's map-making and it is his name which was chosen for the society dedicated to the study of Ordnance Survey maps.

Opposite. Arthur Palmer, Covers of the Ordnance Survey Tourist Maps of
Rothesay & Firth of Clyde (1920, but published in 1922) and *Burns' Country* (1921)

ORDNANCE SURVEY

THE KYLES OF BUTE

TOURIST MAP of

ROTHESAY & FIRTH OF CLYDE

G R

Scale 1 Inch to 1 Mile

Price: Three Shillings

ORDNANCE SURVEY

TOURIST MAP of

BURNS' COUNTRY

R

Scale: 1 Inch to 1 Mile

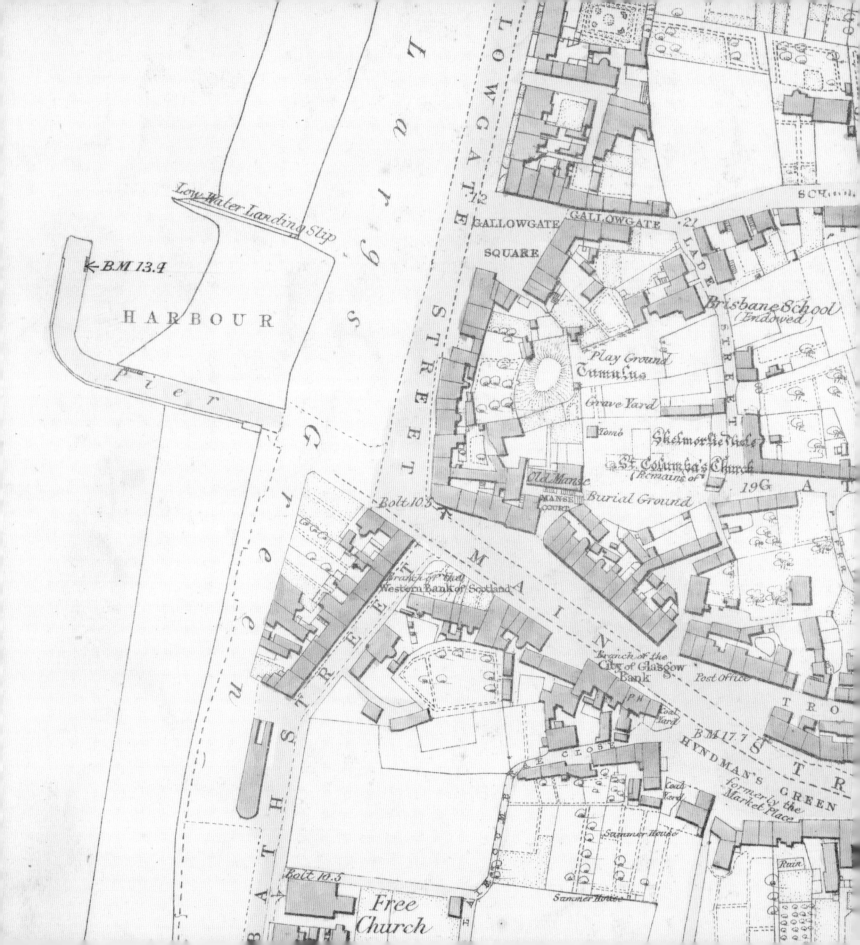

Low Water Landing Slip

← B.M 13.4

HARBOUR

Pier

Largs

Greens STREET

BATH STREET

Bolt 10.5

Free
Church

LOWGATE STREET

GALLOWGATE GALLOWGATE 21

SQUARE

LADE STREET

SCHOOL

Brisbane School
(Endowed)

Play Ground
Tumulus

Grave Yard

Tomb Skelmorlie Aisle

St. Columba's Church
(Remains of)

Old Manse Burial Ground 19 G A T

MANSE
COURT

Bolt 10.5

M A I N

Branch of the
Western Bank of Scotland

Branch of the
City of Glasgow
Bank Post office

P.H Coal
Yard

TRO

CLOSE

BM 17.7 S T R

HYNDMAN'S GREEN

formerly the
Market Place

Coal
Yard

Summer House

Summer House

Ruin

Bolt 10.5

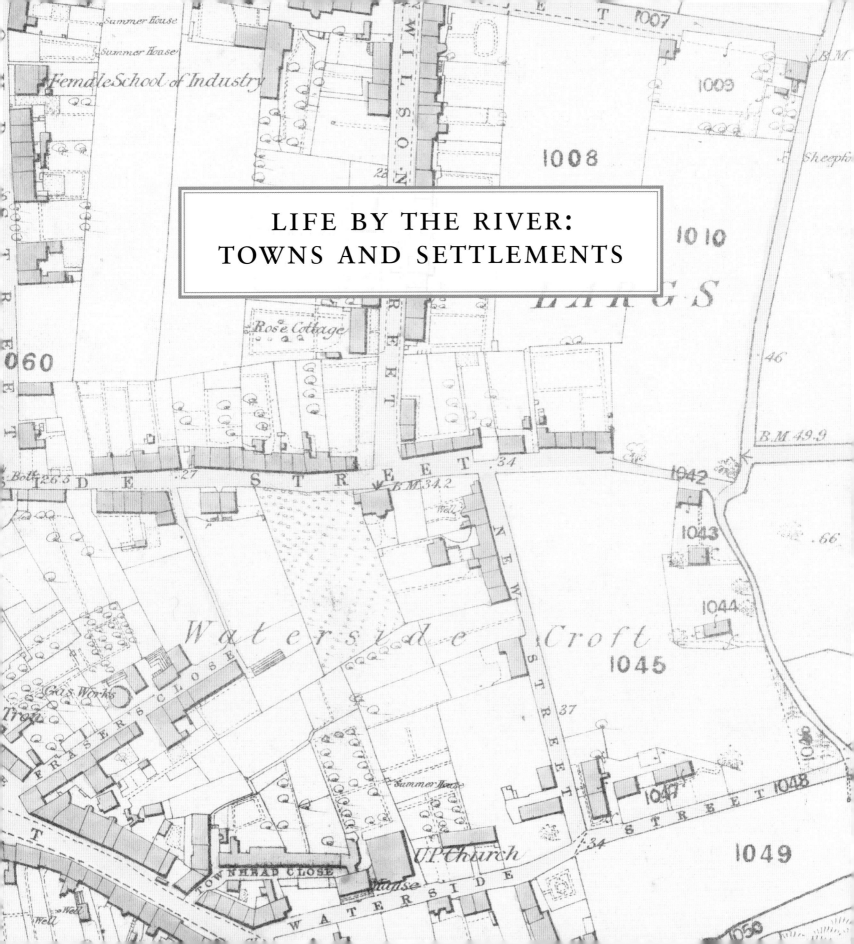

LIFE BY THE RIVER:
TOWNS AND SETTLEMENTS

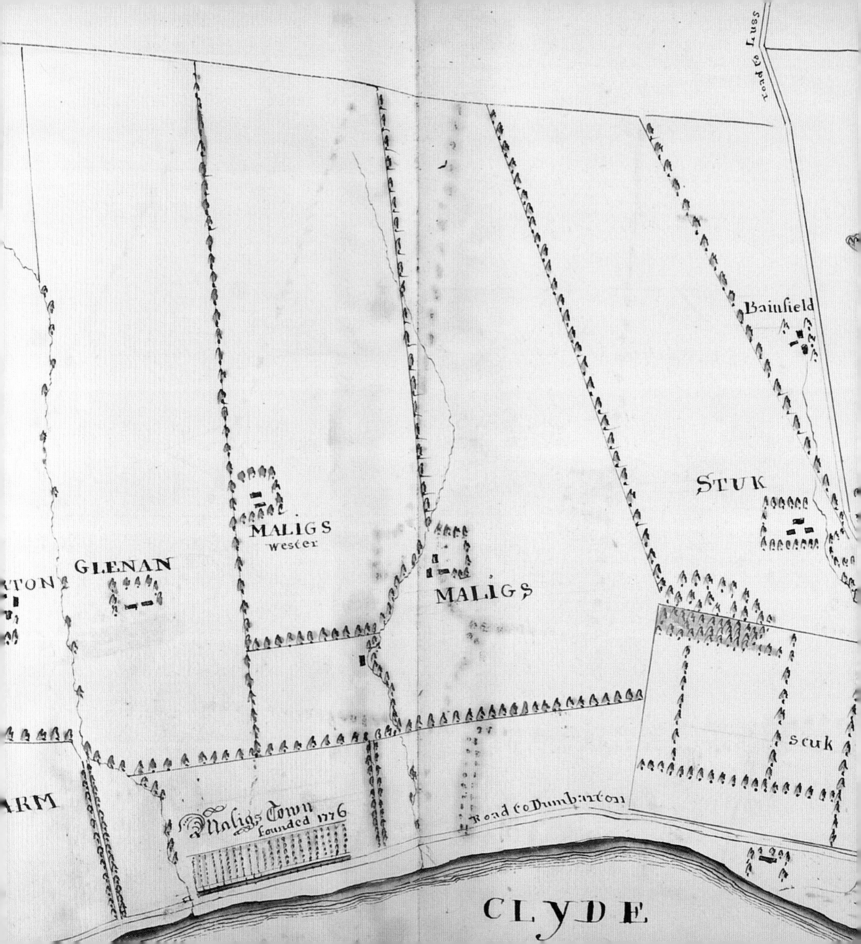

STUK

Baiusfield

MALIGS
wester

GLENAN

TON

MALIGS

scuk

ARM

Maligs Town
Founded 1776

Road to Dumbarton

CLYDE

CHAPTER 44

Helensburgh: the weaving village which became a resort

In early January 1776, the *Glasgow Chronicle* carried an advertisement offering building ground to be feued upon the shore of Malig, on the north side of the Clyde, opposite to Greenock. As an enhancement to those with a potential interest, the notice described the location as lying 'on both sides of the great road leading from Dumbarton to the Kirk of the Row' and that the ground would be regularly laid out for houses and gardens built according to a plan. Feuing was to take place two months later and enquirers were instructed to contact either Sir James Colquhoun or Charles Ross. With an appeal to trade, the details closed with this note 'Bonnet-makers, stocking, linen and woollen weavers will meet with proper encouragement. There is a large boat building at the place, for ferrying men and horses with chaises.'

Sir James Colquhoun of Luss had purchased the lands of Milligs in 1752 but he appears to have delayed any immediate development of the area. Charles Ross was an eminent Renfrewshire land surveyor who had an established business as a nurseryman near Paisley. In the late October of the previous year, he had corresponded with Colquhoun on lime quarrying and estate management in general, having recently drawn a plan for him of the Muir of Leachlaran and its adjacent farms. Two copies of the plans Ross prepared of the Luss estate in 1776 have survived, both clearly showing the settlement at Maligs,

lying between the Glenan and Milligs Burns. In truth, neither depiction shows the settlement in any great detail since Ross's commission was to survey the whole estate. Nonetheless, his large composite plan which may have been used for practical estate management does give a clear image of the regular design of the houses and their backlands. More importantly, both plans identify what was a very small-scale settlement with a markedly limited design.

One interesting addition on the larger version is the note over Ben Bowie indicating that 'Here is the best view in Scotland'. This small hill certainly enjoys stunning views both across the Clyde and to Ben Lomond. A somewhat similar comment is appended to a plan of the barony of Malig which was produced at about the same time but which does not show the newly planned settlement. Ross's notes may have been more for the benefit of his patron than as a selling point to any would-be weaver. The year following this work, Ross was to publish a county map of Dunbartonshire which again includes a clear depiction of Maligs Town as a regular row of houses lying on the north side of the coastal road. Like much of his other work, the plans reflect his naive style and rather limited use of colour.

Within a decade, the town became known as Helensburgh, named after Colquhoun's wife, Lady Helen Sutherland. Things do not appear to have gone to plan and Colquhoun's vision of

Opposite and overleaf. Charles Ross, Plan of Maligs town from *A book of maps of the estate of Luss* (1776)

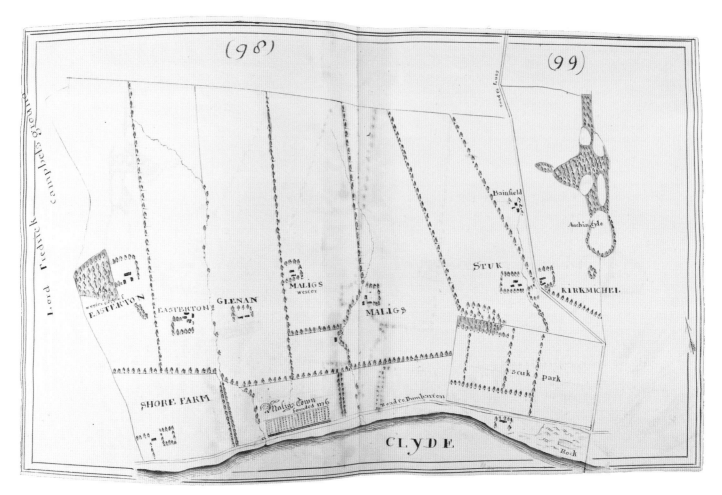

establishing a weaving trade appears never to have materialised. By January 1794, only 17 feuars were recorded in the new settlement. However, writing in the *New Statistical Account* in 1839, the parish minister, the Revd John Laurie, described Helensburgh as a rapidly increasing watering place, observing that 'There are no manufactures or public works in the parish, and consequently a great want of employment for the many individuals . . ., whose labours are but partially required in the neighbourhood.' The 'small and incommodious pier' seems to have kept the number of coasting and coal vessels to a minimum and, despite various proposals, a harbour was never constructed. Regardless, the town was thriving, having grown from a village of around 100 inhabitants to a population of 1,400 'with many excellent houses' and several 'respectable and well educated

families' residing there during the summer months. In fact, more than half of the householders listed in the *Helensburgh Directory* for 1834 offered lodgings or other accommodation for visitors.

The town's popularity was undoubtedly enhanced by the successful introduction of steam-powered navigation in the estuary by its first provost, Henry Bell. Working with Glasgow engineers John Robertson and David Napier, his vessel *Comet* was launched in 1812 and soon began a regular passenger service plying between Glasgow, Greenock and Helensburgh thrice weekly, thereby becoming the first commercial steam passenger service in Europe and inaugurating the Clyde's long association with shipbuilding and marine engineering. Lying directly across the Clyde from Greenock and having a flat and

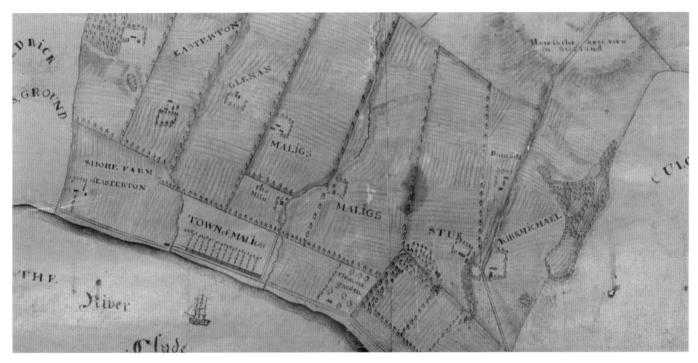

sandy shoreline, the burgh was well placed to attract both holiday-makers and, eventually, commuters.

Slightly less well known is Bell's other contribution to Helensburgh's development, namely the building of the Baths Inn, equipped with hot and cold fresh and seawater therapeutic baths. Opened in 1807, only five years after the granting of a burgh charter, this enterprise reflects a new approach in promoting the town as a resort for the well-to-do, underpinned by a growing fashion for sea bathing and the salubrious air of the Clyde coast. The establishment was run by Bell's wife, certainly more adept in business than her husband. An advertisement in the Edinburgh newspaper *Caledonian Mercury* for August 1809 provides details of the additional facilities that Bell offered. These included a conservatory, public reading room and large assembly room, but equally important was an adjoining lodging house for the use of 'genteel' families. Subsequently, the novelist John Galt was to describe the establishment in his book *The Steam-Boat* which recounted the adventures of Thomas Duffle. Other hotels, including the Tontine on West Clyde Street, extended the facilities. In 1858, the Glasgow and Helensburgh Railway opened and gradually, the town added those features typical of a resort – a bandstand, fine esplanade, putting green and golf course. That regular geometric layout of broad streets parallel to the shore which is characteristic of Helensburgh had, however, been well established by the time of its charter as can be well seen in Peter Fleming's feuing plan of about 1803. Although this design was not fully implemented, it gives a picture of a considerably larger settlement with a manuscript addition of 'baths' on East Clyde Street showing clearly the location of Bell's hotel.

Above. Charles Ross, extract from *A plan of the estate of Luss showing settlement at Maligs and Ben Bowie*

Overleaf. [Peter Fleming], *Feuing plan of Helensburgh* (c.1803)

Bel...
the
Sir James C...

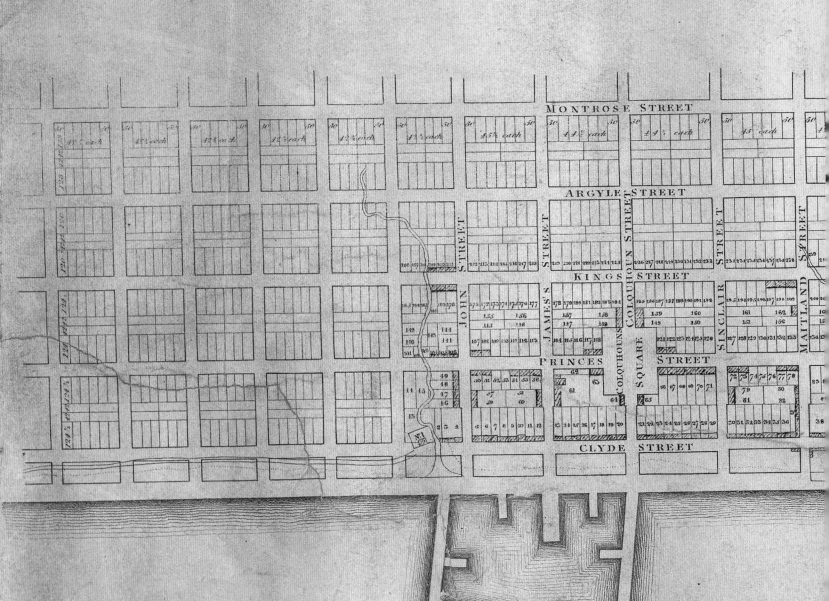

MONTROSE STREET

ARGYLE STREET

JOHN STREET

JAMES'S STREET

COLQUHOUN STREET

SINCLAIR STREET

MAITLAND STREET

KINGS STREET

PRINCES SQUARE STREET

CLYDE STREET

A Plan of the

Old and the New Town of

Largs

In the Pairsh of Largs and the shire of

AYR

The Property of

Thomas Brisbane Esqr

of that Ilk

by

David Owen
1798

9   10   11 12 13 14   15   16   17 18 19 20

BORROW

7   24

the House of Brisbane road to Largs   25

Kirkland   9   6

5

MANSE   4

Nev

Glebe   Mr Hills ground

A
Square of   NEW TOWN OF LARGS
160 feet

Sea

Quay

HARBOUR

A Scale of Scots Chains

CHAPTER 45

An unrealised plan:
Largs in 1798

While a considerable number of plans relating to the improvement of estates, communications or towns have survived from the second half of the eighteenth century, not every one records a proposal which was realised. This speculative plan of old and new Largs is one of a sequence prepared at the turn of the century, designed to attract new residents to the village and bolster the Brisbane family's finances. The Brisbanes had a long association with Largs, owning land in the parish from the beginning of the fifteenth century. They were formally ratified as feudal superiors in the confirmation charter of 1631 which established the burgh. By the time of his birth, Thomas Brisbane's father was managing the estate's affairs because the legal heir, his uncle James, was deemed mentally incapable. Brisbane junior (1720–1812) matriculated at the University of Glasgow in 1738 and was a well-read and cultured young man but, being from a large family, he entered the army. During the Jacobite Rising of 1745, he served under the Duke of Cumberland and participated in the battle of Culloden.

In 1762, three years after his father's death, Brisbane retired to the family estate, but it was to be another eight years before his uncle died and Thomas at last came into his inheritance. He married late in life, but his children included his more famous son Thomas who rose to be Governor of New South Wales and a noted astronomer. Although this was an age of general agricultural improvement, the complexities of settling sizeable debts and the dispensing of various annuities to an extended family stretched the estate's limited finances considerably, thereby restricting the scale of any proposed development.

At the time that this plan was prepared, the principal employment of the inhabitants was handloom weaving, mostly for Paisley manufacturers. However, the condition of the connecting roads and the lack of a good harbour were frequently mentioned as harming the growth of the settlement. Brisbane was keen to promote fishing and to concentrate it in the local area. The plan reflects this vision for the village's future, with a large refuge and quay designed to serve what appears to be an over-optimistically sized new town. The regular street pattern bears all the signs of the geometric approach to urban design which was typical of the period. Land plots are indicated in a symmetrical fashion to a designated and predetermined scale. The contrast between the uniformity of the new town and the somewhat more haphazard huddle of buildings and streets of the original village is evident. Even more striking are the long parcels of land on Borrow Acres to the west of the road to Brisbane House and the size of the manse and glebe lands.

The plan's creator, David Owen, was a Renfrewshire surveyor who possibly began his working life as a gardener or nurseryman in Renfrew itself. From the surviving records, it is possible that

Opposite and overleaf. David Owen, *A Plan of the Old and the New Town of Largs* (1798)

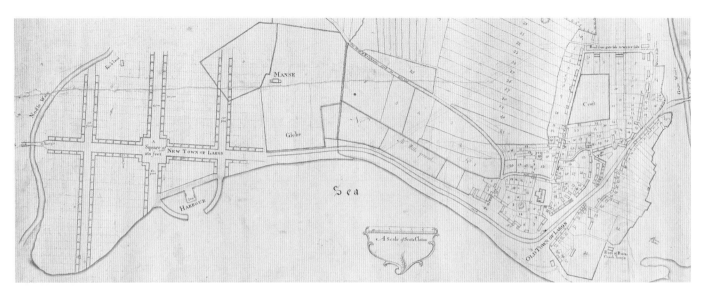

this work for Brisbane was one of his last commissions in a career that spanned in the region of 35 years. Certainly, its style reflects the assuredness and maturity of someone well capable of producing a good design and, probably, at less cost than one of the leading Edinburgh or Glasgow practitioners. During the 1760s and 1770s, Owen did much work measuring estates in his native county for the Spiers family at Elderslie and the Stewarts of Blackhall.

Despite the transport difficulties, Largs was already attractive to visitors from Glasgow and Paisley as a favoured watering place, largely because of its salubrious air, fine local walks and picturesque views over the Cumbraes to Arran, Gilbert Lang, the parish minister noted in the first *Statistical Account* in 1792 that Largs had 'been frequented a good deal of late, in the summer months, by many persons and families, for the sake of health or amusement; and it would be still more, if there were better accommodation'. One notable feature the plan identifies is the Earl of Bute's coach-house close to a small inlet, used by the earl when crossing from Rothesay to his property at Dumfries House near Cumnock.

Improved communications came with the establishment of packet boats and a steamer service to other Clyde locations. It was only in 1833 that a harbour was constructed but this paved the way for the town to develop into an attractive and popular resort, particularly for sea-bathers, due to its gradually sloping shingle beach. By the time of the *New Statistical Account*, written in 1845, it was estimated that upwards of 1,000 visitors would swell the summer population. As can be seen from the Ordnance Survey map published only 12 years later, the harbour was positioned in an entirely different location from that on Owen's depiction. By this date, the town was already spreading north in a pattern distinctly unlike the uniformity suggested in 1798. While no hotels are identified, several large properties set in their own grounds are clearly shown.

Other plans were proposed and were equally left undeveloped. Eventually, the family sold land off in individual feus. While there are several thoroughfares in the immediate area named after them, the closest reminder of the family's association with the town is, perhaps, the Brisbane Aisle lying in the grounds of Largs Old Kirk. Today, Largs remains a popular destination for day-trips and weekend breaks and the views across the Clyde still prove an attraction.

Opposite. Ordnance Survey, 1:2500 *Ayrshire first edition, Sheet III.12* showing the harbour at Largs (1857)

Auchinkean

13

21 N E L 24 S O 26 N

BM 272

Church

Coal Yard

Summer Ho

Summer Ho

Female School

School

SCHOOL STREET 26

Low Water Landing Slip

BM 13.4

HARBOUR

GALLOWGATE STREET

GALLOWGATE
SQUARE

GALLOWGATE 21

Brisbane School
(Endowed)

1060

Play Ground
Tumulus

Grave Yard

Tomb

Shelmorlie Vale

St. Columba's Church
(Remains of)

19 G A T E S I D E

Bolt 126.5

Burial Ground

Old Manse

MANSE
COURT

Bolt 10.5

MAIN

Branch of the
Western Bank of Scotland

STREET

Branch of the
City of Glasgow
Bank

Post Office

P.H.

Coal
Yard

T R O N P L A C E

Gas Works

Tron

FRASER'S C

HYNDMAN'S GREEN
formerly the
Market Place

BM 17.5

S T R E E T

Coal
Yard

Ruin

Well

CLOSE

Coal
Yard

Summer House

Summer House

Free
Church

BATH STREET

THE VENNEL

Bolt 10.5

Free Church
School

Sur 8.2

Pier

Largs

to

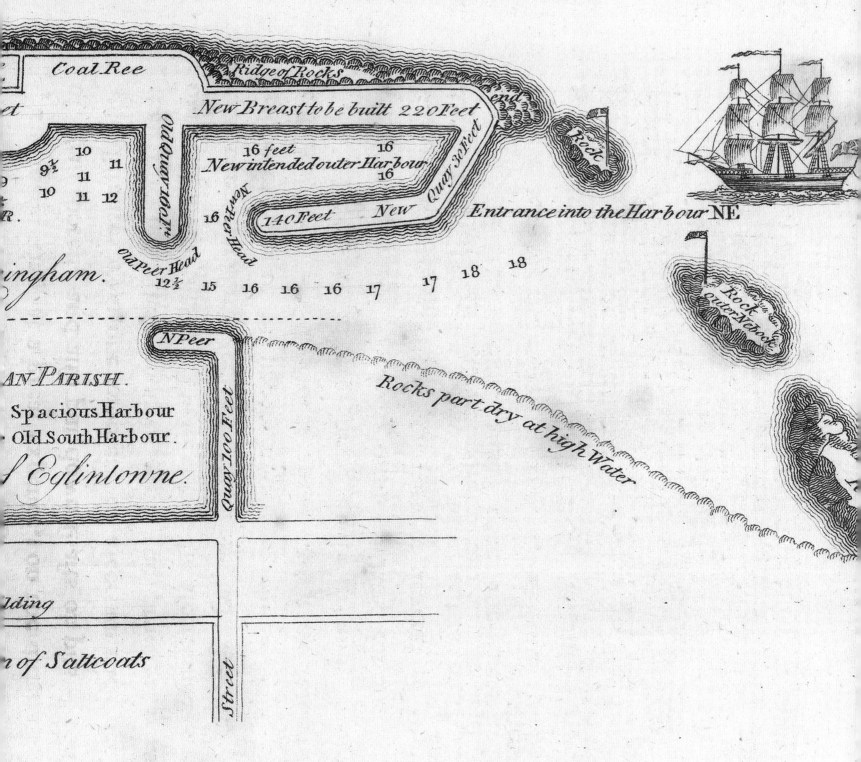

Coal Ree

Ridge of Rocks

New Breast to be built 220 Feet

end

Rock

Old Quay 100 Feet

16 feet 16

New intended outer Harbour

16

Quay 30 Feet

New Peer Head

16

140 Feet New

Entrance into the Harbour NE

Old Peer Head

ingham.

12½ 15 16 16 16 17 17 18 18

9½ 10 11

10 11 11

10 11 12

Rock outer Nabock

N Peer

AN PARISH.

Spacious Harbour

Old South Harbour.

Quay 100 Feet

Rocks part dry at high Water

f Eglintowne.

Street

lding

n of Saltcoats

CHAPTER 46

A tale of two harbours: Saltcoats and Ardrossan

Despite the length of its coastline, Ayrshire has relatively few harbours. During the Elizabethan period, a military report described the Carrick shore as an 'iron coast' emphasising the inhospitable nature of the seaboard north of Galloway. In addition, entry into the harbours of both Ayr and Irvine were hampered by sandbars at their entrances. Saltcoats and Ardrossan lie further north and both were to develop harbour facilities during the eighteenth century. What is more surprising is that they lie within only a little more than a mile of each other. The story behind this situation is one strongly influenced by the competing interests of two local landowners, Robert Reid Cunninghame (1744–1814) and Hugh Montgomerie, 12th Earl of Eglinton (1739–1819).

Unsurprisingly, Saltcoats takes its name from the town's earliest industry, established during the reign of James V when salt was harvested from the saline waters of the Firth of Clyde. At about the same time, it was created a burgh of barony, a settlement subsequently growing up on the headland around the natural harbour. This was improved during the later seventeenth century by the construction of an L-shaped stone pier. The local landowner, Robert Cunningham of Auchenharvie, was the force behind this as his chief interest was the industrial development of the area, particularly through the mining and exportation of coal, along with the building of several new salt pans. In fact,

the width of the harbour quays confirms that it was intended principally for coal shipment rather than the landing of fish.

One major problem for Saltcoats as a harbour was that it lay between two parishes, Ardrossan and Stevenston, and was part-owned by two proprietors. This is clearly seen in this detailed plan of the harbour drawn to accompany Dr James Wodrow's extensive account of the parish of Stevenston for the *Statistical Account of Scotland* in 1791. As the local minister, he recorded several suggestions for improving the locality, including, unsurprisingly, enlarging the harbour. The plan shows an intended outer basin, as well as indicating a new breastwork and various soundings in the Stevenston part of the haven. What it shows is the relatively narrow entry channel between the offshore rocks which, combined with a relatively small port facility, limited the loading of vessels. John Duncan, whose charge was the neighbouring parish of Ardrossan, was equally critical of these handicaps, but his opinions may well have been influenced by the interests of his patron, the Earl of Eglinton. Such awareness of what was needed had been raised by recent activity to improve facilities, which included an accurate survey and the preparation of estimated costs calculated to require investment of about £2,000. Subsequently, in 1803, John Rennie was to investigate Saltcoats as the terminal point for an intended canal from Glasgow but this was never realised, largely because

Opposite and overleaf. Plan of the Harbour of Saltcoats engraved for the 'Old' *Statistical Account* (1791)

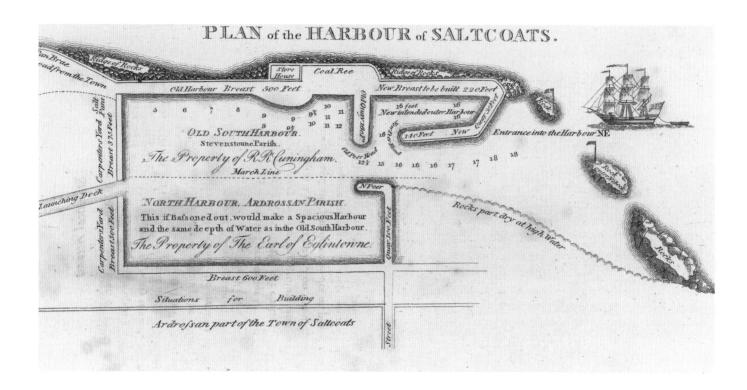

of the expense and unsuitability of the harbour.

The plan and account presented by Wodrow are almost contemporary with the surveying work of John Ainslie which resulted in his outstanding volume of estate plans for Hugh Montgomerie in 1789–90 and which included this finely detailed town plan indicating individual houses and yards. In addition, it shows the harbour, dockyard, windmill and limekilns, and provides a clear impression of the approach into the haven, as well as the offshore Reid and Nebbock Rocks. Looking specifically at the harbour, it is obvious that Cunningham had the better of the division, for the northern portion belonging to the Eglinton family consisted mostly of foul ground mixed with rock and stones. Ainslie included a more general smaller-scale plan of the whole barony of Ardrossan and was also responsible for drawing the map which accompanied Rennie's 1803 canal proposal.

Despite several disadvantages, Saltcoats became the site of the first fully working canal in Scotland. Opened by Robert

Reid Cunninghame in 1772, it was a very basic design without locks or reservoirs, which was extended by subsequent cuttings to newly opened coal pits. Cunninghame sought to capitalise on the Irish demand for coal by linking the neighbouring Stevenston coalfield to his harbour and, in a joint venture with Archibald Montgomerie, 11th Earl of Eglinton, he sought to double its capacity following an Act authorising a new pier extension to ease the difficulties faced by ships queuing to await their coal cargoes. Circumstances changed following the earl's death and the issue of coal transportation resulted in the production of several maps to support both sides of a case brought before the Court of Session.

Hugh Montgomerie, the 12th Earl, was determined to build a rival wet dock at Ardrossan, located entirely within his own lands. He was chairman of the North Ayrshire Turnpike Trust and a decision to locate a turnpike toll to the west of the coal depot was a serious threat to Cunninghame's transport costs, since by this date some 42,000 loads were being shipped annually.

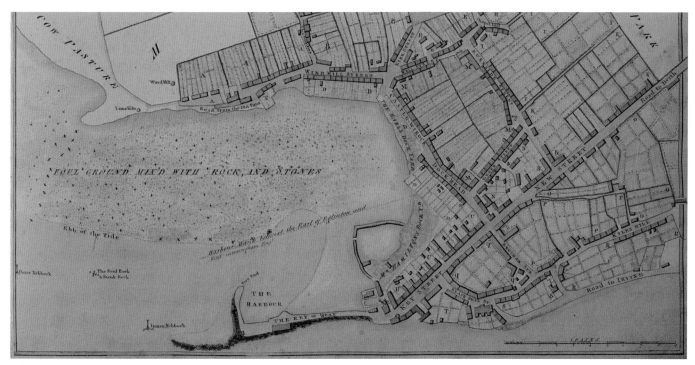

John Ainslie, Plan of Saltcoats from the volume of plans of Eglinton Estate (1789–90)

To circumvent this, Cunninghame started work on an iron rail track along the shoreline beside the toll road. This was challenged in 1811 by the Montgomeries who initiated court proceedings. At the core of the arguments were the issues of ownership of, as well as access to, the coast but also, of course, the impact of enterprise on vested interests. The case was abandoned the following year, but the surviving maps are an important source of detail about Saltcoats in the early nineteenth century.

Montgomerie called in Peter Fleming to draw this plan of the town and the adjoining lands of Townhead to identify his own property, as well as the sands and the coast. Fleming marked the new sections added to the harbour by Cunninghame as part of his improvement scheme but, as has been noted elsewhere, the plan focuses on the area of dispute where, according to the Montgomerie claim, the railway prevented direct access to the beach for sea bathing. With the potential for this to affect the value of seaside properties, it is perhaps understandable why the earl turned his attention to the development of Ardrossan.

The railway eventually was completed to the old quay pier in 1827 but, with the linking of Ardrossan to the Eglinton coalfields and to the railway line to Glasgow, the exporting of coal from Saltcoats dwindled and ceased after 1852. The small shipbuilding industry which had grown up nearby moved out and, with the subsequent development of Ardrossan as a larger harbour and ferry port, trade at Saltcoats declined.

Around this time, Saltcoats was described as the principal watering place in Ayrshire, with between 300 and 500 visitors travelling from Paisley, Glasgow and Hamilton during the summer months to enjoy the sea bathing and the local beaches. Given that the population was recorded as nearly 4,000, it suggests a considerable summer influx of visitors. However, by the advent of the *New Statistical Account*, David Landsborough reflected that it was no longer 'the most fashionable sea-bathing place on the west coast'. Like Largs, the town had seen an increase in the number of weavers, such industry being enhanced by better road communications. Some renovation of the harbour

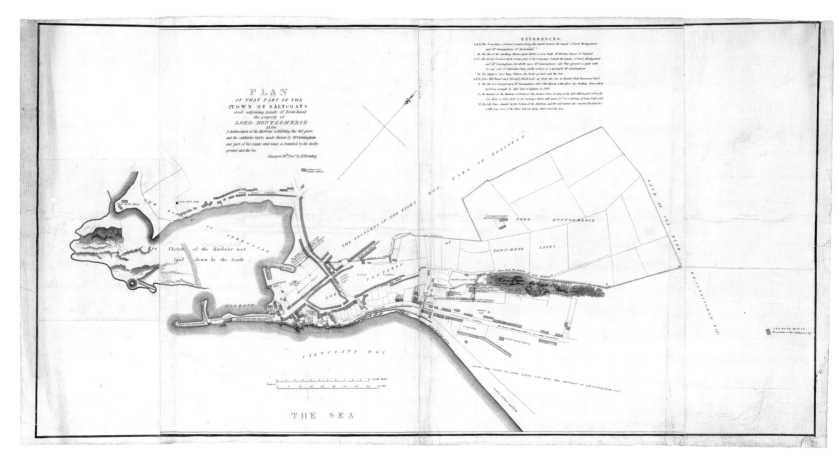

PLAN
OF THAT PART OF THE
TOWN OF SALTCOATS
and adjoining Lands of Town-head
the property of
LORD MONTGOMERIE
1810
A Delineation of the Harbour exhibiting the Old piers
and the additions lately made thereto by McCunningham
and part of his Lands and Sands as bounded by the Rocky
ground and the Sea.
Glasgow 10th Novr by P.Fleming

THE SEA

took place in about 1914 but this appears to have silted up in the 1920s. Despite this and its decline as a seaside resort with the arrival of cheap air travel, the town is still a destination for day-trippers on a sunny summer afternoon. The tidal bathing, yachting and paddling pools on the site of the old salt pans recall busier days but, as an indication of a more contemporary recreation, the Ayrshire Coastal Path and the Coast Cycleway, part of the National Cycle Network, both follow the Saltcoats beach promenade.

In contrast, Ardrossan's growth was the result of the construction of its harbour, begun in 1806. Thomas Telford was consulted by Montgomerie on the feasibility of a separate canal to link Glasgow to a deep-water harbour on the coast and he recommended Ardrossan as the only fit western terminal for such a proposal, protected as it was to the south-west by an extensive ridge of rocks and to the north by Horse Isle. The earl intended to create a much larger deep-water facility here to facilitate the loading of freight at any state of the tide. Further

Above. Peter Fleming, *Plan of that part of the Town of Saltcoats ...* (1810)

Opposite. David Henry, *A Chart of the Bay of Ardrossan on the west coast of Ayrshire with a plan of the intended harbour and wet dock* (1813)

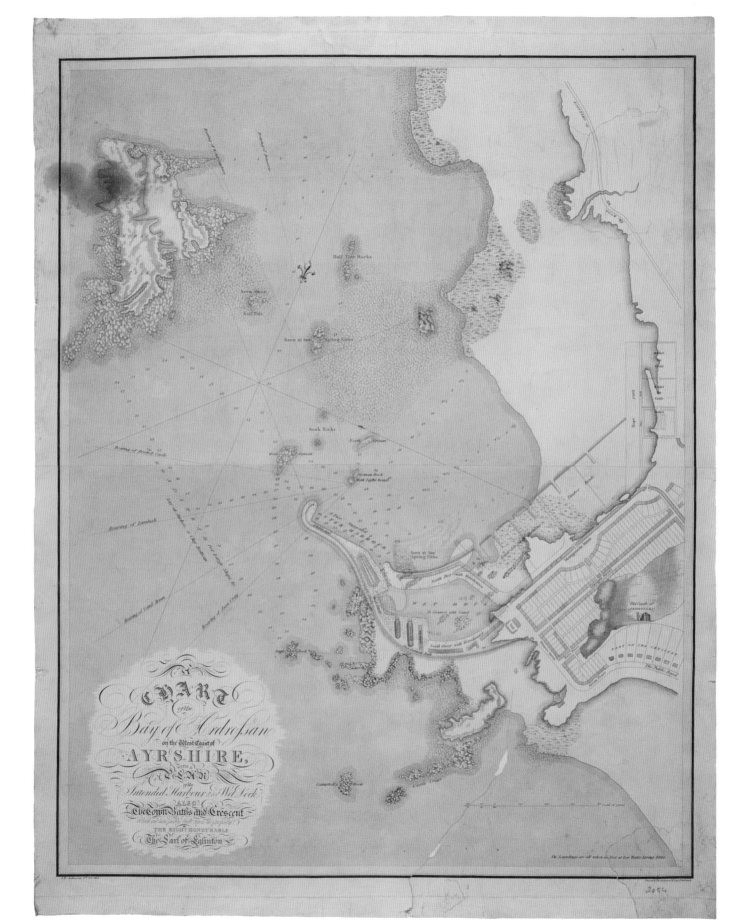

A CHART of the Bay of Ardrossan on the West Coast of AYRSHIRE, with a Plan of the Intended Harbour and Wet Dock ALSO The Town Baths and Crescent Which are now partly built upon the property of THE RIGHT HONOURABLE The Earl of Eglinton

The Soundings are all taken in Feet at Low Water Spring Ebbs.

2054

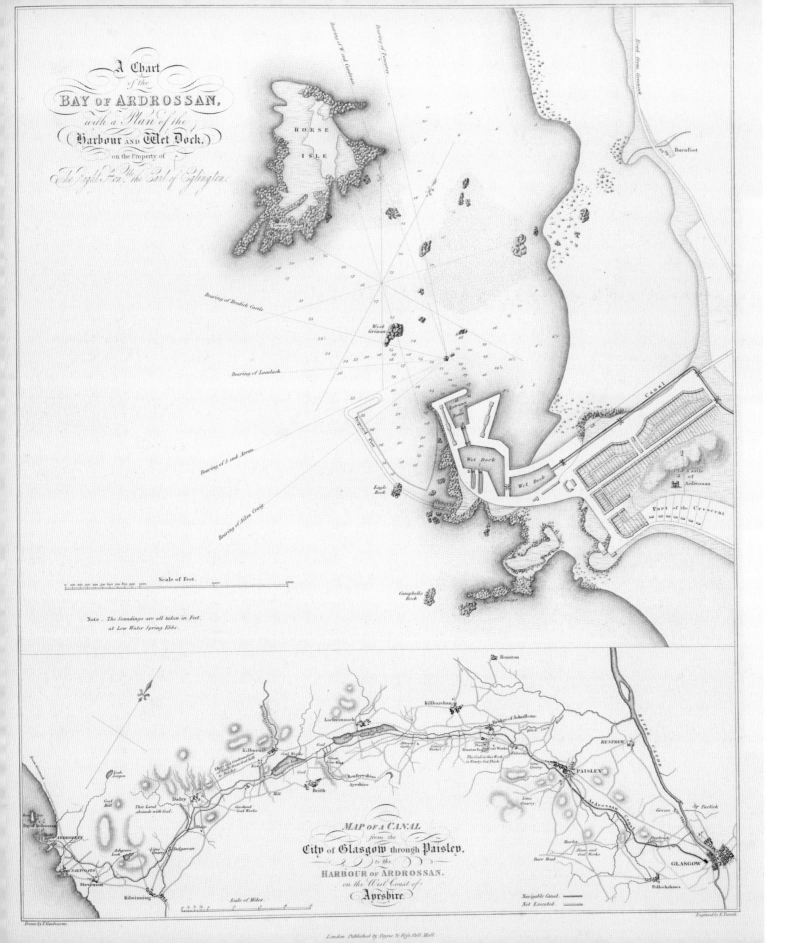

A Chart
of the
BAY OF ARDROSSAN,
with a Plan of the
Harbour AND Wet Dock,
on the Property of
The Right Hon.ble the Earl of Eglinton.

HORSE ISLE

Tower

Bearing of W. and Lamlash

Bearing of Pinmore

Bearing of Brodick Castle

Bearing of Lamlash

Bearing of S. end Arran

Bearing of Ailsa Craig

West Grinan

Eagle Rock

Campbell's Rock

Wet Dock

Entrance Basin

Wet Dock

Canal

Old Castle of Ardrossan

Part of the Crescent

Burnfoot

Road from Greenock

Scale of Feet.

Note. The Soundings are all taken in Feet at Low Water Spring Ebbs.

Drawn by T. Gainsborne.

MAP OF A CANAL
from the
City of Glasgow through Paisley,
to the
HARBOUR OF ARDROSSAN,
on the West Coast of
Ayrshire.

Houston

Killbarchan

Lochwinnoch

Bridge of Johnstone

RENFREW

RIVER CLYDE

Kilburnie

Coal Works

PAISLEY

Loch Jargon

Dalry

Beith

Renfreyshire Ayrshire

Lime Quarry

Ardrossan Canal

Govan

Partick

Bay of Ardrossan

ARDROSSAN

Blair

Coal Hill

This Land abounds with Coal.

Adgreen loch

Lime Quarry

Dalgarcan

Barr Head

Hurlet Alum and Coal Works

Pollockshaws

Dumbreck Colliery

GLASGOW

SALTCOATS

Stevenston

Kilwinning

Scale of Miles.

Navigable Canal

Not Executed

Engraved by E. Turrell.

London, Published by Payne & Foss, Pall Mall.

potential competition came from the nearby natural harbour at Troon which was being promoted by the Duke of Portland, following the construction of Scotland's first public railway to bring coals from his Kilmarnock pits to the coast.

These two charts of the bay at Ardrossan come from the Montgomerie family papers and the *Atlas to the Life of Thomas Telford* published four years after his death. Although they appear to be similar at first glance, a closer scrutiny shows that the earlier design indicates the 'intended' harbour and wet dock. Drawn by local surveyor David Henry in October 1813 and engraved by the Edinburgh firm of James Kirkwood and Son, it shows a far more extensive wet dock area than the Telford atlas plan. Additionally, the attention paid to marking the detail of the bearings, soundings and offshore rocks emphasises the problems of a narrow and difficult entrance. Beyond the immediate harbour area, Henry marks the cattle market, rope yard and areas designated for shipbuilding and timber storage, as well as naming certain buildings and streets. Telford's design shows fewer graving docks but a proposed pier extension to create an outer harbour, with an entrance basin leading to two smaller wet docks. Combined with a lack of space and the eventual collapse of the canal project, the original design was subject to subsequent alteration, as suggested by the later variant.

Montgomerie clearly did nothing by halves for, as part of a larger development of the town, he commissioned Robert Reid, subsequently the King's architect and surveyor, to prepare a grid of well-built villas enhanced by an elegant crescent lying to the east. A plan of the proposals appeared in William Aiton's *General View of the Agriculture of the County of Ayr* published in 1811. It was drawn by Peter Nicholson, a local architect who had been responsible for the design of the temporary timber replacement for Glasgow's Hutcheson Bridge built in 1803, and engraved by James Lumsden and Son. Bearing all the traits of the grand design in its layout, it emphasises space and regularity, all with an eye to attract genteel sea-bathers. Enhanced

by a plan of a proposed cloth market house and elevations of the terraced houses, the document provides an illuminating backdrop to Montgomerie's vision. The main grid to the town makes no allowance for the Castle Hill and is interrupted only by the line of the proposed canal intended to link with Glasgow. Although simple in its conception, the effectiveness of this grid was adhered to for the next five decades. The design was also supported by a series of promotional feuing plans produced by Reid. It is recorded that Telford was sufficiently impressed by Nicholson's work to recommend him for the post of County Surveyor for Cumberland in 1808.

Development of the town, however, was slow and in his contribution to the *New Statistical Account*, the Reverend John Bryce described Ardrossan in 1837 as 'yet only in its infancy'. However, he took pains to list several 'families of distinction' who had frequented the locality recently, before detailing its several key features, including the baths which are identified on the Nicholson plan. It was not until the following year that Ardrossan was erected into a burgh of barony but, significantly, Bryce recorded that 60,000 tons of coal had been carried to the harbour in the previous year. By 1855, the figure had increased to 260,000 tons. The railway link strengthened the growth in passenger and freight transport both inland and by ferry to Stranraer, Arran and, subsequently, Belfast and the Isle of Man.

Within 50 years, the town's population more than quadrupled and major extensions to the harbour took place in the 1880s under the guidance of its chief engineer, John Strain. The final plan of the docks from 1895 indicates the various facilities at what had become a bustling port. Produced by Strain, Robertson and Thomson, consulting engineers in Glasgow, and authorised by John Craig, secretary and general manager of the harbour company, it bears the hallmark of an advertising promotion for the services provided there, with tables of the sizes of the docks, including the graving dock and the repair slipway, as well as the indication of the railway lines and stations for

Opposite. Thomas Telford, A Chart of the Bay of Ardrossan with a Plan of the Harbour and Wet Dock from *Atlas to the Life of Thomas Telford, Civil Engineer* (1838)

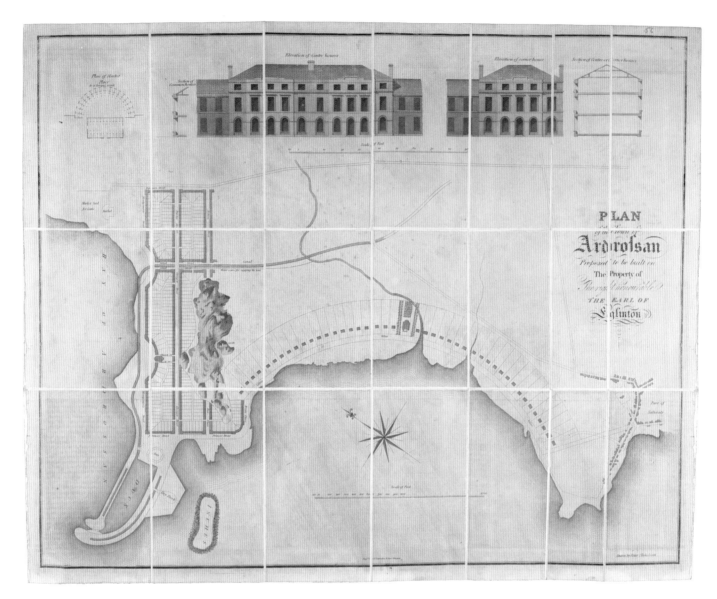

both the Glasgow and South Western and the Caledonian Railways, the shipbuilding yard, engineering works, cranes and warehouses. Additional notes emphasise the links to the coalfields and ironworks of Lanarkshire and Ayrshire, the availability of hydraulic hoists, a good water supply and the steamer links to other ports. Craig must surely have been contented by the success of the port's trade, for by 1900 a million tons of goods were being shipped out of the harbour.

Above. Peter Nicolson, Plan of the Town of Ardrossan proposed to be built; from William Aiton, *General View of the Agriculture of the County of Ayr* (1811)

Opposite. John Strain, *Plan of the Ardrossan harbour and docks* (1895)

246

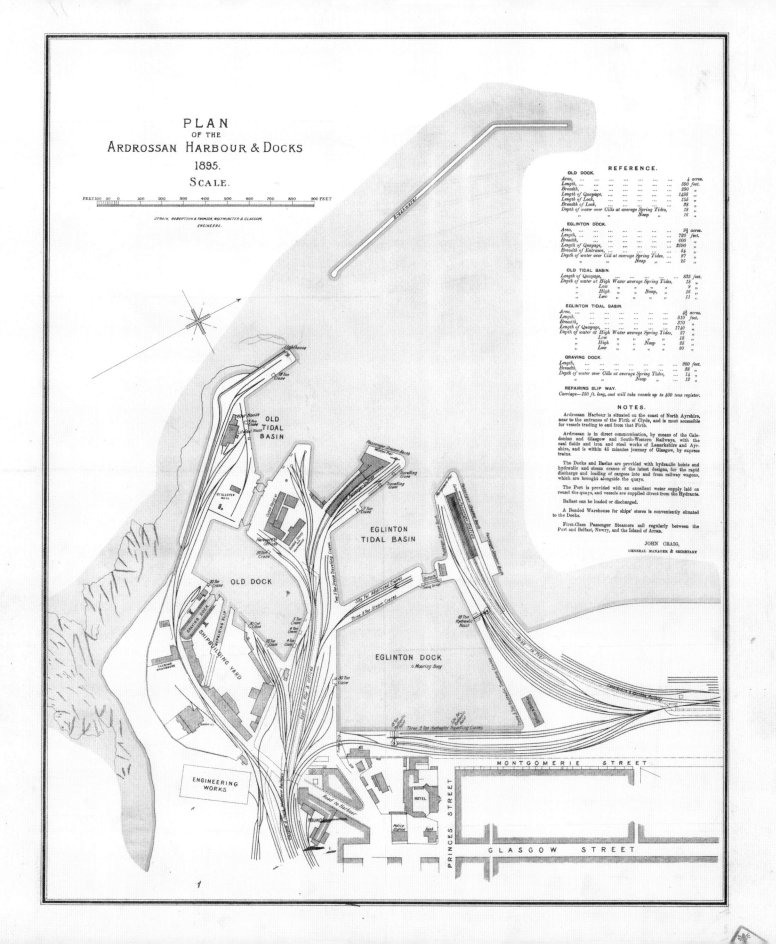

PLAN
OF THE
ARDROSSAN HARBOUR & DOCKS
1895.
SCALE.

FEET 100 50 0   100   200   300   400   500   600   700   800   900 FEET

STRAIN, ROBERTSON & THOMSON, WESTMINSTER & GLASGOW,
ENGINEERS.

REFERENCE.

OLD DOCK.
Area,	...	4 acres.
Length,	...	590 feet.
Breadth,	...	290 "
Length of Quayage,	...	1493 "
Length of Lock,	...	155 "
Breadth of Lock,	...	38 "
Depth of water over Cills at average Spring Tides,	...	18 "
" " Neap	...	16 "

EGLINTON DOCK.
Area,	...	9¼ acres.
Length,	...	720 feet.
Breadth,	...	600 "
Length of Quayage,	...	2590 "
Breadth of Entrance,	...	54 "
Depth of water over Cill at average Spring Tides,	...	27 "
" " Neap	...	25 "

OLD TIDAL BASIN.
Length of Quayage,	...	838 feet.
Depth of water at High Water average Spring Tides,	...	13 "
" Low	...	9 "
" High Neap,	...	16 "
" Low	...	11 "

EGLINTON TIDAL BASIN.
Area,	...	4¼ acres.
Length,	...	510 feet.
Breadth,	...	370 "
Length of Quayage,	...	1740 "
Depth of water at High Water average Spring Tides,	...	27 "
" Low	...	18 "
" High Neap,	...	25 "
" Low	...	20 "

GRAVING DOCK.
Length,	...	260 feet.
Breadth,	...	38 "
Depth of water over Cills at average Spring Tides,	...	14 "
" " Neap	...	12 "

REPAIRING SLIP WAY.
Carriage—150 ft. long, and will take vessels up to 400 tons register.

NOTES.

Ardrossan Harbour is situated on the coast of North Ayrshire, near to the entrance of the Firth of Clyde, and is most accessible for vessels trading to and from that Firth.

Ardrossan is in direct communication, by means of the Caledonian and Glasgow and South-Western Railways, with the coal fields and iron and steel works of Lanarkshire and Ayrshire, and is within 45 minutes journey of Glasgow, by express trains.

The Docks and Basins are provided with hydraulic hoists and hydraulic and steam cranes of the latest designs, for the rapid discharge and loading of cargoes into and from railway wagons, which are brought alongside the quays.

The Port is provided with an excellent water supply laid on round the quays, and vessels are supplied direct from the Hydrants.

Ballast can be loaded or discharged.

A Bonded Warehouse for ships' stores is conveniently situated to the Docks.

First-Class Passenger Steamers sail regularly between the Port and Belfast, Newry, and the Island of Arran.

JOHN CRAIG,
GENERAL MANAGER & SECRETARY

OLD TIDAL BASIN

EGLINTON TIDAL BASIN

OLD DOCK

EGLINTON DOCK

SHIPBUILDING YARD

ENGINEERING WORKS

MONTGOMERIE STREET

PRINCES STREET

GLASGOW STREET

WEST QUAY

THE HARBOUR

MID QUAY

EAST QUAY

SHORE STREET

Ware Houses

DRY DOCK

Engine

Stables

Collectors Close

Fresh Market

Coal Ree

ROAD TO GLASGOW

Garden

CAMPBELL ST STREET

NEW WARK BURYING GROUND

Garden

Cotton Factory

THE ROPE WORK

Rope Walk

GARDEN

Rope Work Close

THE PROPOSED NEW ROAD TO GLASGOW

THE PROPOSED NEW STREET ABOVE THE TOWN

Garden

Windy hall

CHAPTER 47

Port Glasgow in 1799

Due largely to the increase in trade and problems of navigation on the Clyde, the magistrates of Glasgow made several attempts to acquire a site for a harbour of their own. In 1668 they purchased lands beside Newark where they developed a port to accommodate their merchant vessels at the point where the River Clyde ends and the firth begins. The first graving dock in Scotland was built here in the early 1760s and the Glasgow authorities employed both John Watt and James Barry to draw plans of the town. A surviving Barry plan from the 1770s clearly identifies ships in the new dock and both depictions indicate a markedly geometric layout to what was a planned settlement, with the principal streets following the line of the bay. While the site was advantageous for shipping, largely due to the channel close to the shore being reasonably broad and deep, the hinterland of the coastal plain is relatively narrow and backed by a steep hill. Writing in 1818, George Robertson commented that little more than half of the parish had been cultivated to any great extent and this consisted 'chiefly of the gardens belonging to the town, and to the pleasure grounds belonging to numerous villas that have recently been erected in the neighbourhood'.

This elegant plan, prepared by John Ainslie in 1799, shows the town, harbour and those various gardens surrounding the burgh. The design also emphasises the restricted site on which the settlement was founded and which would hamper its later development. It is the first to show Port Glasgow in any detail and dates from a time when the streets and buildings of many Scottish towns were beginning to be recorded meticulously. Based in Edinburgh, Ainslie's work covered a wide range of commissions covering many parts of the country. In the same year that he drew this plan, the Newark magistrates and council petitioned the Glasgow authorities with a proposal to convert the bay area between the east quay and Blackhouse Neuk into a wet dock to improve the facilities for shipping. The Neuk is one of relatively few coastal locations identified on the plan which, interestingly, was to form the basis of an engraved reduction dedicated to the burgh's magistrates and town council only seven years later. This later copy was one of a series prepared in the first decade of the new century, all produced with improvement in mind and suggesting various harbour proposals. It shows a far more extensive development to the north of the quays of the original port, with 20,000 square yards appropriated for new warehouses, based on legislation parliament had passed specifically in 1801 for the maintenance of the harbour. Despite this plan to expand the dock facilities considerably, the proposed new harbour was never built and a simpler scheme based on the wet dock proposals of 1799 was subsequently completed in 1836.

Ainslie's original plan was produced before the burgh's trade was seriously affected by the improvements on the Clyde, partic-

Opposite and overleaf. John Ainslie's original manuscript plan of Port Glasgow (1799)

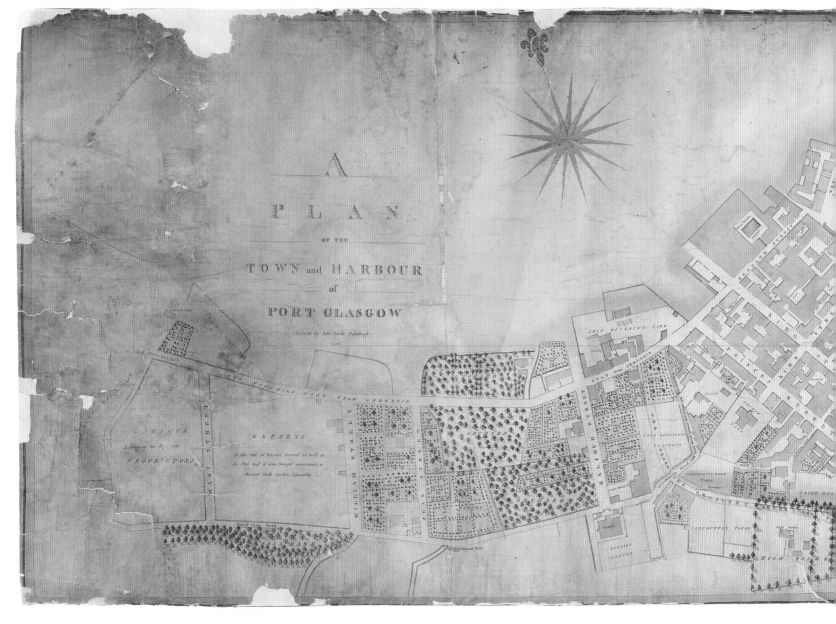

A PLAN OF THE TOWN and HARBOUR of PORT GLASGOW

ularly following those works suggested by Golborne, and identifies two shipbuilding yards, namely that owned by John Wood and Thomas McGill's Newark yard, as well as the warehouses, sheds and quays of the dock, a cotton factory and rope work. One unusual feature is its marked lack of definition of the coast. Like many town maps of the period, it also marks new street and road proposals, reflecting that spirit of improvement which was characteristic of the age. The turnpike road from Greenock

to Glasgow followed the line of the coast and Ainslie marks a proposed new and less circuitous route which was not carried forward to his later engraving.

By 1799, the town had a population of just over 4,000 but, unlike other places growing up along the banks of the Clyde, Port Glasgow was never to develop into a watering place or destination for tourists. Although the harbour was described as among the best in Scotland, its distance from the main market

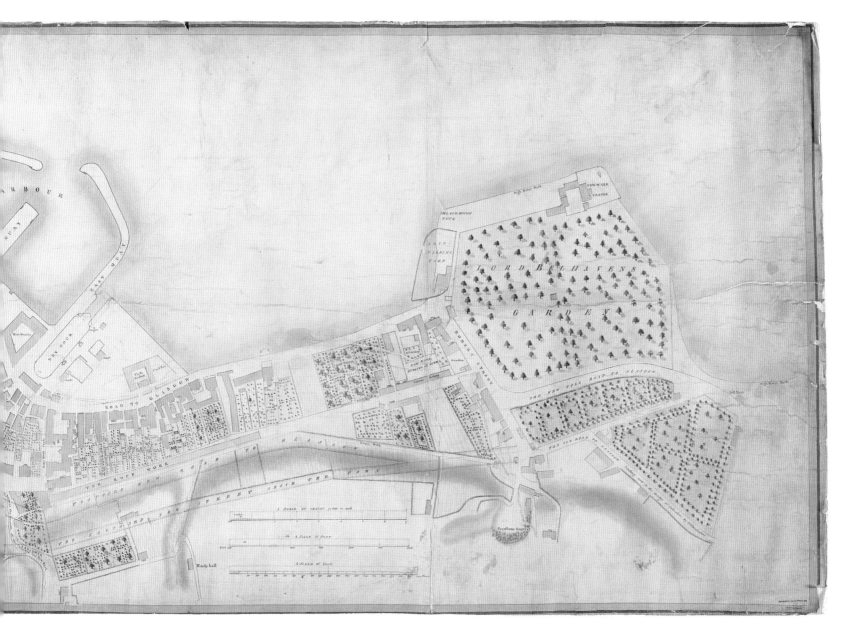

of Glasgow, combined with a loss of the West Indies trade to other ports, road and rail improvements, and the transference of much of the coasting trade to Glasgow, resulted in a decline in shipping itself. However, the port was to develop into a ship-building centre and is celebrated as the place where the first commercial steam vessel in Europe, the paddle steamer *Comet*, was built in 1812. At one stage, it was responsible for about a quarter of the total tonnage launched on the Clyde but, like other places along the river, has suffered from the decline in such heavy industry.

Overleaf. John Ainslie, *Plan of the Town and Harbour of Port Glasgow and Newark …* (1806)

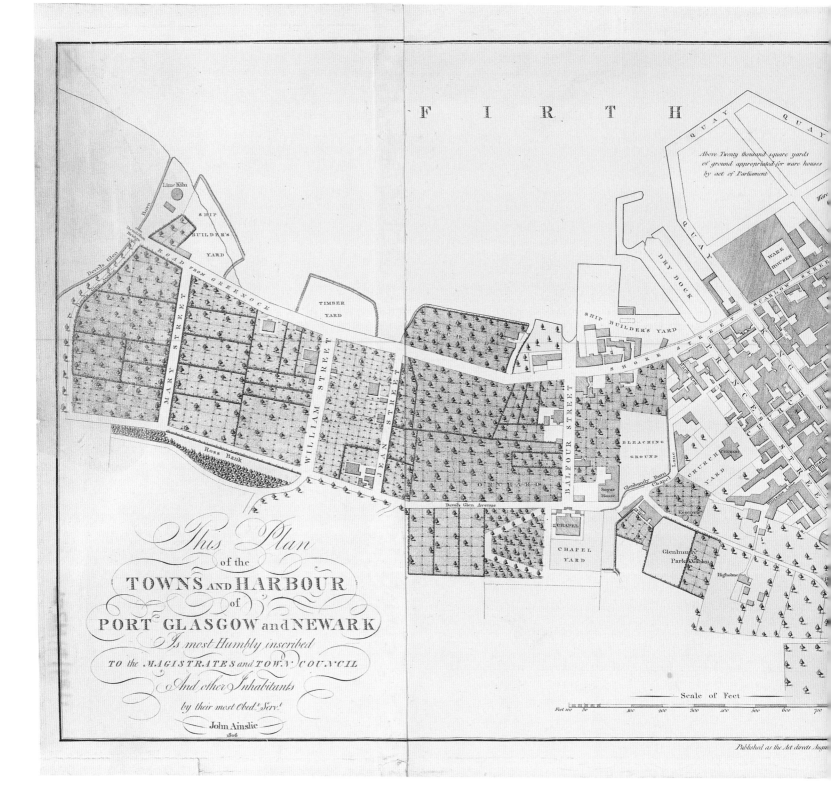

FIRTH

Lime Kiln

SHIP BUILDER'S YARD

Devil's Glen

ROAD FROM GREENOCK

MARY STREET

WILLIAM STREET

TIMBER YARD

Ross Bank

JEAN STREET

Devil's Glen Avenue

ORCHARD

BALFOUR STREET

Sugar House

Glenhunly Burn Chapel

BLEACHING GROUND

Lane

CHAPEL

CHAPEL YARD

Glenhunly Park & Garden

Reservoir

Higholme St

CHURCH YARD

SHIP BUILDER'S YARD

SHORE STREET

DRY DOCK

QUAY

QUAY

QUAY

Above Twenty thousand square yards
of ground appropriated for ware houses
by act of Parliament

Ware

WARE HOUSES

SCARLOW STREET

KING STREET

PRINCES STREET

CHURCH STREET

This Plan
of the
TOWNS AND HARBOUR
of
PORT GLASGOW and NEWARK
Is most Humbly inscribed
TO the MAGISTRATES and TOWN COUNCIL
And other Inhabitants
by their most Obed.t Serv.t
John Ainslie
1806

Scale of Feet
Feet 100 50   100   200   300   400   500   600   700

Published as the Act directs Augu...

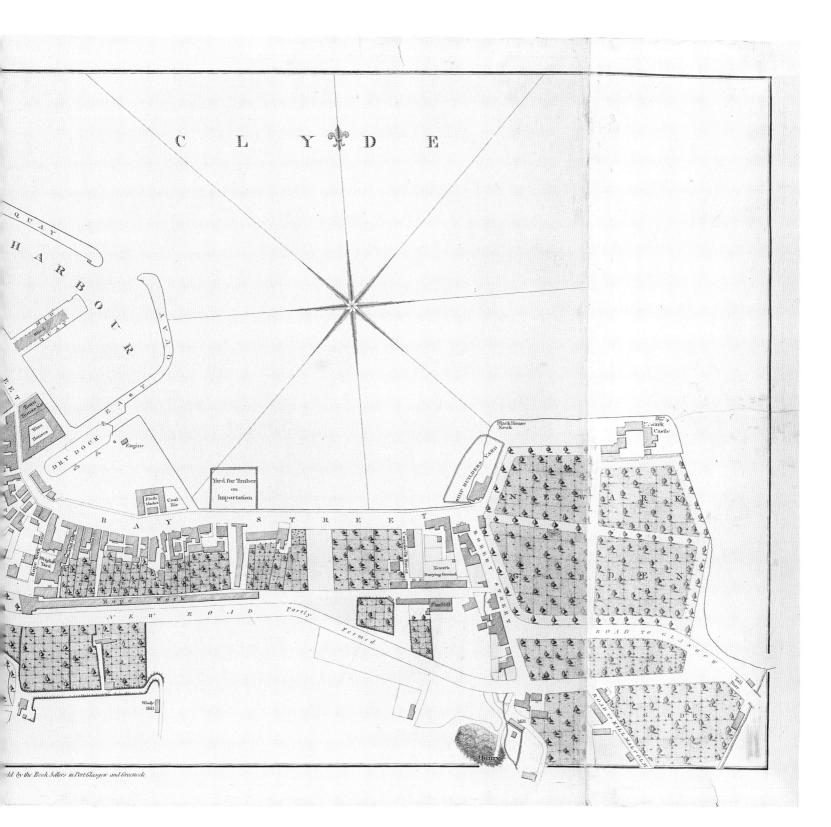

C L Y D E

HARBOUR

QUAY

QUAY EAST

M·D
Shed

QUAY EAST

Town
House &c.

Ware
Houses

DRY DOCK

Engine

Yard. for Timber
on
Importation

BlackHouse
Neuk

Newark
Castle

SHIP BUILDERS YARD

N E W A R K

Flesh
Market

Coal
Rie

BAY STREET

Campbells Street

Rope Work Lane

Wrights
Yard

Newark
Burying Ground

ROBERT STREET

G A R D E N

Rope Work

Flax Mill

NEW ROAD Partly

ROAD TO GLASGOW

Formed

Wind-
Hill

Toll
Bar

Mill

ROAD TO KILMALCOLM

G A R D E N

Library

CHAPTER 48

Dunoon at the high point
of the Clyde's tourist boom

Dunoon, the main town on the Cowal peninsula, has had a chequered history over the past 200 years. At the end of the eighteenth century, the locality was beginning to show signs of change. In 1792, the unknown contributor to the *Statistical Account* provided a local example of migration out of the Gaelic-speaking Highlands, partly through the introduction of sheep. While flavoured with an undercurrent of criticism of urban ways, he mentions the ferry which gave rise to a village with a declining population which, by then, amounted to only a little more than 30 families. Growth was said to be hindered by its openness to the south which prevented the creation of any safe haven for boats. The community had been hard hit by the suppression of local whisky distilling by Excise officers and by the building of the new road to Inveraray which had affected trade. All combined to fuel a slow but steady drift of people to Greenock, only 10 miles across the Clyde. However, five decades later, the *New Statistical Account* of the parish highlighted the major changes wrought by the development of steam navigation in the Firth of Clyde. This inaugurated the beginnings of a tourist trade, with families from Glasgow travelling to Dunoon as a summer resort, as well as the construction of several fine villas by successful businessmen, including James Ewing and David Napier. In fact, the variation in the number of residents at different times of the year merited some comment.

All had been facilitated by the building of a pier in 1835.

By the late 1860s, the place had become a favourite watering place for holiday-makers and an ideal centre for excursions into the Highlands. During the summer months of the 1880s, it was reckoned that the resident population of around 4,500 swelled to more than 7,000, attracted by the scenery and fresh air, in addition to boating and bathing opportunities on the sandy beach of the West Bay – all for a return fare from Glasgow of 3s. At least ten hotels were listed in a guidebook for the period, including the Argyll which is identified on this Ordnance Survey 25-inch scale map from 1869. The map also provides a good impression of the many villas and their grounds laid out along the shoreline. By this date, the town also offered a Convalescent Home, underlining the restorative benefits of a seaside location, and the Royal Clyde Yacht Club.

Thirty years later, the new edition of the Ordnance Survey map indicates several of the changes resulting from the growing number of summer visitors. The new esplanade which greeted the steamer passengers arriving at the extended jetty is a central feature but the town also boasted two bandstands, gardens, a public park and drinking fountains. Several more hotels are marked, including the Crown and Commercial. Interestingly, both maps also carry an inset showing the offshore rocks of the Gantocks and their beacon discussed earlier. By this date,

Opposite. Ordnance Survey, *Argyllshire 1:2500 1st edition sheets 184.5 and 184.6 (surveyed 1864, published 1869)*

such recreational facilities as a bowling green, golf course, yachting pond and gentlemen's bathing station had also been established. Such developments were replicated in many of the Clyde destinations of this period, including Rothesay and Largs.

In the heady days when the MacBrayne steamer *Columba* sailed daily to Tarbert or Ardrishaig, the author of the 1925 official guide to Dunoon praised it thus: 'Nowhere, probably in the British Isles, is there a spot better suited to be the headquarters of a summer holiday . . . lying on the shores of one of the loveliest estuaries in the world.' At that time, the summer population almost quadrupled the number of winter residents, with between 60 and 70 steamers calling every day. Visitors could be catered for in a variety of boarding houses, hotels and private residences, listed on 30 pages of the guide and most promoting their fine sea views.

With the rise in popularity of foreign holiday destinations, Dunoon suffered the same downturn experienced by many Clyde coast resorts and, nearly 50 years ago, a young Billy Connolly, as one of The Humblebums, produced his wistfully bittersweet parody 'Why Don't They Come Back to Dunoon?' which highlighted the dramatic changes of the period. While the lyrics reflected something of the humour of the west of Scotland, they also highlighted a fundamental problem in the lack of adaptability to what was becoming a markedly more sophisticated holiday and leisure market. Since the departure of the US Navy's submarine squadron in the early 1990s, the area and its economy have suffered a major downturn. Today, little is left of the vibrancy of the Edwardian holiday community except the annual Cowal Highland Gathering in late August. However, both the Victorian pier and burgh hall have been recently refurbished and the area can still capitalise on its spectacular scenery, its access to Benmore Botanic Garden and the many walking, running and mountain biking trails in the locality. In something of a return to its Gaelic roots, Dunoon has been host to the Royal National Mòd on seven occasions since 1930 and it is scheduled to return to the town in 2018.

Right. Ordnance Survey, *Argyllshire 1:2500 2nd edition sheets 184.5 and 184.6 (raised 1898, published 1899)*

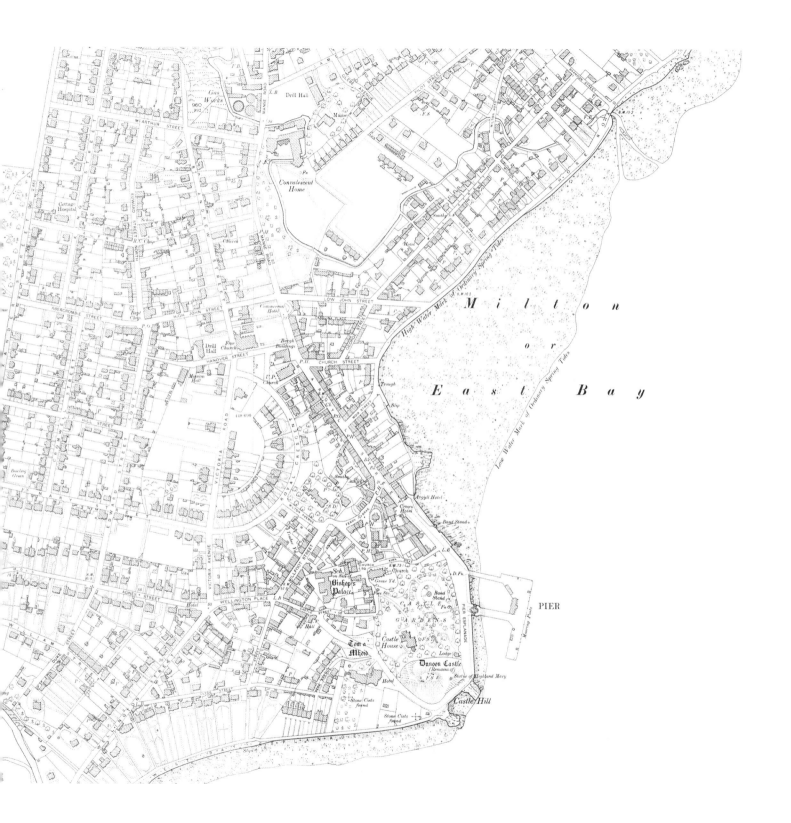

Milton

or

East Bay

PIER

CHAPTER 49

Late nineteenth-century Greenock
and its fire insurance plan

Most of the images in this book come from what can be described as thematic maps – in other words, maps designed to illustrate a particular aspect of the location covered, whether this be its topography, transport network, defence or industry. The illustration chosen here comes from one particular type of thematic map, namely fire insurance plans. Unlike other forms of cartography, these specialist plans were all produced by a single company, namely Charles Goad, and they are still a very much underused source for the local and industrial history of the urban areas they cover. Unfortunately, this coverage is markedly limited and, north of the border, it extends only to the four major Scottish cities, as well as to the ports of Granton, Leith and Greenock, the industrial centre of Paisley and, a little surprisingly, Campbeltown, reflecting the hazards of the number of distilleries and duty-free warehouses in the town.

Most of these plans first appeared in the 1880s and 1890s and were prepared at a slightly larger scale of 1 inch to 40 feet (or 1:480), thereby being more detailed than even the Ordnance Survey's town plans. They focus on supplying the kind of information that a fire insurer needed to determine and assess both the fire risk and the potential damage of each building in the built-up areas of the towns covered. This was particularly important at the end of the nineteenth century when warehouses and industries were located in close proximity to each other and

where the storage of highly flammable liquids (such as whisky) was far less controlled than it is today. As a result of this focus, the maps are colour coded to identify the types of building materials used in construction, such as red for brick or yellow for wood, as well as indicating such features as glass roofs and skylights. Hoists, boilers, sources of water supply, fire alarms and the types of available appliances are understandably also a novel element of such plans. Where they do supply particularly unique information is in the provision of details of the trades and businesses on different levels of an individual building, as well as recording proprietors. When matched to the Post Office directories of the day, a far clearer picture of the local juxtaposition of manufacture, commerce and residence can result. The plans also give a far better record of the use and ownership of individual properties and their street number.

Although born in Surrey, Charles Goad (1848–1910) had started his insurance plan business in Canada where much of the early construction of buildings was in wood and prone to the risk of serious damage by fire. Within a decade, his company had produced more than 1,300 plans of various Canadian locations, having bought over his major competitor, the Sanborn Map Company of New York. In 1875, Goad returned home to set up a London office as a base for what became an international operation providing plans for various European cities,

Opposite. Charles Goad, *Fire Insurance Plan of Greenock, sheet 7* (May 1888)

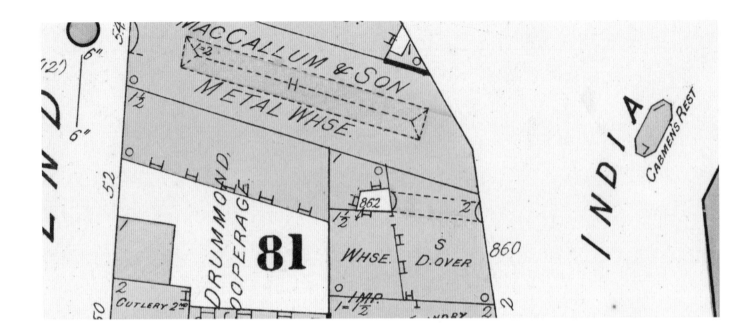

as well as urban areas in the West Indies, Chile, Venezuela and South Africa. The company dominated the market for this type of cartography and remained in business as an independent firm until 1974.

Greenock was initially surveyed between February and April 1888, when the burgh's population was in the region of 65,000, making it Scotland's fifth largest town. Seven individual plans of the central area were prepared and were accompanied by a key plan which contained an explanation of the special symbols and colours used, as well as an index to the streets and special buildings. These included banks, 28 factories, public houses, 42 warehouses, churches and schools. Also noted in the key is the existence of a constant water supply from the works but only one hand fire engine. This sheet provides an impressive record of the town's businesses, indicating that Greenock had a bookbinder, confectioner, fish curer, photographer, upholsterer and three sugar refiners, while the various warehouses stored bedding, furniture, hay, oil and wine and spirits. The plans cover only the buildings of the area between the Albert and Victoria Harbours lying north of a line from West Stewart Street and Regent Street which defines only part of the business core

of the burgh. This is significant because the key shows a considerable number of businesses elsewhere in Greenock not covered by any plan. These include a brewery, distillery, the chemical works in Dellingburn Street and another eight sugar refineries. Other features on the plans include canteens, billiard halls and a model lodging house. Tenements are frequently indicated above business premises. Given the scale and number of the Greenock plans, the compact nature of the commercial centre is quite striking and emphasises how congested cities in late-Victorian Britain were.

Unfortunately, one of the difficulties in using these plans is that they were rarely purchased outright but 'leased' for the duration of a subscription, with an obligation to return superseded editions when major updated versions were produced. Travelling agents would paste sheets with minor corrections over the originals, thereby complicating an understanding of change over time. However, some of the later sheets survive and show, for example, the Marks and Spencer and F.W. Woolworth Bazaars on Hamilton Street in 1937 and the Pavilion Picture House in 1953. More fortunately, urban areas today are less prone to the indiscriminate ravages of major fires in town centres.

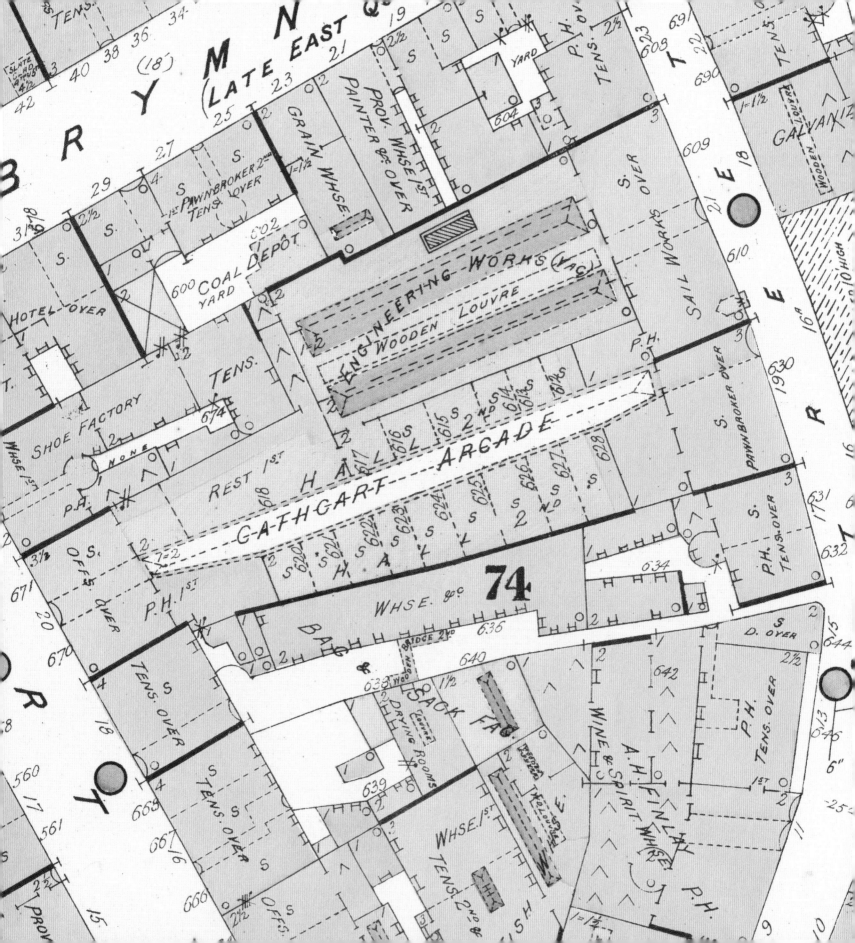

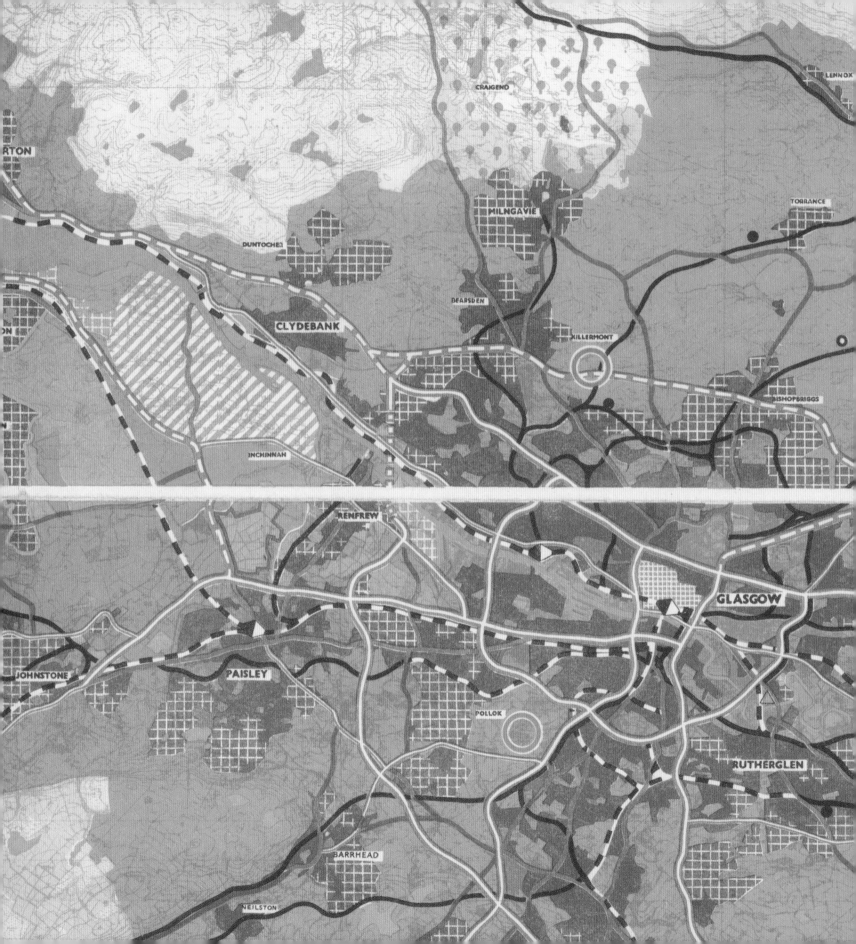

CHAPTER 50

Post-war reconstruction: the
Abercrombie *Clyde Valley Regional Plan*, 1946

Regional planning, overspill and new towns are terms redolent of the attempts made to resolve the housing problems in many British cities following the end of the Second World War. Before its outbreak, there had been widespread recognition of the need for major action to deal with the overcrowded and slum conditions in which many citizens lived. By 1931, Glasgow, the largest urban area in Scotland, had a population of nearly 1.1 million, with a density of more than 16,100 inhabitants per square mile. Glasgow was not heavily bombed during the Second World War and, although it did not face the same degree of reconstruction of infrastructure as many other areas, its Corporation was well aware of the scale of the housing problem, highlighted by Robert Bruce's *First Planning Report to the Highways and Planning Committee* issued in early 1945. His bold and dramatic vision for building a fairer and more equitable society for the modern age was also influenced by political considerations. Glasgow Council was determined to find a solution which would not involve any major loss of population, income and, thereby, power. In 1947, its Planning Committee approved Bruce's scheme but, in the interim, the Clyde Valley Regional Planning Committee commissioned a separate plan from Sir Patrick Abercrombie (1879–1957), one of the leading city planners of his day. Well-connected and charismatic, Abercrombie was responsible for similar proposals covering London, Plymouth, Hull, Bath and Warwick and had the backing of the Scottish Office who published his *Clyde Valley Regional Plan* in 1949. At its core, Abercrombie's scheme suggested the relocation of people away from the existing conurbation, in line with the intention to decentralise and repopulate Scotland as a whole.

With this background, it is clear to envisage the clash between central and local government aspirations, with the city seeking to solve what it saw as its own problems within its own boundaries whereas Abercrombie's proposals took a wider view of the dispersal of considerable numbers of people to smaller satellite communities or 'new towns'. Power to designate such had been granted under the terms of the New Towns Act, passed in 1946. Strongly influenced by both the Arts and Crafts and Garden City movements, Abercrombie's strategy was, in its own way, no less radical than the Bruce report, involving the unprecedented movement of more than a quarter of a million people. By the summer of 1949, the city authorities had rejected the main thrust of the Bruce Plan but subsequently developed a series of initiatives based on Comprehensive Development Areas and peripheral housing estates. Given the scale of the challenge, there was no swift answer and even by 1961 the city's population remained well over 1 million, with a density of more than 15,600 per square mile. Eventually, there was a growing acceptance of the need for some form of overspill programme, with

Opposite and p. 265. Patrick Abercrombie, Clyde Valley Regional Plan 1946 master plan (1949)

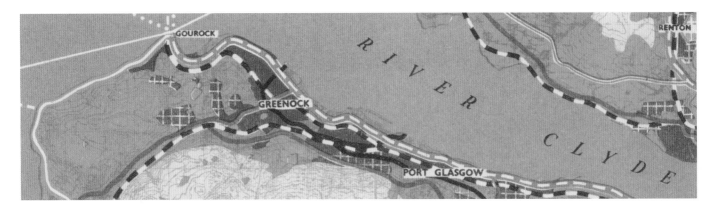

considerable numbers of citizens being encouraged to move within the immediate area to newly constructed housing in East Kilbride and Cumbernauld while arrangements were also made with Glenrothes and Livingston.

Abercrombie's report was supplemented by more than 200 maps, graphs and illustrations, as well as 33 tables. This image is taken from the volume's very sizeable master plan covering the whole Clyde valley. Like others of its type, it indicates residential areas, industries, communications networks and the proposed green belt. Colour is used to differentiate individual elements and, like the plan's text, it focuses on an area downstream from Larkhall. Given the speed with which the report was prepared (less than two years), the quality of the mapping is understandably crude, but it indicates effectively the general trends which are detailed elsewhere in the volume. Certain proposals were never realised, but the plan does identify the suggested national recreation centre at Hamilton Low Parks, the forerunner of the subsequent development of Strathclyde Country Park. In fact, the emphasis on settlement and industry makes it quite difficult to make out the course of the Clyde on the map. Surprisingly, the report, which runs to nearly 400 pages, contains only six short paragraphs on the river itself and these all relate to cross-river communications. Possible tunnels to facilitate north–south journeys are mentioned but, significantly, extreme doubt is cast on the acceptability of a fixed bridge at Erskine. Other than its mention in a very short list of 'favourite resorts of naturalists', there is no further discussion of the river either as an asset or a valuable resource for community use.

In the long run, the question of how and where people should live has been influenced as much by the far wider impact of globalisation, the move to a service economy and, of course, the short-term nature of pragmatic politics. At the 2011 census, Glasgow's population had dropped to under 600,000 and the density had fallen to 8,790 per square mile but the challenges of a regional economy can be seen in the dichotomy between the wishes of many people to enjoy the benefits of a major urban centre without necessarily living there. Undoubtedly, the living conditions of tens of thousands of people were improved over a relatively short time but the resultant breaking-up of communities, the sense of isolation that many experienced in the new towns and the inevitable subsequent impact on the road and transport networks of high levels of commuting cannot be glossed over.

Visions of the needs of society can never be complete or permanent and the volume of information on the myriad and complex factors involved can work against any clear understanding of contemporary society. What Robert Bruce once considered out of date and a hindrance to a new vision of the modern city now forms the core of Glasgow's renewed civic pride. More relevantly to this study, many bodies and interest groups now view the Clyde in a more positive light, seeking to enhance the connection between the human and physical features of the river valley. Attitudes and conditions change. Writing nearly 2,000 years ago, St Paul put it succinctly when he penned his first epistle to the inhabitants of Corinth, 'For now we see through a glass, darkly'.

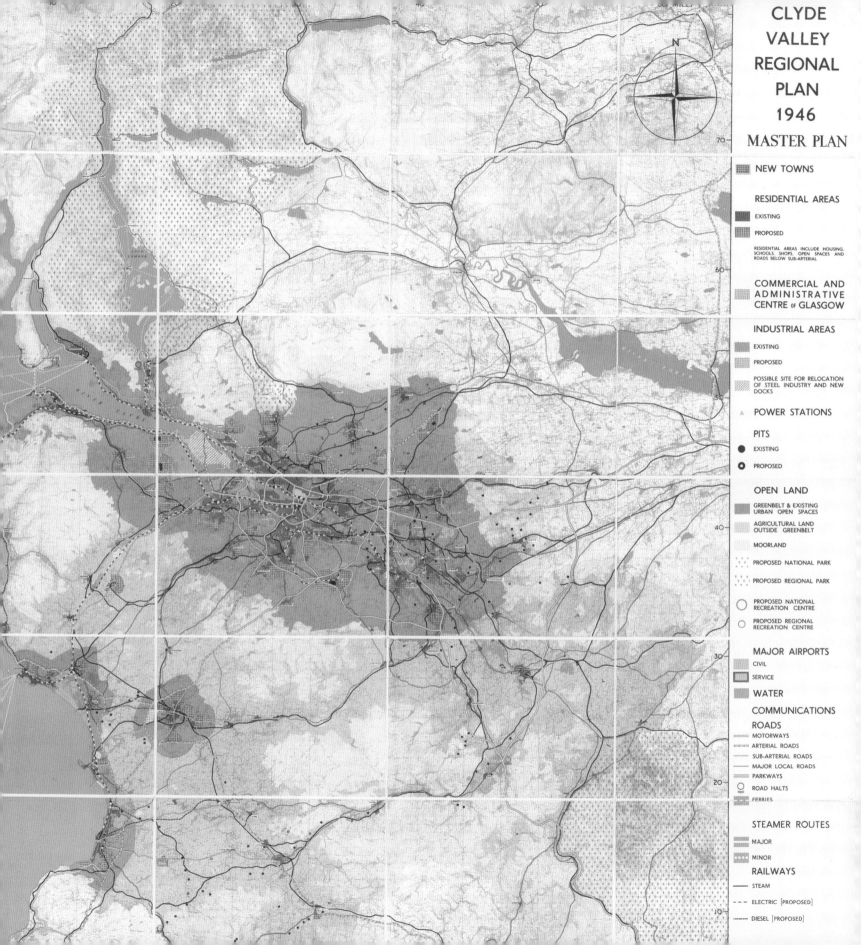

CLYDE VALLEY REGIONAL PLAN 1946

MASTER PLAN

NEW TOWNS

RESIDENTIAL AREAS

EXISTING

PROPOSED

RESIDENTIAL AREAS INCLUDE HOUSING,
SCHOOLS, SHOPS, OPEN SPACES AND
ROADS BELOW SUB-ARTERIAL

COMMERCIAL AND ADMINISTRATIVE CENTRE of GLASGOW

INDUSTRIAL AREAS

EXISTING

PROPOSED

POSSIBLE SITE FOR RELOCATION
OF STEEL INDUSTRY AND NEW
DOCKS

POWER STATIONS

PITS

EXISTING

PROPOSED

OPEN LAND

GREENBELT & EXISTING
URBAN OPEN SPACES

AGRICULTURAL LAND
OUTSIDE GREENBELT

MOORLAND

PROPOSED NATIONAL PARK

PROPOSED REGIONAL PARK

PROPOSED NATIONAL
RECREATION CENTRE

PROPOSED REGIONAL
RECREATION CENTRE

MAJOR AIRPORTS

CIVIL

SERVICE

WATER

COMMUNICATIONS

ROADS

MOTORWAYS

ARTERIAL ROADS

SUB-ARTERIAL ROADS

MAJOR LOCAL ROADS

PARKWAYS

ROAD HALTS

FERRIES

STEAMER ROUTES

MAJOR

MINOR

RAILWAYS

STEAM

ELECTRIC [PROPOSED]

DIESEL [PROPOSED]

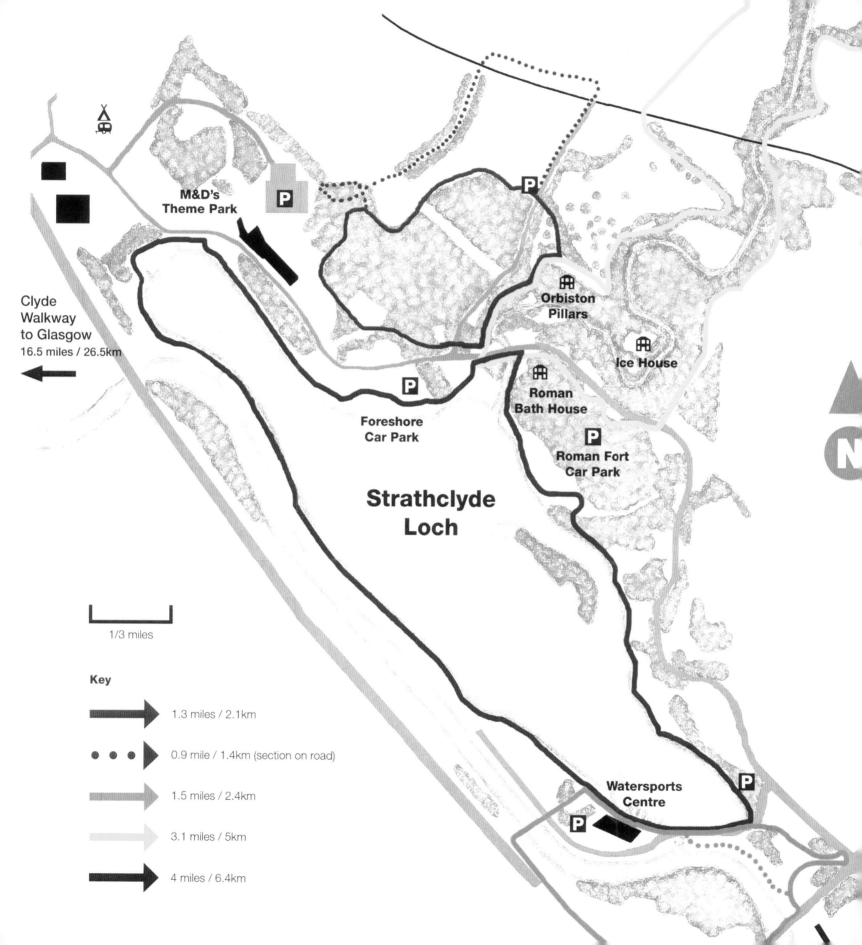

M&D's
Theme Park

Clyde
Walkway
to Glasgow
16.5 miles / 26.5km

Orbiston
Pillars

Ice House

Roman
Bath House

Foreshore
Car Park

Roman Fort
Car Park

**Strathclyde
Loch**

Watersports
Centre

1/3 miles

Key

1.3 miles / 2.1km

0.9 mile / 1.4km (section on road)

1.5 miles / 2.4km

3.1 miles / 5km

4 miles / 6.4km

N

CHAPTER 51

The Clyde on
contemporary maps

The Clyde has had both a varied history and an equally varied cartography. The choice of the maps and plans discussed so far has been influenced by their survival, scope and significance. With the extensive range of available contemporary maps, it is difficult to make a selection which reflects the continued relationships between the river, its wider environment and those who use it in the twenty-first century. It is this interconnection which will be investigated in this final discussion.

Increasingly, the Clyde is being utilised as an important recreational resource for the large urban populations of Glasgow and Lanarkshire. With growing pressure on, and fragmentation of, the green belt in these authority areas, the river has developed into an artery providing a sequence of walkways, cycleways and nature reserves through which something of the original rural nature of the Clyde might still be discerned. There is a growing resurgence in rowing on the river upstream of the weir, particularly since the introduction of indoor rowing to Glasgow secondary schools in 2007. The historic West Boathouse on Glasgow Green which was built in 1905 to designs by Alexander Beith McDonald is home to both the Clydesdale and Clyde Amateur Rowing Clubs, established by 1857 and 1865 respectively, and is currently the subject of development proposals. Scottish Rowing, the national governing body, has identified Glasgow as a key regional centre for the sport and its home at

Strathclyde Country Park regularly hosts international regattas, as well as offering training facilities which include an indoor rowing tank.

While not necessarily regarded as a sport, walking is being promoted for health within the community through the registered charity *Paths for All* and, as a partnership of a number of national organisations, it seeks to develop a path network in Scotland. Acting as a focal point in the local network is the Country Park, lying almost halfway along the Clyde Walkway which links Glasgow and New Lanark. With an overall area of 400 hectares, the park is located close to the north bank of the Clyde which was diverted to create Strathclyde Loch, the park's central feature. Much of the area was formerly part of the Hamilton Palace Low Parks and was engrossed into the amenity when it was originally created.

As can be seen from this map of its facilities prepared by the Countryside and Landscape Services of North Lanarkshire Council, other walking routes emanate out towards Motherwell and Stonehouse. The map is included in a leaflet issued as a guide to a sequence of routes of various lengths. Anyone familiar with the park will know that these can be used by a wide range of folk seeking some form of outdoor exercise, including cyclists, joggers and walkers. While simple in style, the plan meets the present-day requirements for accessibility and presents a clear

Opposite. North Lanarkshire Council, *Strathclyde Country Park map of walking routes*

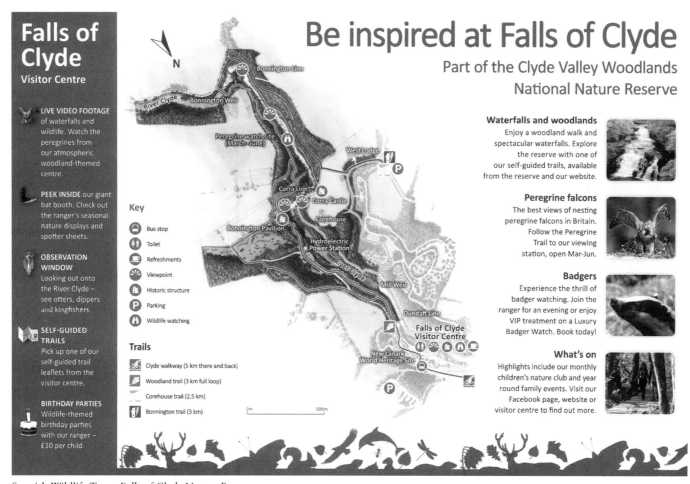

Scottish Wildlife Trust, *Falls of Clyde Nature Reserve map*

impression of both the park's layout and its key features. More importantly, it is an example of a type of freely available cartography which provides information to an audience which may not necessarily be map literate. Apart from rowing, other recreational amenities include coarse angling, kayaking and similar water sports. Of possibly greater significance is the park's role in forming part of a chain of rough wetland and wildlife refuges along the banks of the river. These include the Baron's Haugh, Mauldslie Woods, Garrion Gill, Nethan Gorge and Falls of Clyde Reserves which constitute part of the Clyde Valley Woodlands. Sites are managed by a number of bodies, including the Royal

Society for the Protection of Birds, Scottish Natural Heritage and the Scottish Wildlife Trust under the umbrella organisation of the Clyde and Avon Valley Landscape Partnership. Some reserves (e.g. Garrion Gill) have online maps which can be accessed from their websites, but these tend to be based on recent Ordnance Survey mapping with pertinent information added.

The middle Clyde valley and its tributaries are designated as an Area of Great Landscape Value, largely as a consequence of its incised nature, steep slopes and semi-natural woodland. Within this area can be found stands of a variety of woodland, including oak, ash, rowan and hazel which provide ideal habitats

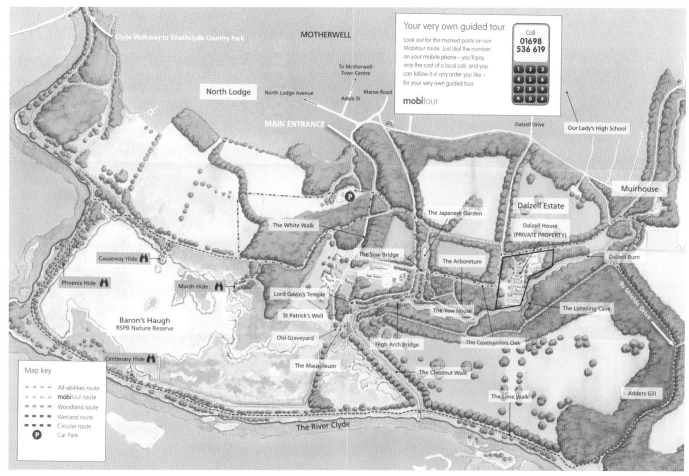

North Lanarkshire Council, *Baron's Haugh Reserve plan*

for wildflowers, birds, invertebrates, insects and mammals. Given that the reserves are easily accessible to more than 40 per cent of Scotland's population, they play not only a vital role in safeguarding our natural heritage but also an important part in the education of an increasingly urbanised population with less immediate experience of the interconnection between humankind and the environment. In this role, the maps and leaflets of the various reserves provide a valuable synthesis of self-guided information on the relevance of these areas, what can be seen and where to look for certain features.

A very good example of this is the illustrated map which is contained within the reserve leaflet issued by the Scottish Wildlife Trust for their Falls of Clyde Visitor Centre. A well-balanced choice of colour allows the map to indicate the various trails to be enjoyed at the reserve and a specialised key aids the identification of particular aspects of the area, such as waterfall viewpoints. More significantly, the map is oriented to suit the visitor coming from New Lanark, with north being located in the south-east corner, and it is drawn at a scale to suit the leaflet size without compromising clarity. Like other designs geared to reach a wider audience, it incorporates important local information and illustrations of selected features.

Baron's Haugh, once part of the Dalzell estate, is an important community reserve on the edge of Motherwell, providing easy access to view wildlife at relatively close quarters. Using an attractive range of colour tones, this plan of the reserve and the neighbouring estate is more than a mere guide to the area. It has neither north point nor scale but clearly identifies such important features as the hides, car park, the various walking routes and other significant elements of the landscape on a backdrop which shows the field and land parcel layout. Of greater relevance to contemporary mapping is the mobile phone illustration indicating the ability to create a personal guided tour using specifically marked posts. In this way, cartography continues to provide a valid support to modern technology, as well as providing a flexibility which is increasingly expected by today's map user. Of possibly greater significance is the contrast with the more general detail of the Strathclyde Park map which may indicate an interesting editorial approach to information provision for different audiences. Considering the three maps together, the user can see a gradual transition from what is a relatively standard cartographic depiction in the park routes map to a markedly more pictorial style for Baron's Haugh.

As in the past, cartography today is used to monitor specific themes. The Scottish Environment Protection Agency (SEPA) employs GIS experts to create a range of maps relevant to its role in regulating and protecting the environment. Assessing river waterbodies is a significant part of its work and this overall river quality classification map of the Clyde basin provides a valuable indication of the river's 'health' to support decision making. It is based on Ordnance Survey data and it classifies the river upstream of Glasgow as generally marked as 'moderate' but with a considerable number of tributary burns in the lower reaches still identified as 'poor' or 'bad', based on a number of variables sensitive to organic pollution, nutrients and toxic substances. Like any mapping, the information shown needs to be placed in context, either with previous depictions or the accompanying discussion of trends. In 2015, the proportion of Scottish river length classed as slightly polluted, polluted or severely polluted was 3.5 per cent, less than half the figure in 1998. While the map reflects the growing improvement in the

condition of the Clyde as suggested by the return of Atlantic salmon to the middle reaches, changes in our relationship with the environment require constant monitoring. The Agency produces other environmental mapping of Scottish waters covering such matters as obstacles to fish migration, bathing water sites and shellfish production areas which all contribute to Scotland's sustainable economic growth. Whether or not this style of cartography has a wide circulation, such mapping provides a vital resource for understanding contemporary Scotland.

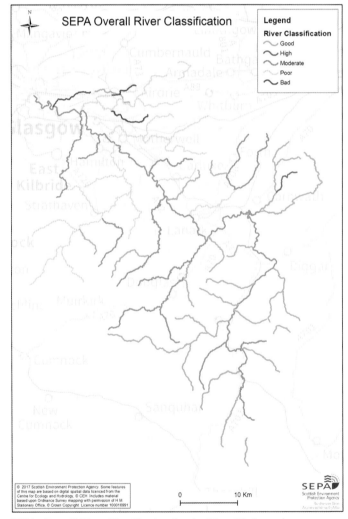

SEPA, *Overall River Classification for the River Clyde catchment area* (2017)

Postscript

Today, we live in a world which has ready access to a bewildering array of cartography through a variety of means from online Google mapping to sat nav applications for iPhones. The facility OpenStreetMap allows communities, engineers and Geographic Information System (GIS) professionals to contribute or update map information globally. Combined with Global Positioning System (GPS) software and web map servers, it allows people to create their own maps for very specific purposes. Digital technologies enhance the synthesis of geospatial data to aid our understanding of social, health and other issues. Maps accompany us when we travel, when we watch television news or weather reports, when we attend sporting or other public events and when we visit parks or similar recreational areas. Many of these are disposable or, at best, transient and are, perhaps, ideally suited to the dynamic nature of twenty-first century life where maps, whether printed or digital, can become quickly out of date. In addition, few of these are circulated beyond a relatively small interest group and the possibility of their long-term survival or potential assessment of their value may be limited.

We also live in a time when the Internet has provided the ordinary citizen with unprecedented levels of access to a constantly expanding range of 'heritage' resources, including the cartography of earlier generations. This is proving to be a double-edged tool in many instances where increased availability of information has enhanced further research but where such access may be heavily dependent on a specific selection process or funding of particular projects. The apparent ease with which earlier mapping can be accessed disguises the complexities behind the cartography and can work against a proper understanding of the story which places the map in context. Of greater concern is the tendency for some to work on the assumption that material does not exist if it is not available electronically. There are strong arguments and pressures for the promotion of the resources, held within our major libraries and archives through a dynamic web presence. However, in a time of financial stringency, many smaller and, indeed, larger collections are under threat through a lack of staff or resources, which presents serious challenges to those responsible for their care and continued survival. During the research for this book, I visited many institutions holding a considerable number of unique items which form part of the story of the mapping of the Clyde in the widest sense but where there is insufficient funding for their cataloguing, promotion or conservation. When any heritage is under threat, the dichotomy between retention in a larger institution where that uniqueness may not be so readily recognised or valued and its safeguarding in a smaller, but possibly more immediately relevant, repository constrained by limited financial resources will challenge those responsible for its care. This lays a heavy responsibility on both providers and users. Like the maps considered in this volume, we will be judged on what survives and what narratives will be drawn from them. The cartographic heritage which is passed on to future generations should continue to reflect the wonderfully diverse and intricate inheritance that is enjoyed today.

Sources and Further Reading

General cartography: Depicting the river from the earliest times

Cunningham, I. C. (ed.), *The Nation Survey'd: Essays on Late Sixteenth-Century Scotland As Depicted by Timothy Pont* (East Linton: Tuckwell Press, in association with the National Library of Scotland, 2001).

Fleet, C., Wilkes, M. and Withers, C.W.J., *Scotland: Mapping the Nation* (Edinburgh: Birlinn, in association with the National Library of Scotland, 2011).

The Glasgow Story, http://www.theglasgowstory.com. Covering all aspects of the city's history, including its association with the River Clyde, with many images of maps, plans and other illustrations.

Hewitt, R., *Map of a Nation: A Biography of the Ordnance Survey* (London: Granta, 2010).

Moir, D.G. (ed.), *The Early Maps of Scotland to 1850*, 2 volumes (Edinburgh: Royal Scottish Geographical Society, 1973 and 1983).

Moore, J.N., *Glasgow: Mapping the City* (Edinburgh: Birlinn, in association with the National Library of Scotland and the University of Glasgow Library, 2015).

Moore, J.N., *The Historical Cartography of Scotland: A Guide to the Literature of Scottish Maps and Mapping Prior to the Ordnance Survey*, O'Dell memorial Monograph No.24 (Aberdeen: University of Aberdeen, Department of Geography, 1991).

Oliver, R.R., *The Ordnance Survey in the Nineteenth Century: Maps, Money and the Growth of Government* (London: Charles Close Society, 2014).

Oliver, R.R., *Ordnance Survey Maps: A Concise Guide for Historians*, 3rd edition (London: Charles Close Society, 2013).

Shannon, W.D., 'Laurence Nowell of Read Hall, Lancashire (c.1530–c.1569): Lexicographer, Toponymist, Cartographer, Enigma', in Stringer, Keith J., *North-West England from the Romans to the Tudors: Essays in Memory of John Macnair Todd*, Extra series 41 (Carlisle: Cumberland and Westmorland Antiquarian and Archaeological Society, 2014).

Smith, D., *Victorian Maps of the British Isles* (London: Batsford, 1985).

Statistical Accounts of Scotland 1791–1845, http://stataccscot.edina.ac.uk. Online access to scanned pages and transcripts of the 'Old' and 'New' Statistical Accounts covering the whole of Scotland.

Woodward, D. (ed.), *The History of Cartography, Vol.3: Cartography in the European Renaissance* (Chicago and London: University of Chicago Press, 2007).

Navigating and improving the river

Blake, G., *Clyde Lighthouses: A Short History of the Clyde Lighthouse Trust, 1756–1956* (Glasgow: Jackson, 1956).

Cunnison, J. and Gilfillan, J.B.S., *The Third Statistical Account of Scotland: Glasgow* (Glasgow: Collins, 1958).

Reed, P. (ed.), *Glasgow: The Forming of the City*, 2nd edition (Edinburgh: Edinburgh University Press, 1999).

Riddell, J. F., *Clyde Navigation: A History of the Development and Deepening of the River Clyde* (Edinburgh, John Donald, 1979).

Robinson, A.H.W., *Marine Cartography in Britain: A History of the Sea Chart to 1855* (Leicester: Leicester University Press, 1962).

Scottish Burgh Records Society, *Extracts from the Records of the Burgh of Glasgow: A.D. 1573–1833* (Glasgow: Scottish Burgh Records Society, 1876–1916).

Defence, security and conflict

Anderson, C.J., 'Constructing the Military Landscape: The Board of Ordnance Maps and Plans of Scotland, 1689–1815'. Unpublished PhD thesis, University of Edinburgh, 2010. (http://www.era.lib.ed.ac.uk/handle/1842/4598).

Barclay, G. J., *The Built Heritage of the First World War in Scotland* (Edinburgh: Historic Scotland & RCAHMS, 2013).

Cavers, K., *A Vision of Scotland: The Nation Observed by John Slezer 1671–1717* (Edinburgh: HMSO, 1993).

Davies, J., 'Uncle Joe Knew Where You Lived: The Story of Soviet Mapping of Britain', *Sheetlines* 72 (2005), 26–38, 73 (2005), 1–15.

Davies, J., 'Soviet Military City Plans of British Isles', *Sheetlines* 89 (2010), 23–24.

Hewitt, R., 'A Family Affair: The Dundas Family of Arniston and the Military Survey of Scotland (1747–1755)', *Imago Mundi* 64 (2012), 60–77.

Hodson, Y., 'William Roy and the Military Survey of Scotland', in Roy, W., *The Great Map: The Military Survey of Scotland 1747–55* (Edinburgh: Birlinn, 2007).

Using the river

Donnachie, I.L. and Hewitt, G., *Historic New Lanark: The Dale and Owen Industrial Community Since 1785* (Edinburgh: Edinburgh University Press, 2015).
Ironside Farrar Ltd., *A Clyde Valley Orchards Survey*. Commissioned Report no.023 (ROAME No.F02LI21). (Lanark: Scottish Natural Heritage, 2004).
Stamp, L.D. (ed.), *The Land of Britain: Report of the Land Utilisation Survey of Britain* (London: Land Utilisation Survey, 1937–46).

Crossing the river

Close, R., Gifford, J. and Walker, F.A., *Lanarkshire and Renfrewshire: The Buildings of Scotland* (New Haven and London: Yale University Press, 2016).
Reid, T., 'Fords, Ferries, Floats, and Bridges Near Lanark', *Proceedings of the Society of Antiquaries of Scotland* 47 (1912–13), 209–256.

Tourism, leisure and recreation

Boyd, J., *The Bonnie Links of Turnberry* (Turnberry: Turnberry Golf Club, 2004).
Browne, J.P., *Map Cover Art: A Pictorial History of Ordnance Survey Cover Illustrations* (Southampton: Ordnance Survey, 1991).
Mackintosh, I.M. (ed.), *Troon Golf Club: Its History from 1878* (Troon: Troon Golf Club, 1974).
Queen Victoria's Journals, http://www.queenvictoriasjournals.org. Online digital images and transcripts of the entire sequence of the monarch's diaries.

Life by the river

Abercrombie, P. and Matthew, R.H., *The Clyde Valley Regional Plan, 1946: A Report Prepared for the Clyde Valley Regional Planning Committee* (Edinburgh, HMSO, 1949).
Fire Insurance Maps and Plans, http://www.bl.uk/onlinegallery/onlineex/firemaps/fireinsurancemaps.html. The British Library's comprehensive holdings of fire insurance plans produced by the firm Charles E. Goad Ltd dating back to 1885, including images of each sheet covering Greenock.
Graham, E.J., *Robert Reid Cunningham of Seabank House: Entrepreneur and Life-Time Manager of the Stevenson Coal Company 1770–1814*, Ayrshire Monograph No.19 (Ayr: Ayrshire Archaeological and Natural History Society, 1997).
Smith, R. and Wannop, U. (eds), *Strategic Planning in Action: The Impact of the Clyde Valley Regional Plan 1946–1982* (Aldershot: Gower, 1985).

Picture Credits

Index